T0176163

BEHAVIORAL BIOMETRICS

BEHAVIORAL BIOMETRICS

A REMOTE ACCESS APPROACH

Kenneth Revett, PhD

Harrow School of Computer Science,
University of Westminster,
UK

A John Wiley and Sons, Ltd., Publication

This edition first published 2008
© 2008 John Wiley & Sons, Ltd

Registered office
John Wiley & Sons Ltd, The Atrium, Southern Gate, Chichester, West Sussex, PO19 8SQ, United Kingdom

For details of our global editorial offices, for customer services and for information about how to apply for permission to reuse the copyright material in this book please see our website at www.wiley.com.

Library of Congress Cataloging-in-Publication Data
Revett, Kenneth.
    Behavioral biometrics : a remote access approach / Kenneth Revett.
        p. cm.
    Includes bibliographical references and index.
    ISBN 978-0-470-51883-0 (cloth)
 1. Biometric identification.   I. Title.
    TK7882.B56R48   2008
    006.4–dc22

                                                   2008024097

A catalogue record for this book is available from the British Library.

ISBN: 978-0-470-51883-0

Set in 10/12pt Times by SNP Best-set Typesetter Ltd., Hong Kong
Printed in Singapore by Markono Print Media Pte Ltd

Contents

1

Introduction to Behavioral Biometrics

1.1 Introduction

This book fills several roles in the biometrics literature. It is intended to serve as a reference source for case studies in behavioral biometrics. There are a number of very useful texts on the topic of biometrics, but they tend to focus on physiological biometrics, or they focus at a generic level, covering the full spectrum, becoming overly general. There are texts that focus on the algorithmic approaches deployed in biometrics, and as such serve as a source of machine learning algorithms. To date, there is no text that is solely dedicated to the topic of behavioral biometrics. This book serves to provide a number of case studies of major implementations within the field of behavioral biometrics. Though not as informative as the actual published work, the case studies are comprehensive and provide the user with a strong sense of the approaches employed in the various subdomains of behavioral biometrics. The intended audience is students, at the advanced undergraduate and postgraduate levels, and researchers wishing to explore this fascinating research topic. In addition, this text will serve as a reference for system integrators, CIOs, and related professionals who are charged with implementing security features at their organization. The reader will be directed to appropriate sources when detailed implementation issues are concerned, especially those involving specific machine learning algorithms. A single text of this size cannot cover both the domain of behavioral biometrics *and* the machine learning algorithms they employ.

Biometrics in the context presented in this book is concerned with a scientific approach to user verification and/or identification. The focus will be on *behavioral* biometrics – the verification and/or identification of individuals based on the way they provide information to the authentication system. For instance, individuals could be required to provide a signature, enunciate a particular phrase, or enter a secret code through an input device in order to provide evidence of their identity. Note that there is an implicit simplicity to behavioral biometrics in that typically, no special machinery/hardware is required for the authentication/identification process other then the computer (or ATM) device itself. In addition, the approaches prevalent in this domain are very familiar to us – practically everyone has provided a signature to verify their identity, and we have one or more passwords for logging into computer

Behavioral Biometrics: A Remote Access Approach. Kenneth Revett
© 2008 John Wiley & Sons, Ltd.

systems. We are simply used to providing proof of identity in these fashions in certain circumstances. These two factors provide the foundation for the behavioral approach to biometrics. These modes of identification are substantially different from the other classes of biometrics: physiological and token-based biometrics. For instance, what is termed physiological (or biological) biometrics requires that we present some aspect of our physicality in order to be identified. Typical instances of physiological biometrics include iris scans, retina scans, and fingerprints. Lastly, token-based biometric systems require the possession of some object such as a bank or identity card. Each class of biometrics is designed to provide an efficient and accurate method of verifying the identity (authentication) and/or the identification of an individual.

1.2 Types of Behavioral Biometrics

There are a variety of subdivisions within the behavioral biometrics domain. Each subdivision has its own characteristics in terms of ease of use, deployability, user acceptance, and quality of the identification/verification task. In order of presentation in this text, the following subdivisions can be identified as

- **Voice Recognition:**

in which users are requested to enunciate text as a means of identifying themselves. Voice can be employed for either speaker identification or speaker authentication. With respect to speaker identification, a person enunciates text, and the speech patterns are analyzed to determine the identity of the speaker. In the literature, this is referred to as speaker-independent recognition. This mode poses several interesting issues, such as what happens if the speaker is not contained within the database of speakers? As in all major forms of biometrics, any individual wishing to utilize the biometric device must, at some stage, introduce themselves to the system, typically in the form of an enrollment process. One of the principal tasks of the enrollment process is to register the person as a potential user of the biometric system (enrollment will be discussed further later in this chapter). In a speaker-independent system, the user's voice pattern is analyzed and compared to all other voice samples in the user database. There are a number of ways this comparison is made, and specific details are provided via case studies in the appropriate chapters (Chapter 2 for voice recognition). The closest match to the particular voice data presented for identification becomes the presumed identity of the speaker. There are three possible outcomes: i) The speaker is correctly identified; ii) the speaker is incorrectly identified as another speaker; or iii) the speaker is not identified as being a member of the system. Clearly, we would like to avoid the last two possibilities, which reflect the false acceptance rate (FAR) (type II error) and the false rejection rate (FRR) (type I error) as much as possible. When speakers attempt an authentication task, the speakers have provided some evidence of their identity, and the purpose of the voice recognition process is to verify that these persons have a legitimate claim to that identity. The result of this approach is a binary decision: either you are verified as the claimed identity or you are not.

The other major division within voice recognition biometrics is whether the enunciated text is fixed or free, that is, do the users enunciate a specific phrase (text dependent), or are

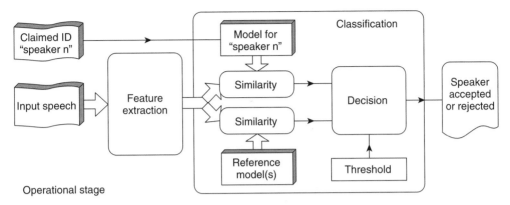

Operational stage

Figure 1.1 An example of a voice recognition processing system (Source: Ganchev, 2005)

they allowed to enunciate any phrase (text-independent)? The speaker-dependent version is easier from a matching perspective, in that the spoken text is directly matched to the information stored in the database. The text-independent approach allows speakers to enunciate any speech they wish to. This approach requires a model of each speaker, which is certainly more computationally expensive than the text-dependent approach. These and other related issues will be discussed further in the next chapter (Figure 1.1).

• **Signature Verification:**

where users are required to present handwritten text for authentication. This is probably the most familiar of all biometrics – though currently not the most prevalent – due to the advent of computer-based passwords. There are two essentially distinct forms of signature-based biometrics: online and off-line. With an online signature verification system, the signature characteristics are extracted as the user writes, and these features are used to immediately authenticate the user. Typically, specialized hardware is required, such as a pressure-sensitive pen (a digital pen) and/or a special writing tablet. These hardware elements are designed to capture the dynamical aspects of writing, such the pen pressure, pen angle, and related information (see Chapter 3 for details). In a remote access approach, where specialized hardware may not be feasible, the online approach is most suitable from a small portable device such as a PDA, where the stylus can be used for writing. The off-line approach utilizes the static features of the signature, such as the length and height of the text, and certain specialized features such as loops (not unlike a fingerprint approach). Typically, the data are acquired through an image of the signature, which may be photocopied or scanned into a computer for subsequent analysis. As in all behavioral biometric approaches, a writing sample must be stored in the authentication database, and the writing sample is compared to the appropriate reference sample before the acceptance/rejection decision to be made. Again, there is the possibility of having text-dependent or text-independent signature verification. The same caveats that apply to voice also apply here – and voice and signature are really very similar technologies – only the mode of communication has changed, which results in a different set of features that can be extracted. An example of an online signature setup is presented in Figure 1.2.

Figure 1.2 An online signature verification system (Source: Interlink Electronics ePad (www.primidi. com/2003/05/31.html))

• **Keystroke Dynamics:**

is a behavioral biometric that relies on the *way we type* on a typical keyboard/keypad type device. As a person types, certain attributes are extracted and used to authenticate or identify the typist. Again, we have two principal options: text-dependent and text-independent versions. The most common form of text-dependent systems requires users to enter their login ID and password (or commonly just their password). In the text-independent version, users are allowed to enter any text string they wish. In some implementations, a third option is used where a user is requested to enter a long text string on the order of 500–1500 characters. Users enroll into the system by entering their text either multiple times if the short text-independent system (i.e. password) is employed, or typically once if the system employs a long text string. From this enrollment process, the user's typing style is acquired and stored for subsequent authentication purposes. This approach is well suited for remote access scenarios: no specialized hardware is required and users are used to providing their login credentials. As discussed in more detail in Chapter 4, some of the attributes that are extracted when a person types are the duration of a key press (dwell time) and the time between striking successive keys (digraph if the time is recorded between successive keys). These features, along with several others, are used to build a model of the way a person types. The security enhancement provided by this technology becomes evident if you leave your password written on a sticky notepad tucked inside your desk, which someone happens to find. Without this level of protection, possession of the password is that that is required for a user to access your account. With the addition of a keystroke dynamics-based biometric, it is not sufficient that the password is acquired: the password has to be entered exactly (or at least within certain tolerance limits) the way the enrolled user entered it during enrollment. If not, the login attempt is rejected. An example of the notion of a digraph is depicted in Figure 1.3.

• **Graphical Authentication Systems:**

are employed as an alternative to textual-based password systems. There are issues with textual-based passwords regarding the strength, which refers to how easy it would be to guess

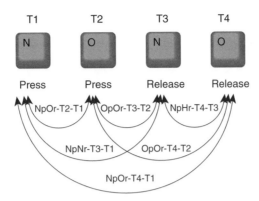

Figure 1.3 The combinations of digraphs that can be generated from the character sequence "N" followed by "O" Note the subscripts "p" and "r" indicate press and release, respectively

someone's password, given free access to the computer system on which they are stored (an off-line attack). Studies have indicated that most people make their passwords easy to remember – such as their names, certain memorable places, etc. Generally speaking, the full password space is not utilized when people are allowed to select their own passwords. On a typical PC-type keyboard, there are 95 printable characters, and for a password of eight characters, there are 95^8 (or 6×10^{15}) possible passwords that can be generated. This is a relatively large search space to exhaustively explore, though not impossible in a realistic time frame with today's modern computing power (and the deployment of a grid of computers). But typically, most users explore a small fraction of this possible password space, and the possibility of a successful off-line attack is very real (see Chapter 4 for some examples). As indicated, the principal reason for the lack of a thorough exploration of password space is the issue of memorability. Here is where graphical passwords take over.

Graphical passwords are composed of a collection of images, each representing an element of the user's password. The images are presented to the user – who must select the password elements – possibly in a predefined order, but more often than not, order is removed from the equation, depending on the implementation. A key difference between textual- and graphical-based passwords is that in the former, recall is required, and in the latter, recognition is involved. The psychological literature has provided ample evidence that recognition is a much easier task than recall. In addition, it appears that we have an innate ability to remember pictures better then text. These two factors combined provide the rationale for the graphical password-based approach. There are a variety of graphical-based password systems that have been developed, and this interesting approach is discussed in some detail in Chapter 6. An example of a classical approach, dubbed Passfaces™, is presented in Figure 1.4. In this system, the user's password is a collection of faces (typically four to six), which must be selected in order form a series of decoy face images.

• **Mouse Dynamics:**

is a biometric approach designed to capture the static and dynamic aspects of using the mouse as a tool for interacting with a user interface, which contains the elements of their password,

Figure 1.4 An example of the Passfaces™ graphical password authentication scheme. Note that on each page of faces, the user is required to select the correct face image; note that in this system, there is an implied order to the selection process (Source: Passfaces website – www.passfaces.com)

typically presented in a graphical fashion. Mouse movement information such as the change in the mouse pointer position over time and space is recorded, providing the basis for determining trajectories and velocity, which can be used to build a reference model of the user. Therefore, mouse dynamics is used in conjunction within a graphical password scenario, though the password may not consist of a collection of images to be identified. Instead, this approach is based on human computer interaction (HCI) features – how one interacts with an application is used to authenticate a user. Provided there is enough entropy in the game – enough possibilities for interacting with it, then one may be able to differentiate users based on this information. Some examples of this approach, which are rather sparsely represented in the literature, are presented in detail in Chapter 6, and an example of a system developed by Ahmed & Traore, (2003) is presented in Figure 1.5.

• **Gait as a Biometric:**

relies on the walking pattern of a person. Even the great Shakespeare himself stated that "For that John Mortimer . . . in face, in gait in speech he doth resemble" (Shakespeare, W., King

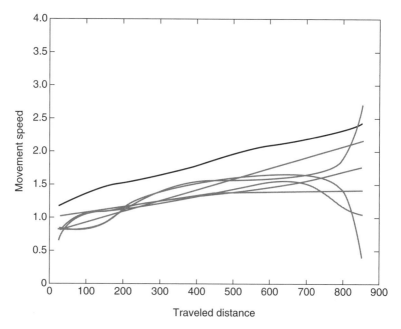

Figure 1.5 A graph presenting the user profile (solid top line versus a series of imposters based on average speed of mouse movements (Source: Awad et al., 2005)

Henry the Sixth, part 2, ca. 1590-1591). As Shakespeare himself intimated, there are subtle differences in the way a person ambulates. The results of a number of gait-based biometrics indicate that these differences are statistically significant – leading equal error rate (EER) values on the order of 5% or less. There are two principal approaches to gait biometrics: machine-vision and sensor-based approaches. The former is the more traditional approach and is suitable for scenarios where the authentication process must be mass produced, such as at airports. In this scenario, a user can be scanned from a distance relative to the authentication point. Provided the data acquisition can occur quickly, this type of approach may be very attractive. The sensor-based approach (see Figure 1.6 for an example of an accelerometer, the typical sensor used in gait analysis) acquires dynamic data, measuring the acceleration in three orthogonal directions. Sensor-based systems are quite suitable for user authentication – as they are obviously attached to the individual accessing the biometric device. Machine-vision based approaches are more general, and are typically employed for user identification.

The feature space of gait biometrics is not as rich as other technologies. This probably reflects the conditions under which the data are acquired – either a machine-vision approach with issues regarding lighting and other factors that typically degrade the performance of related biometrics such as face recognition. Even under the best of conditions (the gold-standard condition – see Appendix A for details), there are really only three degrees of freedom from which to draw features from. The current trend is to focus on dynamic aspects of walking, and the results tend to be somewhat better than static features when comparing EER values. When deployed in a multimodal approach, gait data, in conjunction with speech biometrics, for instance, tend to produce very low EER values (see Appendix A for details).

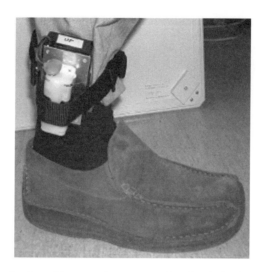

Figure 1.6 A photograph of a subject wearing a sensor-based gait device termed an accelerometer. Note that it is capable of measuring acceleration in three different orthogonal directions (Source: Gafurov et al., 2006)

Research continues to find ways to enhance the feature space of gait biometrics, but considering what is currently available, an EER of 3–5% is quite respectable.

+ **Smile Recognition:**

is a technique that uses high-speed photography, and a zoom lens generates a series of smile maps. These maps are composed of the underlying deformation of the relevant muscles and tiny wrinkles, which move in a characteristic fashion when a person smiles. A collection of directional vectors is produced which form the contours describing the dynamical aspects of smiling. This approach requires further analysis to determine how effective it will be as a behavioral biometrics, as current results are produced from a small study cohort.

+ **Lip Movement Recognition:**

For the purpose of recognizing individuals, we suggest a lip recognition method using shape similarity when vowels are uttered. In the method, we apply mathematical morphology, in which three kinds of structuring elements such as square, vertical line, and horizontal line are used for deriving pattern spectrum. The shapeness vector is compared to the reference vector to recognize the individual from lip shape. According to experimental results with eight lips that uttered five vowels, it is found that the method successfully recognizes lips with 100% accuracy.

+ **Odor as a Biometric:**

is an often-overlooked class of behavioral biometrics based on our sense of smell – olfaction-based biometrics. The human olfactory system is capable of detecting a wide range of odorants using a relatively sparse receptor system (see Freeman, 1991 for an excellent review). There are two principal processes involved in olfaction: stimulus reception and identification. There are questions regarding the specificity and sensitivity of the sense of

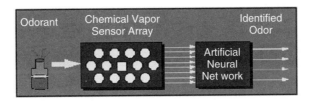

Figure 1.7 The olfactory biometric scheme, highlighting the sensor array and pattern recognition components (Source: Korotkaya, 2003)

smell. There are a number of professions that rely on a keen sense of smell – wine tasters, perfume experts, and human body recovery are a few examples (Yamazaki et al., 2001, Teo et al., 2002). It would therefore seem reasonable to assume that olfaction does have sufficient capacity to accurately identify a wide range of odors with high sensitivity. The question then shifts to whether or not humans exude sufficiently distinct odors such that we can be discriminated by them. Does the use of deodorant, colognes, and perfumes obfuscate our body odor beyond recognition? Lastly, how do we get a computer to perform olfaction?

The answer to the last question relies on the development of an artificial nose – the ENose (Keller, 1999, Korotkaya, 2003) – depicted in Figure 1.7. It is composed of two modules: a sensor array and a pattern recognition system. The sensor array consists of a collection of sensors (typically 10–20) each designed to react with a particular odorant. The pattern recognition system is used to map the activation pattern of the sensor array to a particular odorant pattern. The sensor array can be designed from a variety of materials, conductor sensors:

- made from metal oxide and polymers;
- piezoelectric sensors;
- metal-oxide-silicon field-effect transistors;
- optical fiber sensors.

Each of these technologies can be deployed as the basis for the sensor aspect of an ENose system (for details, please consult Gardner, 1991, Korotkaya, 2003).

There are a number of pattern recognition systems that can be employed – cluster analysis, neural networks, and related classification algorithms can be employed with success. The current operation of the ENose system is essentially a $1:1$ correspondence between sensor array number and odorants. Though the human olfactory system contains a great number of receptors (on the order of 1×10^{6}), they are used in a combinatorial fashion, that is, there is not a $1:1$ correspondence between an odorant and the activation of a particular receptor. It is a distributed system – and ENose, if it is to succeed at all, must adopt a similar approach. To date, there is not a clear direction in this area; it is really up to the neuroengineers to develop the required technology before it can be adapted to the biometrics domain. Though interesting, this approach will have to therefore wait for further parallel advancements in engineering before it can be considered a truly viable behavioral biometric – especially in a remote access context.

- **Biological Signals as a Behavioral Biometric:**

is a novel approach that relies on the measurement of a variety of biological signals. These include the electrocardiogram (ECG), the electroencephalogram (EEG), and the electrooculogram (EOG) to name a few potential candidates. In the late 1970s, Forsen published a report that evaluated the largest collection of potential biometric technologies known at the time (Forsen et al., 1977). Included in this impressive list was the deployment of the ECG and EEG – quite prescient for 1977! The basic approach is to extract the signals from the user during the enrollment period, to extract features, and to generate a classifier. When the user then attempts to log in, the particular class of signal is recorded, and a matching score is computed, which determines the decision outcome. This is really no different than any other behavioral biometric (and physiological for that matter) – the novelty here is the data that are acquired. In order to acquire biological signal data, specialized hardware is required. One of the tenets (or at least selling points) of behavioral biometrics is that no specialized hardware is required. It is anticipated that with the current rate of technological advancement, the amount of hardware required will be reduced to acceptable levels.

- **ECG as a Behavioral Biometric:**

The ECG is simply a recording of the electrical activity associated with the beating of the heart. A series of leads is positioned appropriately over the heart – which picks up the small electrical signals produced by various regions of the heart that generate electricity (i.e. the pacemaker or the sinoatrial node). The recording of the human heartbeat generates a characteristic profile (depicted in Figure 8.3). The question to be addressed is whether there is sufficient variability between individuals such that this signal can form a reliable marker for any particular individual. The data presented in Chapter 8 of this volume indicates that there is plenty of evidence to suggest that *it is* sufficiently discriminating to produce a high degree of classification accuracy (near 100% in some studies). Figure 1.8 presents a typical authentication scheme employing ECG data (taken from Mehta & Lingayat, 2007).

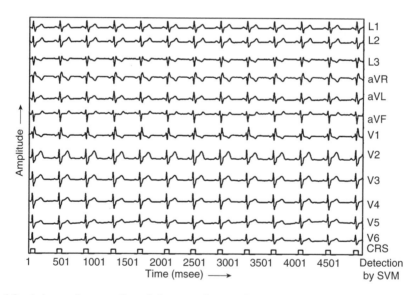

Figure 1.8 A time series recording of electrocardiogram data and some preprocessing results. The *x*-axis is time and the *y*-axis represents the signals acquired from each of the 12 leads. The bottom row represents the SVM detection results (Source: Mehta and Lingayat, 2007)

- **EEG as a Behavioral Biometric:**

The EEG is a recording from the scalp surface of the electrical activity of a collection of synchronously firing, parallel-oriented neurons. The EEG records the electrical activity of the brain and, as such, is continuously active (even for patients in the locked-in-state condition, resulting from a stroke). Embedded within the ongoing EEG activity are changes that occur in a correlated fashion with particular types of cognitive activities. The activities are typical cognitive functions such as thinking of a name, reading aloud, and listening to music. These signals can be isolated from the underlying background activity through a series of filtering and related techniques, which are discussed in some detail in Chapter 8 of this volume (see the references therein for more details). The goal in this approach is to associate particular electrical signatures that occur within the brain with particular cognitive tasks, such as entering a password to playing a video game.

The data obtained from EEG is sufficiently robust to generate a significant amount of intersubject variability, and many studies have produced statistically significant classification results using "raw" EEG data. In addition, through the process of biofeedback, a type of operant conditioning, people can control, to some degree, the activity of the brain in response to particular tasks (Miller, 1969). This is the essence of the brain–computer interface (BCI) (Figure 1.9) and forms the basis of an exciting area of research that is being applied to biometrics. For instance, users can control the movement of a cursor, type on a virtual keyboard, and related activities.

That this technology can be used as an authentication system is receiving serious research efforts, and the results appear to be quite promising, even at this early stage in the evolution of this technology. Again, there are the issues of the requisite hardware, which, as in the case for ECG technologies, can be expected to diminish with time. An example of a typical BCI protocol stack is presented in Figure 1.10.

Figure 1.9 A subject interacting with a virtual keyboard while wearing a standard 10–20 electroencephalogram skullcap (Source: Internet image – www.lce.hut.fi/research/css/bci *Copyright requested)

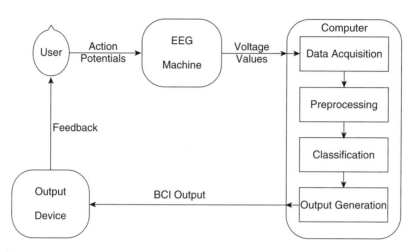

Figure 1.10 An example of a typical BCI protocol stack, displaying the principal features and the feedback loop (Source: Felzer, 2001)

1.3 The Biometric Process

Virtually all biometric-based authentication systems operate in a standard triage fashion: enrollment, model building, and decision logic. This set of processes is depicted in Figure 1.11. The purpose of enrollment is to acquire data from which the other two modules can be generated. In addition, it serves to incorporate a user into the pool of valid users – which is essential if one wishes to authenticate at a later date. The enrollment process varies little across biometrics modalities with respect to the user's participation: to provide samples of data. How much data are required depends on how the biometric operates. Typically, the inherent variability of a biometric modality will have a significant impact on the quality of the data obtained during enrollment. Issues of user acceptability, in terms of the effort to enroll, are a significant constraint and must be taken into account when developing the particular biometric. It is of no use if the system generates 100% classification accuracy if it is too invasive or labor intensive. This is an issue that distinguishes physiological from behavioral biometrics. Physiological biometrics is based on the notion of anatomical constancy and individual variation. One would expect that in this situation, enrollment would be minimal. For instance, in a fingerprint-based system, once all fingers are recorded, there would be no need to repeat the process 10 times for instance. A fingerprint is a fingerprint? The same may not hold true for behavioral biometrics, where there is an inherent variability in the way the process is repeated. Signatures are rarely identical, and the irony of it all is that the technology scrutinizes our behavior at such a low level that it is bound to find some variation even when we as humans, examining two versions of a signature produced by the same individual, find no clear differences.

There are two principal classes of features that can be acquired during enrollment, which can be categorized into static and dynamic features. Typically, static features capture the global aspects of the enrollment data. For instance, in signature verification, the static features capture the width/height ratios, and the overall time interval during which the signature is

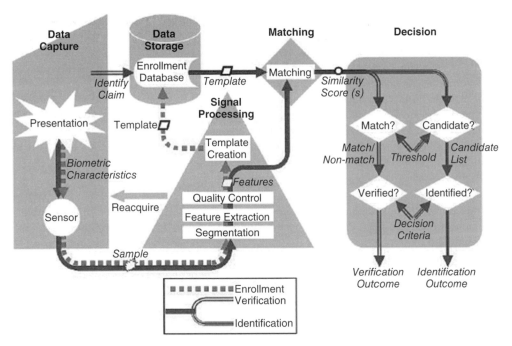

Figure 1.11 The elements that comprise a complete biometric-based system, suitable for both verification (authentication) and identification (Source: ISO/IEC JTC 1/SC 37 N1272, Figure 1 2005-08-30)

entered. Dynamic features include how the enrollment data change while they are being entered, such as the acceleration or the change in typing speed over time. One could envision that the static data are used as a gross approximation, with the dynamical features added in the event of a borderline decision. This presupposes that the static data are less informative than the dynamical data. But at the same time, the issue of constancy might weigh static data more heavily than dynamical data, which tends to be more variable. Finding this balance is a difficult task as it is not known in advance of the study. Typically, the results of the study are used to weigh the features – and different studies produce varying results – as the conditions are rarely identical between studies. There are also issues of data fusion – how does one incorporate a variety of features, which may operate on different timescales and differing magnitudes? These are important issues that will be discussed in Chapter 7, where multimodal biometrics is addressed.

Once these issues have been resolved, the ultimate result of the enrollment process is the generation of a biometric information record (BIR) for each user of the system. How do we transform the data that are collected during enrollment into a useful model? In part, this is a loaded question. On the one hand, one would assume that a model was available prior to collecting the data. But in reality, a lot of exploratory analysis is performed, where one collects all the data that appear possible to collect, and generates a collection of models, trying each to find out which provides the best classification accuracy. But the question is where did the model come from in the first place? This is the way science progresses, so we proceed as normal barring any other indication.

There are a vast number of models that have been employed in behavioral biometrics. It is beyond the scope of this text to explore this area, as it would fill a number of volumes. The case studies that occupy the majority of this text provide some examples of a variety of approaches that have been successfully applied in this domain. Assuming that a BIR is created for each successfully enrolled person, a database is created with the BIR data. There are issues here as well. Should the data be encrypted to help reduce the success of an off-line attack? Generally, the answer is yes, and many systems do employ online encryption technology.

The decision logic is designed to provide an automated mechanism for deciding whether or not to accept or reject a user's attempt to authenticate. When users make a request to authenticate, their details are extracted and compared in some way to the stored BIR. In order to decide whether to accept or reject the request, a decision process must be invoked in order to decide whether or not to accept the request. Typically, this entails comparing the features extracted from the authentication attempt with the stored BIR. There are a number of similarity metrics that have been employed in this domain. A factor that significantly impacts the matching/scoring process is whether or not the system utilizes a static or dynamic approach. For instance, in keystroke dynamics, one can employ a fixed text or a variable text approach to authentication. For a fixed text approach, a specific set of characters are typed – which can be directly compared to the BIR. This is a much easier decision to make than one based on a more dynamic approach, where the characters entered are contained within a much larger search space of possible characters. Of course, the ease with which the decision can be made is contingent upon the model building component but nonetheless has a significant impact on the decision login. Given that a decision has been rendered regarding an authentication attempt, how do we categorize the accuracy of the system? What metrics are available to rate various decision models?

In part, this depends on the exact task at hand: is it a verification or identification task? Clearly an authentication task (also known as identification), the goal is to confirm the identity of the individual. This can simplify the match and scoring processes considerably as it reduces the search task to a 1:1 mapping between the presumed identity and that stored in the database. The verification task is depicted in Figure 1.12.

The task of identification is considerably more difficult then authentication in most cases. The entire database must be examined as there is no information that could narrow down the

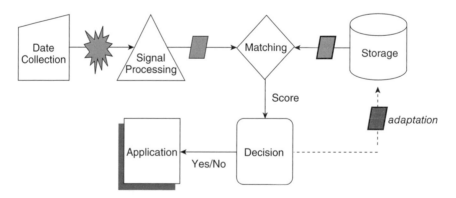

Figure 1.12 A graphical depiction of the verification process model indicating the principal elements and their potential interactions

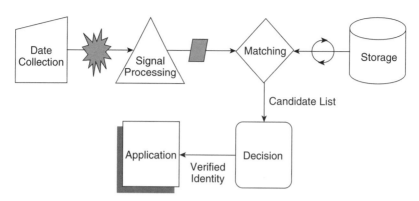

Figure 1.13   The identification process model depicting the principal difference between verification and identification, the candidate list element (see the text for details)

search. As depicted in Figure 1.13, the two process models are similar – barring the candidate list component, found only in the identification model. Another subtle distinction between these two approaches is depicted by the "adaptation" component present in the verification process model (Figure 1.12). Adaptation of the BIR is a vitally important feature of a mature and viable biometrics. Take for instance a keystroke dynamics-based authentication system. After the users complete enrollment and continue entering their password, the typing style might change slightly due to a practice effect or for other reasons. If the user is continuously matched against the enrollment data, the system may begin to falsely reject the genuine user. To prevent such an occurrence, the user's BIR must be updated. How the user's BIR evolves over time is an implementation issue. We tend to keep a rolling tally of the latest 10 success-ful login attempts, updating any statistical metrics every time the user is successfully authen-ticated. This is possible in a verification task – or at least it is easier to implement. In an identification task, the issue is how does the system actually confirm that the identification process has been successful? The system must only update the BIR once it has been success-fully accessed – and this cannot be known without some ancillary mechanism in place to identify the user – sort of a catch-22 scenario. Therefore, adaptation most easily fits into the authentication/verification scheme, as depicted in Figure 1.13.

1.4 Validation Issues

In order to compare different implementations of any biometric, a measure of success and failure must be available in order to benchmark different implementations. Traditionally, within the biometrics literature, type I (FRR) and type II (FAR) errors are used as a measure of success. Figure 1.14 illustrates the relationship between FAR, FRR, and the EER, which is the intersection of FAR and FRR when co-plotted. Note that some authors prefer to use the term crossover error rate (CER) as opposed to the EER, but they refer to identical con-cepts. When reading the literature, one will often find that instead of FAR/FRR, researchers report FAR and the imposter pass rate (IPR). The confusion is that this version of FAR is what most authors' term FRR, and the IPR is the common FRR. Another common metric prevalent in the physiological literature is the false matching rate (FMR) and false

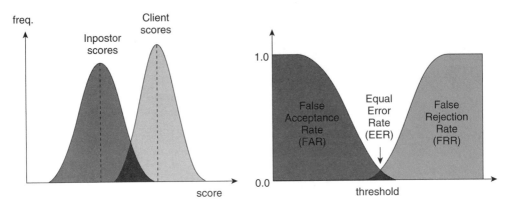

Figure 1.14 When the FAR and FRR are plotted on the same graph, as a function of a classification parameter, the intersection of the two functions is termed the EER or CER (Source: Google image: www.bioid.com/sdk/docs/images/EER_all.gif)

non-matching-rate (FNMR). The FMR is used as an alternative to FAR (FRR). Its use is intended to avoid confusion in applications that reject the claimants (i.e. an imposter) if their biometric data match that of an enrollee. The same caveat applies to FNMR as well.

A common result reported in the literature is the interdependence between the FAR and FRR. Most studies report that one cannot manipulate one of the metrics without producing an inverse effect on the other. Some systems can produce a very low FAR – but this generally means that the system is extremely sensitive and the legitimate user will fail to authenticate (FRR) at an unacceptable level. From a user perspective, this is very undesirable, and from the corporate perspective, this can be quite expensive. If users fail to authenticate, then their account is usually changed, and hence the user will have to reenroll into the system. In addition, the help desk support staff will be impacted negatively in proportion to the user support required to reset the users' account details. On the other hand, when the FRR is reduced to acceptable levels, then the FAR rises, which tends to increase the level of security breeches to unacceptable levels. Currently, there is no direct solution to this problem. One possible approach is to use a multimodal biometric system, employing several technologies. This approach doesn't solve the FAR/FRR interdependency but compensates for the effect by relaxing the stringency of each component biometric such that both FAR and FRR are reduced to acceptable levels without placing an undue burden on the user. The use of a multimodal approach is a very active research area and will be discussed in some detail in Chapter 7.

In addition to FAR/FRR and their variants, it is surprising that the concepts of positive predictive value (*PPV*) and negative predictive value (*NPV*), along with the concepts of sensitivity and specificity, often reported in the classification literature. *PPV* is the positive predictive value and the *NPV* negative predictive value of a classification result. The *PPV* provides the probability that a positive result is actually a true positive (that is a measure of correct classification). The predictive negative value (PNV) provides the probability that a negative result will reflect a true negative result. From a confusion matrix (sometimes referred to as a contingency matrix), one can calculate the *PPV*, *NPV*, sensitivity, specificity, and classification accuracy in a straightforward fashion, as displayed in Table 1.1.

The values for *PPV*, *NPV*, sensitivity, specificity, and overall accuracy can be calculated according to the following formulas (using the data in the confusion matrix):

Table 1.1 A sample confusion matrix for a two-class decision system

	Negative	Positive	
Negative	190 (*TN*)	10 (*FP*)	Specificity
Positive	10 (*FN*)	190 (*TP*)	Sensitivity
	NPV	*PPV*	Accuracy

TN = true negative, *FP* = false positive, *FN* = false negative, *TP* = true positive.

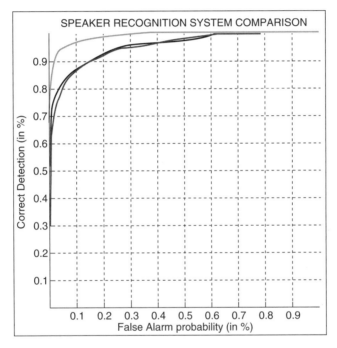

Figure 1.15 An example of an ROC curve, which displays the relationship between specificity and sensitivity (the *x*-axis is 1 specificity), and the *y*-axis is the sensitivity. The closer the curve approaches the *y*-axis, the better the result. Typically, one calculates the area under the curve to generate a scalar measure of the classification accuracy (Source: Martin et al., 2004)

$$\text{Sensitivity} = TP/(FN + TP)$$
$$\text{Specificity} = TN/(TN + FP)$$
$$PPV = TP/(TP + FP)$$
$$NPV = TN/(TN + FN)$$
$$\text{Accuracy} = (TN + TP)/(TN + FP + FN + TP)$$

Furthermore, the use of specificity and sensitivity can be used to produce an receiver operator characteristic (ROC) curve (see Figure 1.15). The ROC curve displays the interplay between

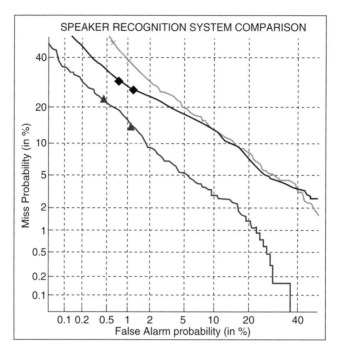

Figure 1.16   An example of a DET curve (using the same data used to plot the ROC curve in Figure 1.15). (Source: Martin et al., 2004)

sensitivity and specificity; it quantifies the relationship between FAR/FRR, in a form that is more quantitative than a simple EER/CER plot. In addition, the likelihood ratio (LR) can be obtained simply by measuring the slope of the tangent line at some cutoff value. These measurements are very useful in assessing the quality of a classification result. They are used quite frequently in the data mining literature and related fields, but for some reason have not found a place in the biometrics literature.

In addition to the above metrics, the detection error trade-off (DET) curve may be reported (see Figure 1.16 for an example of a DET curve). To generate a DET curve, one plots the FAR or equivalent on the x-axis and the FAR or equivalent on the y-axis. Typically, this plot yields a reasonably straight line, and provides uniform treatment to both classes of errors. In addition, by the selection of judicious scaling factors, one can examine the behavior of the errors more closely then the ROC. Of course, the FAR/FRR values are obtained as a function of some threshold parameter. With a complete system in hand, we can now address the important issue of biometric databases – valuable sources of information that can be used to test our particular biometric implementation.

1.5 Relevant Databases

One of the key issues with developing a novel biometric or developing a new classification strategy is to test it on an appropriate dataset. The case studies presented in this book employ a variety of techniques to acquire the data required for biometric analysis. But generally

Table 1.2 FVC2000 summary of the four databases employed in the competition. Note that w is the width and d is the depth (the dimensions of the image)

	Sensor type	Image size	Set A (w × d)	Set B (w × d)	Resolution
DB1	Low-cost optical sensor	300 × 300	100 × 8	10 × 8	500 dpi
DB2	Low-cost capacitive sensor	256 × 364	100 × 8	10 × 8	500 dpi
DB3	Optical sensor	448 × 478	100 × 8	10 × 8	500 dpi
DB4	Synthetic generator	240 × 320	100 × 8	10 × 8	About 500 dpi

Each is distinguished based on the type of sensor that was used to acquire the fingerprints (DB1-3), and DB4 contained synthetic signatures (Source: http://bias.csr.unibo.it/fvc2000 – free access website).

speaking, most people use local data collected in their own particular style. In this section, we will review some examples of databases that have been made publicly available for research purposes (and in Section 1.6, a discussion of ontologies and standards is discussed – both are intimately related).

The majority of biometric databases contain information on fingerprint, voice, and face data (Ortega-Garcia, 2003, Ortega & Bousono-Crespo, 2005). The fingerprint verification competition (FVC2000) databases were started in 2000 as an international competition to test classification algorithms (FVC2000, FVC2002, FVC2004). The FVC2000 competition was the first such event, bringing researchers from academia and industry in to compete. The data consisted of four separate databases (see Table 1.2 for details), which included different types of fingerprint scanners (optical, capacitive, etc.) along with synthetic data. The primary purpose of this competition was to determine how accurately we could identify a fingerprint based on automated techniques (cf. automated fingerprint identification system). The competition was advertised to anyone wishing to enter – with the express purpose of producing a classifier with the lowest EER. The results from this first competition (FVC2000) are summarized in Table 1.3. As can be observed from the results for the EER was approximately 1.7%. Note that this value was the average across all four databases. According to Maio and colleagues (2004), the purpose of this competition can be summarized by this quote from the authors: "The goal of a technology evaluation is to compare competing algorithms from a single technology. Testing of all algorithms is done on a standardized database collected by a 'universal' sensor. Nonetheless, performance against this database will depend upon both the environment and the population in which it was collected. Consequently the 'three bears' rule might be applied, attempting to create a database that is neither too difficult nor too easy for the algorithms to be tested. Although sample or example data may be distributed for developmental or tuning purposes prior to the test, the actual testing must be done on data that has not been previously seen by the algorithm developers. Testing is done using 'off-line' processing of the data. Because the database is fixed, results of technology tests are repeatable" (Table 1.3).

The competitors were judged on several criteria, but the average EER across all four databases was considered the de facto benchmark. As can be seen, the average EER was approximately 1.7%, and the adjusted EER (Avg EER* in Table 1.3) represents an adjustment based on whether there were rejections during the enrollment (see the fourth column in Table 1.3). These results are impressive, and it is interesting to note that the latest competition, FVC2004,

Table 1.3 Summary of the classification results from the first fingerprint verification competition (FVC2000)

Algorithm	Avg EER (%)	Avg EER* (%)	Avg REJ$_{ENROLL}$ (%)	Avg REJ$_{MATCH}$ (%)	Avg enroll time (sec)	Avg match time (sec)
Sag1	1.73	1.73	0.00	0.00	3.18	1.22
Sag2	2.28	2.28	0.00	0.00	1.11	1.11
Cspn	5.19	5.18	0.14	0.31	0.20	0.20
Cetp	6.32	6.29	0.00	0.02	0.95	1.06
Cwai	7.08	4.66	4.46	3.14	0.27	0.35
Krdl	10.94	7.59	6.86	6.52	1.08	1.58
Utwe	15.24	15.24	0.00	0.00	10.42	2.67
Fpin	15.94	15.94	0.00	0.00	1.22	1.27
Uinh	19.33	17.31	3.75	5.23	0.71	0.76
Diti	20.97	20.97	0.00	0.00	1.24	1.32
Ncmi	47.84	47.88	0.00	0.09	1.44	1.71

Please note that for a correct interpretation of the results, Avg EER alone is not an exhaustive metric, but Avg REJ$_{ENROLL}$ should be also taken into account (Source: http://bias.csr.unibo.it/fvc2000 – free access website).

yielded a slightly higher average EEG, just over 2%. Presumably, the technology – both from a signal acquisition and classification perspective, had increased during the 4 years between these competitions. This interesting fact alludes to the caution that should be applied when considering the classification results obtained from such studies. These were large-scale datasets – one should be cautious when examining much smaller datasets – how well do they cover the possible spectrum of events possible within the domain of interest? Have the classification algorithms been tailored to the data? A common issue of over-fitting may result if one is not careful. Ideally, after one has developed a classification algorithm that works well with a local database – in essence treating it as the training case – then the algorithms(s) should then be applied to a non-training database to see how well the results extrapolate. For more details on these datasets, please consult Maio and colleagues (2003).

The next dataset to be examined is from the behavioral biometrics literature. The signature verification competition (SVC2004) premiered in 2004, in conjunction with the FVC2004 and the FAC2004 (the latter being a face verification competition using the BANCA dataset, sponsored by the International Conference on Biometric Authentication (http://www.cse.ust. hk/svc2004/). Two datasets were used in this competition: the first (DB1) contained static information regarding the coordinate position of the pen, and the second (DB2) contained coordinate information plus pen orientation and pen pressure. The signatures contained controls and forgeries – the latter consisted of skilled forgeries and causal forgeries (see Chapter 3 for details on different types of forgeries). Generally, the skilled forgeries were obtained from participants who could see the actual signature being entered and had some amount of time to practice. The results from this study are summarized in Table 1.4. It is interesting to note that the average EER for signature was not very different from that of the fingerprint competition (for FVC2004, the best average EER was 2.07% versus 2.84% for signature verification; see Yeung et al., 2004 for more details). Note also that there was a very considerable range of EER values obtained (see Table 1.4) in the signature verification competition.

Table 1.4 Summary of the classification results from the first signature verification competition (SVC2004) sponsored by the International Conference on Biometrics consortium (Source: http://www.cse.ust.hk/svc2004/#introduction – free access website)

Test set (60 users):

Team ID	10 genuine signatures + 20 skilled forgeries				10 genuine signatures + 20 random forgeries			
	Avg EER (%)	SD EER (%)	Max EER (%)	Min EER (%)	Avg EER (%)	SD EER (%)	Max EER (%)	Min EER (%)
106	2.84	5.64	30.00	0.00	2.79	5.89	50.00	0.00
124	4.37	6.52	25.00	0.00	1.85	2.97	15.00	0.00
126	5.79	10.30	52.63	0.00	5.11	9.06	50.00	0.00
119b	5.88	9.21	50.00	0.00	2.12	3.29	15.00	0.00
119c	6.05	9.39	50.00	0.00	2.13	3.29	15.00	0.00
115	6.22	9.38	50.00	0.00	2.04	3.16	15.00	0.00
119a	6.88	9.54	50.00	0.00	2.18	3.54	22.50	0.00
114	8.77	12.24	57.14	0.00	2.93	5.91	40.00	0.00
118	11.81	12.90	50.00	0.00	4.39	6.08	40.00	0.00
117	11.85	12.07	70.00	0.00	3.83	5.66	40.00	0.00
116	13.53	12.99	70.00	0.00	3.47	6.90	52.63	0.00
104	16.22	13.49	66.67	0.00	6.89	9.20	48.57	0.00
112	28.89	15.95	80.00	0.00	12.47	10.29	55.00	0.00

This variability in the results must be reported – and the use of an average EER goes some way toward presenting the variability in the results. One will also notice that the details of the collection of the datasets is generally underdetermined – in that even for SVC2004, there are significant differences in the description of the datasets between DB1 and DB2 – making it difficult at best to produce these databases. These issues will be discussed next in the context of international standards and ontologies.

1.6 International Standards

The biometrics industry has undergone a renaissance with respect to the development and deployment of a variety of physiological and behavioral biometrics. Physiological biometrics such as fingerprints and iris and retinal scanners were developed first, followed by behavioral-based biometric technologies such as gait, signature, and computer interaction dynamics. These developments were driven for the most part by the needs of e-commerce and homeland security issues. Both driving forces have become borderless and hence must be compatible with a variety of customs and technological practices in our global society. Thus, the need arose to impose a standardization practice in order to facilitate interoperability between different instantiations of biometric-based security. As of 1996, the only standard available was the forensic fingerprint standards. Standards bodies such as the National Institute of Standards (NIST) and the International Standards Organization (ISO) have become directly involved in creating a set of standards to align most of the major biometric methodologies into a common

Figure 1.17 The three blocks contained within the CBEFF standard template for biometric data storage. The "SBH" block is the standard biometric header; the "BSMB" is the biometric specific memory block, and the "SB" block is an optional signature block (Source: Podio et al., 2001 (Figure2))

framework for interoperability purposes (http://www.iso.org/). The first major standardization effort was initiated in 1999 by the NIST (http://www.nist.gov/). Through a meeting with the major biometric industry players, a decision as to whether a standard template could be generated that would suit all of the industry leaders was examined. In the end, no agreement was met, but within a year, the Common Biometrics Exchange File Format (CBEFF) format was proposed. The CBEFF 1.0 was finalized as a standard in 2001 under the auspices of the NIST/Biometric Consortium (BC) and was made publicly available under an NIST publication NISTIR 6529 (January 2001). In 2005, CBEFF 1.1 was released under ANSI/INCITS 398-2005, and CBEFF 2.0 was released under the auspices of ISO/IEC JTC1 (ISO/IEC 19785-1) in 2006 (http://www.incits.org/). The overall structure of the CBEFF is depicted in Figure 1.17. It consists of three blocks onto which the required information is mapped onto. The purpose of the CBEFF was to provide biometric vendors a standard format for storing data for the sole purpose of interoperability. The basic format of the CBEFF is depicted in Figure 1.17. It consists of three elements – a header block, the data block, and an optional signature block (SB). Each block consists of a number fields that are either mandatory or optional. The essential features of the CBEFF template are

- facilitating biometric data interchange between different system components or systems;
- promoting interoperability of biometric-based application programs and systems;
- providing forward compatibility for technology improvements;
- simplifying the software and hardware integration process.

In summary, the standard biometric header (SBH) is used to identify the source and the type of biometric data – the format owner, the format type, and security options – these fields are mandatory. There are, in addition, several optional fields that are used by the BioAPI (discussed later in this chapter). The biometric specific memory block (BSMB) contains details on the format and the actual data associated with the particular biometric, and its specific format is not specified. Lastly, the optional SB is an optional signature that can be used for source/destination verification purposes. Table 1.5 lists the fields contained within the CBEFF blocks. For more details, please consult Reynolds (2005).

In addition to the development of the CBEFF standardized template, several variations and/or enhancements have been added to facilitate application development and to enhance security. In particular, the International Biometrics Industry Association (IBIA) is the body responsible for ensuring that all biometric patrons are properly registered and provided with a unique ID number (http://www.bioapi.org/). Clients can then register their biometric solutions with an appropriate patron. This patron/client relationship is depicted in Figure 1.18.

The CBEFF template does not specify at any level how the applications that acquire and utilize biometric information should be developed. To enhance the software development

Table 1.5 A depiction of the fields within the standard CBEFF template. (Source: International Standards Organization, ANSI/INCITS 398-2005)

Ident	Cond Code	Field Number	Field Name	Char Type	Field size per occurrence		Occur count		Max byte count
					min	max	min	max	
LEN	M	18.001	LOGICAL RECORD LENGTH	N	4	10	1	1	15
IDC	M	18.002	IMAGE DESIGNATION CHARACTER	N	2	5	1	1	12
RSV	–	18.003	RESERVED FOR FUTURE	–	–	–	–	–	–
		18.099	INCLUSION						
HDV	M	18.100	CBEFF HEADER VERSION	N	5	5	1	1	12
BTY	M	18.101	BIMOETRIC TYPE	N	9	9	1	1	16
BDQ	M	18.102	BIOMETRIC DATA QUALITY	AN	2	4	1	1	11
BFO	M	18.103	BDB FORMAT OWNER	AN	5	5	1	1	12
BFT	M	18.104	BDB FORMAT TYPE	AN	5	5	1	1	12
RSV	–	18.105	RESERVED FOR FUTURE	–	–	–	–	–	–
		18.199	INCLUSION						
UDF	0	18.200	USER-DEFINED	–	–	–	–	–	–
		18.998	FIELDS						
BDB	M	18.999	BIOMETRIC DATA	B	2	–	1	1	–

cycle, the BioAPI was developed – and indeed was part of the driving force for the development of the CBEFF. The BioAPI has its own version of the CBEFF – defined as a biometric identification record (BIR) (In later versions, BIR is used more generically and stands for biometric information record). A BIR refers to any biometric data that is returned to the application, including raw data, intermediate data, processed sample(s) ready for verification or identification, as well as enrollment data. The BIR inherits the standard structure of CBEFF and inserts detailed information into the SBH which makes it possible to be interpreted by BioAPI devices. The BioAPI has extended the original CBEFF by developing a suite of software development tools. By subsuming the CBEFF (via inheritance), it provides a complete program development environment for creating a variety of biometric applications. For more details, please consult BioAPI (http://www.nationalbiometric.org/) (Figure 1.19).

The last issue that has been addressed with regards to biometric standards is that of enhanced security – which was not part of the original CBEFF model. To enhance the security features of this model, the X9.84 specification was created. It was originally designed to integrate biometrics within the financial industry. Subsequently, the security features can be used in biometric applications regardless of the nature of the end user. In 2000, ANSI X9.84-

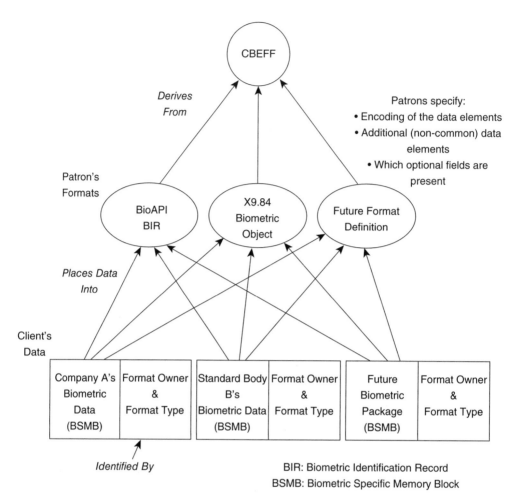

Figure 1.18   Patron/client architecture of the current working model. A client must register with a patron, who has the responsibility to ensure that the standards are adhered to and that any new technologies are properly defined and subsequently registered appropriately (Source: Tilton, 2003)

2002, Biometric Information Management and Security for the Financial Services Industry, was published (http://www.incits.org/tc_home/m1htm/docs/m1050246.htm). This standard provides guidelines for the secure implementation of biometric systems, applicable not only to financial environments and transactions but far beyond. The scope of X9.84-2002 covers security and management of biometric data across its life cycle, usage of biometric technology for *verification* and *identification* for banking customers and employees, application of biometric technology for physical and logical access controls, encapsulation of biometric data, techniques for securely transmitting and storing biometric data, and security of the physical hardware (Tilton, 2003). X9.84 begins by defining a biometric data processing framework. This framework defines common processing components and transmission paths within a biometrically enabled system that must be secured. Figure 1.19 summarizes the X9.84 specification.

Basic Functions	Primitive Functions
Module Management BioAPI_ModuleLoad BioAPI_ModuleAttach	**BioAPI_Capture** Captures raw/intermediate data from sensor
Data Handling BioAPI_GetBIRFromHandle BioAPI_GetHeaderFromHandle	**BioAPI_Process** Converts raw sample into processed template for matching
Callback & Event Operations BioAPI_SetStreamCallback	**BioAPI_CreateTemplate** Converts raw sample(s) into processed template for enrollment
Biometric Operations *BioAPI_Enroll* – Captures biometric data and creates template	**BioAPI_VerifyMatch** Performs a 1:1 match
BioAPI_Verify – Captures live biometric data and matches it against one enrolled template	**BioAPI_IdentifyMatch** Performs a 1:N match
BioAPI_Identify – Captures live biometric data and matches it against a set of enrolled template	**BioAPI_Import** Imports non-real-time data for processing

Figure 1.19 Summary of some of the major modules within the BioAPI version 1.1 framework. See BioAPI (http://www.nationalbiometric.org/) for details. This list contains many (but not all) of the primitive and basic functions required for the Win32 reference implementation of the BioAPI framework (Source: International Standards Organization, ANSI/INCITS 398-2005)

Note that recently, the BioAPI has been updated to version 2.0, which extends the previous version (ISO/IEC-19794-1, 2005). The principal change is the expansion of the patron/client model – which now includes devices, allowing for a proper multimodal approach. This should help facilitate interoperability – as it has moved the emphasis from the business collaboration perspective down to particular implementations. We will have to wait and see if this enhancement facilitates.

To summarize what is available in terms of a standard for biometric data interchange, we essentially have an available application programming interface Application Programming Interface (BioAPI), a security layer (X9.84), and a standardized template (BIR and CBEFF). The API is used to integrate the client (biometric applications) via a common template to other biometric clients implementing implements the interoperability requirement set forth by the standards organization. If you examine the patron list (http://www.ibia.org/), you will notice that there are no behavioral biometric patrons. This could be explained by a paucity of biometric clients, but if you look at the literature, there are a number of behavioral-based biometrics in the marketplace. Consider BioPassword®, a leader in keystroke dynamics-based biometrics. They claim to be driving forward via an initiative with INCITS, a keystroke dynamics-based interchange format (CEBFF compliant) BSMB. Yet they have not yet registered as a patron/client with IBIA – it simply might be a matter of time. In addition to Bio-Password®, there are a number of other vendors with behavioral-based biometrics – employing gait analysis, signature verification, and voice detection as viable biometric solutions. Why no behavioral biometric solution has registered is an interesting question (although BioPassword® is spearheading the registration of their keystroke dynamics product, BioPassword®).

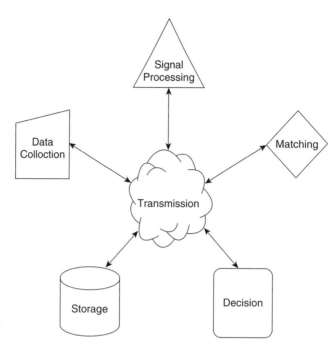

Figure 1.20 Depiction of the X9.84 biometric framework for secure transmission of biometric data over data channel that requires security

This could be the result of the difficulty in establishing a new patron or inherent differences between physiological versus behavioral biometrics.

As is displayed in Figure 1.18, there are only a few patrons – BioAPI and X9.84. These patrons are the result of a large organizational structure that is an amalgamation of international standard bodies and industry leaders. In order to augment the list of patrons, the industry must be willing to cooperate and work with these standards bodies in order to assert their standards with the constraint of being CBEFF compliant. At the client level, organizations (standards or industry) can produce a CBEFF-compliant BSMB for instance, but any additional changes are made at the API level and hence are proprietary in a sense.

Another possibility for the lack of behavioral biometric patrons is the inherent difference(s) between physiological and behavioral biometrics. For instance – though both classes of biometrics require an enrollment process – enrollment in behavioral biometrics may be significantly different than the method employed in physiological biometrics. For instance, enrolling in a fingerprint or retinal scanner may be a more straightforward task then enrolling in a keystroke or mouse dynamics-based biometric. In addition, there is a temporal factor in some behavioral-based biometrics. With keystroke dynamics-based systems, typing styles may change over time or a users' typing style may adapt as they learn their login details through a practice effect. The temporal changes must be captured if the authentication module is to perform at optimal levels. The same considerations apply to mouse dynamics, which are similar to keystroke dynamics except that they are applied to a graphical authentication system. Signature-based authentication systems tend to be more stable than keystroke/mouse dynamics – and so may be more similar to physiological biometrics in this respect. Are these considerations worthy of addressing? If so, how can the existing standards address these issues?

The primary consideration in this chapter is that the BioAPI/X9.84 standards are not robust enough to allow a complete integration of all extant biometric modalities. Though all must conform to the general framework (depicted in Figure 1.19) if they are to be considered for inclusion. The common denominator is that all clients must conform to the CBEFF template format. If you examine the format, you will notice that the vast majority of the fields are optional (17/20 for the SBH alone). Of those that are required, there is a limited vocabulary that is available to choose from – principally codes for format type, etc. An erroneous entry for a field value is handled by the client software and is not included directly as part of the standard. The values for optional fields do not conform to any standard and hence are, from an ontology perspective, ineffectual. Lastly, the "ontology" engendered by either patron has only minimal support for behavioral biometrics such as keystroke/mouse dynamics. We propose that an existing or a new patron be developed that can address these issues at the level of the standard itself – not at the level of the implementation. We propose that a proper ontology must be created in order to ensure that standards are developed properly and encompass all the extant biometric tools that are currently available, from an interoperability and research perspective (Revett, 2007a). An analogy with existing ontologies may be useful in this regard.

One useful ontology that has been very successful is the microarray gene expression data (MGED) ontology (http://www.mged.org/). This ontology describes how gene expression data should be annotated in order to facilitate sharing data across various laboratories around the globe. The ontology is actual in that it has a data model that incorporates named fields and values for each field. It has separate modules that relate to the acquisition of the experimental material, a model for how an experiment was performed, and lastly, a module for storing the data in a Web-accessible format. This ontology has been very successful – as many research laboratories around the world are using them – allowing seamless sharing of data. We propose a similar sort of structure for a behavioral biometric-based ontology, which includes first and foremost a true ontology where data fields are required and values for these fields are from a controlled list. A data structure similar to the CBEFF can be used, but it is not *the* single point of commonality between different biometric systems. Rather, the CBEFF is simply a data storage module that can be used by any biometric system. The fields contained within the data storage module must be more comprehensive and must be generated in the form of some type of object model, similar to the MGED standard.

This discussion has described the need for a comprehensive ontology for behavioral biometrics. The need for such an ontology is premised on the examples of how the attribute selection process and testing protocol can influence the results at all stages of the software development cycle of biometric software. Poor attribute selection will invariably produce a product that is inferior with respect to generation of adequate FAR/FRR results. Even if the attributes are selected reasonably, how they are utilized in the authentication algorithm is highly instance dependent and will clearly vary from one implementation to another. Skewed testing phase results will generally produce a negative impact on the quality of the resultant biometric – possibly increasing the duration of the testing phase – and certainly will increase the cost of product development. In addition, without knowledge of how attribute extraction and the testing protocol, it will be impossible to compare the results of different

authentication algorithms even on the same dataset. The differences might result from variations in the protocol more so than on the authentication algorithm per se.

What we are proposing in this chapter is a comprehensive ontology – not just a data template as the CBEFF standard provides. The CBEFF has too many optional fields and does
not include sufficient data regarding the biometric implementation to allow comparisons
between different methodologies. Though this may not have been the original intention, issues
highlighted in this chapter suggest that this is a critical aspect of such an effort. Interoperability between various biometrics is a noble goal. But the current standards appear to be biased
toward physiological-based biometrics. Granted these are fairly stable technologies – and the
attribute extraction process is well posed – they are incomplete with respect to the inclusion
of behavioral-based biometrics. In addition, the ability of various researchers (both in academia and industry) to explore the same data – for corroboration and analysis purposes – is
greatly hindered, resulting in duplication of effort.

This is a critical feature of a standard. The standards essentially neglect behavioral biometrics, yielding a divide between the two technologies. A proper ontology may be the
answer. The MGED standards has proven extremely effective with regards to a very complicated domain – DNA microarray experiments. Something akin to the MGED ontology may
be what is required to achieve interoperability between the two classes of biometrics. Having
such an ontology in hand would not impede the production of new biometric solutions; in
contrast, it would streamline the development process in most cases. In terms of proprietary
product development – in terms of proprietary product development – an ontology does not
imply that data and algorithms will be shared across the community, divulging trade secrets.
Trademark work can still maintain its anonymity – there is no need to disclose secrets during
the development process. When a product has reached the marketplace, intellectual property
rights will have been acquired, and this protection will be incorporated into the ontology by
definition. What will be made available is how the process was performed: details regarding
study conditions, the attribute selection process, data preprocessing, classification algorithms,
and data analysis protocols are the principal foci of the proposed ontology. The details of the
classification algorithms do not have to be disclosed.

To date, there is a single proposal for an ontology/standard that encompasses a behavioral
biometric authentication scheme, propounded by BioPassword (termed the Keystroke Dynamics Format for Data Interchange), published by Samantha Reynolds, from BioPassword
(Reynolds, 2005). A summary of the keystroke dynamics format is presented in Table 4.13.
It is unfortunate that this data format summary (or mini ontology) has so many incomplete
fields, especially within the "valid values" column. One of the key features of an ontology
is that is serves as a named vocabulary. All field values must be selected from a finite set of
values. Still, this is a very solid start toward the development of an ontology for behavioral
biometrics, and hopefully will be completed in the near future. But during this evolutionary
process, it is hoped that it will be able to incorporate other types of behavioral biometrics as
well. The ultimate aim would be to unite physiological and behavioral biometrics into a
common universally encompassing standard.

1.7 Conclusions

The chapter has highlighted some of the major issues involved in behavioral biometrics. A
summary of the principal behavioral biometrics was presented (though the coverage was not

exhaustive) highlighting the principal techniques. The focus of this book is on a remote access approach to biometrics, and as such, there is an implicit constraint that a minimal amount of hardware is required to deploy the system. One will note that in the list of behavioral biometrics, ECG, EEG, and gait were added. These approaches require some additional hardware over and above what is typically supplied with a standard PC. Their inclusion is to set the background for Chapter 8, which discusses the future of behavioral biometrics. Therefore, it should be noted that these technologies may not fall under our current working definition of a remote access approach, which can be defined as "a technique for authenticating an individual who is requesting authentication on a machine which is distinct from the server which performs the authentication process." But if behavioral biometrics is to expand its horizons, we may have to consider other options from traditional ones such as voice, signature, and keystroke interactions. Who knows what the future of technology will bring to us – which might make these possibilities and others a feasible option in the near future.

It is hoped that this text will highlight some of the advances of behavioral biometrics into the foreground by highlighting some of the success stories (through case study analysis) that warrant a second look at this approach to biometrics. There are a variety of techniques that have been attempted, each very creative and imaginative, and based on solid computational approaches. Unfortunately, the machine learning approaches cannot be addressed in a book of this length, so the reader is directed as appropriate to a selection of sources that can be consulted as the need arises. In the final analysis, this author believes that behavioral biometrics – either alone or in conjunction with physiological biometrics – either is standard reality or in virtual reality – can provide the required security to enable users to feel confident that their space on a computer system is fully trustworthy. This applies to a standard PC, ATM, PDA, or mobile phone.

1.8 Research Topics

1. Odor has been claimed to be a useful behavioral biometric – how would one explore the individuality of this biometric?
2. Is it theoretically possible to make FAR and FRR independent of one another?
3. Do lip movements suffer the same degree of light dependence as face recognition in general?
4. Can DNA be practically implemented as a biometric, and if so, would it be best utilized as a physiological or behavioral biometric tool?
5. What factors are important in the development of a biometric ontology? How do the current standards need to be enhanced to produce a unified biometric ontology (incorporating physiological and behavioral biometrics)?
6. What new behavioral biometric lie on the horizon? Have we exhausted the possibilities?

2

Voice Identification

2.1 Introduction

The deployment of speech as a biometric from a remote access approach is principally based on speech recognition – a $1:1$ mapping between the users' request for authentication and their speech pattern. Generally speaking, the user will be required to enunciate a fixed speech pattern, which could be a password or a fixed authentication string – consisting of a sequence of words spoken in a particular order. This paradigm is typically referred to as a *text-dependent* approach, in contrast to a *text-independent* approach, where the speaker is allowed to enunciate a random speech pattern. Text-dependent speaker verification is generally considered more appropriate – and more effective in a remote access approach, as the amount of data available for authentication is at a premium. This is a reflection of the potentially unbounded number of potential users of the system – as the number of users increases, the computational complexity necessarily rises.

The data generated from voice signals are captured by a microphone attached to a digital device, typically a computer of some sort (though this includes mobile phones and PDAs). The signals generated by speech are analogue signals, which must be digitized at a certain frequency. Typically, most moderate grade microphones employed have a sampling rate of approximately 32 kHz. The typical dynamic range of the human vocal cord is on the order of 8 kHz, though the absolute dynamic range is approximately 1–20 kHz). The Nyquist sampling theorem states that a signal must be sampled at least twice per cycle, so a 32 kHz sampling rate is generally more than sufficient for human voice patterns. If the signal is sampled less than the Nyquist sampling rate, then aliasing will occur, which will corrupt the frequency aspect of the signal (see Figure 2.1 for an example). In addition to capturing the frequency aspect of voice signals, the amplitude of the signal must be faithfully captured, otherwise the pitch (reflected in the amplitude) will be truncated, resulting in information loss at higher frequencies. Therefore, for reliable signal acquisition of voice data, the frequency and amplitude of the signal must be acquired with high fidelity. This is an issue with speakers with a large high-frequency component, such as women and children. Typically, most modern recording devices are capable of digitizing voice data at 16 bits or more, providing more then sufficient dynamic range to cover human speech patterns. In addition, if the data are to be collected over a telephone type device, the data are truncated into a small dynamic range of typically 4 kHz.

Behavioral Biometrics: A Remote Access Approach. Kenneth Revett
© 2008 John Wiley & Sons, Ltd.

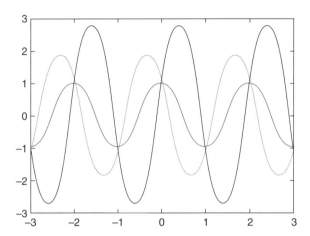

Figure 2.1 The Nyquist sampling theorem and its effect on the recovered frequency (Source: http://en.wikipedia.org/wiki/Nyquist%E2%80%93Shannon_sampling_theorem)

Before we begin by presenting a series of case studies exploring the underlying technologies employed in voice-based recognition, we must digress somewhat to explain some of the terminologies that are associated with speech recognition. Of all the classes of behavioral biometrics, voice recognition is probably ensconced within the realm of signal analysis more so than any other. Therefore, a brief introduction to some of the underlying techniques involved in signal processing may be in order. The literature on this topic has a long and venerable history, of which I cannot do justice to in a chapter of this nature. Instead, the interested reader will be directed to key papers on specified topics as they appear in context. First, we start off with a brief summary of the human speech apparatus.

The human cochlea, the organ responsible for sound reception, has a wide dynamic range, from 20 to 20 kHz. Typically, we can identify a human speaker by using a small fraction of this dynamic range, as for instance, we can recognize speech presented over telephone lines, which are low-pass filtered to approximately 4 kHz. In fact, the elements of the human speech apparatus can be viewed as a collection of filters. Sound is composed of a variable pressure wave modulated by the glottis, the vocal cords, the nasal tract, and the lips (the throat, tongue, teeth, and lips form what is referred to as the vocal tract). There are three basic types of speech sounds: voiced, unvoiced, and plosive. *Voiced* sounds are produced through the use of the glottis, through which air is passed over the vocal cords, producing vibrations. This generates a quasi-periodic waveform as the air passes across the vocal chords. This is the mechanism by which vowel sounds are created. *Unvoiced* sounds are produced by a steady force of air across a narrowed vocal tract (also termed fricative), and do not require any vibratory action of the vocal chords. The signal appears in spectrograms to be similar to noise in that there is no evident signature corresponding to different fricatives (i.e. the /S/ or /SH/ phonemes). *Plosives* are sounds that are produced by a sudden buildup of air, which is then passed through the vocal chord, that is, there is an initial silence, followed by a sudden burst of air pressure passing through the speech apparatus. Examples of this speech sound is the /P/ sound. Plosives are somewhat difficult to characterize as they are affected by previous phonemes and they tend to be transient in nature (see Rangayyan, 2002). Voice data can be viewed as the concatenation of speech sounds (the *linear predictive* model discussed below). There are generally two steps involved in speech analysis: *spectral shaping* and *spectral analysis*. Each of these processing stages will be discussed in turn in the next section.

The purpose of spectral shaping is to transform the basic speech data, which is a continuous time series of acoustic waveforms, into a discretized form for subsequent digital analysis. This process of speech production per se may be included in this processing stage, though most approaches do not incorporate a direct model of speech production process (though see Rahman & Shimamura, 2006 for a detailed example). If it is to be included, this process requires incorporating the generators of speech itself into the processing pipeline. The glottis, vocal chords, trachea, and lips are all involved in the production of the waveforms associated with speech. Each anatomical element acts in a sense as a filter, modulating the output (waveforms) from the previous element in the chain. The estimation of the glottal waveforms from the speech waveforms is a very computationally intense task (Rahman & Shimamura, 2006). Therefore, most studies forgo this process, which may yield a slight reduction in classification performance (see Shao et al., 2007 for a quantitative estimate of the performance degradation).

In spectral analysis, the speech time series is analyzed at short intervals, typically on the order of 10–30 ms. A pre-emphasis filter may be applied to the data to compensate for the decrease in spectral energy that occurs at higher frequencies. The intensity of speech sound is not linear with respect to frequency: it drops at approximately 6 dB per octave. The purpose of pre-emphasis is to account for this effect (Bimbot et al., 2004, Rosell, 2006). Typically, a first-order finite impulse response (FIR) filter is be used for this purpose (Xafopoulos, 2001, Rangayyan, 2002). After any pre-emphasis processing, the signal is typically converted into a series of frames. The frame length is typically taken to be 20–30 ms, which reflects physiological constraints of sound production such as a few periods of the glottis. The overlap in the frames is such that their centers are typically only 10 ms apart. This yields a series of signal frame each representing 20–30 ms of real time, which corresponds to approximately 320 windows/second if sampled at 16 kHz. Note that the size of the frame is a parameter in most applications, and hence will tend to vary around these values. It should be noted that since the data is typically analyzed using a discrete Fourier transform (DFT), the frame/window size is typically adjusted such that it is a power of two, which maximizes the efficiency of the DFT algorithm. After framing the signal, a window is applied which minimizes signal discontinuities at the frame edges. There are a number of windowing functions that can be applied – and many authors opt to apply either a Hamming or a Hanning filter (Bimbot et al., 2004, Orsag, 2004). With this preprocessing (spectral shaping) completed, the stage is ready to perform the spectral analysis phase, which will produce the features required for speech recognition.

2.1.1 Spectral Analysis

There are two principal spectral analysis methods that have been applied with considerable success to speech data: *linear prediction* (LP) and *cepstral analysis*. Both of these approaches assume that the data consist of a series of stationary time series sources, which is more or less assured by the windowing preprocessing step. The basic processing steps in LP analysis is presented in Figure 2.2. In this scheme, the vocal tract is modeled as a digital all-pole filter (Rabiner & Shafer, 1978, Hermansky, 1990). The signal is modeled as a linear combination of previous speech samples, according to equation 2.1:

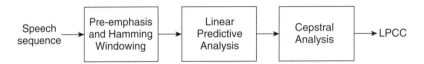

Figure 2.2 A summary of the processing stream based on the linear predictive modeling scheme employed in the production of speech features (Source: Cheng et al., 2005)

$$s(n) = \hat{s}(n) + e(n) = \sum N_{LP}(i)s(n-i) + e(n) \qquad (2.1)$$

where $\hat{s}(n)$ is the model; a_{LP} is a set of coefficients that must be determined; N_{LP} is the number of coefficients to be determined, and $e(n)$ is the model error or the residual (Bimbot et al., 2004). The coefficients are determined typically by applying an auto-regression (AR) model, which is then termed the linear prediction coefficient (LPC). These coefficients, possibly with the addition of a power term, can be used as features for a classifier. Typically, a transformation of the data is performed prior to obtaining the coefficients, in order to map the spectra onto the physiology of the human auditory system. More specifically, the signal is Fourier transformed and mapped onto a physiologically relevant scale (typically the mel scale). This step takes into account the fact that the human auditory system displays unequal sensitivity to different frequencies. Specifically, the system is more sensitive to low frequencies than to high frequencies. This feature is depicted in Figure 2.3. This transformation, termed the perceptual linear prediction (PLP), was introduced by Hermansky (1990).

Note that the human ear is not linear with respect to its response to sound of varying frequencies. Essentially, the human auditory system responds linearly to frequencies up to approximately 1 kHz. Beyond this frequency, the auditory system acts in a logarithmic fashion, typically described as the mel scale (Stevens et al., 1937). More specifically, the mel scale is a perceptual scale of pitches judged by listeners to be equal in distance (frequency) from one another. Also note that the term "mel" is derived from the word "melody" to denote that the scale is based on pitch information (Stevens et al., 1937, Mermelstein, 1976, Davis & Mermelstein, 1980). Figure 2.3 provides a graphical measure of the mel scale, depicting the nonlinearity of the pitch perception of the human auditory system. This feature must be taken into account when extracting frequency information (or alternatively power information) from the time series data.

The LP (and PLP) approaches utilize the AR model to acquire values for the coefficients to characterize the signal within each frame. The deployment of the AR model yields a set of coefficients (in Section 2.1) that are highly correlated. This tends to reduce the classification accuracy of this approach (see Atal & Hanauer, 1971 and Ouzounov, 2003 for examples of this approach). To overcome this limitation, many speech recognition systems employ the use of cepstral coefficients.

2.1.2 Cepstral Analysis

The cepstrum (a word produced by shuffling the spelling of "spectrum") is the time domain representation of a signal. Also note that the word "quefrency" is used to denote the time used in cepstral analysis – a shuffling of the term "frequency." It reflects the juxtaposition of time and frequency that occurs when performing this type of analysis.

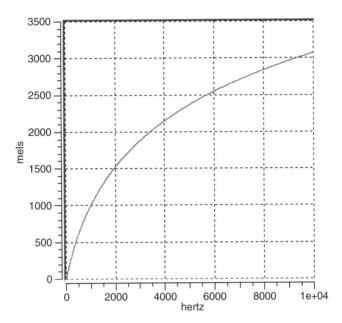

Figure 2.3 The mel frequency scale, which is typically implemented using the following equation: $m = 2595 \times \log(1 + f/700$ Hz$)$ (Source: http://en.wikipedia.org/wiki/Mel_scale)

In the context of speech recognition, one usually begins with a model of the spectral pattern of speech, which can be modeled as the product of the vocal tract impulse response and glottal excitation, as depicted in equation 2.2.

$$S(n) = g(n) \oplus v(n) \tag{2.2}$$

where $g(n)$ is an excitation signal (via the glottis), and $v(n)$ is the output of the vocal tract filter. This convolution is then transformed into the frequency domain (via the Fourier transform) to yield the product

$$S(f) = G(f)V(f) \tag{2.3}$$

By taking the log of this product, the two aspects become additive. The task then becomes one of eliminating the glottal excitation component of speech ($G(f)$). Note that the excitation elements (the glottal components) will tend to yield a higher frequency than the vocal tract elements. This fact can be used to remove the glottal ($\log|G(f)|^2$) components by effectively low-pass filtering the data. To do this, the inverse Fourier transform (iFT) can be applied to the log transformed power spectrum. This will transform the data into the time domain (quefrency), yielding the so-called cepstrum (Rabiner & Shafer, 1978). This process smooths out (cepstral smoothing) any peaks, leaving the glottal excitation components, which appear as a large peak in the smoothed signal. The peak can be removed by filtering the signal, zeroing out the point in the signal where the large peak occurred (the glottal excitation peak), and by transforming the data back into the frequency domain. This effectively removes $G(f)$, leaving on the vocal tract signal, which is the important aspect of the speech signal in terms of identification of the speech formants.

The time domain data can be used directly as features representing the frame of speech data, along with several other parameters such as the power and statistical measurements of the cepstral coefficients. The coefficients produced by this process correspond to the center frequencies transformed onto the mel scale, which reflect the frequency components (harmonics with respect to the fundamental frequency). Usually, only the lower order coefficients are discriminating, and most studies utilize the first 12 coefficients (representing the low-frequency components) as features for recognition tasks.

2.1.3 Additional Features and Classification Algorithms

There are a number of additional features that can be extracted from speech signals in addition to the cepstral coefficients. These include the energy, the zero-crossing rate, the instantaneous frequency from phase information (Paliwal & Atal, 2003), and statistical measures of the cepstral coefficients that have been successfully deployed (Xafopoulos, 2001, Bimbot et al., 2004, Orsag, 2004). The feature space of voice is therefore quite substantial – with typically 15–30 features used to encode a particular speech signal (Furui, 1981a). In addition, there are a number of subsamples that are available from a particular speech sample. Typically, the speech stream is windowed at approximately 20–30 ms – generating a large number of samples for even 1 minutes worth of speech. This large volume of data allows a variety of classification algorithms to be deployed. Only a small sample of the approaches will be explored – as the literature is just too vast to explore the full range of applications that have been developed. Also, note that the principal focus of this chapter is for voice recognition in a biometrics context; the focus will be on text-dependent and speaker-dependent applications. In the next section, a series of case studies is presented, highlighting the specific features of each class of applications with respect to the static and dynamics features of speech based biometrics.

2.2 Case Studies in Speaker-Dependent Voice Recognition

Niesen and Pfister (2004) explored the use of artificial neural networks (ANNs) for speaker verification in a text-dependent fashion. A text-dependent speaker verification task requires that the speaker enunciates a particular corpus of text. This can simplify the verification task as the data can be aligned with a reference corpus – usually by way of a distance metric. With text-independent speaker verification, the speaker is allowed unconstrained speech production, which means a more general model of the speaker must be developed. The central issue in this paper is the alignment of the cepstral components between a reference sample and a test sample. In text-dependent speech, aligning the cepstral coefficients is typically performed by minimizing the Euclidean distance between the cepstral coefficients between the samples (Furui, 1981b). The authors argue that this task can be performed more efficiently through the use of ANNs. The distance between two speech samples in the case of text-dependent speech is the same; the total distance between the two samples (in a global sense) is the summation of the differences between the local windowed samples of both spectra. The authors claim that the use of the dynamic time warping (DTW) algorithm is not suitable for speaker verification because there are two processes that require alignment: one at the local window level, and the other at the global level. The authors indicate that these are very different processes, and the use of the DTW approach may not be suitable for these tasks. Instead, the authors use the DTW for the local windowing comparisons, but use these local windows as an input to an ANN to produce the global alignment.

The input to the ANN is a pair of DTW time-aligned speech signals, which employs the Euclidean cepstral distance to optimally align the signal pairs. For each frame (subset of the speech window), the first 12 coefficients of the LPC cepstrum were extracted from the reference and test samples were used as inputs to the ANN, which yields a local distance metric for the frames. The local distances are then used to calculate the global distance, and this value is used to make the decision of authentic or imposter test sample.

The ANN employed was a multilayer feedforward network with a hyperbolic tangent activation function. The network was trained using the back-propagation algorithm, using an adaptive learning rate. There were 24 input nodes (corresponding to the 12 cepstral coefficients for test and reference data) and a single output node. There were two hidden layers, with 60 and 18 nodes, respectively (this was determined empirically from the datasets). Note that the inputs to the ANN were normalized by a linear transformation to yield a zero mean and diagonal covariance matrix (they employed principal component analysis [PCA] for this transformation). One property of the system that was investigated was the issue of symmetry – it should not matter which order the coefficients were added – as the distance between the two sets should be order invariant. To facilitate the invariance, the authors employed a function that coded the input such that it computes the sum and the absolute difference between the pair of inputs.

An important issue in this work is the local transition behavior – what happens during the frame transitions. This relates to edge effects that tend to distort the signal (the reason why most researchers use a non-rectangular frame/window when subsampling speech signals). The authors employed the use of the first and second time derivatives for each window, which essentially corresponds to the delta and delta–delta cepstrum (see Mason & Zhang, 1991, Orsag, 2004 for details). To take into account the transitional information, 24 addition features were required for input into the ANN. The results from the augmented input scheme produced reduced classification accuracy at the global level, compared to omitting these additional features. At the local level, the transitions increased the classification accuracy – as the effect is to lengthen the regression window, which enhances the signal-to-noise ratio (SNR). Yet the contribution of the local windows is reduced with respect to the information imparted onto the global feature. The issue is to strike a balance between these two competing processes (a common issue throughout the biometrics field unfortunately!). To solve this problem, the authors employed three separate ANNs used in parallel, one for the instantaneous features and one for each of the transitional features (delta and delta–delta cepstra). The local distances (between the reference and test frames) were calculated from a linear combination of the ANN outputs (0.86, 0.46, and 0.22, respectively, for the instantaneous and the two transitional features, respectively).

After developing their classification system, it was tested on a set of 30 male speakers. The data were collected over a period of several months, during which time each speaker produced 10 sessions of speech (3 hours in total), over a telephone system. The LPC cepstral coefficients were extracted from 37.5 ms speech frames with a frameshift of 15 ms. The dataset consisted of approximately 500,000 feature pairs from 20 speakers; the rest of the speaker data were used for testing purposes. The authors reported the performance of the system via the equal error probability (EEP), which was 5.3% for approximately 1 second of speech signal from the 10 test speakers.

The results from this study were quite impressive – producing a reasonably low EEP of approximately 5%. The authors employed local (instantaneous) and regional information (the delta and delta–delta cepstra) as the only features of this system. It would have been interesting if the authors employed a larger range of features, both at the local and global levels. Further note that the system was tested using speech produced over the telephone, which has a tendency to reduce the dynamic range of the data. Though not directly applicable as a technique for remote access, this study did present an interesting example of the approach used in speaker verification. It would prove interesting to see if the results can be improved upon by utilizing data from a computer microphone, where the dynamic range is considerably larger than that of a typical telephony system.

Benzeghiba and Bourlard (2003) published an interesting paper describing how speech could be used for password-based authentication, that is, the password is spoken instead of typed. Their approach used a hybrid hidden Markov model (HMM)/ANN approach, where the ANN was used to estimate emission probabilities of the HMM and Gaussian mixture models (GMMs). More specifically, the ANN aspect of this approach captures the lexical component of the speech, while the HMM/GMM captured the user-specific details. By merging these two processes together into a single system, it is believed that this system will be able to perform well when validating user-spoken passwords (termed speaker verification on user-customized passwords [SV-UCP]).

Given an acoustic signal (X), the task required of SV-UCP is to estimate the joint posterior probability that the correct speaker (S_k) has uttered the correct password (M_k), that is, $P(M_k, S_k|X)$. A set of decision rules is generated that will allow the system to make a decision as to the probability that the current correctly uttered password is generated by the correct speaker. The posterior probability of a speaker S pronouncing the utterance M is

$$P(M_k, S_k|X) \geq P(M, S|X) \tag{2.4}$$

where M is represented as an ergodic HMM (Benzeghiba & Bourlard, 2003). The posterior probability of a speaker S pronouncing correctly the correct password M_k is given in equation 2.5:

$$P(Mk, Sk|X) \geq P(Mk, S|X) \tag{2.5}$$

Using Bayes rule, equation 2.4 can be rewritten as

$$\frac{P(X|M_k, S_k)}{P(X|M_k, S)} \geq \frac{P(M, S)}{P(M_k, S_k)} \tag{2.6}$$

and the decision rule from equation 2.5 can be written as

$$\frac{P(X|M_k, S_k)}{P(X|M_k, S)} \geq \frac{P(M_k, S)}{P(M_k, S_k)} \tag{2.7}$$

where equations 2.6 and 2.7 become decision thresholds. Rule 2.7 is superior to 2.6 in that it is based on the assumption that the imposter could pronounce the correct password, as opposed to pronouncing the right password correctly (and is thus a stronger rule).

The denominator in equation 2.6 is estimated as an ergodic HMM which serves as the world model (i.e. the incorrect speakers amalgamated into a single speaker). The authors refer to the to this as the "unconstrained HMM." The denominator in equation 2.7 is estimated using a forced Viterbi alignment performed on the password HMM model M_k. This is referred to by the authors as the "constrained HMM."

Two databases were employed in this study – the Swiss French Polyphone database and a large telephone database which contains prompted and natural sentences pronounced by a large number of speakers, containing 10 phonetically rich sentences read by 400 users (Chollet et al., 1996). These databases were used to train different HMM and HMM/ANN speaker-independent speech recognizers. The speaker verification experiments in this work employed the PolyVar database, as this one was designed to measure inter-speaker variability. The database contains telephone records of 143 speakers, with each speaker recording anywhere from 1 to 229 sessions. Each session consisted of one repetition of the same set of 17 words common for all the speakers. The authors selected a subset from the database, which contained 19 speakers (12 males and 7 females) each of which had more than 26 sessions each in the database. The first five sessions for each of the 19 speakers was used as training data, and the rest as testing data. A different subset of 19 speakers was used to serve as imposters.

Two types of acoustic parameters were utilized: RASTA-PLP (<u>Rel</u><u>A</u>tive <u>Spec</u><u>Tr</u><u>Al</u> <u>P</u>erceptual <u>L</u>inear <u>P</u>redictive) coefficients for HMM inference and mel-frequency cepstral coefficients (MFCCs) were used for speaker verification. Twelve RASTA-PLP coefficients and their first- and second-order temporal derivatives of the log energy were calculated at 10 ms intervals over 30 ms windows, resulting in a toal of 26 coefficients. These coefficients were used to train a speaker-independent multilayer perceptron (SI-MLP) which was used to infer the password of the user. In order to retain the features of the user, the MFCCs were used for speaker adaptation. Twelve MFCCs with an associated energy value derived from the first derivative were calculated every 10 ms over the 30 ms window, which produced another set of 26 coefficients.

Each of the study participants enrolled into the system by uttering a password (derived from phonemes stored in the PolyVar database) five times, three of which were used for inference data and the remaining two entries for cross-validation purposes. The result of the enrollment process is to ascertain a set of three parameters required to estimate the normalized log likelihood ratio to compute the final score that is compared to a speaker-independent threshold.

The results of this system were tested under two conditions: in one, the same password was used for all users, and in the other, each user had a different password. In the same password experiment (which was "annulation"), 19 subjects pronounced 27 utterances for testing, 5 being incorrect passwords, and the other 22 were correct utterances of the password. All the imposters were from the PolyVar database (and hence different from the training participants employed in this study). Each imposter had two entries – one of which was the correct password and the other incorrect (i.e. not one typically used by that user – inferred). This yielded 420 true study accesses and 779 false imposter accesses (which includes correct subjects entering the inferred password). A speaker-independent threshold was set a posteriori to yield an equal false acceptance rate (FAR) and false rejection rate (FRR). The results indicate that when the correct password was used, the equal error rate (EER) was approximately 1.5% for the constrained HMM model. The corresponding EER value was 2.08%. When the subjects were allowed to choose different passwords (which is typically the case), the EER for the unconstrained HMM was 4.1% when entering the correct password, and 2.6% when using the inferred password.

The results of this study yielded a very reasonable value for the EER, on the order of 2.6% when the users uttered passwords they were not accustomed to (imposters or not). This is the typical case, where imposters are expected to utter the password of another user – one which they are not accustomed to entering. The system proposed is fairly complicated – and requires the training of a fairly significant multilayer perceptron (MLP) (234 inputs – nine consecutive 26 dimensional acoustic frames, 600 hidden units, and 36 outputs, each associated with a different phone). An MLP network of this dimension will take some time to train – an issue that may have to be addressed for execution efficiency issues. Another issue to be addressed in this work is the fusion at the score level, which in this work assumes equal weight between the utterance verification and speaker verification model. It may be that these different models will have to be weighted in a user-specific manner – see Chapter 7 in this volume for a brief discussion on fusion models in the context of multimodal biometrics.

In a study published by Masuko and colleagues (1999), the effect of a spoofing technique for speaker verification where synthesized speech was used to attack a system is presented. This study builds on previous work by the authors that sought to develop a speech synthesis system that utilizes HMMs to generate smooth and natural speech (Masuko et al., 1996). This paper describes the use of an HMM-based speech synthesis system that attempts to attack another HMM-based system!

The imposter-based system is derived from an HMM-based speech synthesizer that consists of two parts: a training and a synthesis component. For the training component, the mel-cepstral coefficients are acquired from speech database via mel-cepstral analysis. Dynamic features, such as delta and delta–delta coefficients, were calculated from mel-cepstral coefficients. The phoneme HMMs were trained using the dynamic features (mel-cepstral coefficients and their delta and delta–delta coefficients). The authors employ a mel log spectral approximation (MLSA) filter, which then generates speech from the mel-cepstral coefficients directly. For the synthesis aspect, an arbitrary text to be synthesized is transformed into a phoneme sequence. The phonemes are then concatenated to form arbitrary strings (sentences) from the collection of learned phonemes.

The text used in this system was acquired from the Japanese speech database, which consists of sentences uttered by 20 male speakers, each generating a set of 150 sentences. Ten of the speakers were used as genuine speakers and the remainder served as imposters. The database was divided into three partitions, each containing 50 sentences for each of the speakers. One set was used to determine the thresholds of a normalized log likelihood; another set was used to train the speech synthesis system, and the last set was used to test the system. The speech was sampled at 10 kHz and was segmented into 48 phonemes based on labels included in the database.

The authors then employed an HMM-based text-dependent speaker verification system (Matsui & Furui, 1994). The state sequence is generated by a combination of static and dynamic features, and the output distribution of each state forms a single Gaussian distribution. An overview of their system is presented in Figure 2.4. The synthesized speech (i.e. a collection of HMM-generated phonemes) was windowed by a 25.6 ms Blackman window with a 5 ms shift, and the cepstral coefficients were calculated by 15th-order LPC analysis. The feature vector therefore consisted of 16 cepstral coefficients, which included the zeroth-order coefficient, and the corresponding deltas and delta–deltas. The speaker-dependent phoneme model was trained on the 50 sentences. The speaker-independent phoneme models were trained using the entire set of sentences from all speakers. After calculating the log

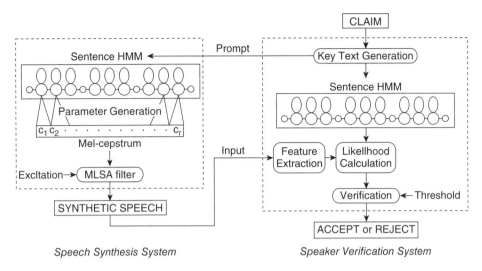

| CLAIM |
Sentence HMM ←	Prompt	Key Text Generation
Parameter Generation		Sentence HMM
$c_1 c_2 \cdots c_r$		
Mel-cepstrum	Input	Feature Extraction — Likelihood Calculation
Excitation → MLSA filter		Verification ← Threshold
SYNTHETIC SPEECH		ACCEPT or REJECT
Speech Synthesis System		*Speaker Verification System*

Figure 2.4 An overview of the HMM-based imposter detection system of Masuko and colleagues, depicting the HMM-based speech synthesis component and the speaker verification (HMM-based) component (Source: Masuko et al., 1999)

likelihoods of speaker-dependent and speaker-independent models (genuine versus imposter utterances), speaker-defined thresholds based on training data were generated. The authors employed several state models, ranging from two to four states. The baseline system FRR (with a FAR of 0%) ranged from approximately 7% to 10%. The number of training samples was varied from one to five, which tended to decrease the FRR slightly as well.

Next, the system was tested using synthesized speech, employing the same phonemes as in the baseline experiment. The data were processed in exactly the same way as the baseline case, though some of the feature parameters were different in the two experiments (whose features were not indicated in the paper). Also note that the system was trained using a different set of 50 sentences from the baseline case. The results with respect to FAR/FRR yielded a FAR well over 70%, indicating that the imitation aspect of the synthesized speech was quite accurate, relative to the baseline training case.

The results from this study indicate that synthesized speech can be used with some degree of success as a way to spoof a voice recognition system. In this study, a speech synthesis system, based on an HMM, was used to generate test data and also was used as a discriminatory function for synthesized data consisting of the same phonemes. The authors noted that for their system, the incorporation of dynamic data (delta, delta–delta cepstral coefficients) was critical with respect to false acceptance rates. They also noted that the number of states in the HMM was also important, indicating the dependency on the amount of available training data. With an increased number of states, more parameters values are required to be fit, which requires more training data. It would be interesting to see how well the system would perform if the sentences used to train the model were different from the ultimate test sentences – even if they contained the same phonemes, but in a different order.

The dynamical elements in speech signals was analyzed in terms of its contribution to classification error in a study by Ortega-Mendoza and colleagues (2006). The authors investigated dynamic features in a speaker identification task, where the purpose is to select a particular speaker from a set of possible speakers. Generally speaking, most successful speaker identification systems employ a text-dependent paradigm, where the speakers utter a fixed text. This reduces the complexity of the problem to one of template or frame matching. In this study, the authors generalize speaker identification using a *text-independent* paradigm. In addition, the system attempts to cross language-based barriers by focusing on the speech signals directly, without any reliance on phonetic recognition. The authors focus on the information content of the MFCC as the principal source of dynamic information. The cepstral coefficients are used to compute a unique set of features that capture and utilize the temporal signatures within the speech signal, which are integrated into a model of the speaker. The authors employ a naive Bayes and a support vector machine (SVM) for automatic classification purposes.

The speech signal is framed into 30 ms windows, which are non-overlapping. For each segment, 16 MFCCs are extracted, instead of the usual 12 which are normally used for characterizing the dynamical content of windowed speech signals. Typically, the upper cepstral coefficients possess information regarding the upper frequencies contained within the window (see Ganchev et al., 2005). In addition to the 16 MFCCs, the derivatives are calculated as well (equivalent to the delta), and the authors take the minimum, maximum, average, and variance of the change in the coefficients in each frame (yielding a total of 64 features/frame). This data forms the signature for each speaker, and is used as the input into the classification system (naive Bayes or SVM).

Very briefly, a naive Bayes classifier assumes that the features are conditionally independent of one another with respect to class membership. The features are in conjunctive form, and the decision outcome can take on any finite value. What is required to apply this approach, the conditional probability density and the probability that class X has some particular value, j, both of which must be obtained from the training data. An SVM is a computationally efficient classifier for learning how to create separating hyperplanes in a high-dimensional feature space (Cristianni & Shawe-Taylor, 2000). These classification tools were deployed on data extracted from the DIMEx100 corpus (Pineda et al., 2004).

This corpus contains speech in Mexican Spanish from 100 individuals who were native speakers, recorded at 44 kHz. Each speaker recorded 50 *different* phrases, each 3.5 seconds in length (approximately 4.9 hours of speech in total). For the experiments described in this paper, 3 seconds worth of speech from 50 randomly selected speakers were used. The speech signals were partitioned into fixed length, nonoverlapping 30 ms segments. The first 16 MFCCs were extracted from each of the segments and were used for all subsequent analyses. The authors examined a variety of feature combinations to determine, based on the classification accuracy, their information content. The best classification accuracy was obtained by utilizing the dynamic features of the first 16 MFCCs (the minimum, maximum, average, and variance). The resulting classification accuracy was 94.56% and 97.56% for the naive Bayes and SVM classifiers, respectively (note that these results were generated by a 10-fold cross-validation scheme). Another observation from this study was that the SVM classification error was typically lower than the naive Bayes classifier. Also note that the deployment of the dynamical aspects of the first 12 cepstral coefficients reduced the classification accuracy (89.59% and 94.28% for the naive Bayes and SVM classifiers, respectively). This highlights the information gain by including some higher cepstral coefficients (which correspond to slightly higher waveform frequencies). In contrast, without the full complement of dynamic data, the classification accuracies ranged from 85.55% to 90.47% (the range for both classifiers).

The results from this study indicate that dynamic information improved the classification accuracy, regardless of the classifier employed (at least for naive Bayes and SVM as deployed in this study). It would be interesting to try this approach on different datasets to see how well these results generalize – especially across different languages – as the authors claim this approach is language independent. In addition, it would be interesting to measure the impact of each of the statistical measures of the coefficients on the classification accuracy – higher-order statistics may also be useful – although the measures employed in this study were straightforward to compute.

2.3 Standards

Generally speaking, voice is an underrepresented element in the international standards for biometrics. According to the Common Biometrics Exchange File Format (CBEFF) framework, Amendment 1, there is a slot for lip motion! Of the behavioral biometrics, keystroke dynamics has the largest representation, and this is possibly a reflection of the interest in this area generated by BioPassword, a keystroke dynamics-based authentication product (see Chapter 4 for details), whom have pushed for its incorporation into the CBEFF. The same sentiment holds true for the BioAPI specification, which includes signature/sign behavioral data as part of its specification, but nothing regarding voice as a biometric (Dessimoz & Richiardi, 2006).

There is clearly an under-representation of speech as a mainstream behavioral biometric in the standards industry. Even though there are a number of commercial implementations, the industry proper has not pressed for its dissemination to any significant degree. Generally, this dissemination comes in the form of international competitions – such as the fingerprint and signature verification events (Fingerprint Verification Competition [FVC], Signature Verification Competition [SVC], etc.). The National Institute of Standards (NIST) speaker recognition evaluation (SRE) has been ongoing since 1996, which consists of a subject cohort of 20 males and 20 females (Doddington et al., 2000). Unfortunately, the focus has been on telephone speech, which may not be suitable for the purposes discussed here. Clearly, the results are reasonable, and there is a need for increasing the profile of this underrated behavioral biometric.

2.4 Conclusions

The results from the case studies presented in this chapter suggests that this biometric modality provides a range of accuracies, depending on the features that are utilized when creating the verification system. When systems employ dynamic information such as the derivatives of the cepstral coefficients (delta and delta–delta), in addition to the static features such as the MFCC, the classification accuracy (as measured by EER or detection error trade-off [DET]) ends toward a maximum somewhere around 3–5%. This result appears to be independent of the classification approach (see the study by Ortega-Mendoza et al., 2006). This may represent an upper bound to the classification accuracy of voice bioemtrics.

A variety of classification algorithms have been employed in this domain, including dynamic time warping for a template-matching approach, to HMMs and GMMs (for speaker-dependent versus speaker-independent systems), neural networks, Bayesian techniques, and SVMs. Unfortunately, very few studies employ a multi-classification approach using the same datasets and the same preprocessing strategy – so direct comparison of the different strategies, with respect to classification accuracy, is difficult to quantify. It is interesting to note that as mentioned by Paliwal and Atal (2003), only half of the available information is typically utilized in most studies, namely, the power spectrum. These authors make the important observation that the other half of speech information – the phase components, is rarely utilized in most studies. Though not examined as a case study in this chapter, the classification rate, in the absence of noise, was approximately 80%, much lower than most of the case studies presented in this paper (Paliwal & Atal, 2003). The study was quite small, involving only a few speakers, and used a modified mel frequency feature encoding scheme. It would be interesting to apply the use of phase information in a more typical type of experimental protocol to judge its effect on the classification rate.

It is also interesting to note that the use of wavelet analysis in voice recognition is an underrepresented technique. Wassner and Chollet (1996) present the results of a study where they employed wavelets instead of the Fourier transform for the generation of cepstral coefficients. The results indicate that, when compared to a Fourier transform-derived cepstral coefficients, the classification accuracy improved slightly. Speech does possess some non-stationarity – so the deployment of a wavelet approach to spectrum production is justified – and in this study provided enhanced results. It must be noted that the authors employed two separate databases, and the classification results differed significantly between the two. This highlights a very important issue: the availability of test data.

As mentioned in the introduction, there are a variety of databases that can be used for testing feature extraction and classification accuracies. It should be noted that there is a wide variation in the content of these databases. Much of the data are collected from telephone conversations and hence may have a significant amount of noise and filtering relative to unconstrained human text. Other issues involve the fact that a variety of languages are employed, which may have an impact on the classification accuracy if one doesn't provide a language-independent feature space and classification algorithm (see Ortega-Mendoza et al., 2006 for this type of approach). If the voice verification system is to be employed over an e-commerce framework, clearly a *lingua franca* approach must be adopted.

It is also interesting to note that most voice recognition systems adopt a text-independent approach. In the current context – voice as a biometric verification process – it is sufficient to produce a text-dependent approach (such as the Benzeghiba & Bourland [2003] approach – this chapter) where the speakers are only required to enunciate their password. This raises an interesting question with regard to the training process and the overall classification accuracy: is it better to work with a small amount of data using a template-matching or HMM approach or is it better to produce a more generic model, utilizing GMMs? What is the impact on training and classification accuracy? It might be useful for a speech based password system to allow the user to select from a larger set of phonemes from which they can use to select a password. When users are required to change their password, they may not have to retrain the system. But can we assume that the conditions and the speaker will remain constant over time? These are relevant issues that need to be addressed in addition to the more standard feature extraction and classification issues that are omnipresent in this type of research.

2.5 Research Topics

1. How can the range of dynamic features be enhanced – over and above the first and second derivatives of the cepstral coefficients?
2. How can the speech model itself be improved and incorporated into the recognition model?
3. There are a number of features that are employed for speech recognition – yet there are no detailed studies indicating the relative importance of the features – what would be the best way to rank these features with respect to speaker identification accuracy?
4. How does speech recognition generalize across devices such as mobile phones and PC microphones? What issues would have to be addressed to account for device-specific characteristics when building a speech-based verification system?
5. How does one decouple noise from speaker data? This is especially true for telephone-based systems.
6. What standards information is required to allow this technology to be incorporated into the CBEFF framework?
7. The databases are very disparate – containing different types of speech, different languages, variable gender makeup, and variable speech patterns. A large all-encompassing database would facilitate field testing – what issues are involved in this type of project?
8. What other biometric modalities are compatible with speech – how could they be integrated into a multimodal biometric system? What considerations at the fusion level would be required for this integrated approach?

3

Signature Verification

3.1 Introduction

Signature-based identity verification is a venerable technique for presenting ourselves in an official capacity, with a legal implication of authenticity. Prior to automated biometrics, signatures were checked by visual inspection, often by people with little or no formal training. Exactly what is it about a signature that allows us to differentiate the real from a cleverly (or even not so cleverly) crafted forgery? One answer might be that we are not really looking for cleverly crafted forgeries – those produced by skilled attempts. We simply do not have the time to examine a signature at the level required to attempt to differentiate a valid from a forged version. After all, if someone has access to our signature and practices long enough, he will probably be able to reproduce it to a degree that is indiscernible from the authentic version. If this is the case, then we (as humans) probably rely on other cues in addition to the signature for verification purposes. For instance, the emotional state of the person (i.e. do they appear nervous), does the person enter their signature with considerable effort as if enacting a rehearsed event, etc. How can we devise an authentication system, based on signature authentication alone, that is trustworthy enough to allow access to vital information contained within an electronic environment? If humans find this task difficult, is it possible to produce a machine-executable algorithm that is able to exceed the human capacity for this task? The evidence from the case studies presented in this chapter indicates that *it is* possible to produce an accurate signature recognition system.

There are two basic approaches to signature verification. In an approach termed *online* signature verification, the signature is verified immediately after it has been entered. The other approach is termed *off-line* verification and occurs sometime after the signature has been produced. In an online approach, information about how the signature has been produced is extracted and used for verification purposes. Typically, specialized hardware in the form of pressure-sensitive writing implements (digital pens) and/or writing surfaces (pads) is used to gather information about how individuals produce their signature. For instance, pen pressure and pen angle can be measured, which provides information over and above the actual writing sample users produce when presenting their signature. That is, there is both a *static* and *dynamic* aspect to signatures that can be used to infer with greater accuracy the authenticity of a signature. This is the primary reason why an automated system, which records and utilizes

Behavioral Biometrics: A Remote Access Approach. Kenneth Revett
© 2008 John Wiley & Sons, Ltd.

this information, can exceed the capacity of a human expert (forensic experts are generally only accurate in 70% of suspected forgery cases!). In contrast, an off-line system only has access to the static (spatial information) aspects of a signature – the actual writing per se, without any record of the dynamics (temporal information) deployed in its production. Such systems tend to produce lower classification accuracy rates compared with online systems (see Jain et al., 2003).

Signature feature space can also be classified based on whether the feature attributes are generated in a *static* or *dynamic* fashion. Generally speaking, dynamic attributes capture temporal features, and static attributes capture the spatial features of a signature. *Dynamic* features of a signature provide information regarding how the signature changes as it is written, examining at discrete (or possibly continuous) time points various features of the signature. These include position ($\langle x, y \rangle$ coordinates), curvature, acceleration, distance between successive sampling times, and related information (see the case studies for more details). In general, these attributes are made available by the enabling technologies – digital pens and pressure-sensitive tablets provide the means to capture this data with sub-millisecond temporal resolution in many cases. The *static* features include the degree of slant, the bounding box (horizontal and vertical dimensions that contain the signature), and pen width. Another classification that is relevant in this context is *global* versus *local* feature space. *Global* features describe how the signature is produced and includes techniques such as the discrete wavelet transform (Deng et al., 1999, Nakanishi et al., 2004), the Hough transform (Kaewkongka et al., 1999), and projections (Kholmatov, 2003). *Local* features are typically extracted from at the stroke level (a stroke is a portion of the signature that is produced while the writing implement is on the writing surface) and include ballistic movement, local shape features, and slant/orientation information (Quek & Zhou, 2002). Aspects of this rich feature space have been exploited in order to enhance the classification efficacy of online and off-line signature verification systems, as discussed in the case studies presented below.

Another taxonomic category that must be emphasized in this chapter is the type of forgery that one is investigating. Signature verification is performed to detect whether or not a signature is authentic, that is, was it produced by the genuine individual or by someone forging another's signature? There are two basic classes of forgers: skilled and random forger. A skilled (or professional) forger is someone who has access to the signature to be forged and has considerable skill and practice at copying the signature. A random (or casual) forger is one who is asked to copy a signature that he has never seen before, and is not adept at the skill. It is very important to realize that for the most part, studies *do not* examine skilled forgery cases, as the data are difficult to acquire. That is, the false acceptance rate (FAR) data are generated by other study participants who are not skilled at the art of forgery, and hence do not represent forgery in the truest sense. That is, a user is asked to produce the signature of another study member; this is sometimes termed a simple forgery scenario. To address the issue of skilled forgery versus zero-effort forgery, the forgers will be allowed to copy and practice entering the signature that they are trying to reproduce. This will certainly help, moving the "forger" from a zero-effort forger (no knowledge of the signature to reproduce), but may not be sufficient to mimic a trained professional forger. This caveat must be kept in mind when examining the literature on this topic.

In this chapter, and this text generally, the emphasis is on biometric authentication from a remote access approach. The use of an online signature verification provides better classification results (though see below in the off-line case studies for possible exceptions) and would therefore be the method of choice for very secure installations/transactions. Yet the online approach may require special hardware such as pressure-sensitive pads/tablets and/or digital pens, which violates one of the basic tenets of behavioral biometrics: no special hardware is required. Therefore, the case studies presented will emphasize the range of techniques applied and how they may be tailored to suit a remote access approach, both from an off-line and online approach, when appropriate.

3.2 Off-Line Signature Verification

Off-line signature verification systems typically utilize an image of a signature. As such, they contain the static features of a signature, such as the slant, bounding box, and pen width. In addition to a minimal set of features to work with, the quality of the data may vary depending on the quality of the image containing the signature and related aspects of the signature acquisition process. Typically, the image may need to be preprocessed, in order to remove any artifacts that may have become integrated with the signature sample (i.e. slightly blurred image, speckled background, etc.). After this preprocessing step, work can begin on verifying the signature. In order to develop a signature verification scheme, like any other biometric, a reference sample must be available. Users will typically be asked to produce their signature a number of times, and these data are then used to form a reference (biometrics information record – BIR) signature that will be utilized for subsequent authentication/verification purposes. Typically, the preprocessing stage involves background cleansing and employing some sort of two-dimensional (2-D) Gaussian filtering scheme, which preserves edges in the image (Kholmatov, 2003). The next stage entailed binarization of the image, using a thresholding scheme. After cleansing, there are several additional preprocessing steps that may be considered. Another preprocessing step involves normalizing the image with respect to the horizontal and vertical dimensions. This may be necessary when comparing images of varying sizes, which may occur when the signatures are produced in different environments. For instance, a signature on a PDA will typically differ in spatial dimensions from that entered on a paper form. If the verification algorithm employs a direct overlay approach, then the variation in the signature dimensions will negatively impact the comparison process. In this case, scaling the signature will allow a direct comparison to be made. But this scaling process may then distort some information contained within the signature that is user specific, and so this option should only be employed when absolutely necessary. Other related issues include pen width, which will alter the overall dimensions of the signature, as well as possibly distort some of the local information such as curvature and related features. Once the data has been preprocessed and normalized, the stage is set to perform the signature verification steps. This entails feature extraction, reference model building, and classification strategies. Specific examples of implementations are presented next, but first it must be noted that the literature in this field is extremely vast, and therefore only a small sample of approaches can be discussed in detail.

3.2.1 Off-Line Verification Case Studies

Kholmatov's MSc dissertation provides a thorough description of the process employed in performing off-line signature verification (Kholmatov, 2003). He preprocessed a collection of signature images using a 2-D Gaussian filter, and then binarized the signature using a sample threshold procedure. Any isolated points or holes in the remaining image were filled in using appropriate morphological operators. The signature images were normalized with respect to their horizontal and vertical dimensions, providing feature vectors of the same length. In order to perform the verification stage, a reference profile was produced by asking the study participants to enter their signature several times. The signatures were evaluated with respect to certain similarity metrics, and these metrics were used as the BIR – the actual signature is typically not utilized (and hence not stored) during the verification stage. This has the advantage of reducing the storage footprint for each user, which may be substantial when storing a large database of users. The metrics captured from the enrollment data consisted of the average of the pairwise distance metrics, average distances to the nearest signatures, and the average distances to the farthest neighbors. If there are N signatures employed for the reference signature, then there are a total of $N(N-1)/2$ measures that were calculated, from which the three statistics were calculated, yielding a 3-tuple for each measurement point, which served as the user's BIR. The features that were extracted in this study were the upper and lower envelopes, and the vertical and horizontal projections (depicted in Figure 3.1). These features have been reported by others as factors which enhance, or at least are correlated with, the reproducibility of signature production (Maarse & Thomassen, 1983). For instance, the upper envelope captures the upward strokes produced during writing and reflects how we write with respect to the horizontal progression of written text. In addition, the

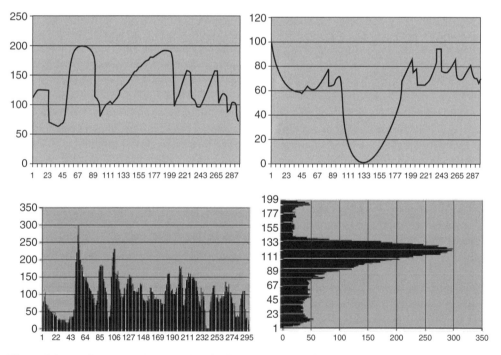

Figure 3.1 Attributes (envelopes) and projections employed as features in the Kholmatov study. Note that the figures represent the upper and lower envelopes (top row), and the vertical and horizontal projections (Source: Kholmatov, 2003)

upstrokes contain information about how we link together letters. The downstrokes appear to be involved in letter formation directly. An interesting research question is how do the upper and lower envelopes affect the horizontal (and possibly the vertical) projections? If these features are in fact correlated in some way, then there is perhaps some redundancy with respect to these parameters. This hypothesis can only be examined through appropriately controlled experiments.

With the feature vectors available for each user of the system, a classification algorithm is required to determine how close two signatures are to one another. The others employ a dynamic time warping (DTW) algorithm for this purpose, as it can be employed to compare two vectors (which can be of varying lengths) in a nonlinear fashion (see Niels, 2004, Neils & Vuurpijl, 2005 for a review of DTW in the context of signature verification). Very briefly, the DTW is a modification of the basic dynamic programming algorithm, which has been used very successfully in many fields (i.e. bioinformatics) to compare two or more vectors that may differ in length. The results of the DTW algorithm are an optimal alignment between two or more vectors in a least squares sense.

For the verification stage, the same features are extracted and the DTW (dynamic programming implementation) is used to compare the authentication attempt to each of the reference vectors associated with the a particular signature (note that each signature has an associated ID, which is matched during signature verification). The result of the matching algorithm is a sequence of matching scores, which are passed as inputs into a final decision classifier model (after normalization), yielding a 3-tuple score. The authors further reduce the matching score using principal component analysis (PCA) which yields a single scalar value. The authors employed 20 genuine and 20 forgery signatures to determine the principal component and threshold values for each user.

When the test consisted of distinguishing between genuine signatures and forgeries, the skilled forgery detection rate was 25% and a 20% error rate when accepting genuine signatures. Note that the authors considered users to be "skilled forgers" if they were able to trace and practice the signature several times before attempting to perform the actual forgery attempt. Whether these results extrapolate to actual skilled forgers is still an open question. Other classification techniques could have been applied, and some of the other off-line case studies presented in this chapter examine alternative classification approaches.

Coetzer and colleagues (2004) proposed a combined approach utilizing a discrete radon transform (DRT) and a hidden Markov model (HMM) for off-line signature verification. Note that typically, systems developed to distinguish casual from genuine users tend to deploy global features, as these are computationally tractable and provide reasonable results in most cases. When skilled forgery is investigated, the systems tend to deploy both global and local features. It is of interest to note that this study developed an automated forgery identification system using scanned images (an off-line approach) and only global signature features.

In this study, signatures were scanned in as a binary image with a resolution of 300 dpi, which were median filtered to remove speckling. Next, the DRT is calculated for each signature, and forms the principal feature used in the classification task. Very briefly, the DRT is a technique for imparting pseudo-temporal information to a static feature. The signature is mapped onto a 2-D grid, with user-specified spatial dimensions. The grid is examined regionally, using what are termed beams which are projected onto the grid at some given angle. The grid is covered by the beams, each of which are parallel (nonoverlapping). There are two parameters that can be adjusted: the beam angle and the number of partitions (beams). The beam angle is allowed to rotate through 360° (because of symmetry, this results in twice the number of features; 180°–360° is symmetrical with 0°–180°). The radon transform then is the summation of the product of a weight times the pixel intensity contained within a beam (see Coetzer et al., 2004, p. 564 for more details). When moving through the full circle with the beam, transitions occur in the corresponding radon, which can be treated as a temporal sequence. It is this process of generating pseudo-temporal information from static signatures that is novel about this approach. A feature vector is created that depends on the number of steps (angles through 360°) that are taken. Each of the vectors is normalized by the variance of the intensity of all the feature vectors. These vectors are then used to train a collection of HMMs, one per signature.

The HMM employed has a circular topology, which maps directly onto the beam angles employed in the feature vector selection process. Note that the ends of the HMM are connected together and that each node represents the feature at a particular beam angle in the radon transform. The model for each user is trained using the Viterbi reestimation technique, and is trained with a small number of samples. The distance metric between each transformed signature and the trained HMM is based on the Euclidean distance metric (for specific details, see Coetzer et al., 2004, p. 566). A sliding *global* threshold is used to decide whether to accept or reject a signature as genuine or not. This system was tested with two separate datasets (one from Stellenbosch (see Coetzer et al., 2004) and the other from Dolfing, 1998).

The Stellenbosch dataset consisted of 924 signatures from 22 writers. For enrollment purposes, 10 signatures from each writer were used (all off-line). Thirty-two test signatures were deployed, consisting of 20 genuine users, 6 skilled forgeries, and 6 casual forgeries, obtained over a 2-week period. The casual forgers only had access to the name of the person (no access to their signatures). The skilled forgers were provided with samples of the genuine signatures that they could practice from. The Dolfing dataset consisted of 4800 signatures from 51 writers, originally derived in an online fashion (Dolfing, 1998a,b). The data was digitized, transforming it into an off-line database. For the Dolfing dataset study, 30 genuine signatures were used for each writer, with half used for training and the other for testing. The Dolfing dataset also contained both professional and amateur forgers, with no casual forgers as in the Stellenbosch dataset. Note that amateur forgers are a subclass of professional forgers, except that they are not well versed in handwriting strategies and analysis, but do have access to an actual signature that is to be forged. The results from the Stellenbosch dataset yielded an equal error rate (EER) of 18% when only skilled forgers were considered, and 4.5% when casual forgers were measured. For the Dolfing study, the EER was 12.2% when only amateur forgers were considered. Note that the amateur forgers are much closer to professional forgers then casual forgers are, so these results are consistent with expectation.

This study examined only global features of the data, derived from a collection of static signatures. The EER values from this study were quite low, and comparable to many studies employing local features (within an off-line system). The number of training samples was within the typical range of 5–20 as reported by many studies in the field (see Jain et al., 2005 for a brief discussion on this topic). The radon transform is computationally feasible to calculate, and tends to be quite robust with respect to noise, and is rotation and scale invariant (see Coetzer et al., 2004). It would be an interesting experiment to examine other purely global features to see how these results compare. In addition, other global features and a variety of local features could be added to see if the classification accuracy could be enhanced.

Ozgunduz and colleagues explored the use of support vector machines (SVMs) for forgery detection in an off-line signature scheme (Ozgunduz et al., 2003, 2005). Utilizing high-resolution gray scale images, the signatures were preprocessed by eliminating any background details, noise reduction, width normalization, and thinning. Briefly, background elimination was performed after cropping the signatures – a smoothing filter was applied using a binary threshold process, where the signature elements were a "1" and all the other pixels were a "0" of they were not part of the signature. Any residual background pixels that were not removed from the background elimination were removed using a morphological operator, with a window size of eight pixels. That is, if within a window of eight pixels, if the number of background pixels was less than the number of foreground pixels, the background was converted into foreground. Next width normalization was applied, where the width was adjusted to a default value and the height was changed such that there was no change in the height-to-width ratio. Lastly, the writing thickness was normalized by making the width of each point equal to one pixel (the authors employed the Hilditch algorithm for this).

After preprocessing, the next stage is feature extraction. Three sets of features were utilized in this study: global features, which provided information about the specifics of the shape of the signatures, mask features, which provided information regarding the directions of the lines of the signatures, and grid features, which provided information about the overall appearance of the signatures. More specifically, the global features generated a set of sub-features that were used for classifier training and testing. The signature area was extracted by counting the number of pixels occupied by the signature, which, for variable grid sizes, provides information about the fractional occupancy of the grid, or equivalently, the pixel density. The height-to-width ratio was calculated, which remains fairly constant for a given person, but can be quite variable with respect to potential forgers. The maximum horizontal and vertical row histograms were also utilized, and the authors recorded the row/column with the largest pixel occupancy. The center of image gravity was calculated by finding the horizontal and vertical center of the image. The number of local maxima of the signature was calculated in both the vertical and horizontal positions. This utilized the same histograms used to find the maxima. Lastly, the number of signature edge points was calculated. An edge point is defined as a pixel that has only one neighbor in an eight-pixel neighborhood. The mask feature provided directional information, and was obtained by applying a set (eight) of 3×3 mask which systematically covered the signature portion of the image (including all edges). Each time a portion of the image corresponded to one of the masks, a frequency counter was updated. The grid features were used to calculate pixel densities, and the authors employed a set of 60 grid features. The signature was divided into 60 disjoint regions, and density values were obtained for each and were used as part of the feature space. The features were used to create a feature vector with 77 elements (9 global, 8 masks, and 60 grid values), normalized onto the interval [0, 1].

The signature database employed in this study consisted of 1320 signatures from 70 persons. For training, a total of 480 signatures were employed, 12 signatures for 40 of the subjects. Of the 12, eight were genuine signatures and the remaining were forgeries (produced by the other 30 participants – a casual forgery system). For the testing phase, a total of 320 genuine and 320 forgeries from the same set of 40 participants were employed. SVMs are generally two-class recognizers, so the authors utilized the SVM approach by a one-against-all scenario, where each class was trained against all other classes. Since the critical task in this study was to distinguish forgers from genuine signatures, the data were partitioned in genuine and forgers (a mixture of skilled and random forgers). The authors did not indicate the type of forgers specifically, but it would appear that the "skilled" forgers were causal forgers who practiced entering the required signatures, but had no professional skill at this task. Therefore, the genuine and forger participants were randomly selected such that all signatures used in this part of the study were used for training in an exhaustive fashion. They employed a radial basis function kernel, which the authors state provided the best classification performance. After training the SVM, the system was tested for both verification and recognition. The FAR for recognition was 11%, and the false rejection rate (FRR) was 2%. For the recognition task, the authors report the true classification ratio, which was 95%, and the false classification ratio, which yielded a value of 5%.

The results from this study indicate that the deployment of an SVM is suitable for a multi-class recognition task such as signature verification. The classification results were quite reasonable, on the order of 6.5% for the average error rate (AER) for the verification results. The authors did employ a substantial number of attributes in this study, which were predominantly associated with image density (60 of the 77 features). Why the image was partitioned into 60 regions was not made clear in their paper. Clearly, in the limit of partitioning onto every occupied voxel would increase the number of features, but whether this would have enhanced the classification accuracy remains to be determined. Exactly how informative is each class of the feature set is an important question that is typically not addressed in most papers. The mask attribute, which captured the line directions, was extracted using a collection (eight) of 3×3 windows, providing some detail with regard to the spatial orientation of various elements of a signature (other authors have utilized the slant in a similar fashion). This is an interesting attribute, in that it captures local information, but when applied to an entire image, it provides global information (in a sense, it represents a gradient field over the entire image – a simplified DRT operation).

Deng and colleagues (1999) applied a wavelet-based approach to off-line signature classification. The authors utilized images acquired using a 600 pixel per inch image scanner for their analysis of off-line signature verification. The signatures were preprocessed using four principal steps. First, the images were binarized to remove background imperfections, leaving only a clean signature on a white background. Next, a morphological dilation process was applied to remove gaps that might exist between portions of the signature (excluding inter-word gaps such as between the forename and surnames). Then, any closed contours were removed by tracing their outline and removing any inner closed surface, yielding only the outer contour – yielding the largest closed-contour shape (see Deng et al., 1999, p. 176 for details). These preprocessing steps are applied consistently for all signatures employed in this study. Note that the result of this preprocessing is that each signature is represented as a series of closed contours. The next stage entails the feature extraction process, for which they utilized Mallat's (1991) discrete dyadic orthogonal wavelet transform. Wavelets can be considered as performing multi-resolution filtering steps, which decompose signals into low-pass (low-frequency signal) and high-pass (high-frequency signal) components. These components are sometimes referred to as the *approximation* and *detail* levels, respectively. The mother wavelet employed in this study is the second derivative of a smoothing function, so the zero crossings of the transformed data indicate transition points within the data. The authors extract the following features from the transformed data (via preprocessing and the application of the wavelet transform): i) the total number of closed contours in the signature, ii) the zero crossings in the high-pass data, which include three additional attributes: i) the

amplitude

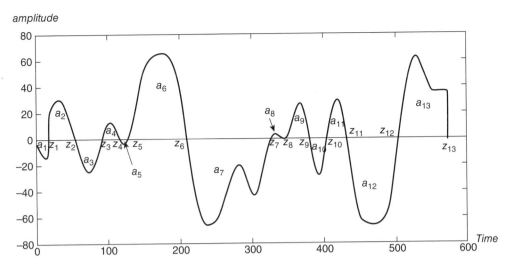

Figure 3.2 An example of the zero-crossing points generated by the application of the wavelet transform (Source: Deng et al., 1999)

abscissa of the zero crossing, ii) the integral between successive zero crossings, taken from positive time (left-hand side), and iii) the amplitude of the corresponding low-pass filter abscissa position. Figure 3.2 illustrates the signal decomposition result when applying the wavelet to a signature. One property of this transform that is useful as a relevant feature for signature verification is that the integral measure allows a definition of the L^2 norm to be generated from the zero-crossing points.

With the preprocessing and wavelet-transformed data, the authors generate the actual features that will be used to characterize each signature. Since each signature will vary as it is written, a local threshold is used for each user, as opposed to a global threshold. The individual threshold (T_i) is determined from a set of features, which includes the number of closed contours (K_i) and the optimal resolution from the wavelet (L_i), for each user's signature i. The number of closed contours in a given instance of a signature can vary, and so there is an issue of extracting the most stable value for this feature, which maximizes classification performance. With respect to the optimal resolution feature, it must be noted that the number of zero crossings for a closed contour may vary from one signature instance to the next. Essentially, we may be faced with an instance of vectors with unequal lengths, and so the authors employ a delayed time warping algorithm. DTW is used to expand or contract the time axis such that the number of zero crossings is matched between two instances of a closed-contour element within signatures. A Euclidean distance metric is applied, across different levels, in order to determine which level best matches the examples of a particular closed contour, across all contours for a given set of signatures. This yields a dissimilarity degree, which is based on the values for K and L. This process establishes the unique value of L for each signature. Next, the values of K and L that minimize the classification error are explored. Note that there is a nonlinearity in determining the value of these two parameters, as they both depend on the same mean and standard deviation in a nonlinear form (see Deng et al., 1999, p. 184 for details). The authors opt to fix a value for L_i, then determine the value for K_i. Once K_i and L_i have been determined, it is a straightforward matter to compute T_i. With the individual thresholds acquired for each user, a series of experiments were performed to determine the classification efficacy of this system.

The authors employed a signature database that contained a collection of genuine signatures and a collection of forgeries. For each genuine user, 10 signatures were used to generate the person's reference signature. For the forgeries, amateur forgeries were produced, and they were classified into different categories based on the amount of time each forger had to learn the signatures to forge (from 0–3 minutes to unlimited time). This process generated five classes of forgeries, and 10 samples from each class were produced for each genuine signature. The signatures were randomized within the database, and also note that the database consisted of English and Chinese signatures. The match score for the verification process consisted of determining the number of closed contours in the verification attempt, along with the boundary lengths for each close contour pair, and a measure of dissimilarity (based on the Euclidean distance between the zero crossings). If the dissimilarity score was below the individual threshold, then the signature was rejected. Note that the dissimilarity score indirectly incorporates the values of K and L. The results from a study generated an AER of approximately 8.3% for English signatures (best type I error of 5.2% and best type II error of 12.24%) and 6.9% for Chinese signatures (best type I error of 5.5% and best type II error of 7.9%).

The results of this study indicate that using the wavelet transform of signatures can be a very useful attribute in differentiating forged from genuine signatures. Although due to the length of this paper not all results were summarized, it must be noted that in this study, the authors examined the classification rate based on the level of forgery skill. The skill level was based on the amount of time the "forger" had to practice writing a signature. For those forgers with no time to practice (zero-effort forgery), the misclassification rate was 0%. Those that had an unlimited amount of time to parties yielded a misclassification error rate of approximately 21%, still superior to many forensic experts generally. The features extracted from this study focused on extracting a set of closed contours, which are regions within a signature that may be quite unique to a given individual. The value of such features with respect to the classification needs to be more fully explored. There are a range of other mother wavelets that could have been used – it might be worth exploring how other wavelet transforms perform in this application.

3.3 Online Signature Verification

Online signature verification refers to a machine-based method for automating signature verification (identification is allowed as well) that occurs essentially in real time. The challenges for online systems are therefore different from an off-line approach, both in terms of the processing requirements (i.e. time to decision) and the nature of the information available to generate the authentication decision. Most authors make the distinction between static and dynamic features of the input data, and that there is a decided advantage when both forms of data can be incorporated into a signature model. Still other authors report that dynamical data alone provide more discriminating capacity than static features (Dolfing, 1998, Plamondon, R., & Parizeau, 1988). This section explores the development of *online* signature verification systems, again from a case study approach in order to provide data that will allow informed persons to generate their own decision – in an off-line style.

3.3.1 On-Line Verification Case Studies

The mouse-driven signature verification scheme deployed by Syukri and colleagues (1998) relies on the use of a mouse as an input device for entering one's signature. This system works in an online fashion, using a standard PC (which could be implemented on a PDA-type device using a stylus instead of a mouse). The mouse is used to enter a user's signature, which is then utilized for authentication purposes. The system extracts a number of features from users as they enter their signature, such as the number of signature points, $\langle x, y \rangle$ coordinates of the points, signature writing time, velocity, and acceleration. These features are extracted during an enrollment process, wherein each user is required to enter their signature three times. These data are preprocessed by normalizing the data by a scaling procedure utilizing the leftmost and top aspects of the input, such that the horizontal and vertical signature area is consistent across samples. When users wish to be authenticated, their entry is normalized to the reference sample such that they are in spatial alignment with one another (on a point-by-point basis). If the alignment requires the point be moved more than a threshold distance (typically 50 pixels), then the point is rejected; otherwise, it is accepted. A count of the number of matched points is recorded, and if it is greater than some threshold (typically 70%), then the attempt is authenticated; otherwise, it is rejected. Figure 3.3 presents the user interface to this system.

After parameter selection, preprocessing, and enrollment, the authors conducted several experiments to test the efficacy of their system. They also investigated the effect of a *static* versus a *dynamic* user database. In the dynamic database version, when users successfully

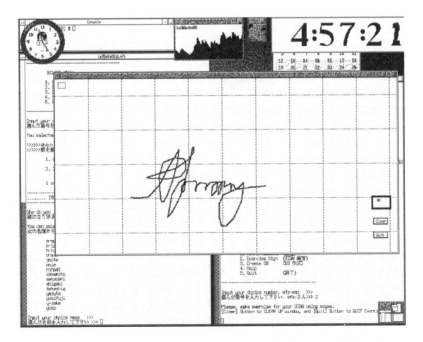

Figure 3.3 The interface presented to a user to authenticate via the mouse-driven signature scheme of Syukri and colleagues (Source: Syukri et al., 1993)

authenticate, their details are updated reflecting the latest successful entry, which updates the reference profile. The static version does not update the reference profiles of users who have successfully authenticated. The authors employ the use of *geometric average means* as opposed to arithmetic average means for their user verification scheme.

The experiments consisted of 21 users, each of which enrolled in the system by presenting his signature three times. The results were reported as FAR and FRR values, and imposter attempts were generated by the other users within the study cohort (amateur forgers). In general, the system was able to correctly classify authentic users with an average 91% of the time for the static database. The value was 93% for the dynamic database. It was also noted that a user's signature becomes stable after approximately 80 trials, with regard to the features utilized in this study. This in effect provides a measure of the power law of practice, which indicates the increased reproducibility of a task as a function of practice (see Chapter 4 for details). It appears from this study that it takes longer for a signature to stabilize than it does entering a login ID/password.

This study is the only one that entails the deployment of a mouse for signature entry as far as this author is aware. The mouse is not typically used for such purposes, and the fact that the classification results are so high may be somewhat surprising. The authors did note that since the subjects were not typically used to entering a signature as such, the signatures entered tended to be fairly simple in their construction. This might work in both direction, reducing the FRR, but also might enhance the FAR. One potential way to address this issue is to repeat this experiment with subject cohorts who are used to entering their signature for verification purposes. Another very interesting aspect of this study is that it inadvertently (possibly not?) highlights the structural aspects of signature production. Clearly, there is no pressure sensor, no angle of the pen, and related attributes used in this study. The study did collect the speed of drawing, as a point process so did incorporate some dynamical behavior, but this was clearly a minimal amount. The essence of the attributes selected was related to the more static features of the signature process. The results with this approach yielded classification accuracies above 90% – at least for this particular study cohort. Whether this result generalizes will have to wait for subsequent work. The values were consistent with other off-line approaches – and serves as a benchmark for the contribution of dynamically oriented features in more traditional online approaches.

Jain and colleagues published a report on an implementation of an online signature verification study (Jain et al., 2003). The signatures are acquired using a digitized tablet (IBM CrossPad), which has a data capture rate of 100–150 Hz. After users enter their signatures onto the tablet, the signatures are preprocessed to clean up the data. First, the signature is smoothed using a Gaussian filter. Certain aspects of the data, such as critical points and temporal features, are first detected and collected prior to preprocessing. These are part of the ultimate feature vector that will be used to characterize each signature. To preserve the spatial features of the signatures, the temporal aspects are eliminated, by resampling the signature at an equidistant spatial location. The critical points are also retained throughout the feature extraction process. The same holds true for the temporal aspects of the discovered prior to the resampling process. The critical points refer to features associated with pen strokes, which refer to the writing that occurs when the pen is placed down on the tablet. A signature may consist of a number of strokes, and each possesses information about the writer. The strokes are concatenated, and the number of strokes is a global feature used in the feature space for each signature. The $\langle x, y \rangle$ coordinates of the image provide local features that are used to formulate the feature vector. These features can be partitioned into spatial and temporal features, as described below.

The local features that were extracted were the i) $\langle x, y \rangle$ coordinate differences between two consecutive points, ii) the absolute y coordinate with respect to the center of the signature, iii) the sine and cosine of the angle with respect to the x axis, iv) the curvature, and v) the gray values in a 9×9 pixel neighborhood. In addition, features such as the writing speed at particular points were measured. The authors measured the relative and absolute speed (the latter is the absolute speed normalized by the average signature speed), recorded at each of the resampled points in the signature. In addition, the absolute and relative speed between consecutive critical points was also recorded.

These features were extracted for each sample point in the signature and were utilized as the reference vector for each signature stored in the system database. Two strings are compared, and a measure of similarity (or distance) is generated, which is used to score two signatures (which are really just a sequence of features concatenated according to the sampling points. Two samples of the same signature may have different lengths, and so the distance metric must be able to account for this. The typical approach is to use some form of DTW, which allows vectors of differing lengths to be aligned. Typically, a dynamic programming method is employed, with appropriate penalties for stroke mismatches and other forms of insertion/deletion operations. After the alignment process, the difference between the number of strokes between the two aligned strings is recorded and used as part of the decision feature space. Essentially, the authors employ an edit distance measure, which computes the distance between two strings, normalized by the possible amount of difference from strings of that size (see Connell & Jain, 2001 for more details).

During verification, the test signature is compared against all the extant reference signatures in the database. The authors suggest three different methods for combining the dissimilarity scores: i) the minimum dissimilarity score, ii) the average dissimilarity score, or iii) the maximum dissimilarity score. With a scalar dissimilarity score at hand, the decision must be made whether to accept or reject the test signature – this is accomplished through the use of a threshold. An important point addressed in this study was whether a single global threshold could be used, or must a threshold be extracted for each signature in the database? The issue is affected by the amount of training data that is available. Generally speaking, data are scarce, and so the authors circumvent this issue by starting with a global "guess" so to speak, and then tuning it for each user. The tuning of the user-specific threshold can be accomplished by an additive term to the guess, which can be generated by computing the i) minimum distance between all reference samples, ii) the average distance between all references, or iii) the maximum distance between all reference samples.

This system was tested on a database containing 1232 signatures from 102 different writers. In addition, a second database was used, containing 520 signatures from 52 writers (each containing approximately 10 samples/writer). In addition, 60 forgeries were generated, three each for 20 of the writers in the database. Note that the forgers were allowed to view the signatures, but were not professional forgers, and hence would be considered as random forgers. Also note that the signatures of 17 writers were collected (10 signatures each) over an extended period of time (up to 1 year), providing a temporal aspect to the dataset, at least for a fraction of the writers.

The authors investigated the performance of the classification of the system as a function of the feature vectors and the threshold type: common or writer dependent. With respect to a common threshold, the features that generated the best results were the sine and cosine angles, and the x- and y-coordinate differences between two consecutive points, combined with the speed features. These "best results" relate to the decision plane between genuine signatures and forgeries, related to the setting of the threshold. The genuine values above threshold (i.e. accepted genuine signatures) and the number of forgeries below threshold (rejected false attempts) were approximately 9.5% and 4.6% for the common and writer-dependent thresholds, respectively. Further testing with writer-dependent thresholds and various speed features generated very similar results in terms of balancing false acceptance and false rejection, more or less indicating that the choice of the speed feature was largely independent of the overall classification accuracy. This result highlights the importance of the sine and cosine angles and Cartesian distance between successive points as being the principal attributes responsible for accurate classification. Lastly, a general trend in the author's results is that the skilled forgers (those with practice as opposed to random forgers) generally yielded larger error rates than random forgers or the genuine writers.

The results from this study indicate that certain local features were important in the ability to produce an automated signature verification system. The dynamic features such as speed did not have a significant impact on the classification results – at least when utilized in conjunction with some of the local spatial features. It would have been more informative if the classification results were produced for the dynamic and spatial features separately. Only then could a direct comparison between the two classes of features be directly compared. The databases employed contained a relatively small number of samples from each user – approximately 10. The number of forged signatures was 60 – a very small fraction relative to the number of genuine signatures. This unequal distribution between genuine signatures and imposters may have skewed the results somewhat. It may have been appropriate to start with equal numbers of genuine signatures and imposters and increase the number of genuine signatures, recording the results along the way. Lastly, the authors make a point of discussing how to use an evolving signature base. They do employ signatures that have been acquired over the course of 1 year. It would have been an interesting result to determine if signatures acquired over a long period of time impact the classification results. This effect could have been measured by separating out the two classes of signatures and by repeating the authentication attempts directly with them. This would have also been in line with the small number of forgery cases as well. In addition, the authors suggest that signatures evolve, and that possibly, there is the need to incorporate successful signature authentication signatures into the database, and of subsequently updating the reference signature (writer-dependent threshold) accordingly. We have suggested this for keystroke dynamics (see Chapter 4 of this volume) – the question is whether it is prudent to do so for signatures.

An interesting approach by Xuhua and colleagues (1995a, 1995b) investigated the use of a genetic algorithm (GA) as a machine learning technique for online signature verification which captures "virtual strokes." The authors make use of the notion of strokes, more specifically, virtual strokes, as a method for hiding the characteristic features of a signature (see Parizeau & Plamondon, 1990 for details). Virtual strokes are produced when the pen is raised from the writing surface and moved to a new position and then placed back onto the writing surface. As such, this movement leaves no trace and hence would be extremely difficult to reproduce. The question is whether or not there is enough information to capture these virtual strokes through a set of reliable features. The authors employ a GA to explore the possible feature space – as they are suitable for difficult optimization problems generally (Goldberg,

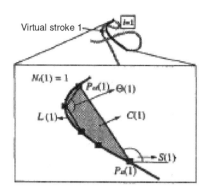

Figure 3.4   The notion of a virtual stroke (Source: Xuhua et al., 1995b)

1989). Figure 3.4 presents the concept of a virtual stroke, depicting the successive pen-up operations.

The system employs a digitized tablet that records both pen-up and pen-down events. Only the pen-up events are used to define a virtual stroke. Their system extracts six features associated with each virtual stroke, which form the feature set used for subsequent classification purposes. The features are the stroke length, the slope, the largest angle (Θ in Figure 3.4), the local curvature, and the relative location of the stroke (with respect to the x and y axes). The purpose of the GA is to find the optimal values for the features that result in maximal classification accuracy. The authors utilize a two-step process to perform the feature optimization process: i) extract the partial curve that contains the characteristic features and ii) determine which of the features optimize the classification by searching through the feature space.

The chromosomes are variable length, and each allele contains a set of values for each of the features. If there are N chromosomes in a particular generation, chromosome 1 is selected for processing. Locus 1 is then selected first, and cloned with mutation such that five copies are produced. Each gene, with the remaining loci, is evaluated with respect to the classification task. One gene from the five with the highest fitness is selected in subsequent generations. This process is repeated for all loci, one by one, until all have been evaluated. Note that the fitness function is related to the minimization of the type I and type II errors (see Xuhua et al., 1995a, p. 173 for details). This process generates a single chromosome that is optimal from the given population and is processed as in a typical GA, via the genetic operators (reproduction, crossover, and mutation).

Once a set of features has been produced, the system employs a fuzzy network to perform the verification process. The inputs to the fuzzy network are the values of the alleles for each of the chromosomes generated during the training process. A switch is associated with each gene, which decides whether or not the gene should be used in the verification task. When the switch is set to a "1," the feature will be used and the grade of the membership function is calculated. When the switch is set to "0," the feature will not be used and the grade of the membership function is set to "1." All the values of the features are inputted to their corresponding membership functions (when set appropriately via the switch). The grades of each membership function are multiplied as the output of the fuzzy network. The output of the fuzzy network is utilized in the fitness function (as a delta term, which uses the difference between the value of the feature in a training vector and the output from the fuzzy network). The value of the training exemplars is set to 1 for genuine signatures and 0 for forgeries. The shapes of the membership functions are determined by five of the signatures in the signature training set. Each feature contained within the chromosomes is calculated for the five training signatures. The maximum and minimum values of each feature are calculated based on the values of the five reference signatures. The center of each of the membership functions for each feature is calculated as the average of the maximum and minimum values. The width is calculated as the difference between the maximum and minimum, and is multiplied by a weighting factor, which is meant to capture the inherent variability contained within the reference signatures.

This system was tested using a database of 250 signatures, generated from 20 subjects. The number of genuine signatures and forgeries was 120 and 130, respectively. Of the forgeries, 15 were produced by directly tracing over signatures contained within the database. From the signatures (excluding the traced forgeries), 90 were used for training purposes, which included 45 genuine signatures and 45 forgeries. Further, five genuine signatures were chosen randomly to build the membership functions. The remaining signatures were used for testing purposes (75 genuine and 85 forgeries). The results reported were from 20 trials, and the initial population size was set to 50. The mutation rate was set to 10%.

The average type I error rate was 6% and the type II error was 0.8%, based on the average of the 20 trials. For the 15 forgeries generated by tracing, the type II error was 10% on average. These results compare favorably from the results of their previous study where they utilized both real and virtual strokes. The forgery type II error was 14% on average, compared to 10% in this case (using only virtual strokes) (see Xuhua et al., 1995b). Lastly, the authors examined how significant each of the six features was in terms of the classification accuracy. The general findings were that deletion of any of the genes resulted in reduced classification accuracy – this was especially evident when reducing the number of partial curves. These results indicate that the feature selection, at least for the values selected by their approach, was optimal and required.

This paper takes a fresh approach to signature verification by examining what is NOT left on the paper, as much as other systems rely exclusively on what IS on the paper! A virtual stroke is that part of a signature that resides between real strokes, a filling in process, with characteristics that can be reproduced and identified. In this study, a set of local spatial features and the speed were selected to represent the typing characteristics of the writer's signature. These features were incorporated into a GA, which was designed to explore and exploit regularities within the typing samples. In order to accommodate the inherent variability associated with multiple instances of a user's signature, the output of the GA was fed into a fuzzy network. The fitness function was related to the difference between the reference sample and the output of the fuzzy network. When the selected attributes were used for testing purposes, the results yield an EER of approximately 3.4% – very reasonable results. The authors further explored the impact each of the features had on the classification accuracy. The results indicate that the features were all required – but especially the number of local curvature points was critical with respect to the classification accuracy. It is also interesting to note that the system was able to detect traced forgeries 90% of the time. How accurately the signatures were traced could be an issue, but one would assume that the forgery would be quite difficult to spot. The size of the database was fairly moderate – though consistent with many others reported in the literature. This type of approach, using virtual strokes, may be somewhat difficult to generalize across signatures that do not contain many pen-up events – signatures with a low stroke count. It would also be an interesting study to examine a richer feature set. The number of attributes/features is quite large – well over 40 features (without a lot of duplicity have been reported in the literature (see Gupta & McCabe, 1997, Nalwa, 1997, Guo, 2000).

Fierrez-Aguilar and colleagues (2005) presented the results of an interesting study which integrates the use of local and regional information to online signature verification. The authors utilized the Signature Verification Competition Database developed in 2004 (SVC2004) to test two different approaches to signature verification. The local approach focused on the deployment of DTW, and the regional approach was based on the use of an HMM. The question is whether the fusion of these two approaches enhances the classification accuracy compared to the individual application of either approach.

The authors make the distinction between a feature-based approach and a functional-based approach to online signature verification. The feature-based approach typically extracts global features from the signature, whereas the functional approach tends to extract temporal aspects of the signature, such as pen velocity, pressure, and position trajectory (Fierrez-Aguilar et al., 2005). The authors further classify functional approaches into those that utilize local or regional features. In a localist approach, specific elements of a signature are registered with a reference signature. These elements are typically $\langle x, y \rangle$ coordinates, and related information that are extracted at fixed time intervals. In order to compare two such feature vectors, some form of registration algorithm is employed. Since signatures may vary in length, a simple Hamming distance or Euclidean distance metric is not suitable. Instead, the use of DTW can be utilized, which allows vectors of different lengths to be co-registered with one another (see Jain et al., 2005 in this chapter). This process is typically implemented using some form of dynamic programming algorithm for computational tractability reasons. The regional approach utilizes features that fit somewhere between local and global features. Such approaches, exemplified by HMMs, have been deployed with great success in signature verification and other biometric modalities (see Rigoll & Kosmala, 1998, Coetzer et al., 2004 in this chapter and elsewhere in this text). The question is can these modalities be combined such that the classification accuracy is enhanced relative to the corresponding unimodal approaches (see Chapter 7 for a discussion on multimodal biometrics)? The experimental design is briefly described next.

For the DTW system, the data were preprocessed such that all strokes were concatenated and the data were normalized. The following three features were extracted at each time point: the δx, δy, and p, the pen pressure. Note that the δ terms correspond to the change in the x and y directions, respectively. The matching algorithm employed the DTW algorithm (see Jain et al., 2005 for details), where the penalty (gap penalty) is proportional to the Euclidean distance between the two points, multiplied by a constant. Score normalization was employed, which was user dependent, according to the scheme employed by Kholmatov (Kholmatov & Yanikoglu, 2004). The matching results in a 3-tuple consisting of the minimum, maximum, and average distances relative to the training signature. The resulting score vector is mapped down to a scalar using PCA.

For the HMM system, the signature trajectories were initially preprocessed by performing position and rotation normalization. Seven attributes were extracted for each time point and, together with their derivatives, yielded a 14-tuple feature vector. The original seven features were x and y coordinates, pressure, path tangent angle, path velocity magnitude, log curvature radius, and total acceleration magnitude. A z-score transformation was applied to each of the discretized feature vector elements. The matching process then employed a left-to-right HMM without transition skips between states which was used for signature verification. The authors employed a multivariate Gaussian mixture density approach to model the observations generated from the training data.

With respect to data fusion, the scores from each approach were normalized using a logistic function, mapping them onto the interval [0, 1], prior to the fusion process. The fusion strategies utilized in this study were based on the max, product, and sum rules, and the results from each approach were compared with respect to classification accuracy.

The signature database employed in this study was generated by the First International Signature Verification Competition initiative, which had the admiral goal of generating an internationally available signature database, established in 2004. The signature corpus consisted of 40 sets of signatures (from the SVC2004 database), 20 genuine signatures acquired in two separate sessions, and 20 forged signatures. The forgeries were produced by five other subjects. Also note that the signatures were either in English or Chinese. Training samples were randomly acquired, and 10 runs on the training samples were conducted. For each user, 10 genuine signatures acquired from the second session and 20 skilled forgeries were used for testing. Also note that this study included random forgers, and these forgery results were compared with skilled forgers. It should also be noted that the signatures used by the subjects in this study were not their own – they were asked to enter signatures selected from the SVC2004 database. Also note that the skilled forgers had access to the signature shape and the signature dynamics. Lastly, the training data were acquired in a different session from the testing data. With these caveats in mind, the authors report the results (EER values) of the approaches individually, and the different fusion approaches.

Generally speaking, the EER tended to be lower for skilled forgers when the HMM approach was used. This general trend held whether a global or user-dependent decision threshold was used, though the EERs were considerably lower in all cases. For random forgeries, the DTW approach performed significantly better for user-independent thresholds relative to the HMM approach. The HMM performed the best when user-dependent thresholds were employed (i.e. EER of 0% when 10 signatures were used for training, random forgeries, and employing user-dependent thresholds). For skilled forgeries, the lowest EER was generated from the analogous skilled forgery conditions (yielding an EER of 4.5%).

The authors then examined the use of fusion approaches to see if this could enhance the discriminability of the system. For skilled forgeries, the lowest EER result was obtained using the sum fusion rule (in fact this held true generally across all four conditions: skilled versus unskilled, and user-independent versus user-dependent thresholds. Also note that these results were based on the use of five signatures for generating the references. The results were quite impressive – in that their results for user-independent random forgeries were all well below the best results from the SVC2004 competition (which was 3.02%). The results from this study, in the same category, were 0.19%, 0.14%, and 0.15% for max, product, and sum fusion rules, respectively. It must be noted, though, that the local versus regional results for the same category were 0.24% and 0.34%, respectively, already below the best SVC2004 results before the fusion process.

The results from this study indicate that neither approach alone (DTW or HMM) was a clear winner with respect to forgery class (skilled or random). The fusion process reduced the EER rates significantly across all categories, but the differences were minor in many instances between the various fusion approaches. It should be noted that the methodology employed in this study possibly may have made the task more difficult than in other studies. For one, the training and testing data were acquired at different time points. The writers did not have any visual feedback when entering their signature. The signatures utilized were not the owner's signatures – this in essence made every participant a random forger! Yet given these caveats, the results from the fusion approach were quite remarkable in terms of the low EER values obtained. These factors will certainly impact the classification accuracy of any system deploying this dataset.

Rigoll and Kosmala (1998) describe an interesting study where they evaluated the use of an HMM for *both* off-line and online systems, thereby evaluating the efficacy of the HMM approach. The signatures were obtained from a digitizing tablet, and the data were used either directly in real time for the online approach, or scanned and saved as an image file for the off-line approach. The features that were extracted included the i) angle between two consecutive sampling points, ii) the angle between the current angle and the angle of the previous set of points, iii) a sliding bitmap window, iv) speed in the horizontal and vertical directions, and v) the vertical motion as a function of horizontal displacement (the slope). Note that the sliding bitmap window occupied 30×30 pixels, which slides along the pen trajectory and generates a nine-dimensional vector. Note that there was no resampling as in their previous work, as this might reduce the writer-dependent features such as speed and stroke rhythm (see Rigoll et al., 1996). The window was evaluated using a discrete Fourier transform (DFT) (window size was 10), and the absolute values of the Fourier spectrum forms a 10-dimensional vector that describes any frequency components contained within the data. The final feature vector contained the absolute angles (sine and cosine), the difference angles, the bitmap, velocity, acceleration, and the frequency vector, yielding a total of 23 features for the *online* signatures. The feature vector for the off-line system was similar, but excluded the dynamical elements contained within the online version, leaving essentially the pixel image as a source of features. Essentially, for the off-line feature set, the image of the signature (which was previously preprocessed to remove noise and was binarized) was discretized based on the dimensions of the signature. The vertical dimension was measured and partitioned into approximately 6–10 squares (depicted in Figure 3.5). Each square consisted of approximately 100 pixels (10×10), for each of which the gray scale values were computed. The signature is partitioned into a series of columns, each of which is characterized by 6–10 gray scale values. The number of columns is determined by the length of the signature and the dimensions of the squares used in the vertical direction (i.e. essentially modulated by the height of the signature).

The feature extraction process described above was applied to a database of 20 individuals, each of whom presented 20 signatures. The HMM was trained with 16 samples from each user, and the remaining samples were used for testing purposes. The forgery samples (60 in total) were used to test the discriminatory power of the resultant HMMs. Note that 40 of the forgery samples were considered "skilled forgeries," and the remaining 20 forgeries were random forgeries. Note that the skilled forgeries were really generated from casual forgeries, where the forger had access to the signatures and had time to practice entering it.

With feature vectors for both the online and off-line systems, the next stage was to develop the appropriate HMM for the features, which produces the ultimate classification/decision outcome for the system (i.e. genuine or forgery). The authors deployed a discrete HMM, where the probability density function for a state emitting a particular output was generated

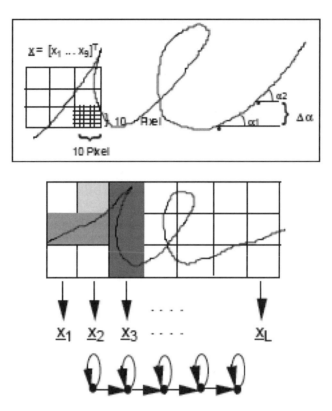

Figure 3.5   The top panel illustrates the dynamic acquisition scheme. The middle panel illustrates the spatial partitioning of the signature utilized in the static scheme. The bottom panel is a schematic of the HMM (Source: Rigoll & Kosmala, 1998)

from a discrete distribution. The distribution was obtained from the users during the training session (where a reference signature was developed during multiple entries), which was based on a vector quantizer. The authors employed a multiple codebook approach, and the feature vectors were partitioned into seven different streams for angle, delta angle, bitmap, pressure, velocity, acceleration, and Fourier features (for the online system). For the off-line system, only the bitmap codebook was trained. The codebook size for the bitmap feature was set at 100. Note that in order to investigate the effect of the various features on the classification task, the authors used a range of 2–30 codebooks for training in the online case.

The HMM was trained with 16 samples from each user to be recognized. The Viterbi algorithm was used for computing the probability that the input feature stream belonged to a given writer. The output of the Viterbi was used in the final decision outcome, which was normalized by the difference between the observation sequence length and the length of the signature. This normalized outcome would be accepted if it fell within the expected value ± the variation (variance). Note that the variance is user specific, derived during the training process, and hence the decision boundary is local to each user.

The authors reported the error rates as a function of feature category. The bitmap feature produced the highest classification rate of 92.2%. The classification rate is defined as the number of correctly accepted genuine signatures and the number of rejected forgeries. The least informative feature was the acceleration (66.0%), yet the velocity was considerably higher (86.4%). Lastly, the authors explored some of the combinations of attributes, and found that the bitmap, velocity, Fourier spectrum, and pressure were highly informative, accounting for 99.0% of the classification accuracy for the online scenario. The best classification result for the off-line scenario was 98.1%, using only the bitmap feature vector (codebook size of 30). The difference between the online and off-line scenarios may not be statistically significant. One can argue therefore that the dynamic aspects of signatures may not yield a significant effect on the classification accuracy in online signature verification. This conclusion is contrary to some authors (Plamondon, 1998), but is consistent with the claims of other researchers (see Nalwa, 1997 for a discussion on this issue). As far as the classification accuracy results reported in this paper, the off-line values are consistent with literature reports (El-Yacoubi et al., 2000). Their online recognition rates were on par with several studies, but there appears to be more variability in online HMM studies (see Fuentes et al., 2002, but cf. Yang et al., 1995, Dolfing, 1998, and Fierrez et al., 2007). The direct comparison of an online and off-line approach is a very useful experiment that provides some insights into the classification accuracy of the features that were extracted. Since the online approach allows one to capture the static and dynamic aspects of a user's signature entry, by subtraction, one could quantify the contribution of the spatial features associated with signature verification. A proper study would require the inclusion of the full repertoire of features associated with off-line signature verification systems which are those that are essentially spatial in nature (see Nalwa, 1998 for a useful discussion on this topic). The results would obviously depend on the classification approach that was used, so clearly, there is a considerable amount of effort required.

Trevathan and McCabe (2005) presented a study investigating an approach to remote signature verification. The authors propose a basic client–server model, where clients make requests from the server for authentication based on the production of the required signature. The signature reference database is stored secured on the server, and is utilized whenever users wish to authenticate themselves. The authors note that since signatures can change with time, due to natural aging or the physical health of the user, the reference signatures must be updated over time. The verification process is local to the user's machine, though the reference signature is derived from the server side, and the decision outcome is generated from the server, which notifies the client of the decision. Note that in this paper, the reference signature was generated from five samples provided by the user. The reference profile is then based on the average of these reference samples, along with some statistical information. In addition, the reference profiles should be updated over time, according to some schedule.

The authors suggest that the features extracted are transformed into a string representation before being passed onto the server. The features are generated by a process that traces the path of the signature and extracts both the static and dynamic details of the signature. These attributes are encoded into a string, which could carry positional information, and along each position is a particular value for the particular feature (much like a GA-based chromosome). The string representation of the feature values is then transmitted, in encrypted format, to the server. The server then utilizes a string matching algorithm to compare the submitted sample to a reference profile. Note that since this is a verification task, the ID of the user must also be encoded in the string and used for lookup on the server when extracting the reference profile. There is a wide range of efficient string matching algorithms available, and the authors suggest the use of the Wagner–Fischer algorithm because it was the most successful strategy in their system (Stephen, 1994, McCabe, 1997). A user-specific acceptance threshold is required, which is used to decide whether or not to accept the signature. The authors also suggest the use of time stamping, which can help reduce the problem of signature capture and reuse. When the request for authentication is made, the time stamp is examined. It must be up-to-date and within some tolerance range; otherwise, the request will be denied. Another solution to the capturing problem, suggested by McCabe (2000) is to employ a signed password, as opposed to a signature to validate a user. This allows the "signature" to be changed periodically, and will help reduce the impact of stolen signatures.

This forms the basis of a remote access approach to signature verification. It is presented in very general terms and emphasizes the need to secure all data transfers and the reference profile database. These are generic issues associated with any biometric-based system that is employed in a distributed computing environment. The other important issue is the mode of signature collection.

Syukri et al., presented an interesting approach that allows users to use a mouse to enter their signature. This method does not require any special hardware, and their results were quite significant in terms of the classification rate. This approach is suitable for PCs and laptops, which accounts for a significant proportion of remote access users. Alternatively, users with PDAs can use a stylus type of device to enter their signatures. Once these hurdles have been traversed, the techniques discussed in this chapter, which are merely a very small sample of what is available, can be deployed. With increased usage of remote signature verification implementations comes the need to produce standards. This important issue is described in the next section.

3.4 Signature Verification Standards

There are two critical issues with regard to standards in biometrics: one involves testing comparative methodologies and the other involves international implementation regulations. The first issue is intimately related to ways of evaluating biometric systems in an objective and verifiable fashion. This chapter has presented a small sample of the various ways signature verification systems are developed, each in isolation, without the ability to compare one system to another. In this modern era, biometrics, especially those deployed in a remote access environment, will undoubtedly entail the crossing of one or more borders. International standards are required to ensure interoperability across borders. Both of these issues will be discussed in turn.

With regard to comparative studies, there are several issues that must be tackled. In the context of signature biometrics, the critical issue is that of standards for forgeries. The principal task of signature-based biometrics is to distinguish a genuine signature from a forgery. As mentioned earlier in this chapter, there is a significant difficulty in acquiring forgeries – at least skilled forgeries. Most studies utilize other study participants to act as forgers, with or without practice on the signatures they are to forge. Whether this is a realistic test is debatable, but this author and probably many others believe this is not sufficient. How are we going to generate realistic forgeries in the numbers required for statistical validity? One approach is to recruit professional forgers, asking them to spend time to input some number of forged signatures. This may not be an appealing way to proceed, but if the forgeries were stored on an anonymous database, this might indeed work quite reasonably. Another approach is to trace the signature of another, which should yield, with some practice, a reasonably accurate forgery. The only problem with this approach is that one can only capture the *static* aspects of the forgery. If the verification algorithm requires dynamical data, then this approach will certainly not be viable. This highlights the importance of research into the classification accuracy of static versus dynamic features (see Nalwa, 1998 for a detailed discussion on this topic). If it is found that static features are sufficient, then this is possibly a viable approach. If dynamic attributes are required, then possibly the use of machine-based signatures may be required. This author is personally willing to consider the deployment of robots – or similar devices – as a device for generating forged signatures. Several literature reports have provided evidence that the level of control required to reproduce writing in robots is sufficient for legibility (Wahl et al., 2006). For instance, dynamic measurements such as pressure and velocity have been reproduced in attempts to automate forgery (Franke & Koppen, 2005). The development of the ink deposition model (IDM) provides an analytical framework to examine the use of writing implements within a robotics-based framework, suitable for examining the entire signature production process (Franke & Rose, 2004). The deployment of suitable forgeries may soon be an impediment of the past.

There are of course many other considerations with regard to the production of a framework for comparative signature verification studies. The type of features that are extracted is a critical factor in the verification results. The debate still continues with respect to static versus dynamic features. Within each class of features, the issue of consistency in their measurement is an unresolved issue. Lastly, the verification algorithms proper is a major area of discordance between studies, even when applying the same basic approach (e.g. the application of HMMs as mentioned earlier in this chapter). Granted there is considerable room for exploration with the verification algorithm, stock should be taken when considering the range of verification results generated when the same approach is taken. If there is a disparity between two relatively similar studies, this should sound a warning bell (see Lei & Govindaraju, 2004 for a nice summary of these topics).

With respect to international standards, there are a series of standards that focus principally on physiological-based biometrics. The National Institute of Standards (NIST) and the ISO Joint Technical Committee 1 (JCT1) have chartered a sub-commission on biometrics, called Subcommittee 37 (SC37), established in 2002 (see http://www.jtc1.org/). This technical committee was established to help set the international standards for a range of biometric technologies. One of the outcomes of this committee (in part produced in parallel by other international standards organizations) was the Common Biometrics Exchange File Format (CBEFF), spearheaded by the NIST. The purpose of the CBEFF is to provide a format for data storage (essentially a data header) that allows biometric data to be shared, in a multimodal fashion. The header does have an entry for signature dynamics (see the field value type, 0×80), but does not contain a framework to allow a proper signature verification experiment to be encoded within this framework. The Multimodal Biometrics for Identity Documents (MbioID), via the BioAPI specification version 1.1, was designed to promote interoperability between vendors. There is an entry for signature/sign behavioral data, but it is not yet complete (see the latest BioAPI version 2.0 standard, http://MITproject.com/). What is clear from the standards literature is that physiological biometrics is well represented within this technical committees. That behavioral biometrics has lagged behind in this arena is a cause for concern. These issues are discussed in more detail toward the end of Chapter 4.

3.5 Conclusions

This chapter has presented a series of case studies involving off-line and online signature verification studies. It must be noted first that the classification errors associated with each approach are quite low, on the order of 1–20%, depending on the type of study. The general consensus is that online approaches are more accurate, in terms of accepting genuine signatures and rejecting forgeries. One reason for this "consensus" is that online signature verification systems can extract more information than off-line approaches. The incorporation of static and dynamic features provides a wider range of classification criteria, from which to build a classification system capable of differentiating genuine signatures from forgeries. One clear issue is that the range of features that can be utilized for signature verification is highly variable, at least based on the small sample of case studies presented in this chapter. But unfortunately, one has to scour hundreds of papers on the topic to acquire an inkling as to the features that have been employed in this domain. It is a very rare occurrence that two papers utilize the same features (whether static, dynamic, or both). Gupta and McCabe (1997) provide a very comprehensive overview of the variety of features that have been exploited in signature verification systems. Though somewhat dated, this study is still relevant today. Some of their conclusions are as follows:

1. Systems that employ user-dependent thresholds are better than those that employ a global threshold.
2. The performance of a signature verification system is enhanced when incorporating more signatures when building a reference signature.

Throughout the literature, the use of user-dependent thresholds generally produces a more accurate model that yields lower classification error rates than global thresholds (see case studies in this chapter for examples). This is true regardless of the biometric modality (see Chapter 4 for examples within the keystroke dynamics literature). It is probably safe to indicate that *all* biometric studies *should* produce user-dependent thresholds as part of the model training process. As to the second conclusion, the more signatures available, the more data available generally, the more accurate the model will be. The question really is how much is enough? This may be modality dependent, and will certainly be influenced by the type of model utilized in the study. These are areas of intense active research in the field.

Nalwa (1997) presents an interesting set of conclusions in his paper, which discusses the issues associated with online verification systems). His principal contention is that signature verification should be based on the shape of the signature. Humans rarely ensure that the pen angle, pen pressure, and related dynamic features are foremost on their minds when signatures are generated. Again, his comments may be somewhat dated, but the conclusions are still relevant today. Some of his conclusions are

1. Building a model from signatures entered over many sessions results in a more realistic and accurate model.
2. Models should be designed to cover a range of feature resolutions.
3. Fine-tuning a signature verification system for a particular database is an unrealistic prospect.

The notion of an adaptive signature database is a very important feature of behavioral biometrics, which tend to vary over time. Whether the variation is linear in some direction is debatable, but clearly, signatures and typing styles change with time. The ability to include dynamic reference values must be incorporated into the model from which we base the acceptance criterion on. The issue of multiple scales or resolutions is important − as the quality of the data may vary over time − and the number of data points may vary from one signature to another. The ability of the model to scale with the quality and/or quantity of the data, in an adaptive way, is important in a system that is fully automated. Lastly, the issue of fine-tuning the verification system for a particular database of signatures speaks of the importance of avoiding overtraining the classifier. Clearly, given enough time and models, a given collection of signatures can be classified with virtually 100% accuracy. Whether this system will generalize is a completely different matter. This is a very critical factor in developing an online/remote access signature verification system. This aspect can only be examined by having a range of testing data, fully specified within a standard ontology, that allows for interoperability between various biometric implementations. These issues will be discussed throughout the course of this text.

3.6 Research Topics

1. Examine how the use of a stylus, for remote PDA signature verification, compares in terms of accuracy to a traditional digital pen.
2. What constitutes a proper number of reference samples? Clearly, the more the better, but is there a way to quantify the relationship between number of reference samples and the quality of a given modeling process generally?
3. How should one measure the distances between training samples, and test and training samples? Currently, the DTW or some variant is the predominant technique. Can the penalties and related issues be fine-tuned to enhance the scoring outcome?
4. Can the level of skilled forgeries be increased in order to provide a more robust testing scenario? This may require some form of automated signature production scheme, which could possibly employ the use of state-of-the-art robotics technology.
5. In relation to 4 above, how can signature databases be expanded to include a much larger number of signatures, in a variety of languages? In the case studies presented in this chapter, the predominant languages are English and Chinese. Clearly, if this technology is to be universally applied, does the language of the signature have an impact on the classification strategy?
6. International standards must be expanded to allow interoperability between different research groups. This would entail the creation of a relevant ontology that would allow researchers to share data and to provide the means for incorporating signature verification biometrics into the broader realm of biometrics for fusion analysis studies.

4

Keystroke Dynamics

4.1 Introduction

This chapter examines a behavioral biometric based on keystroke dynamics. Essentially, this technology focuses on extracting quantitative information from the interactions between a user and a keypad/keyboard device and using this information to automate user authentication and/or identification. The basic idea is that each user interacts with a keyboard in a particular way, yielding a unique pattern that can be associated with that particular user. The bulk of the research in this domain has focused on identifying which aspects of our interactions with such devices are sufficiently individualistic as to provide a unique reference signature. With a signature in hand, the next task is to develop an automated method for distinguishing one reference signature from the set of all reference signatures – essentially a classification task. How accurately this process can be performed is the principal research goal – what factors influence the classification accuracy? Is it the attributes, the classification algorithm, or a combination of the two? In order to address these critical issues, this chapter will present several case studies in varying degrees of detail, with the aim of analyzing their underlying assumptions with respect to the classification result(s). Due to the substantial body of research published in this area, only a sample of reported experimental designs and results will be presented. The survey will focus on several factors: i) the selection of attributes for authentication, ii) the automation methodology (classification schemes), iii) the use of modeling techniques, and iv) the experimental design. No attempt is made to explicitly rate these various implementations. The pros and cons of the experimental approach will be evaluated – in terms of the effectiveness of the system. The data will be interpreted in light of the experimental design and the inherent value of the underlying assumptions.

4.2 Attribute Selection Process

In the broadest sense, keystroke dynamics-based authentication entails a three-stage process. First, attributes are selected from a user; a model is developed, and a classifier is produced based on the values of the attributes with respect to the model. Probably, the most critical aspect of keystroke dynamics is attribute selection. What attributes can be extracted by examining how a person types? The purpose of attribute selection is to extract features that

Behavioral Biometrics: A Remote Access Approach. Kenneth Revett
© 2008 John Wiley & Sons, Ltd.

are discriminating with respect to the way users interact with a keyboard. The majority of studies have identified three fundamental attributes: scan code, dwell time, and time of flight.

The scan code is a unique numeric value that is associated with each key on a standard PC keyboard (see Appendix B for a brief discussion of the history of the keyboard). This attribute identifies uniquely which key is pressed. It becomes significant when users are required to enter a capitalized letter for instance and have to hold down a shift key. Some users may deploy the left and some the right shift key. This is an individual choice that may reflect typing style or may be influenced by which side of the keyboard the letter to be capitalized is located. In addition, if digits are to be entered, does the person use the digits above the letters, or does he use the numeric keypad? The keypad "1" has a different scan code from the upper row "1" found above the letters. Further still, the rest of the keys on the numeric pad (the arithmetic operators and the "enter" key) have a different scan code from the rest of the keyboard. Evidence will be presented later in this chapter indicating that the use of the scan code does produce a more complete model with enhanced discriminatory capacity.

The dwell time (or key-press duration time) refers to the length of time a user depresses a key when typing. Typical values are on the order of 10 seconds of milliseconds, but may vary considerably between users. Assembly language code or even high-level languages like C# and Java are able to detect events such as key-down and key-up with very little programming effort. The press-down and release events associated with pressing a key can be used to calculate another important typing attribute, the inter-key latency (also termed n-graphs).

An n-graph is the time taken to press n-keys, and typically the value of n is 2 or 3 (referred to as digraphs and trigraphs, respectively). Dwell time and n-graph times provide indirect information about typing speed. It is interesting to note that there are only a couple of studies that utilize typing speed directly (see Monrose & Rubin, 1997, Gunetti & Picardi, 2003, Revett et al., 2005a). The values of n-graphs are generally larger than those for dwell times – and typically range on the order of 50–200 ms for digraphs – and essentially scale linearly for larger values of n. Also note that there are several different means for obtaining an n-graph. The variations depend on which stage of the key press one monitors. There is a leading edge, which occurs when a key is pressed, and a trailing edge that occurs when the key is released. For instance, when entering the digraph "NO," there are six combinations of press and release events that could be used to record the digraph (please see Figure 4.1 for details). Generally, there does not appear to be a quantitative difference between choosing the press-down versus the release event – as long as they are consistently collected. There is evidence that trigraphs are generally slightly more reliable than digraphs or tetragraphs (Gunetti & Picardi 2002). The only consideration is that the larger the n-graph is, the fewer examples one is likely to collect from the data – and hence may negatively impact the quality of the model developed for the user. This is a design issue that must be taken into consideration when developing the biometrics solution.

In addition to these essential attributes, the use of specialized keyboards that record the amount of pressure exerted when a key is pressed has been used as an attribute in keystroke dynamics (Sommerich et al., 1996, Kotani & Horii, 2005). The results indicate that this is a very useful attribute, which in the study by Kotani & Horii, 2005 yielded an equal error rate (equal error rate) of approximately 2.4%. This study employed several attributes used in combination (digraph latencies, dwell times) in addition to keying force, so the exact contri-

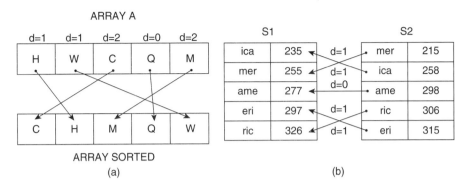

Figure 4.1 A sample of the algorithm for matching up two sets of digraphs generated from typing samples. On the left is an array version, demonstrating alignment of individual array elements. The same process appears on the right, where the ordering of trigraphs is based on trigraph timings. (Source: Bergadano et al., 2002)

bution to the classification accuracy directly attributable to keying pressure still remains to be quantified. Keying force will not be discussed further as it violates one of the driving forces behind keystroke dynamics-based biometrics: it does not require any additional hardware facilities for its implementation. Using pressure-sensitive keyboards would obviously require replacing the standard keyboard with one that costs significantly more.

Other attributes such as the sounds produced when striking a key have been suggested by several authors (Asonov & Agrawal, 2004, , Zhuang et al., 2005, Berger et al., 2006). The idea is that these acoustic emanations generated when striking a key can be used to identify which keys on the keyboard have been pressed. In addition, with careful monitoring of the acoustic emanations, events such as the press and release of a key provide an audible signal that could be used to measure key-press duration, for example, providing direct values for timing information. The results indicate that this technique has produced classification accuracies up to 98% when applied to small sets of users. The limited research in this area has yielded results that indicate that this aspect of typing can be a useful feature in the discrimination of different users. This attribute will not be discussed further in this chapter, but the interested reader should consult the references cited above for more details (especially Asonov & Agrawal, 2004).

There are several other attributes that could be utilized in the context of extracting typing characteristics that fall within the confines of a software-based solution. For one, the time required to type specific portions of a text string could be recorded. This measure provides some additional useful discriminatory information over and above typing speed, which is a more global measure of typing skill level (see Revett et al., 2005a,d). The effect of practice could be measured – and quantified within the framework of the so-called practice effect (please consult Appendix C for more details on the power law of practice derived from the experimental psychology domain). The practice effect is well known within the human–computer interaction domain, in the context of examining how a user's response time changes with repetition. This effect was first quantified by Newell and has been coined the "power law of practice" (Newell & Rosenbloom, 1981). Typically, this metric can be used in the context of keystroke dynamics by maintaining a record of task performance (e.g. typing speed) over a number of repeated trials. A log–log plot of task performance over repeated trials yields a linear function, the slope (A) and Y-intercept (B) of which can be a quantitative measure of task performance that may be unique to an individual at some point in time. Generally speaking, this metric is most useful in continuous mode authentication/identification schemes, as this approach will provide more samples through which one can determine the values for A and B, which can be compared with the authentic user via an extrapolation process. This metric will be discussed later in this chapter in more detail.

In order to enhance the range of attributes, a few second-order attributes have been utilized. One key second-order attribute is based on the entropy contained within a typing sample. Entropy in this context is an information theoretic concept that describes the order (or amount of variability) found in an input stream such as in the vector of attributes contained within a typing sample. Several authors have used the concept of entropy as a convenient measure of the information content of typing samples and the password space of a given biometric model (i.e. textual versus graphical passwords) (Monrose et al., 2001, Bergadano et al., 2002, Gunetti & Picardi, 2003, Revett et al., 2005a,b). Another interesting secondary attribute reported by Modi (Modi, 2005) is the use of the difference in successive keystroke latencies and/or n-graph timings, which they call the "slopes of the shape." More specifically, the difference between the slopes of the reference signature and an authentication attempt may contain significant discrimination capacity (Modi & Elliot, 2004). To the author's knowledge, these are the most significant second-order attributes that have been published within the context of keystroke dynamics-based user authentication. Certainly, there are derivative measures based on the statistical properties of the attributes – such as the mean and variance/standard deviation (SD) of attributes. These measures have been applied both on a global scale (Leggett & Williams, 1988) and locally (Mahar et al., 1995). Yet the statistical properties of collected data hardly qualify as secondary attributes in the sense that entropy and slope shape do. These really are measures of data quality, and form a very important part of the modeling process, which will be discussed at length further in this chapter.

With a small set of attributes, their use in a classification scheme is highly dependent upon their reliability. Virtually all keystroke dynamics-based authentication systems require users to register their details for subsequent model development and classifier training purposes. The purpose of registration is to extract typing samples from which a model of the typing style can be generated. In most studies, registration comes in the form of an enrollment process where users are required to provide details regarding their keyboard interaction style via a typing sample.

4.3 The Enrollment Process

The purpose of enrollment is to extract user-specific details in order to construct the profile of a given user. There are essentially two versions of enrollment – *static* and *dynamic*. The distinction between these two methods is somewhat blurred within the literature. For instance, some authors refer to static in the temporal sense – *when* the user enrolls into the system – which occurs generally before the authentication process can begin. In a dynamic version of enrollment, the users enroll during and/or after they have gained access to the system (see Gunetti & Picardi, 2003 for a discussion on this topic). The terms static/dynamic may also refer to the type of text that the user inputs for enrollment. The distinction is whether or not the text is fixed or free (sometimes referred to as "structured" and "nonstructured," respectively; Monrose & Rubin, 1997). In the former version, a fixed string of characters must be entered specifically. In the free text form, the user is allowed to type in any text that they choose – for instance, while typing with a word processor. In other scenarios, the user will enter a combination of fixed and free text.

Whether the enrollment is dynamic or static, the users are required to enter text in order to provide a measurable sample of their typing characteristics. In the long text version, a user is asked to enter a string of text that has been carefully selected to contain a range of attributes such as digraphs, trigraphs, and dwell time measurements (with a minimal amount of repetition for statistical validation purposes). Typically, a long text string may contain anywhere from 100 to 1500 characters. A commercial implementation using this strategy is Psylock (http://www.psylock.com/). The results indicate that the accuracy of the classification process is related to the length of the enrollment string – though the exact nature of this relationship remains to be quantified empirically (see Gaines et al., 1980). An interesting research issue is whether certain digraphs (or trigraphs) are more discriminatory than others. For instance, Leggett and Williams (1991) found that five digraphs were sufficient for the purpose of user authentication. In another study by Revett (2005a), particular digraphs were very informative with respect to classification accuracy. Further evidence for the discriminatory power of n-graphs was derived from a set of experiments published by Sim and Janakiraman (2007). Their results indicate that digraphs were more discriminatory than other n-graphs, but only when examined in a context-dependent manner. That is, n-graphs contained within the context of a larger word contained more discriminatory power than the n-graph appearing on its own. The enhancement of context-dependent n-graphs will be more significant in the context of free text as opposed to fixed-length text – as there is also a frequency component involved in the discriminatory effect as well. In addition, how many examples of a digraph/trigraph are required for statistically significant results – another interesting research topic with as yet no definitive answer. Typically, studies employ some standard value such as 5 – without any statistical substantiation for this value. These are critical issues that must be examined from both a theoretical and empirical perspective.

The short text form (which is typically static) requires users to enter the same string of characters (i.e. login ID and password) multiple times (typically 10–15). A commercial implementation using this strategy is BioPassword (http://www.biopassword.com/). Typically, a user/login ID and password are from six to eight characters each, providing approximately 14 characters on average from which to extract attributes from. By repeating this process 10–15 times, one has a significant amount of repeated entries from which to build a statistical model of the attributes. This method balances the trade-off between a small subset of the total attribute space for repeatability. A key advantage of this strategy is that is minimizes the enrollment effort (quantified as the cost of enrollment [COE]).

The long text input mode (static version) of enrollment has the drawback that it may be cumbersome to the user. Typically, the user will enter up to 10 times more text than the repeated entry version. One advantage of long text enrollments is that they are insensitive to typing errors. Generally, if the enrollment text is selected properly, there are sufficient duplicates within the text string that typing errors can be tolerated without degrading system performance. In most fixed, short text enrollment implementations, any input that contains a typing error is discarded and the user must replace any entries that are incorrect. The majority of studies have utilized the repeated entry version. Unfortunately, there are very few studies that have directly compared the two approaches. The only comparisons have been made at the study level, that is, a collection of study participants will enroll using one form or the other, and the classification results will be based on the type of enrollment each study group employs. A carefully controlled study involving the same participants, using both forms of enrollment (deploying the same underlying set of attributes) must be implemented in order to obtain a more rigorous comparison between these two strategies. Unfortunately, this type of study has not been published to date, and forms the basis for an active area of research.

In addition to static enrollment (short or long text string versions), another approach relies on the *continuous* monitoring of a user's typing style. This enrollment approach monitors the typing style of the users as they interact with the computer – for example, when using a word processor. This monitoring can begin at the authentication process (using the standard login ID/password access method) and subsequently when a user interacts with the system. One of the key advantages of this approach is that a user does not have to enroll per se. The users interact with the computer as normal, and the attributes are extracted and used for subsequent model building and authentication. Another advantage of the continuous approach is that it may be able to determine at randomly selected time intervals whether the typing style has changed relative to some previous time point. If the system notices a change in the typing style, this might signal the possibility that the current is not the same individual that has been using the system at some previous time point. For instance, once a person logs into a computer – he may leave for a moment and someone else could gain access to the computer and use it for his own purposes. In a static enrollment protocol, the authentication process could be tied into the screen saver login process. In this situation, the timing of the inactivity (screen saver) process must be fairly short, which might place an undue burden on the user, requiring the user to authenticate frequently. This safety feature is difficult to incorporate into a continuous enrollment protocol where there is no single point in time where users authenticate themselves. Instead, a sample of typing must be examined before a decision of authenticity can be rendered. By that time, the damage may have already been done. In addition, another key disadvantage of continuous enrollment is that users may feel their privacy is being invaded. The privacy issue can have a major impact on the users' perception of the system and has to be carefully considered before choosing an approach.

Ideally, the machine that users enroll on must be similar to the machine they will be expected to use. Issues such as typing on a laptop versus desktop as well as moving from one desktop to another have been raised, where results indicate that moving between a desktop and laptop and vice versa influence (usually in a negative fashion) the consistency of user authentication/identification (Monrose et al., 2001, Revett et al., 2005). How to cope with this problem is a serious design issue that must be addressed from an administrative standpoint. To approach this problem, research into how a person's typing style may change when moving from one type of input device to another (when typing the same text) must be fully investigated. One would anticipate that the changes would be of a relative nature – the consistency would be the same – but the base timing might be altered. This assumes that the keyboard essentially remains the same with respect to authentication input. If this is the case, then using relative timing information might be a more feasible approach, rather than absolute timing information. If the keyboard changes with respect to its layout, such as when using one with a different country locale, then the user might be required to reenroll onto that computer. This may be an unavoidable consequence of the added provided security. More specific research into this area is required to fully comprehend the extent of this phenomenon.

Lastly, the selection of the text to be entered during authentication is vitally important with respect to authentication efficacy, that is, should the users be allowed to select their own authentication details, or should they be system provided?

Typical of static enrollment processes, the user is required to enter a predetermined string of characters. This is generally true whether the system employs short fixed text or long string text. In the model employed by BioPassword, users are required to select their own login ID and password and to repeatedly enter them until some given stability-based criterion has been met. In our research, which employs the same strategy, users are required to enter their login ID/password 10 times. The stability criterion can take different forms – but typically is based on an entropy-like measure – where differences between successive entries are bound by some measure of similarity. Typically, this would entail recording the attributes and ensuring that they are within some range – such as the mean $\pm n$ SDs, where n is typically 1 or 2. There are other measures as well, but clearly, the more consistent the enrollment samples are, the better the resultant model will be. This decision to accept individual authentication entries can only be addressed by looking at a more local level. For instance, how many of the attributes must meet some predefined stability criterion is extremely important. Are all attributes required to meet the stability criterion, or a fraction – in our work at least 50% of the attributes are required for successful enrollment (Revett et al., 2005b,c). Leggett and Williams (1988) required 60% of the attributes to be within 1.5 SD of the mean reference value; otherwise, they were excluded and the entry would have to be repeated. Others have used slightly different values, but generally, the figure used by Leggett and Williams is optimal (see Mahar et al., 1995, Napier et al., 1995 for a full discussion on this issue). This acceptance criterion is an implementation issue – and will have a direct influence on the perceived usability of the system. If the criterion is set too stringently, then failure to enroll (FTE) will increase. A high FTE is an extremely undesirable side effect of biometric authentication schemes, which should be avoided whenever possible. FTE values are very low with keystroke dynamics-based systems compared with fingerprint and related technologies (Jain et al., 2005). This issue becomes even more significant if users have multiple passwords that need to be changed on a regular basis. The balance between ease of use and security needs to be struck. The long text string enrollment process requires that a user types in a string of selected text. Attributes such as digraph/trigraphs are recorded and the text string incorporates multiplicity with respect to the attributes to be extracted. If there is a lack of consistency with respect to the desired attributes, the user may be forced to reenter the text string. Whether FTE is higher with long text string versus short text-string enrollment procedures has not been fully investigated. This would be an interesting area for further study.

In continuous enrollment schemes, the notion of FTE does not really exist. The user types normally within a variety of different software-based environments, from word processors to programming languages. The system must develop an ongoing model of the user's typing dynamics, and typically has at its disposal a very large amount of data from which to build a model of the typing dynamics of the user. This is one of the key advantages of this type of enrollment system, but the results from published studies indicate that the classification error from this approach is no less than that generated from static enrollment schemes (see Gaines et al., 1980, Gunnetti & Picardi, 2003). A possible reason for this lack of performance is that the model becomes blurred through the incorporation of a large amount of data that is acquired over a considerable period of time (typically, static enrollment takes on the order of seconds to minutes to acquire). The typing style of the users may change during the course of time, unless they are professional typists, and this fact must be taken into account when the reference model profile is generated. Otherwise, the distributions become wide and overlapping with respect to variations in the attributes. For instance, a "tr" digraph may overlap considerably with a "th" digraph, thereby reducing the discriminatory power of these attribute instances. If the classification is based solely on values for this class of attribute, then the total discriminatory capacity of the system is thereby reduced. Very few studies employ an evolving measure of the user's typing style (see Revett et al., 2006 for an example implementation). How much does the typing style of a *typical* computer user change over time? This is a very interesting area of research that needs systematic exploration.

A hybrid approach to user authentication entails the idea of spontaneously generated authentication strings. For instance, in the case of spontaneously generated passwords, Modi and Elliot (2004) generated a user profile based on users entering 15 different words 10 times. The user is then subsequently authenticated on text that has not been employed during the enrollment process, but which is composed of elements that are contained within the authentication text. This approach allows a variety of passwords to be used, which may augment the password space. As long as the passwords contain elements found in the authentication text strings, the user can still be authenticated. Typically, the passwords are generated by the system – and indeed the password could even be presented on the screen for the user to type. This would remove the cognitive load of password memorability without compromising system performance. This approach was not fully examined in the Modi paper though – they presented a single password that the user was required to enter for authentication. The results from this study indicate that the classification error is quite low, with values on the order of a few percents (combined error rate), depending on the classification algorithm employed. This approach may be likened to a "cancelable"-based biometric, and has the attractive feature that a user does not have to enter the same password twice. If users are allowed to select their own password, then the burden is on the user to ensure their selection meets some minimal overlap between attributes contained within their password and the enrollment data. This generally would necessitate having a much more stringent enrollment process – following essentially the long text format. These issues will be discussed later in this chapter.

4.4 Generation of the Reference Profile

Once users have enrolled into the system, a model of their typing dynamics is constructed and stored for the purposes of authentication and/or identification. Typically, the enrollment data is stored in a data structure typically referred to as a biometric information record (BIR). The BIR should be stored in encrypted format on a server and is accessed when a user wishes to be authenticated and/or identified. This may make the BIR susceptible to an off-line attack. Substantial efforts have been undertaken to reduce the success rate of off-line attacks (see Monrose et al., 2001) by deploying methods such as password hardening and related concepts that strive to increase the entropy of the authentication data space. The issue of authentication data entropy space and related topics will be deferred until the end of the chapter (also see the introduction for some comments on this important topic as well). Lastly, some formal specification for the storage of BIR data is vitally important. The ability of one laboratory to exchange data with another is essentially nonexistent at the moment. This may reflect the lack of a standard storage format (e.g. the Common Biometric Exchange File Format

[CBEFF]), especially within the behavioral biometrics arena. This issue will be discussed later in this chapter.

With a suitable storage format for the BIR, the next phase entails the deployment of a classifier that uses information extracted from an authentication attempt and the contents of the associated BIR. The bulk of the literature on keystroke dynamics-based authentication focus on the classification accuracy can be manipulated with respect to the deployment of a particular classification scheme. There have been a substantial number of schemes deployed in this domain, from simple statistical models, a variety of machine learning algorithms, and complex mixture models. The classification process can operate in one of two modes: user authentication and user identification. The overwhelming majority of literature reports focus on the deployment of keystroke dynamics for user authentication. Authentication is a simpler task than identification, in that it entails a $1:1$ mapping between the login details and the associated BIR. When a person logs into a computer, the same attributes that have been collected during enrollment (stored in some form within the BIR) are extracted and compared to the associated BIR. If they match, then the user is authenticated; otherwise, their attempt to login is rejected. A critical question in this regard is how many chances does a user have to be authenticated/identified? In a typical Windows environment, we have three chances to authenticate ourselves. It is surprising how many studies do not adhere to this operational definition of authentication. This issue will be discussed later in this chapter. Identification requires searching for the BIR that most closely matches the input characteristics of a login ID/password. This requires searching through every record in the BIR database, which could be extremely large in our e-commerce-based society. An effective solution may require partitioning the BIRs according to some optimization-based criteria.

Another interesting question is when do users have to authenticate themselves? In a Windows environment, there are three separate login sessions. BioPassword integrates their authentication scheme within the Microsoft login facility, MSGina. Therefore, the user's login details are checked by the authentication algorithm before being passed onto the standard Windows authentication scheme (see BioPassword white materials for a fuller discussion). Since the authentication is integrated into the operating system's native authentication mechanism, anytime Windows requires the user to authenticate, the keystroke dynamics-based authentication scheme is also deployed. This is a very useful feature, but is more of an operational detail. It may place a constraint on the implementation – especially in the context of continuous authentication schemes. As mentioned previously, continuous authentication and/ or identification monitors the keystroke dynamics of the user multiple times. Thus, imposters who enter the system using someone else's login session can be detected. This places a greater burden on the authentication process, as it will have to occur for each user at some predetermined time interval. How this is integrated into the operating system becomes a real consideration. Issues such as ensuring attackers cannot turn off this facility become important – and cannot be overlooked if the system is to be deployed in a large-scale operation.

In addition, there are quantitative measures associated with enrollment, such as FTE and COE, sometimes referred to as CUE, the cost of user enrollment. FTE is a measure of the number of enrollment failures. As previously mentioned, FTE is fairly low with keystroke dynamics-based biometrics – as opposed to physiological biometrics such as fingerprints. The reason is that if a person does not have fingerprints for whatever reason, he will not be able to change that. With a behavioral technique, if users find the enrollment process difficult, they can continue trying until they get it right. The COE is a measure of the amount of user effort required to enroll into the system. This is typically measured in terms of the number of keystrokes required to enroll.

The stage is now set to begin to evaluate several examples of keystroke dynamics-based authentication systems that have been reported in the literature. This literature is quite large, and it is not even possible in the space provided to survey all the major classes of algorithms that have been employed. Most authentication (which applies to identification as well) approaches use some form of automated machine learning algorithm(s). To provide a structured approach to the survey, the literature will be partitioned according to a set of categories. The first principal category within keystroke dynamics-based biometric implementations reported in the literature is whether the data is one-class or two-class. For instance, if we start off with enrollment data only, then we have a one-class decision system. We have examples of only successful authentication attempts. The goal of the authentication mechanism is to distinguish valid from invalid authentication attempts. If the classifier works by examples – such as most typical supervised learning techniques such as neural networks – then one must consider how to train the system wit a single class of data. Two-class systems have examples of authentic user data as well as imposter data. This type of data is very amenable to a supervised learning strategy such as support vector machines (SVMs) and rough sets. As specific implementations are presented, solutions to the one-class problem will be highlighted in the context of their implementation discussion.

Another taxonomic category is based on the distance metrics employed to distinguish authentic from non-authentic users. Virtually all systems generate a reference model of an authentic user (stored as a BIR). The resulting classifier must determine if an authentication attempt is sufficiently close to the BIR for that user based on some distance metric. There are a variety of distance metrics that have been employed, from simple Hamming distances, edit distances, and higher-order statistical measures. This is a very important aspect of the classification algorithm, and various examples will be discussed in turn.

The following section presents a survey of implementations organized according to these taxonomic categories. The literature reveals that these taxonomic categories are not mutually exclusive, and that a variety of different measures have been examined in various combinations, looking to find the best classification accuracy (in terms of reduced EER). Let us begin by looking at some of the earliest works in this field, published by Gaines et al. (1980).

4.5 Case Studies

In 1980, a RAND report was published by Gaines entitled "Authentication by Keystroke Timing: Some Preliminary Results" (Gaines et al., 1980). This was the first large-scale study of keystroke-based biometrics. The purpose of this study was to investigate whether or not a small collection of professional typists (six) could be identified based on their keystroke timing. The typists were given a paragraph of prose (long text – approximately 260 words, 1500 characters) to type, and the times between successive keystrokes (digraphs) were recorded. In addition, the experiment also investigated whether *what we type* might have an impact on the classification task. To this end, the authors asked the professional typists to enter three different texts: i) ordinary English text, ii) collection of random English words, and iii) a collection of "random" phrases. There were no significant differences between the three categories of text based on their analysis, and the authors concluded that there was insufficient information in the three texts to allow a discrimination to be made. The entries were pooled together for each of the subjects, treating them as one long continuous text (approximately 5000 characters in length). The typists were then asked to repeat their entry 4 months later.

The attributes that were extracted from the text entries were digraphs, although the authors of the study acknowledged that other attributes such as trigraphs could have been used for the analysis as well. The digraph times ranged from 75 milliseconds to several seconds and were measured with a resolution of 1 millisecond. From this data, they generated a statistical model that was to be used to identify the typist who entered the text on both occasions. As a further consequence of this study, the authors postulated that this system could be used for user authentication. The person (they term the "originator") who will later gain access to a computer types some predefined text, from which information regarding digraphs will be extracted. At some later time, a person ("claimant") wishing to gain access to the computer system enters the same predefined text. The system then compares the two entries and decides whether or not the two entries are produced by the same person. This is the essence of keystroke dynamics-based user authentication.

The basis of their decision system is a statistical model that utilizes hypothesis testing for discrimination. Their null hypothesis (H_0) is that the originator and claimant is one-and-the-same person. The experimental hypothesis (H_1) is the samples are not produced by the same typists. In their terminology, they generated the following equations:

$$\alpha = P\{\text{rejecting } H_0 | H_0\} = P(\text{making a secondary error}) \qquad (4.1)$$

$$\beta = P\{\text{rejecting } H_1 | H_1\} = P(\text{making a primary error}) \qquad (4.2)$$

Generally, α is taken to be something on the order of 0.01 or 0.05, a typical value for a statistical significance threshold. What the authors wished to do was reduce both α and β, amounting to reducing both false rejection rate (FRR) (type I error) and false acceptance rate (FAR) (type II error), respectively. These authors pointed out that this generally was not possible in practice, so like most studies still performed today, they fixed α (equation 4.1) and then tried to minimize β (equation 4.2). The authors further claim that the test statistic U must reflect differences in digraph times (keystroke dynamic attributes generally) between the originator and claimant (authentic user and imposter in today's parlance). The magnitude of U should be small if the originator and claimant as the same, and hence the p-value should be large (≥ 0.05). The opposite would hold true if the originator and claimant were not the same – that is, their digraphs were significantly different from one another compared to expected random variations from an originator.

The long text contains a significant number of digraphs, and the identical digraphs are grouped together. Even though the originator and claimant typed the same text string on the two occasions, a mistake may have been made and hence the number of digraphs may vary between the two samples. The authors selected the minimal number of complete digraphs from the whole set to use for statistical analysis. There were a total of 87 unique digraphs that were used for the user comparisons. They further assumed that the repeated digraphs were independent of one another, which is a reasonable assumption. They also assumed that the digraphs were normally distributed with approximately equal variance. Whether these assumptions hold has to be determined empirically, and for this study, the assumption held true for the most part. They preprocessed their data by using a low-pass filter, removing any digraphs that had a duration of 500 milliseconds or greater. After the filtering process, the averages were recalculated.

With the data ready for significance testing, the authors deployed a *t*-test against each of the log-transformed digraphs contained within the text. In effect, they used a likelihood ratio test, which was a slightly modified *t*-statistic (see Gaines et al., 1980, Appendix A for details on the derivation of the statistical model). They compared each typing sample against all others, including one by the same typist generated at the other time point (yielding a total of 55 separate tests). The results using the full dataset yielded no primary errors (FAR) with only two secondary errors (FRR). These are significant results, even by today's standards using much more sophisticated machine learning techniques. The authors went further still, asking some very relevant questions such as i) is there any correlation between the attributes (digraphs used) and the secondary error (FRR)? and ii) could the cardinality of the input vector (87 digraphs) be reduced without compromising the classification accuracy? These are very relevant questions that still remain to be answered (addressed further in this chapter and in Chapter 7).

The author's reduced the dimensionality of the digraphs from 87 down to five in a two-stage process. First, they examined the digraphs with respect to their handedness – whether they were made with left–left (LL), right–right, or left–right (LR)/right–left (RL) finger combinations. They noticed that right–right digraphs yielded no classification errors , and so we able to reduce the number of digraphs down to 11 with this observation. Lastly, they noticed that certain digraphs were very effective at discriminating users and found that five were sufficient for their classification task (*in*, *io*, *no*, *on*, and *ul*). This was an extremely significant result which has not been properly corroborated in other studies published in the literature. Lastly, they analyzed the results in terms of the *strength* of the classification process.

The question they addressed is how strong was the decision – either to reject or accept an input as belonging to one of the typist? That is, was the input close to being accepted or rejected – a boarderline case? Their method employed simply viewing the *p*-values – those very close to the threshold were considered marginal. Again, this is a very useful piece of information that provides discriminatory information with respect to the attributes used in the classification task. This notion of strength is rarely addressed in any of the relevant literature – though the use of rough sets by Revett (2007b) does address this issue directly.

This work has been instrumental in setting the direction by which virtually all keystroke dynamics-based authentic systems operate. All extract typing information from the users and build some sort of model of their dynamical interaction with the key input device (keyboard, keypad, or mobile phone). The use of digraphs is a novel approach and serves as the primary attribute in today's systems. They employ a long text static enrollment process – similar to many implementations in use today (see Psylock at http://www.psylock.com/). A minimal amount of preprocessing is required to remove outliers (using a simple low-pass filter). One issue raised by Mahar and Napier (Mahar et al., 1995, Napier et al., 1995) is that the Gaines study employed a global threshold for their low-pass filter. This implies that all users will produce the same level of typing variability. In the Gaines' study, this might be a valid assumption as all users were professional typists. Whether it holds true for all subjects is a matter of empirical study, which will be addressed later in this chapter.

Although Gaines' study was not the earliest mention of keystroke dynamics (see Forsen et al., 1977), it was the first to systematically examine the feasibility of the approach and produced some interesting results. The next case study discussion will focus on a paper published by David Umphress and Glen Williams in 1985. This paper extends significantly the work of Gaines et al. because it incorporated a model of typing based on Card's keystroke-level model (Card et al., 1980). Please note that the Card paper was published just before the Gaines publication and hence might not have been available for them to consult prior to the development of their system.

In Umphress and William's 1985 paper (Umphress & Williams, 1985), the authors examined the question of whether there were any cognitive factors that could be used in order to distinguish one person's typing characteristics from another. If so, these characteristics should be incorporated into a model for each user and could serve as a means of user authentication. As in previous work, a reference profile was generated which was used for subsequent authentication. The authors used two principal attributes for the production of the user's reference profile: i) mean and SD keystroke latency and ii) the latency between all adjacent letter combinations. The latter was maintained in a 26×26 matrix, where the rows corresponded to the first letter of the digraph and the columns to the next letter in the digraph (Umphress & Williams, pp. 267). Note that each cell in the matrix represented the average value for the particular digraphs. The data for the reference profile was preprocessed quite differently from the Gaines' study.

The keystroke-level model was designed to serve as a test bed to examine human–computer interaction-based systems. More specifically, the model examined factors which effect the time required to perform particular tasks when interacting with computers, such as selecting items from a menu, selection of items with the mouse, and entering text (typing). Performance was quantified by examining the level of errors, learning, functionality, and recall.

In terms of task performance, the model is based on the notion of a collection of physical-motor operators. They identify four such operators as relevant to computer-based task performance: **K** (keystroking), **P** (pointing), **H** (homing), and **D** (drawing). In addition, they also incorporate a mental operator **M**, and a response operator **R**. Their model states that the execution time of a task is the linear summation of these operators:

$$T_{\text{execute}} = T_K + T_P + T_H + T_D + T_M + T_R \tag{4.3}$$

The authors assumed that most of the operators take constant time to be performed (e.g. $T_K = n_K t_K$, where n_K is the number of characters to type and t_K is the time per keystroke). The most frequently occurring operator is **K|P**, representing a keystroke or mouse click event, respectively. Considering a constant time for **K|P**, this would reflect the speed of the user, and so task performance would be predominantly affected by a person's speed – which can vary considerably – with world record speeds over 130 words per minute for typing. It is interesting to note that very few studies involving keystroke dynamics employ this attribute directly, but see the discussion later in this chapter. The same observation can be made for most mouse dynamics-based systems as well (see Chapter 6 for details). The homing factor **H** represents the actual movement around the keyboard – this factor can be influenced by the position of the characters to be entered. The study by Revett highlights this issue – in the context of keyboard gridding, where the position of characters in a login request is placed strategically in order to maximize variations in **H**. The operator **D** represents the use of a mouse in drawing lines and will not be discussed until the chapter on mouse dynamics (Chapter 6). The mental preparation required to perform a task (or subtask) is embodied in the operator **M**. This is a highly variable operator and was estimated to be a constant by Card

(Card et al., 1980), as well as by Umphress and Williams. The exact value of this operator is to be determined in a more general context and might prove to be extremely useful in the context of accentuating differences in typing a login string. The last operator proposed by car is the response operator **R**, which represents the response time in seconds. This is useful in the context of an interactive system, which is appropriate for Human Computer Interaction (HCI) but not necessarily so in the current context, and hence will not be discussed further. These factors may have a significant impact on how a user interacts with the keyboard when entering textual passwords. In addition, these factors will have a significant impact on the use of graphical interfaces, and will be discussed further in the chapter on graphical pass-words. Lastly, the model also predicts that the way a person uses a mouse pointer will be affected by the task, and this will be discussed in the chapter on mouse dynamics.

The Umphress and Williams study employed a subset of the operators discussed by Card, 1980. Specifically, they examined operators **K** and **M** in their work. The authors assumed that during typing, the typist would acquire the necessary information for the task, storing the information in chunks of approximately six to eight characters at a time. Employing the terminology and basic model of human performance of the keystroke-level model, they assumed that typing was performed according to the following model:

$$T_{\text{Task}} = T_{\text{acquire}} + T_{\text{execute}} \tag{4.4}$$

where T_{Task} is the time required to perform the task; T_{acquire} is the time required to assess the task, and T_{execute} is the time required to actually perform the task. The T_{acquire} term is the time required to assess the task and to build a model of what needs to be accomplished to complete the task. The authors assume this term is not quantifiable, and hence cannot be used to char-acterize individuals. They therefore reduced deduce T_{Task} after they ascertained the other terms in equation 4.4. The authors further divided T_{execute} into two separate terms that represent the time required to enter the information and the mental preparation time (T_{K} and T_{M}, respec-tively). The authors further indicate that the entry and preparation phases are intermixed within the context of the given task, and so used the following equation to describe this process:

$$T_{\text{execute}} = \sum (T_{\text{mi}} + Tk_{\text{i}}) \tag{4.5}$$

This formulation indicates that the execution time is a summation of mental and keystroke activity times. With regard to short text entry systems, this factor may not be extremely sig-nificant. With respect to long text entry systems, T_{execute} could be extremely significant, yet there is no or little data reported in the literature.

The keystroke-level model was instrumental in the Umphress study, primarily with respect to data preprocessing. The users (seventeen in total) were required to enter a reference profile that consisted of 1400 characters. Note that the participants were not professional typists and exhibited a typical range in typing speed. If any mistakes were made during the transcription process; they were discarded. The reason for this was that typing mistakes would cause the participant to pause and hence create a cognitive boundary that might obscure subsequent keystroke entries. In addition, they used chunks of the input data – using only the first six keystrokes from each word that was entered (the input was considered a continuous string of characters). This again reflects the idea that mental processes are involved in the task (T_{mi} in equation 4.5) and will directly influence task performance. From the input, a collection of digraphs was obtained and used for subsequent authentication/identification as discussed above. The digraphs were low-passed filtered (threshold was 750 milliseconds), and each digraph was collected with 10 millisecond resolution. This data served as the reference profile which was stored for use during the authentication process. During authentication, the user would type in text (300 characters), and the same attributes and conditions used to generate the reference string would be performed. Note that the authentication text was not specified in the paper – the question is whether it was a proper subset of the training samples. The critical issue then becomes how to score the authentication request in lieu of the reference profile. The authors state that two tests were used: one based on keystroke intervals and the other test appraises the overall typing characteristics.

In the first test, the authors matched the digraph using the reference matrix and considered it valid if it was within the reference digraph ± 0.5 SD (60% of the digraphs had to match for success). They maintained a count of the number of valid digraphs, and the ratio of valid to total digraphs was recorded and used for authentication purposes. In the second test, all digraphs were used to generate an authentication vector that was compared against the reference vector (using only the common digraphs from the two samples) via a two-tailed t-test (assuming a normal distribution). The null hypothesis is similar to Gaines' – that there is no difference between the sample and the authentication input and the reference input ($p < 0.05$). The final results of this study yielded an FRR of 12%, and the worst case FAR was approximately 6%. That is, out of the 17 subjects, two failed to be authenticated, and for the FAR, 16 out of the 272 comparisons failed.

Though the results of the Umphress and Williams study with respect to FAR and FRR were not as impressive as those of Gaines' study, it did provide a new approach to the problem. The use of a cognitive model was certainly novel – ideas borrowed from the human–computer interaction literature were used in an appropriate manner. The concept of chunking – where information is read into a "memory buffer" – has certainly proved useful in related domains (Miller, 1956). The authors used the first six characters of each word – neglecting word boundaries. It would have been interesting to extend this to seven and eight characters. The question is whether six was a sufficient number of characters – yielding only five digraphs per word. The rest of the preprocessing steps included low-pass filtering to ensure that the repeat digraphs were uniformly distributed. This is an assumption that has generally been held in subsequent work, but may not be the most suitable distribution. This is an active area of research that has not been completely addressed in a systematic large-scale study. In addition, the use of a cognitive model extends the applicability to other forms of authentication biometrics such as graphical password and mouse dynamics-based systems. These issues will be discussed further in Chapters 5 and 6, respectively. Lastly, their system, like that of Gaines' could be used for dynamic static or continuous identity *verification*.

Leggett et al. published a report in 1987 that was an extension of the Umphress and Williams paper (Leggett & Williams, 1991). Williams was an author on both of these papers, and the approach taken in the two studies was very similar. They employed the idea of typing a long text string – 537 characters of prose, which was entered twice. The first was used to generate a reference profile and the second was entered 1 month later, used for the test profile. The authors extracted several attributes from the typing sample including unigraphs, digraphs, trigraphs, and tetragraphs from 36 participants. Note that the participants were not professional typists. They discarded words that contained errors, used only the first six characters of each word, and discarded any latencies exceeding 75 milliseconds. They employed the same measures of similarity, based on individual n-graphs (their data suggested that digraphs were sufficient) in the profile and reference samples. If the profile was within 0.5 SD of the reference digraph (mean value, again assuming a uniform distribution), the digraph was accepted, and a count was made of the ratio of the total number of accepted digraphs over total digraphs. This ratio was deployed as the principal discriminatory criterion. In the second test, the vector of the profile digraphs was compared against the reference digraphs, and a two-tailed t-test statistic was computed, with $p < 0.05$. These measures were used to assess the confidence that the same person typed by the reference and the profile samples. The confidence was coded as either high ("H," medium, "M" or low – which they left as a blank in their table) (see figure 1, Leggett & Williams, 1987, p. 69). This was the same approach taken by the 1980 Gaines and Williams study.

The authors employed a set of 23 filtering methods, based on latency cutoffs, frequency, and handedness of the digraphs. For instance, they used three different latency thresholds of 30, 50 and 75 milliseconds. They used a threshold for the most frequent digraphs – 6 and 15. They also investigated handedness digraphs, such as LL, LR, and the RL and LR combinations. Again the metric for success was based on type I (FRR) and type II (FAR) measures. The authors report that the lowest value for FRR was 5.5% with a corresponding FAR of 5.0%. These results were obtained using a 50 millisecond threshold for digraph values and the same filtering used in the Umphress and Williams study. They also report that the 30 millisecond digraph threshold was too stringent, resulting in high FRR, though the FAR was reduced in some cases – though this was dependent on the preprocessing filter that was employed (see table 2, Leggett & Williams, 1987, p. 74). Also note that of the two metrics for measuring the confidence – the global method utilizing the full range of digraphs proved most effective and was used to produce the final results in this study.

This work essentially extended some of the parameter space of the Umphress and Williams study, examining a wider range of preprocessing filters. The results cannot be directly compared though, as the subjects in this study were not professional typists. One would expect that professionally trained and experienced typists might yield much more consistent digraph times than novice typists. Unfortunately, this factor is not analyzed in this study – nor has it been addressed systematically in any other reported study as far as this author is aware of. In 1990, Leggett et al. published a second paper on keystroke dynamics, introducing the issues associated with dynamic identity verification.

The previous studies discussed so far have employed a static authentication process. The static indicates that the reference profile is generated completely prior to the authentication/identification phase. With dynamic authentication/identification, the data used to generate the reference profile is collected while the user is interacting with the system and is developed strictly through this interactive process. In this paper, the authors employ the same basic strategy reported in Leggett and Williams (1988). What was added in this work was a means of extracting profile reference data in a dynamic fashion – based on the statistical properties of the users' keystroke dynamics. Briefly, a reference model for each user is created using the frequency, mean, and SD for each digraph. As in their previous work, the digraph data is stored on a tabular data structure composed of a 26×26 grid, representing each character of the alphabet (excluding case and nonalphabetic characters). As the user attempts to authenticate, each attribute (digraph value) has a sequential statistic applied that compares the profile to the reference value(s) in order to determine if the input should be authenticated. The key to this version is the development of the sequential statistical analysis.

The study in question uses a simple z-score system to determine whether or not the profile digraph falls within an acceptable range with respect to the value for the reference profile digraph. The difficulty is that the system needs to compute the test digraph mean value before all of the digraphs have been accepted. To accomplish this task, the authors proposed computing the probability density function (pdf) of the test digraphs and the range of acceptance (the spread of the data around the mean – the variance). The authors generated two pdfs, one for the positive tail and one for the negative tail of the standard distribution (see Leggett & Williams, 1990, p. 867 for details). This amounts to determining whether the test digraph was within the mean $\pm \delta$ SD, where δ represents the number of SD units from the mean used. If the sample digraph was close to the reference profile value, the ratio of the two pdfs would approach unity in the case of an exact match. A threshold value was selected such that if the ratio of the pdfs differed significantly from unity, the attempt was rejected; otherwise, it was accepted.

The results from this study produced a type I error of approximately of 11% and a type II error of approximately 13%. The authors clearly indicate that a critical issue with their approach was the number of digraph exemplars from which to build their statistical model. Their results were based on the top eight digraphs from approximately a 500-character text. Using digraphs with lower frequencies tended to reduce the classification accuracy (measured via FRR/FAR). The authors conclude that ideally, 20 digraphs (unique and independent) would produce the most robust authentication system, though how this result was obtained was not mentioned in their paper. Though the results from this study produced a modestly accurate system, it was the first attempt at constructing a dynamical keystroke dynamics-based authentication system. Most existing systems today are generated based on a static architecture. The principal reason for developing a dynamic system is that the classifier can be generated from a single training class of data – a very important issue that will be discussed later in this chapter.

At around the time of the second Leggett and Williams (Leggett & Williams, 1991) paper was published, Joyce and Gupta published a review article on the topic which included some of their latest research in this field (Joyce & Gupta, 1990). In this study, they employed a combination of short text entry (based on login ID and password), but supplemented it with two additional strings that were familiar to the user, for example, their first and last names. Their study cohort consisted of 33 college university students, aged 20–45, with a wide variation in their typing skill level. Users entered their reference profile text (login ID, password, and their first and last names) a total of eight times. After the enrollment phase (reference generation), users logged into their own account five times, producing 165 self-login attempts. A subset of the study cohort was selected randomly and used to attack the other accounts (27). Thus, there were 810 total imposter login attempts.

The reference profile was generated statically from eight trials (enrollment trials). Initially, the authors calculated the mean and SD for each of the digraph latencies. Any outliers (more than 3 SD from the mean) were discarded and the statistics recalculated based on the remaining entries. The authors initially applied the same approach as in Umphress and Williams (1985), requiring that the authentication digraphs were within 0.5 SD of each of the corresponding digraphs in the reference profile. The authors (Joyce & Gupta, 1990) pointed out that this approach had several weaknesses in that some of the digraph latencies could vary considerably (the local test), yet could still authenticate. The reason for this might be that the digraph latency vectors could still match if the threshold criteria were not sufficiently stringent enough – in that variation either side of the mean could cancel out and yield a successful authentication. Setting the stringency is a difficult task and may not be possible on a global scale. The authors claimed that a slightly more suitable metric was based on calculating the norm of the difference between the reference "signature" and the authentication trial signature. They proposed computing a mean reference vector for each of the four strings and determining the magnitude of the difference between them (as the norm). What they next proposed was that the threshold for deciding whether to accept a login attempt (the difference between the login attempt and the reference) should be based on individual typing characteristics, such as the local variance. Instead of assuming a hard rule of the mean ± δ SD, the authors proposed using a measure of the inherent variance with regard to the reference signature. This idea was implemented in Revett et al., but was not apparently utilized in the Joyce and Gupta (1990) paper. Instead, they chose to fix δ at 1.5 SD for their study. The authors also proposed another interesting idea when they suggested that the slope of the latency times, when plotted consecutively, could be used as an additional measure to decide on the success or failure of an access attempt. This idea was not fully implemented in this work – and has not really been applied successfully within the keystroke dynamics literature, though clearly it has been used in signature verification (see Chapter 3 for details). They measured the success of their system via a measure of type I and II errors.

The FRR rate for this study was 16.67%, with a FAR of 0.25%. The authors discussed ways in which these figures can be reduced further – and indicated that in this study, the two measures of success can be decoupled such that each can be reduced without raising the other. Certainly, raising the threshold for acceptance as measured by the distance between the reference and an access attempt will lower the FRR, but will generally increase the FAR. The paper presents results that indicate raising the δ to 2 SD reduced FRR without appreciably raising FAR (see figure 9 in Joyce & Gupta, 1990). This yielded an FRR to 6.67%, and the FAR was still under 1%. The authors made some additional interesting observations based on this and their earlier (1989) study.

For one, authentication strings are easy to remember tend to be entered more consistently, with minimal entropy and variance. Generally, most studies in this domain fail to examine this criterion directly. A paper by Revett et al., using randomly generated login IDs and passwords, yielded an EER on the order of 1–2% with a cohort of 20 subjects that had similar characteristics to those employed in this study. Although that study did not directly address familiar versus non-familiar authentication details, it does indicate that a low EER can be achieved using foreign authentication details. In addition, as alluded to earlier, the authors suggest that the slope of digraph latencies could be used as an additional attribute. They suggest further that the slopes between adjacent digraphs could be easily measured and added as another attribute to be matched. The authors indicated that if this measure alone was used as the basis for authentication, the authentication accuracy was reasonable, with error rates slightly above those obtained using the method discussed in this study. They suggested that their combination may be able to reduce both FAR and FRR to very acceptable levels. Lastly, the authors suggested that if users can add some natural variability into their typing characteristics, this would make their reference signature more difficult to forge. We suggest entering the authentication string following the beat or words of a familiar song or piece of music – the addition of prosody may be quite effective in this regard. This again is a matter of ongoing research.

4.5.1 A Bioinformatics Approach

Several papers have been published recently employing the use of some fundamental algorithms commonly employed in the bioinformatics literature. In 2002, Bergadano published a paper on keystroke dynamics that employed the use of the edit distance between n-graphs generated from keystroke latencies (Bergadano et al., 2002). In this study, a cohort of 44 faculty members from a computing department were asked to enter a long text string containing 683 characters, repeated five times (yielding a total of 220 samples). A further 110 subjects were asked to provide a single sample of the same text (produces the imposter samples). It should be noted that the text string entered contained a mixture of Italian and English words. All participants were native Italian speakers, who were also familiar with the English language. In addition, all participants were used to typing and using computer keyboards, though there was a considerable range in typing speeds and typing skills generally. Also note that all participants used the same keyboard on the same computer in similar circumstances (lighting, office location etc.; see Bergadano et al., 2002, p. 372). The introduction of errors was not considered problematic in this study. When a typing mistake was made, users were allowed to correct them, but in essence, the actual number of n-graphs was reduced accordingly. The difference in this regard with respect to other studies is that the typing sample containing one or more errors was not discarded. There were a total of 350 unique trigraphs contained in the long text string, but on average, users shared approximately 272. By using trigraphs only, this work specifically relies on typing speed. It would be interesting to perform a detailed analysis to determine the effect of and the information content of typing errors.

The task investigated in this study was to be able to assign a typing sample to one of the subjects in the study (via a distance metric and reference profiles). The study design employed the five samples of the long text string provided by each of the 44 subjects. These samples were designated as the legal authentic users of the system. The system was attacked 110 times by the 110 volunteers who each provided one sample of the same text (which was used as the imposter samples). In addition, the system was also attacked by the five instances of all the other legal users of the system (a total of 215). When a legal user attacked the system, their entries were removed to ensure that they did not match one of their existing typing samples, as would normally be expected to occur. The authors state that there were a total of 71 500 attacks on the system, yet the total number of attacks indicated in the paper indicates a smaller figure (325×153) of approximately 49 725. This number reflects 325 attacks (110 + 215) entered by 153 (110 + 43) possible intruders.

It is very interesting to note that this study does not make use of a single averaged referenced profile like most previous studies. Instead, each of the subject's typing sample is used individually. This has the immediate effect of increasing the numbers with respect to calculating FAR and FRR. Whether using each individual sample versus an averaged reference sample influences FAR/FRR measurements was not directly addressed by this study, nor any other study as far as this author is aware of. This should serve as an interesting area of research to pursue. What the authors of this paper do present in this regard is the authentication/identification as a function of the number of samples of each user. The data indicates that the classification accuracy varied little when the number of samples was reduced from four to one (100.0–96.9%). The classification error was calculated as the number of misclassified cases out of the total number of cases (possible comparisons). The total number of cases was

Fly: GAKKVIISAPSAD-APM--F
Human: GAKRVIISAPSAD-APM--F
Yeast: GAKKVVSTAPSS-TPM--F

Figure 4.2 Multiple sequence alignment of a portion of the glyceraldehyde3-phosphate dehydroge-
nase (GADPH) protein from three different animal species. Note the dashes indicate gaps – insertions/
deletions in the alignment. Also note that there is a considerable amount of sequence identity, that is,
symbols that are the same across all three sequences (Source: Revett, 2007 ICGeS 2007. © IEEE
Computer Society)

calculated from the sample permutations. For instance, if there were three samples used for
a person's typing sample (their model), 10 different models were available for the user (5
choose 3); 44 users would generate 440 samples. These can be tested against the remaining
two samples, yielding a total of 880 test cases.

The authors employ the edit distance as an automated method for calculating the difference
between two typing samples (collection of n-graphs). The edit distance is a measure of the
entropy between two strings. In the bioinformatics literature, the classic strings are DNA and
protein sequences. DNA sequences are simply a string of nucleotides, where each character
is contained within the set (a, c, g, t). A more diverse string is obtainable from protein
sequences, which contain 20 elements, usually represented as single-character abbreviations
("acdefghiklmnpqrstvwy"). A common task in bioinformatics is to determine the phyloge-
netic relationship between two or more protein sequences (see Figure 4.2 for an example).
One simple method is to directly compare the aligned sequences (by align, they must be co-
registered at their start of the sequences) and assign a score to those elements that are exact
matches. The total number of matches normalized by the length of the shortest sequence
provides a measure of the similarity between the two strings. The value of this match score
varies between 0 and 1 – the latter indicating a perfect match. This is rarely the case for full-
length sequences, but quite often there will be segments within the sequence that do produce
a high match score. Usually, these segments (subsequences) may provide valuable insight
into functionally important elements within the protein sequence. This issue will be discussed
further later in this chapter. For the present study, the authors employ a similarity metric that
employs the edit distance, a measure of the order (entropy) of the sequences.

The basic idea behind the edit distance (also termed the Levenshtein distance) is to determine how many moves of the elements in both strings must be made in order for them to
become perfectly aligned. It is a measure of the entropy difference between two systems,
which is proportional to the number of shift that must be made for perfect or best alignment.
The strings that must be aligned in this study were based on trigraph latencies, which were
arranged in ascending temporal order (always and matched to the particular trigraph). This
operation was performed every time a sample was used for authentication against all collected
samples in the database. If there were duplicate trigraphs, the average was recorded. If two
or more trigraphs yielded the same exact latencies, they were arranged in lexical order
(ascending based on the starting character). Note that the temporal resolution of the trigraph
latencies was low, but variable – certainly on the order of 10 milliseconds. The reason for
this was that the users logged into the system via a terminal connected via a relatively slow
modem in a network with variable traffic levels. The degree of disorder (the entropy) was
calculated, yielding a maximal disorder equal to the half the length of the string if the two
strings were completely reversed. This value was normalized by dividing the entropy by the

maximal possible entropy for a string of a given length (both strings must be equal in length) N, yielding a value between 0 and 1 inclusive (see equation 4.6 below)

$$N = \frac{|V|^2}{2} \text{ (if } V \text{ was even); } \quad \frac{|V|^2 - 1}{2} \text{ (if } V \text{ was odd)} \tag{4.6}$$

An example of the algorithm is illustrated in Figure 4.1. The entries in the left column are the trigraph times sorted in ascending order, with the corresponding trigraphs in the right columns. The numbers above the arrows indicate the number of moves required to match all the trigraph characters.

The entropy (edit distance measure) was used to determine how closely two typing samples were to one another. When comparing a typing sample U against all other typing samples, the basic assumption is that the sample U should be closer to other samples of the same user then it is to other samples. This notion still requires the use of a similarity metric. The authors use the empirical result that entropy tends to be nonlinear function of the number of elements. This result was computed based on randomly generated arrays. They state that among 10 million different randomly sorted arrays of 100 elements, only 573 yielded a disorder measure (edit distance) in the interval [0.44–0.5]; the remaining arrays were in the interval of [0.5–0.9] (Bergadano et al., 2002, p. 370). This is a rather unusual result and may need further systematic clarification. They use these results in order to build a distance metric that can be used to unequivocally discriminate users through their keystroke dynamics (based on the edit distance from trigraphs). Using all typing samples for each user (total of five in this study), they build a distance metric termed the *mean difference* (*md*), which is a weighted sum of the differences between a typing sample to be identified and all typing samples for all users in the system. The classification assigns the typing sample with the user in the system that yields the smallest *md*. This method yielded, with 0% FRR, and FAR (they use imposter pass rate, IPR) of 2.3%, a fairly significant result. The authors further claim that this classification accuracy can be improved upon based on the following observation. They argue that the absolute mean differences alone may not be sufficient to correctly classify a sample data to the appropriate owner. If a sample X is to be classified as belonging to user A, then the following constraints must be satisfied: i) the *md* of X to A ($md(A, X)$) is smallest and ii) $md(A, X)$ is closer to the average value of A (indicated as $m(A)$ in their paper) than to any other *md* for all other users in the system ($md(B, X)$). These constraints are implemented as a statistical measure of closeness used by Gaines et al. (1980) and Leggett and Williams (1991). Their formulation is presented in equation 4.7:

$$md(A, X) < m(A) + |\mathbf{k}(md(B, X) - m(A))| \tag{4.7}$$

The previous results used an implicit value of 1.0 for k, and the authors examine the classification accuracy as a function of k. The best results were obtained when $k = 0.66$, resulting in an FAR of 0.1371% and an FRR of 0%. Essentially $\mathbf{k}$ is a stringency factor – which will have an impact on the FAR|FAR values. A small value for $\mathbf{k}$ (which is allowed to vary from 1 to 0) makes the system more stringent, and will tend to increase the FRR value while decreasing FAR. This is indeed born out by their results, with a FAR of 0% and an FRR of 7.27% with a value of $\mathbf{k} = 0.3$.

Lastly, the authors claim that they can produce a system that can yield perfect classification if the following additional constraint is added: the sample must not only be closer to a particular user's model than to any other model (the previous constraint), but must it must also be sufficiently close to all the samples in the claimed model. This closeness with respect to the samples in a particular model is implemented using the SD of the samples in the model. This constraint can be implemented in the following manner (equation 4.8):

$$Md(A, X) < m(A) + \alpha \times \text{MAX}\, d(A) + \beta \times \text{SD}\, d(A) \qquad (4.8)$$

where α and β are real valued constants that must be empirically derived for each user (or set of samples). The purpose of these two terms is to strike the required balance between FAR and FRR. The values for the parameters are also affected by the value of **k**, so for a complete system, all three factors must be determined. The authors claim that by a judicious selection of values for the three parameters, an FAR/FRR value of 0% can be obtained. This required tuning the values of these three terms for each user in the system.

The authors claim that a key advance in this work is the notion of using relative rather than absolute keystroke dynamics. This may help to nullify changes in typing speed – provided any change in speed is consistent across all characters. Using absolute values for trigraphs in the decision model may produce misleading results, which will tend to increase the FAR/FRR values. The edit distance is a relative measure of typing dynamics – and will yield the same result independent of typing speed, provided it is uniform across the characters typed. The users used a long text string (683 characters), which was entered five times. This is a rather burdensome enrollment requirement, requiring 3415 characters to be typed. The authors investigated whether this number could be reduced – not directly but by using a fraction of the trigraphs. As the number of trigraphs used to build the model of the user decreased, the error rates (measured as FAR/FRR) increased considerably, especially with lower values of the parameter **k**. The FRR increased from 0.9 to 5.4% when half the digraphs were used, and the value of **k** changed from 1.0 to 0.5. These results were obtained using the full 683 character inputs – but taking either the first half or second half of the trigraphs (or whichever fraction they choose to test with). One might expect that the later trigraphs might be more consistent than the first – based on a minor practice affect. This result implies that reducing the size of the input may significantly reduce the classification accuracy of this method. This effect will have to be determined experimentally.

An extension of the 2002 work by Bergadano was published by two of the co-authors in 2003 (Gunetti & Picardi, 2003). The study cohort was considerably larger, with 205 subjects. The text entry system was also different, in that they used a continuous free text data acquisition protocol. The authors believe that short text entries will not supply the required data to generate an accurate model sufficient for classification purposes. Asking users to type in long text within a single trial may not be feasible – or at least not attractive to the users. Their alternative is to extract keystroke dynamic-related data while subjects are interacting with a computer. This approach is termed free text by the authors – and is also a continuous mode of data collection – in that user data is extracted during and may be used to authenticate after a user has access to the computer system. The authors also employed a different similarity/ scoring metric than their 2002 work. Lastly, digraphs were used instead of trigraphs as in their previous work.

Gunetti and Picardi (2003) state that there may be a difficulty when using a relative keystroke dynamics scheme for user authentication – as in the Bergadano study (Bergadano et al., 2002). The difficulty can be explained by a simple example: if two users enter the same text with exactly the same dynamics, but at two different typing speeds, they will not be discriminated as different users by the Bergadano scheme. This is a consequence of using a relative scheme. Gunetti proposes in their 2003 paper to extend the classification scheme to include both the relative and absolute measures (referred to as R and A measures, respectively in their paper). The R measure is identical to that employed by Bergadano et al., 2002, based on statistical measures of edit distance values. The A measure reflects actual typing speed of each pair of identical n-graphs. More formally, they define a similarity measure metric based on the duration of the same n-graphs occurring is two typing samples S1 and S2. This metric, which they term $G_{Si,di}$ are treated as *similar* if $1 < \max(d1, d2)/\min(d1, d2) \leq t$, where t is a constant greater than 1. Note that $d1$ and $d2$ refer to the duration of the digraphs from typing samples S1 and S2. They then defined the A distance between S1 and S2 over the common n-graphs for a given value of t, as provided in equation 4.9.

$$A(S1, S2) = 1 - (\text{number of similar } n\text{-graphs for S1 and S2}) / \left(\sum n\text{-graphs shared by S1 and S2} \right) \tag{4.9}$$

The authors then combined the R and A metrics for the process of user authentication and/or identification, using essentially an additive formulation. The classification accuracy of this system, in terms of FAR/FRR, was similar to the values obtained in the Bergadano study (Bergadano et al., 2002). The authors experimented with various combinations of digraphs, trigraphs, and tetragraphs) with R and A values, and the data suggest unequivocally that the R values outperformed the A value in terms of classification error. The authors then combined R and A measures to see if this could enhance the classification accuracy of the system. The authors tested various combinations of the two measures and found the classification error was significantly reduced (to less then 1%), similar to the results from using R alone in the 2002 Bergadano paper. Note that the error is simply a misclassification error. The authors do report FAR/FRR data – and these results indicate that for a very low value for FAR (less than 1%), the FRR ranged from 5% to 14%.

The addition of absolute typing dynamics (i.e. typing speed) did not appreciably enhance the accuracy of this system (on the contrary, it generally reduced the overall FAR/FRR compared to their previous work). Part of the reason for the variability in their results may be due to the long time frame over which data was collected – subjects were given 6 months to enter the required data. The input devices varied between office computers and personal laptops, which might have affected the consistency of the typing dynamics of the study participants. In addition, there are several other issues with this study that need further elaboration. For one, the similarity measure does not allow for duplicate digraph entries, as the quotient in the similarity metric must be larger than 1. Second, the A measure is really just a version of the Hamming distance though the authors argue against this issue (see Gunetti & Picardi, 2003, pp. 321–322 for their reply). The amount of text provided by the users was quite substantial in many cases, with an average character length of 700–900 characters, repeated 14 times. This may be a prohibitive amount of data to collect other than in a continuous free text format. Lastly, the essential difficulties with the 2002 work are generally applicable to this study, as both studies employ essentially the same classification processes. Lastly, one may wish to examine how well edit distance classifies text when employed on much shorter strings.

Choras and Mroczkowsi (2007a,b) have applied a similar approach using the equivalent of the edit distance as a measure of similarity between keystroke dynamics based biometrics.

In these works, the use of the edit distance for digraphs/trigraphs as defined by Bergadano (Bergadano et al., 2002) and Gunetti & Picardi, 2003, was employed on a short text string (login ID and password). The 2007a study employed 18 subjects who were required to enter their login ID and passwords (which was their full name in forename/surname format) 10 times to establish a reference for each of the subjects. To test the system, 20 login attempts by each participant were used for FRR calculations and 10 attempts for FAR calculations. The authors employed a series of thresholds (0.25, 0.3, 0.35 and 0.4) to decide whether or not to accept an authentication attempt. The FRR results yielded an average value of approximately 22% (range 0–55%). The FAR results were more remarkable, with a value of 0% for all but two users (1.9% and 8.1%, respectively). Their 2007b paper (Choras & Mroczkowsi, 2007b) performed a very similar analysis, examining the use of digraphs and trigraphs, via an edit distance measure to estimate values for FAR and FRR. The results indicate that digraphs provided a significantly reduced FAR/FRR compared to the use of trigraphs. The authors indicate that the thresholds should be larger for digraphs than trigraphs, indicating that digraphs were more reliable/discriminating than trigraphs.

The results from the Choras and Mroczkowsi studies indicate that using edit distance for short text strings results in a much higher FAR/FRR value than for long text strings. In their studies, they required users to enter their authentication string 10 times, yielding at most 10 samples of each digraph. Although not stated explicitly, the average length of the authentication string should be on the order of 10–15 characters (the average number of characters in a person's name), yielding 13 and 14 digraphs/trigraphs, respectively. This is a relatively small sample size compared to the Bergadano and Gunetti studies. Their use of a hard threshold value for discriminating users may not be a suitable approach as well. One could generally question whether the edit distance per se is a sufficiently robust similarity measure. In the last paper examined in the domain of bioinformatics, the concept of local and global alignment will be discussed in the context of user authentication.

The next study was performed by the author of this chapter and will be discussed in more detail than the other examples, which served as overviews of their work. The interested reader is encouraged to consult the original papers for further details. Also, since this paper serves to introduce the central concepts of bioinformatics more rigorously than previous work, an in-depth overview of the relevant bioinformatics concepts will be introduced, prior to presenting the results from this study.

4.5.2 Molecular Biology and Biometrics

The central dogma in molecular biology is fairly straightforward: DNA begets RNA and RNA begets protein. How this dogma is manifested is as amazing as it is complex. Proteins are complex molecules that are involved in all life-supporting activities – from respiration to thinking. The structure of a protein is usually represented schematically as a sequence of units that are joined together through chemical bonding. The units are termed amino acids and in humans – there are approximately 20 naturally occurring amino acids. It is the specific combination of amino acids, which is specified through the sequence of nucleotides found in DNA, that imparts specificity in terms of function to proteins. All organisms need to respire and perform similar functions, which implies that there are certain genes in common across most organisms. Similarity between the genome of organisms is a major theme within the bioinformatics community. From a computer science perspective – this issue is one of pattern matching and search – how closely related are two strings which represent the amino acid sequence of a particular gene between two species? What is the difference between a person with a disease that has a genetic basis from normal controls? These are interesting questions in their own right and form the basis for the bioinformatics approach used in this study.

To place these ideas into the current context, imagine that a login attempt can be converted into a string of characters. To do this, the attributes extracted from the login attempt must be mapped onto a string within a given alphabet. The principal attributes extracted from key-stroke dynamics include digraphs, trigraphs, and key-press duration (dwell time). These attributes are then mapped onto an alphabet – in this work, the amino acid (AA) alphabet, which contains 20 elements. This mapped version of the input attributes becomes a query sequence and the task then is to determine the closest match to a database of sequences derived in exactly the same manner from each user of the system. We then have a similar situation to that of a bioinformaticist – can we determine which sequence in the database is the closest match to the query sequence? This type of question has been addressed repeatedly within the bioinformatics community for over three decades now – with quite satisfactory results in most cases. The principal tool of the bioinformaticist is the sequence alignment problem, which is illustrated in Figure 4.2.

The strings of characters in Figure 4.2 represent a short hand notation for amino acids, which can be viewed as a string of these symbols. Of course there is biological meaning to them, but for the most part, bioinformaticists can treat them symbolically simply as a string of characters (Smith & Waterman, 1981). In this work, the digraph times, dwell time, and trigraph times are discretized into an AA alphabet which yields a string of characters similar to that found in a protein but is considerably shorter (42 residues in length). We can then apply the huge amount practical and theoretical research that has been successfully developed in bioinformatics to the task of authentication.

In order to determine the relative alignment between a given query sequence and a database of 1000 s of sequences, one must have a metric – called the alignment score. For instance, if two elements match at a given position (in vertical register), then a score of +1 is recorded. If the characters at a particular position do not match, a score of −1 is recorded. Gaps can be introduced in global alignments that serve to increase the overall score. If for instance two sequences were similar at some point but one had an insertion/deletion mutation, then these mutations would cause a misalignment between the sequences from this point forward, reducing the overall alignment score. Gaps can be placed in either the query or the target sequence, and as many as required can be added. They also serve to ensure that the two sequences are the same length. When gaps are added, they are penalized and reduce the score, but if they are effective at realigning the sequence further downstream, then the penalty may be cancelled out by a higher match score. Otherwise, the effect is to reduce the overall score, which is required because any two sequences can be aligned given enough gaps placed within them.

In this work, the sequence alignment algorithm employed is against a set of sequences stored as motifs (obtained via a position-specific scoring matrix [PSSM]). This process entails aligning each column in the series of sequences and calculating the frequency of each amino acid within each column. A matrix is generated that scores the relative frequency of each of the 20 amino acids at each column position. This data can be used to generate a motif where high scoring positions (corresponding to frequently occurring residues) are important features of the data. There are two dimensions that can be employed in PSSM: the magnitude of the frequency within a column and the number of columns (and whether they are consecutive or not). The process of generating the motif from the training data is extremely fast – on the order of a few milliseconds – which was a constraint placed on this system – it must be able to operate in a real-time environment. One can vary the mapping alphabet in order to vary the resolution of the resulting mapped string. For instance, a mapping onto the digits 0–9 would produce a much coarser map that would generate longer motifs. The number of keys on a piano (typically 88) would provide a much more refined mapping – yielding shorter motifs. The choice of the AA alphabet was based on a compromise between motif length between the two extremes mentioned and also to map directly into the bioinformatics literature. The actual extraction of these motifs is described next, followed by a brief description of the dataset.

There were 20 participants in this study, all computer science undergraduate students from a Polish University. The users were provided with eight-character login IDs and passwords, generated randomly by a computer program. The enrollment process required users to enter their login ID/password 10 times successfully. Each participant enrolled on to a single machine located on campus for both phases of this study. After successfully enrolling (10 trials), the participants were asked to perform 100 self-logins (for FRR) and 100 attacks on other accounts (for FAR data). The following regime was used for non-enrollment logins: each participant was asked to self-login 100 times over a 7 day period. Therefore, the participants logged into their own account approximately 15 times per day. In addition, students were instructed to login at three different periods of the day: morning (09:00–10:00), noon (12:00–13:00) and early evening (17:00–18:00). At each period, students were asked to either perform self-login or nonself logins five times. This simulates the way users would normally access their computer systems, logging in at various periods during the course of a workday.

With the enrollment data collected, the enrollment trials were discretized using the 20-letter AA alphabet. To do this, the largest time (with a resolution of 1 ms) for each of the digraphs, dwell times, and trigraphs was identified (column-wise) from the enrollment process and was used to normalize each attribute. This process was repeated for each of the three sets of attributes collected in this study. The normalized data yielded values from 0 to 1. The range was then partitioned equally into 20 bins corresponding to each of the 20 amino acids available from the alphabet. Next, each bin was assigned to one of the 20 elements from the AA alphabet (which were arranged in ascending alphabetical order). The corresponding collection of mapped attributes (now contained within a string of amino acids) was ordered in the following fashion: digraphs, dwell time, and trigraph times, and this order was used consistently throughout this work. The next stage was the development of a motif for each of the enrollment entries – which would be stored in the query database for verification/identification. A PSSM was generated from the enrollment trials (10 for each user). Briefly, the frequency of each amino acid in each column was calculated and stored in a separate table (the PSSM). The data was not converted into a log-likelihood value as the expected frequencies were not available from a limited set of data. Instead, the values could be interpreted as probabilities of a given residue appearing at each position. There were two parameters that were examined with respect to motif formation: the frequency of each amino acid residue at each position – and the number of elements within the motif (whether they were consecutive or not). These are tunable parameters that can automatically be set based on the data from the enrollment process. The stringency of the motif-based signature is based on these parameters: for high-level security application, positions with a very high frequency, that is, greater than 80% and for a minimum of 50% of the residues, can be deployed. Likewise, reduced stringency is accomplished by relaxing these values. If during the enrollment process the frequency within a column and the number of consistent columns was below some minimal threshold (50%), then the user would either be requested to reenroll, or the normalization time could be increased iteratively until the minimal threshold was achieved.

The normalization time (and hence the bin times) was stored with each database entry (all three stored separately) in order to allow for a re-mapping of the attributes to sequence values if it became necessary. The mapped entries from the enrollment process and the resulting motifs for all 20 users formed the query database which was used for both verification and identification. The run time for the motif extraction phase was fairly constant at approximately 2–8 milliseconds. The efficiency in this particular case is related to the short length of the sequences (many proteins contain 100 s of residues) and the large degree of similarity between the sequences – these were generated from the enrollment sequence. The generation of the motif is performed immediately after enrollment, and for all intensive purposes is so short that the user can then login to the system straight away and be authenticated by the resulting model.

The authentication algorithm works as follows: the user enters their login credentials. It is discretized into the AA alphabet based on the normalization time associated with the login details associated with a given login ID/password combination. The authentication sequence is then compared with the stored motif for the login ID and given a score based on the algorithm specified in (eq 4.10) using a simple global alignment algorithm. Generally, a match is scored +1 and a mismatch is scored −1, and "−" in either the probe of the query sequence has a score of 0. The score is computed and if it is above a specified threshold q, then the entry is authentication, else it is rejected. Note that the score q can be based on both the frequency threshold at a specific column and the number of columns (as well as whether the columns are contiguous or not). The user has three attempts before system lockout. The value of q was set equal to the motif length (number of non-blank "−" entries) in this particular study, although in principle, it could be varied in order to control the level of security required. The identification algorithm works as follows: the normalization factor is extracted from the user during the authentication attempt. Then, we proceed exactly as in the authentication phase, except we compare the resulting motif against all motifs stored in the database. Duplicate motifs are expected to be a rare event considering the number of expected entries in the motifs and the range of values at each. In this pilot study, the average cardinality of the motifs was 42 (14 digraphs, 16 dwell times, and 12 trigraphs). Each element in a motif could contain up to 20 different values, yielding an average of $42^{20}/l$ (where "l" is the motif length) possible motifs. In actuality, the full range of the sequence alphabet may not be fully covered. If there was a tie between two or more entries from the database, then this login attempt is rejected and the users are asked to reenter their login details. Lastly, please note that the data stored in the DB is updated every time a user successfully logs into the system. The oldest entry is removed, replaced by the latest, and the PSSM value is updated and a new motif is generated for each user ID. The next section describes the results obtained from this study, and fills in experimental details as required.

All 20 users were requested to enroll and authenticate during a 1 week period of this study. In Table 4.1 below, we present a typical enrollment dataset that consists solely of the digraph times for the username/password extracted during the enrollment period. The first stage in

Table 4.1 Sample of an enrollment of 10 consecutive entries of the username/password for a randomly selected participant (Source: Revett, 2007 ICGeS2007. © IEEE Computer Society)

#1	#2	#3	#4	#5	#6	#7	#8
25	34	33	21	31	58	66	63
19	28	25	29	28	69	64	75
23	34	29	23	24	48	78	68
28	31	25	25	38	47	56	78
21	35	33	32	30	44	54	82
19	42	22	24	28	68	78	75
28	34	27	25	26	47	38	59
25	32	23	26	29	78	46	64
30	28	35	41	24	44	65	61
26	24	42	33	26	57	58	69

The numbers represent time in milliseconds and each column represents a digraph (only eight are displayed).

Table 4.2 Discretization of an enrollment entry (corresponding to the raw data presented in Table 4.1) using the AA alphabet (Source: Revett, 2007 ICGeS2007. © IEEE Computer Society)

F	G	E	E	G	F	N	M
E	F	F	E	F	M	S	P
Y	G	E	E	F	H	Q	Q
F	G	F	F	H	I	L	Q
E	G	F	E	G	I	H	P
E	H	E	E	F	Q	Q	P
E	G	E	F	F	I	H	L
E	F	F	F	F	Q	E	K
E	E	F	E	F	I	F	G
E	E	E	E	F	N	F	L

Note that the maximal normalization value was 0.063 s.

our algorithm is to discretize the enrollment data since the values obtained are essentially continuous (to a resolution of 1 ms). This stage requires obtaining the largest digraph (which in this was 1.37 – see Table 4.1 for an example) and normalizing all digraph values. Then binning was performed, where each digraph was assigned its ordinal position within the discretization alphabet: A = "ACDEFGHIKLMNPQRSTVWY" – the single letter code for amino acids in ascending lexical order. This resulted in the following dataset displayed in Table 4.2. In our previous work, the maximal frequency of each element within each column corresponds to the range of values that were obtained for each digraph (Revett, 2007). This same approach was taken in this study as it proved to be quite effective with the previous data collected from a new participant cohort. The consensus sequence for the example in Figure 4.2 is EGEEFI-, where the "-" symbol indicates that there is no unique dominant symbol within the column(s) – although the exact frequency of each amino acid is maintained across all columns. The sequence above is the consensus sequence for this enrollment instance. It represents the average behavior in that it captures the most frequently entered digraph values. This amounts to an un-weighted voting scheme, with a threshold for inclusion (set to 0.5 in this study).

The entries within the consensus sequence (motif) also possess information regarding the typing speed and the consistency possessed by the person entering it. This is the value of the normalization factor and influences the spread of the digraphs (and hence amino acid symbols) within the generated sequence. If an imposter attempts to input this particular username/password, the maximal digraph value would more than likely differ from this particular one, and hence the normalization process may yield a different set of elements within the consensus sequence. Please note that the maximal digraph value for each enrollment is stored with the user's data, and it is this value that is used to discretize all subsequent authentic successful login attempts. Also note that for each subsequent successful login attempt, the data for this account is updated, such that the oldest entry is removed and the consensus sequence is updated, along with the longest digraph value (the normalization factor). This allows the system to evolve with the user as his/her typing of their login details changes over time, which invariably happens as the users become more familiar with their login details.

For the authentication process (verification and identification), the username and password entered is discretized using the stored maximal value for digraph time. Equation 4.10 provides the values used when performing the motif matching algorithm. It is a very simple algorithm – which was the intention – as there may be 1000 s of entries in the database. The results from our preliminary study indicate that it took on average 19 ms to compare the motifs over the 20 entries, yielding a value of 106 matches per second. In equation 4.10 below, the match indicates the same symbol in each sequence at the same site; a mismatch means that a non-match and non-blank, and the "−" blank indicate that this position was not part of the motif.

$$+1\} \quad \text{match}$$
$$-1\} \quad \text{mismatch} \qquad\qquad (4.10)$$
$$0\} \quad \text{"−" in either sequence}$$

The algorithm just described may present complications if the enrollment was only marginally successful. That is, in the example provided in (1) above, there were clear-cut dominant entries within each column (except for column 7). If there were less than a threshold level of unique entries in the consensus sequence (a system defined parameter set at a default value of 0.5), then the system automatically recalculates the normalization factor. This re-scaling occurs iteratively until there is at least a threshold level of entries in the consensus sequence. For higher-level security installations, the threshold value can be raised – requiring more consistency during the enrollment. This enhanced stringency, though, has a negative impact on the FRR as it imparts greater stringency on the user during subsequent login attempts. Also note that the AA alphabet is just one of many choices – the greater the cardinality, the more refined the bin size for a constant normalization value. This, too, results in a reduction in the number of elements contained within the consensus sequence. Our results with a 10 (decimal) and 16 (hexadecimal) lettered alphabet yielded results that reduced the discriminatory capacity of the system. The value for the length of the discretization alphabet can be

Table 4.3 Summary of FAR/FRR results as a function of the consistency threshold for elements within the consensus sequence (motif) (Source: Revett, 2007 ICGeS2007. © IEEE Computer Society)

Threshold	FAR (%)	FRR (%)
1.0	0.0	0.8
0.80	0.0	0.5
0.60	0.1	0.2
0.40	0.4	0.0

These results are randomly selected values from a series of one hundred experiments.

examined by looking at the FAR – which was as high as 13% with the decimal and 6% with the hexadecimal-based alphabets. We therefore decided to stick with the AA alphabet and adjust the normalization factor when necessary. The system as just described resulted in an overall FAR of 0.6% and an FRR of 0.4% – a total error rate of 1.0% (for a consistency threshold of 0.5). This result is comparable to that found in other keystroke dynamic-based systems ([14], [15]). Please note that this result is measured for individual login attempts, that is, eight attempts were unsuccessful on an individual login attempt (FRR), but no user was locked out because he failed to log in within three attempts.

When the consistency threshold was raised to 0.80 (rounded upward when necessary), the FAR was 0.0%, but the FRR increased to 0.5%, yielding a total error rate of 0.5%. In Table 4.3, the results for FAR/FRR are summarized with respect to the threshold for dominant consensus elements. Note that in this experiment, the same 20 users were used, and each logged into their own accounts 100 times (FRR measurement), and each participant logged into the other 19 accounts 100 times each (a total of 1900 FRR attempts/account and 100 FAR attempts/account).

In addition to the frequency threshold data that was presented in Table 4.3, another parameter, based on the total number of elements in the consensus sequence, was also investigated in this study. The two parameters are somewhat related in that for a given position to be significant, it must have a specific frequency value. In this part of the study, a frequency value of 0.5 was used as a first approximation, and the focus was on the total number of matching entries within the motifs which are stored for a given loginID/password sequence. Table 4.4 presents a summary of the data as a function of the fractional percentage of the motif cardinality.

Lastly, a critical issue in this paper was the ability of the system to be able to perform user identification – an issue that has not been addressed within the keystroke dynamics literature at all in any significant degree. The data in Table 4.5 presents the results of the identification where the 20 users were to be identified based on a single login transaction as a function of column consistency threshold and column length. Note that the threshold for all consistent attributes was approximately 50% (20) or 75% (32).

The results from this study and others indicate that behavioral-based biometrics generally and keystroke dynamics specifically provide a level of security that rivals many physiological-based systems in terms of error rates. The advantages of keystroke dynamics are

Table 4.4 Sample results from an experiment in which the length (total number) of consensus sites matched the stored record for a set of randomly selected login attempts (Source: Revett, 2007 ICGeS2007. © IEEE Computer Society)

Threshold	FAR (%)	FRR (%)
30	0.0	0.6
25	0.1	0.5
20	0.1	0.1
15	0.3	0.0

Table 4.5 Results indicating the identification capacity of the system with respect to fractional occupancy at each site and the total length of sites consistent with the stored sequence (not contiguous) (Source: Revett, 2007 ICGeS2007. © IEEE Computer Society)

Threshold	FAR (%)	FRR (%)
0.5 (0.50)	0.0	0.1
0.5 (0.75)	0.0	0.0
0.6 (0.50)	0.0	0.0
0.6 (0.75)	0.0	0.0
0.7 (0.50)	0.0	0.0
0.7 (0.75)	0.0	0.0
0.8 (0.50)	0.0	0.0
0.8 (0.75)	0.0	0.0
0.9 (0.50)	0.0	0.0
0.9 (0.75)	0.0	0.0

- that it is a software-based system;
- entering a username/password combination is virtually universally accepted;
- it is unobtrusive;
- it can be used over the Internet

These advantages make this approach a very attractive alternative to expensive and cumbersome hardware-based (i.e. physiological) biometrics. What is left to remain is whether the error rates achieved with this approach can compare with fingerprinting and iris scanners. Clearly, iris scanners provide the lowest total error rate – on the order of 10^{-6} in many cases. Even fingerprints provide an error rate on the order of 10^{-2}. The results from this study indicate that an error rate, measured as the combined FAR + FRR, is comparable to that of typical commercially available fingerprint scanners. What is left is to find ways to enhance the error rate in keystroke dynamics-based biometrics. To accomplish this goal, one must examine the sources of error(s) and try to compensate for them whenever possible.

In this study, the preliminary estimate of the major error is of course the typing consistency between enrollment and subsequent login attempts. The approach that was adopted in this work attempted to remove this potential variability by using a novel approach – one that has not been published according to this author's knowledge. Using the concept of sequence similarity in this domain has provided results that are comparable to any other existing keystroke dynamics-based authentication scheme. Discretizing the input attributes into an AA alphabet captures the statistical variability in the way the user has enrolled into the system. The number of bins that the input was discretized into effectively places upper and lower bounds to the range of allowable values for the particular attribute in question. The motif extraction algorithm employed was able to find motifs very efficiently due to the small number of sequences and their relatively short length. The process of generating the motif is performed in an off-line fashion – so speed is not truly critical – it places a lower bound on how quickly after enrollment a user can access the system. In general, waiting 2–4 seconds is not prohibitive.

The motif matching algorithm is very efficient – it was implemented as a simple pattern matching scheme written in C++. It takes approximately 1 S/search, and so 106 searches can be performed per second. The motif matching algorithm is employed in both the authentication and the identification algorithm. In this paper, the ability to perform identification was explored to demonstrate that it is a task that is feasible within a unified framework. In keystroke-based dynamic systems that employ an online continuous monitoring of the user's typing style, identification of the user would be a necessity. In this study, we were able to identify all users (20) with 100% accuracy.

Lastly, it must be noted that the approach taken in this study is both very efficient and can be used in an online manner. Neural network-based classifiers generally require examples of all decision classes during the training process in order to be able to accurately generalize during testing. A difficulty with keystroke dynamics-based biometrics is that generally, one does not know which category a login belongs to: is it an authentic owner or imposter? That is the question that needs to be addressed by the classifier. The approach taken in this work does not require this prior knowledge; therefore, it can be utilized immediately without the need to accumulate a large sample of imposter logins.

4.5.3 Hidden Markov Model (HMM) Approach to Keystroke Dynamics-Based Authentication

HMMs have been used extensively in speech recognition systems (see Rabiner, 1989 for a comprehensive review) and handwriting analysis (El-Yacoubi et al., 2000, Coetzer et al., 2004), in addition to many successful applications in the bioinformatics domain (Durbin, 1998, Eddy 1995). It would seem reasonable that this approach to stochastic modeling would be suitable to apply to keystroke dynamics. This section describes a series of articles published on the application of HMM to user authentication based on keystroke dynamics. No attempt is made to fully describe the theoretical background of HMMs – for this, there are several very well-written and comprehensive tutorials available in the public domain (Rabiner, 1989, Dugad & Desai, 1996).

In Chen and Chang (2004), a HMM was used to authenticate a collection of 20 users based on n-graphs collected from typing in a login ID/password combination. The users were instructed to enter their login ID and password 20 times, from which a reference profile was generated, the distribution of which they assumed to be normal. To collect data for FRR, each of the 20 users also entered the names of all participants 10 times (yielding a total 190 imposter attempts [FAR] and 200 self-login attempts [FRR]). The attributes that they extracted were the scan code, press time, and release time (the latter two with a resolution of 1 ms). From this data, the hold time (dwell time) and delay time (n-graph latency) can be calculated. The authors subsequently normalized the data to range from 0 to 1. This step made the typing pattern independent of the typing speed (total time spent entering the text). The user profile for each user was learned by an HMM, and the authentication step was accomplished using the trained HMM.

The training process was based on the observation that the sequence of key-press events could be considered as a series of stochastic independent events based on two probability distributions. One was based on the adjacency occurrence from one key to the next, which they modeled as the following probability, $a_{ij} \in A$, which is the state transition probability distribution of all the key pairs occurring in all of the text:

$$a_{ij} = P[key_i | key_i]$$ (4.11)

In addition, for each key entered, there are four events that are possible: press, release, hold, and delay, which they represented as a 4-tuple $o_t = [p, r, h, d]$. They associate with each o_t a set of probabilities $\{b_k(t)\}$ which is the likelihood of o_t being in a class region v_t that contains the event vector generated by some key event $\{key_k\}$, such that

$$b_k(t) = P[o_t \in v_t | key_k]$$ (4.12)

where v_t contains the class in which o_t is a member. Lastly, note that in equation 4.13, B is the observation probability distribution of events generated by all keys:

$$\sum b_k(t) = 1 \text{ and } \{b_k(t)\} \in B$$ (4.13)

In order to develop the model, the transition and emission probabilities must be determined from the data. The transition probability matrix A is based on the total key pairs (for digraphs) in the corpus of text entered during the training process (see equation 4.11). The authors calculate each entry in A via the following algorithm:

1. $C(i, j)$ is the number of times key_i that was entered at some time t and key_j is entered at $t + 1$ and
2. $C(i, x)$ is the number of instances that time key_i is entered (at time t) followed by any key_x at time $t + 1$

yielding a value for $a_{ij} = C(i \cdot j)/C(i \cdot x)$. This process is applied for each a_{ij}, which results in the construction of the transition probability matrix A. The observation probability matrix B is obtained (i.e. each entry in equation 4.13) by performing the following calculations:

1. The instances I_k of observations generated by a key key_k is acquired from the training samples.
2. The probability of key_k being observed as o_t and v_t is the ratio between $D(k, t)$, the instance count of observations in I_k that fall within v_t and the size of I_k, yielding

$$b_k(t) = D(k, t)/|I_k|$$ (4.14)

Note that each I_k really represents a distribution generated by different users entering the same keys and also the multiple entries of the key from the same user. The observation probability matrix then can be viewed as a clustering technique, and what is measured is the ratio of each key_k to the size of each cluster, for each key in the text string. Given an observation sequence $O = 0_1, 0_2, \ldots, 0_T$, what is required is the probability that this sequence occurred given the training data and the resultant model. This amounts to maximizing the product of the two probabilities:

$$\text{argmax}\{\max \prod_{t=1}^{T} \{b_j(t) \cdot a_{ij}\}\} \tag{4.15}$$

This formulation can be further reduced by noting that the path sequence is deterministic in that the sequence to be typed is fixed, and hence $a_{ij} = 1$, and equation 4.15 reduces to

$$P_u = \prod_{t=1}^{T} \{B_j(t)\} \tag{4.16}$$

where the subscript u indicates the entered login details are unique for user u, which has a total length of T. The classification task then reduces to determining if the probability P_u is above a given threshold, given as θ by the authors, that is, if $P_u > \theta$, the entry is accepted. The last step is to produce an aggregate acceptance threshold η, which is the product of the acceptance threshold for each $b_j^t(t)$, the probability of observing an event $o_i \in v_t$ from a key_j at time t over the total time T. The authors use this model to classify the 20 users via the model generated during the enrollment process (20 samples for each user). The results were presented as classification accuracy (FAR/FRR) as a function of the aggregate acceptance threshold (η). The results indicate an EER of approximately 2% for this study ($\eta = 0.74$).

In subsequent work, one of the authors (Chang, 2005) addressed the issue of refining the acceptance threshold using the concept of a "similarity histogram." In essence, the enhancement uses the distance of an observation from the centroid of the matching cluster. This enhancement provides a more adaptable value for η, and hence a more accurate threshold for input acceptance. With this enhancement, the author was able (using the exact same data) to reduce the EER to approximately 1.1%, an improvement from the previous work (without the similarity histogram).

In essence, this work produces a cluster of probabilities for each of the state transitions (press, release, hold, and delay), and the cluster associated with each transition is taken. The ratio $D(k, t)$ to I_k is used to measure the emission probability (or observation probability). $D(k, t)$ is essentially a count of observations that fall within the cluster divided by the size of the cluster. The larger this ratio, the more likely the observation (the more probable it is). Provided the training regions (author's term) or clusters (my term) are larger than the number of samples (number of unique key presses), then the system will not tend to over-fit the data. The authors indicate that a ratio of 3:1 produced reasonable results. Since the text entered was fixed and deterministic, the transition probabilities could be omitted (treated as a constant). This would not be the case for a variable/free text strategy, and hence may limit the applicability of the current system. Samples of all possible keys would have to be obtained in order to generate the appropriate model. This is a very interesting area of active research.

Another application of HMM was published by Song and colleagues (2001), who investigated the issue of packet timing when entering login details through an secure shell (SSH) connection. One of the weaknesses of the SSH protocol is that every keystroke entered by a user is sent as a separate packet immediately after the key is pressed. This reveals the timing information, which may be used as a means of extracting critical information with respect to a keystroke dynamics-based biometrics. This is especially true when issuing the super user (SU) command, from which the keystroke timing of the password can be gathered by carefully monitoring the packet stream (for more details, consult Song et al., 2001). The authors developed a system (*Herbivore*) as an attacker that could extract key sequences from timing information in SSH sessions. The success of *Herbivore* reflects the success of the model that they developed.

The attributes that the authors extracted were key-press latencies (digraphs), as packets are only sent when a key is pressed (as opposed to being released). They restricted the use of random passwords to a set of 10 letter keys and five number keys, and the users practiced entering these passwords until they were comfortable with them. The authors further claimed that users typically typed passwords in groups of three to four characters, and paused between these boundary chunks. This would distort the digraph latencies for the boundary cases and would therefore be an inefficient method – requiring a substantial number of trials to generate reliable data. This is reminiscent of the chunking issue mentioned previously (Miller, 1956). Instead, the authors asked the participants to type sets of key pairs 30–40 times (there were 142 key pairs), and gathered timing data from these examples. The key pairs were uniformly distributed across the keyboard, but the exact key pairs were not disclosed in the paper. Statistics such as the mean and SD was collected from each of the 142 digraphs, which the authors confirmed followed essentially a Gaussian distribution. They further divided the digraphs into five disjoint sets, based on the handedness of the key presses. The differences were based on whether the keys were pressed using the same or alternate hands. The addition of number (from the keypad) and letters also tended to have a consistent effect on the length of the digraph latencies as well (see Song et al., 2005, Section 3.2). They split the latency range into six bins. They assigned a digraph latency into the appropriate bin (based on closeness of the mean digraph latency to the bin range). They performed a frequency histogram (similar to Chang, 2005), where each bar represented the ratio of the number of character pairs in the bin over the total number of character pairs in the category. The finding indicates that there was very little overlap between the six bins, indicating that the class of input – same hand versus different hand – could yield consistently different digraph latencies. Therefore, if someone is monitoring packets and obtains a particular timing value after an SU command was issued, they could make an educated guess about what category the input was generated from (i.e. which bin). The issue left to solve therefore is mapping these bins to typing style (handedness, letters versus numbers, etc.), that is, how much information digraph latencies can provide regarding which characters were typed.

The data suggests that digraph latencies form a Gaussian, unimodal distribution. The authors employed a maximum likelihood estimation to derive the mean and SD for each character pair. The distribution becomes useful when using information theoretic concepts such as *information gain* and *mutual information*. The authors used these concepts to form the upper bound on how much information an attacker can extract from timing information. If a character pair is selected at random from the character space, the entropy of the probability distribution of character pairs is

$$H_o[q] = -\sum_{q \in Q} Pr[q] \log_2 Pr[q] = \log_2 |Q| \tag{4.17}$$

where q is a character pair out of the total set Q. If the latency y_0 between two keystrokes is ascertained, the estimated entropy of the probability of character pairs to the attacker is

$$H_1[q|y = y_0] = -\sum_{q \in Q} Pr[q|y_0] \log_2 Pr[q|y_0] \qquad (4.18)$$

where $Pr[q|y_0] = Pr[y_0|q] \times Pr[q]]/\Sigma_{q \in Q} Q\ Pr[y_0|q] \times Pr[q]$, and $Pr[y_0|q]$ is computed using the Gaussian distribution via the parameter estimation (μ_q and σ_q) via the maximum likelihood estimation (MLE). The result is that the information gain generated via the latency timing information is the difference between the two entropies: $H_0[q] - H_1[q|y = y_0]$. This formulation can be applied to all 142 character pairs and plotted as a function of latency time. The results (see figure 6 in Song et al., 2001) indicate a convex (for information gain) or concave (entropy formulation) curve. The information gain, as measured by the mutual information $I[q, y] = H_0[q] = H_1[q|y]$, is on the order of 1.2 bits per character pair, when the character pair follows a uniform distribution. This implies that the attacker extracts 1.2 bits of information from each character pair just by using timing information (latency) alone. The last stage then is to infer the character sequences given the latency information. This is where the HMM is used in this work.

The authors considered each character pair as a hidden (non-observable) state, and the latency between the keystrokes as the observable outputs. Each state is a pair of characters, and the typing sequence goes through a series of T states, corresponding to $q_1, \ldots, q_T$. Note that $yt(1 \leq t \leq T)$ denotes the observed latency at some state q_t. Then the typing of some character sequence can be modeled as an HMM given the following two assumptions: i) the probability of a transition from one state to the next is dependent only on the current state, not on the previous path, and ii) the probability distribution of the latency observation is dependent only on the current character pair and not on previous characters entered in the sequence. The first condition holds in this case as the characters in the password are randomly selected. The second assumption may not hold – since previous characters may place the hands in a state that makes the next character sequence more difficult to enter than normal. This is an issue that was addressed peripherally in the keyboard gridding experiment work published in 2005 (Revett et al., 2005). In general, keyboard gridding tries to partition the keyboard characters in such a way as to disrupt the normal typing pattern to determine if this provides enhanced discrimination capacity. The results from Revett et al. indicate that the FAR/FRR can be reduced significantly with this approach. Barring this effect, the authors assumed the second condition held and proceeded to develop their HMM model. The authors used a modified version of the Viterbi algorithm, which is used to find the best path through the sequence based on maximizing the product of the transition and emission probabilities using a dynamic programming algorithm (Rabiner & Shafer, 1978). In this work, the digraph latencies for all 142 character pairs overlapped considerably, and hence the probability of yielding the correct sequence was considered too low. Instead, the authors modified the Viterbi algorithm in such as way as to find the best n paths – they termed this the n-Viterbi algorithm. The idea is that by selecting the correct value for n, the most likely sequence would be contained within the n sequences. The issue is selecting a threshold value for n that maximizes the likelihood that the best sequence is actually contained in the n sequences, while minimizing the computational complexity. A measure of the efficacy of their selection of n, the upper bound can be estimated from the mutual information contained in the timing data for each character pair, which was 1.2 bits. If there are a total of T character pairs, then the upper bound is simply $1.2T$. When the value of n is plotted against the probability of success (measured via known samples) they found that a value of approximately 70 yields a classification accuracy of 90%, which they denote as n^*. Therefore, $\log_2(|Q|/n^*) = 1$ is the approximate number of bits per character pair extracted by the algorithm. This value is close to the expected number of optimal bits, $1.2T$. The embodiment of the HMM in the form of *Herbivore* and the results from this work are presented next.

Herbivore has been developed to serve as an attack engine for passwords issued under SU via an SSH connection. It monitors the connections, looks for SSH password, and measures the inter-arrival time of the characters within the password packets. It then uses the HMM (via the modified n-Viterbi algorithm) to identify the character sequence of the password using only timing information. The algorithm generates a set of passwords (containing n elements) and sorts them in decreasing order of their probability $Pr[q^*|y]$. The position of the real password is known, and can be used to quantify the accuracy of the classification task. In their experiments, the authors noted that users tended to pause when about three to four characters were entered (this was noted for each case). They therefore broke up the timing information into chunks corresponding to the edge of the pauses. Tests on 10 different passwords each with a length of eight characters were used in their experiments. Their results indicate that the real passwords were detected within the top 2.7% of the candidate list (ranked in descending order of probability). The median position was 1%, which indicates that approximately half of the passwords are in the top 1% of the list. This result indicates a 50-fold reduction in the number of attacks required for a brute force search of the password space. This results in a total of 5.7 bits of information learned per password using latency information alone.

These results are quite impressive, but seem to assume that an attacker must have detailed statistical information regarding the distribution of character pairs. This is a prohibitive expectation and, if so required, would reduce the usefulness of *Herbivore* (and the approach generally). To test the generality of this technique, they performed an experiment where a person used his own typing latencies to infer passwords typed by another user. They asked two users to enter the password a number of times and collected their statistics. The authors found that 75% of the character pairs were within 1 SD of each other. They inferred that this trend may be generally applicable – that the variation between users for entering key pairs typed with alternate hands tend to be much lower than those typed with the same hand. They tested this hypothesis by asking four users (including the two previously mentioned) to enter randomly generated passwords, and based on the statistics from the original two users, determined the accuracy of the classification task (as measured by the percentage of the search space examined before finding the correct password). The accuracy was generally very high except for a couple of cases – on the order of 2–5% of the search space was examined before finding the correct password.

The primary result from this experiment indicates that the training data from one user can be successfully applied to infer the passwords typed by another user. The assumptions under which these results hold may need to be examined, however. For one, user passwords may not contain the handedness variability contained within the passwords used in this study. A paper published on keyboard gridding/partitioning by Revett et al. indicate that the location of the characters within authentication text can have an impact on the classification accuracy (Revett & Khan, 2005c). The error rate was reduced by more than 50% when the user was asked to enter characters that were selected from a partitioned keyboard, as is illustrated in Figure 4.3.

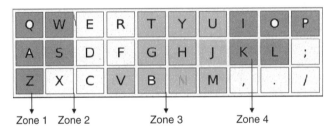

Figure 4.3 The partitioning scheme where the keyboard is partitioned into four distinct regions. Typically, textual login details are randomly generated such that no two characters come from the same contiguous partition. See Revett and Khan (2005) and Revett et al. (2007) for more details (Source: Revett and Khan, 2005)

The authors claim that the inter-subject variability was less then 1 SD, but this was obtained from a relatively small sample size (10 trials) over a small number of character pairs. It would be interesting to see if this trend held over a wider distribution. Lastly, though *Herbivore* was successful at reducing the search space for passwords, it would be interesting to see if this approach would work for longer text strings – as is typically found in free text or continuous authentication schemes. Barring these considerations in mind, this approach was quite successful. It also has the added advantage of working on one-class scenarios, where what is available is data from authentic samples – as opposed to building a model that requires a two-class decision process, where authentic and imposter data is required to build the model. This approach will be discussed in the next section, where a variety of neural network-based approaches to keystroke dynamics are discussed.

4.5.4 Neural Network-Based Approaches to User Authentication

A variety of papers have been published which present reliable and accurate classification of keystroke dynamics-based data for user authentication (see the introduction for a comprehensive listing). In this section, a detailed survey of a few representative techniques will be presented. Due to the extensive amount of literature in this area, only a small survey can be presented. Those papers selected will reflect a prototypical approach – as opposed to any particular criteria such as accuracy or popularity within the literature. In addition, related approaches such as fuzzy logic will also be given space in this section, as fuzzy logic is often embodied within the context of neural networks (i.e. artificial neural networks and fuzzy information systems (ANFIS)).

Typically, most typical neural networks are trained to map inputs to outputs. In the context of keystroke dynamics, the inputs tend to be attributes, presented as exemplars from two classes: the authentic owners and imposters. This is quite distinct from the previous statistical models examined (i.e. HMM). There are several exceptions though, and examples will be discussed as appropriate. We start off by looking at one of the earliest papers on the subject published in 1994 (Obaidat & Macchairolo, 1994).

In Obaidat and Macchairolo, keystroke dynamics data from a collection of six subjects were collected over a 6 week period. The dynamics were extracted from the typing of a password, which contained 30 characters. Only the first 15 were used in this study, as the authors indicated the results were not significantly different when employing the full range of characters. The 15-character vector was repeated 40 times, yielding a total of 600 character vectors per user, yielding a total of 3600 vectors (raw data). The authors then used various combinations of the raw data for training purposes. For instance, a training set termed "Odd-20" indicates that only the odd patterns from each of the 40 trials/user were employed, and the trials were taken as a grand average for that user, resulting in one pattern per user. These processing steps were used to examine the generalization capacity of the trained neural network. Each input pattern was associated with a local representation of an output class, using a six-node output layer. For instance, user designated as "1" had an output the vector: "1 0 0 0 0 0."

The neural network architecture was feedforward, with 15 input units, 4 or 5 hidden units (with a single hidden layer) and 6 output units. Two different learning algorithms were used in this study: back propagation and the sum of products. The principal difference between the two learning algorithms is that in the former, the interconnection scheme is additive, that is, the inputs to a given node are the sum of the outputs from the previous layer. The sum-of-products learning algorithm, as the name implies, employs a multiplicative input to a given node, which is the product of the inputs. Each of these products is termed the conjunct (see Rumelhart & McClelland, 1986). Further, let w_{kij} represent the weight of the conjunct between input node i and j into unit k. The output of unit k is

$$O_k = \mathbf{f}\left(\sum\nolimits_{i,j} w_{kij} o_i o_j\right) \qquad (4.19)$$

where $\mathbf{f}$ if 4.17 is a semi-linear activation function. A closed form of the expression for the number of inputs (N) is as follows:

$$N = n(n-1)/2 \qquad (4.20)$$

Once the inputs are presented, the calculation of the output is similar to that used in the back-propagation algorithm. The actual back-propagation learning algorithm will not be discussed, but there are a number of very suitable surveys that can be found in the literature (Rummelhart & McClelland, 1986, Hertz et al., 1991). Both learning algorithms are supervised in that there is quantitative feedback regarding how close the actual output is to the "real" or desired value. This difference is termed the error E, which is the summation of all the δ terms. The goal of back-propagation-based learning is to reduce the magnitude of E (via δ) below some given threshold ε (typically 0.05). This is accomplished by presenting examples of the inputs (exemplars) and adjusting the weights – the tunable parameters – until the δ at each output node produce an E that is below the desired level. This process embodies what has been termed the "delta rule."

The sum-of-products learning rule also works with the delta rule with a minor extension. The principal change in the sum-of-products rule is that the change in weights contains two output values instead of one, reflecting the product of the inputs to a node in the next layer. The last change requires that the delta term for node k (δ_k) must take into account the *conjunct* units. For a detailed discussion of the differences between the two learning algorithms, please consult Rummelhart and McClelland (1986). The essential point here is that the two learning algorithms can operate within the same neural network architecture with only minor modifications. The operational difference entails a substantially larger number of weights because the number of interconnections grows by a factor of $m \times n(n-1)$ for n nodes feeding into a layer of m units, compared to $m \times n$ weights for a back-propagation algorithm. Generally speaking, the larger the number of weights in a neural network, the longer it takes to train it. The authors therefore proposed a hybrid model, which would maintain the non-linearity of the sum-of-products algorithm while reducing the training time via a slight modification as discussed next.

In the hybrid sum-of-square architecture, the connections between the input layer and the hidden layer are trained using the standard back-propagation architecture. . . . The nodes between the hidden layer and output layer follow the sum-of-products architecture, with the addition of conjunct units. Since the number of output nodes generally is small compared to the number of input nodes, this reduces the number of weights in the system considerably, compared to a full sum-of-squares architecture. The update rule for the weights is also hybridized, in that changes between the input and hidden nodes follow the standard back-propagation learning rule, and those between the hidden and output nodes employ the sum-of-squares rule. With this system in place, the authors employed the standard back-propagation, sum of products, and the hybrid sum-of-squares neural networks to classify the data from the six users. The reason for employing both techniques is that the back-propagation is fairly well trusted within the computational community, but the sum of squares, and especially the hybrid sum of squares, is a relatively new invention. Therefore, the back-propagation architecture provides some corroborative information of the latter two.

The networks were all trained in the exact same way, with a total summed squared (TSS) error of 0.05 as the termination criteria (equivalent to the E term mentioned previously). Note the learning rate and momentum were set to 0.5 for the back-propagation trained network, while the learning rate and momentum were set to 0.5 and 0.3, respectively, for the sum-of-products and the hybrid sum-of-products networks (HSOPs). After the networks were trained, the full sample set (240) was presented and used to determine the error for each of the three networks. The best results from this study were obtained using the standard back-propagation training algorithm, yielding a minimal error of 2.5%. The sum-of-products network produced substantially larger errors, a minimum of 6.3%, and the hybrid version provided intermediate errors, with a minimum of 3.8%. The authors indicated that this might be due to the large number of weights in the sum-of-products model, which is ameliorated in the hybrid version. In the final analysis, this work presents data that indicates that neural networks can be used quite successfully to classify training samples of keystroke dynamics-based data. The results were more or less independent of which data was presented – the first 20 odd or 20 even did not make a significant difference in the classification results (e.g. 7.1% versus 7.9% for the back-propagation results). Though these results may not be impressive by today's standards, it was one of the first systematic studies employing neural networks within the domain of keystroke dynamics-based authentication.

Marcus and Rogers published a paper in 1993 where they presented the results of a study employing a several neural networks for use in user authentication employing keystroke dynamics data (Brown & Rogers, 1993). They also introduced the use of a self-organizing neural network – the Kohonen neural network – as a preprocessing clustering step. In their approach, subjects were asked to enter their names several times (approximately 25 times), interspersed with other names (approximately 43 times), as indicated by the program generated by the authors. The participants were not allowed to correct mistakes, and samples with errors were discarded. The program collected dwell times and digraph latency timing information. This was of the earliest studies to use this particular combination of keystroke attributes. The data samples, collected in an open laboratory on a university campus, were collected over several weeks.

The collected data was divided into two sets. The samples collected during the first session served as the reference data, and the second session served to test the system with respect to FAR and FRR calculations. In addition, a collection of 15 volunteers (not involved in the training/testing process) also typed in their names two times each, providing an additional pool of 30 imposter samples for testing the authentication method. This data was used for all subsequent analysis.

The first phase in the analysis entailed cleansing the data of outliers. The preprocessing step employed a Kohonen self-organizing map (see Kohonen, 1982 for a detailed description of this neural network). Their network contained 25 nodes (corresponding roughly to the number of samples for self-authentication), arranged as a two-dimensional (2-D) grid (5×5) of nodes. Each node is assigned a random weight vector with the same dimensions as the input data. The neighborhood size was set to three; the learning rate decreased from an initial value of 35.0–0.5%, and was trained over 10 000 iterations. After the network terminated, three filters were applied to the data:

1. The first filter removed clusters of authentic data that contained imposter samples, with a tolerance of one imposter to six authentic samples per cluster.
2. The next filter removed any authentic samples that appeared as single-member clusters.
3. The last filter employed both steps 1 and 2.

After these preprocessing steps were performed, the data was used to train two neural networks (disregarding their distance analysis method, which is described in Brown & Rogers, 1993, p. 1009): an adaptive linear element (ADALINE) and back-propagation neural network (BPNN). Very briefly, an ADALINE is a processing construct developed by Bernard Widrow (1962), which takes multiple inputs and generates a single output (the classification). It is a linear processing element and hence cannot properly classify data that is nonlinear (such as the classic XOR problem of Minsky & Papert, 1969). The multilayer feedforward neural network (MLFN) architecture is a collection of ADALINE units, connected in such a way as to be able to process nonlinear input–output relationships. This ability is made possible by the introduction of one of more hidden layer units (for more details, see Haykin, 1999 for a comprehensive description of neural network architectures). What was interesting about the MLFN architecture was that there were direct connections between the input and output nodes – generally not considered as standard for this architecture. The output layer consisted of a single node (indicating either authentic or imposter), and the input layer had the same dimensions as the input vector. When fully trained, this network generated weights that were essentially 0, except for the connections between the input and output nodes, creating in effect a collection of ADALINEs. This process entailed removal of the hidden layer. The authors subsequently treated this network approach as an ADALINE and hence continued processing the data using ADALINEs. One advantage of this type of network is that there are no local **minima**, so a global error minimum is guaranteed to be found (see the perceptron learning rule, Haykin, 1999). The outputs produced by ADALINEs (and most neural networks in general) are not 0 and 1, but some real value close to these extremes. Therefore, a threshold is selected that is used to classify the input during the training process. The authors used the imposter sample with the lowest value as the threshold, thus ensuring that the FAR was 0.

The MLFN trained with the back propagation was also employed, with random weights on the interval [−1.0 . . . 1.0], a learning rate of 45%, and a momentum term set to 9%. The network was trained until the network produced an FAR/FRR of 0, or 1000 training iterations had transpired. An output of 0 indicated an authentic sample and a 1 indicated an imposter, using the same threshold values obtained from the ADALINE system. The classification results for the ADALINE network yielded an FRR of 17.4%, and the MLFN trained with back-propagation yielded an FRR of 12.0% for the test samples. The imposter samples yielded an FRR of 40.0% for the ADALINE and an FRR of 21.2% for the MLFN trained with back-propagation. The authors also employed another classification process, where they selected the technique that provided the lowest FRR value. This approach yielded an FRR of 4.2% for the training cases and 11.5% for the test (imposter) cases.

The results from this study were not as encouraging as those provided by the Obaidat and Macchairolo (1994) study. It should be noted, though, that the results presented for this study were predicated on a 0% FAR. They did not attempt to measure the EER, which most certainly would have reduced the FRR values to more "acceptable" levels. The authors noted that the second group of participants was less familiar with the computing environment than the first group. No other reasonable explanation for these results was provided in their paper. It may be necessary to examine their data using other techniques to determine if the source of the error was at the sample end or the classification end.

In 1997, Obaidat and Sadoun (1997a) published a paper describing the application of a series of different classification techniques for keystroke dynamics-based user authentication. The authors employed clustering via K-means, distance metrics, and Bayes' decision rules as well as a variety of neural network-based approaches to user authentication. This discussion will be limited to their application of neural networks to this task.

The data was generated by 15 participants (informed) when they entered their login user ID 15 times per day, over an 8 week period (yielding 225 samples per day for each login ID). Note that the login IDs contained seven characters on average. The participants were able to enter the required data as they chose during the allotted time period. Key press and release times were recorded to an accuracy of 0.1 ms, along with the key's scan code. Incorrect login attempts were discarded. Imposter data was generated from attempts to login of the 15 IDs by each of the 15 participants. The data was partitioned equally into training and testing datasets. A commercial neural network package was used to evaluate the data. The authors employed several different neural network architectures, in addition to their 1994 work.

The authors applied several neural network algorithms including BPNN, counter-propagation neural network (CPNN), fuzzy artmap (FuART), radial basis function (RBF), learning vector quantization (LVQ), reinforcement neural network (RNN), sum-of-product network (SOP), and HSOP. It would take a book similar in scope to Haykin's (1999) or related efforts to describe all of these neural networks. The interested reader is encouraged to consult Rummelhart and McClelland (1986), Hecht-Nielsen (1990), and Haykin (1999) for a comprehensive review of these topics.

The BPNN they employed is similar to the standard version (see the previous discussion of Obaidat & Macchariolo, 1994 earlier in this chapter for details). The CPNN is a hybrid neural network incorporating a self-organized map and a Grossberg layer (see Hecht-Nielsen, 1990 for details). It is essentially a two-layer feedforward network. The FuART is a fuzzified adaptive resonance theory network based on an extension of Carpenter and Grossberg's original ART network (see Carpenter et al., 1992). The RBF network makes use of radially symmetric and radially bounded transfer functions in the hidden layer (see Leonard & Kramer, 1991 for details). LVQ was proposed by Kohonen, which is an unsupervised clustering algorithm (see Kohonen, 1991 for details). The RNN network is based on the concept of reinforcement learning which falls in between supervised (aided by a teacher – the expected output) and unsupervised learning (without a teacher). For more details, please consult Haykin (1999) for details. Each of these neural network techniques were applied to the dataset and evaluated in terms of the resulting FAR and FRR results.

The authors examined both dwell times and digraph latencies with these technologies and generated a variety of values for FAR and FRR. The authors indicate that the dwell time gave better results in terms of FAR/FRR than the digraph latency values for virtually all of the classification algorithms employed in this study. The combination of dwell time and digraph latency provided the most accurate classification values. For example, the type I error was 4.7% for digraph latency alone, 2.2% for dwell time alone, and 1.9% for the combined approach. A similar trend held for type II errors as well.

These impressive results were obtained using input strings with an average length of seven characters. The results from this study generally had lower type I and type II errors then in their previous study. The data from this study indicate that the SOP and HSOP algorithms also yielded poorer results than most of the other types of neural networks, so even though the data used in the two experiments were different, the trend from this experiment was consistent with their previous work. This lack of consistency with data over a variety of classification algorithms makes it very difficult to compare results from different studies. This issue will be addressed later in this chapter.

In 2000, Haider and colleagues published a paper that presented a combined approach to user authentication – in this case, they employed three approaches in parallel: statistical methods, neural networks, and fuzzy logic (Haider et al., 2000). The input data consisted of a password (user selected) limited to seven characters, which was repeated 15 times for the enrollment process. It is interesting to note that the authors did not state the number of participants involved in this study. Entries with mistakes were discarded and repeated as necessary. The system acquired the delays between successive characters (digraph latencies), though the authors did not specify whether it was key press or key release, or any combination thereof. The timing of the digraph latencies had a resolution of 10 ms. The authors then used this data for all subsequent analysis.

For the fuzzy logic system, they employed membership functions for digraph latencies with five distinct categories: very fast, fast, moderate, slow, and very slow. Each digraph was passed to the membership function and assigned to the corresponding. Next, they calculated the center of gravity using equation 4.21:

$$I = \sum \mu_i / \sum \mu \qquad (4.21)$$

The resulting value generated by the application of the center of gravity (first moment of inertia) was passed back to the membership function, and the category with maximal membership was taken to represent that particular digraph. This process was performed across all digraphs for each user, forming a reference profile for that user. When the same password was entered into the system, the same attributes were extracted and processed according to the fuzzy rules generated by the reference profile. The authors did not explore the acceptance criteria with their fuzzy system. It is certainly a rule-based system, but there is also the possibility that only a fraction of the digraphs will pass. What fraction is sufficient for a successful entry? If all digraphs must meet the rule specified for the user, then this might reduce the FAR considerably, but might increase the FRR to the same extent. Leggett and Williams,

Mahar, and Napier all described the deployment of an acceptance criterion with respect to the number of digraphs that must pass threshold before a decision can be made (Leggett & Williams, 1988, Mahar et al., 1995, Napier et al., 1995). Their results indicate that 60–70% is an optimal value. Certainly fuzzy systems provide some flexibility in the categorization process, as do most other studies in the form of accepting a difference between the sample and reference in terms of some number of SD units. For example, Leggett and Williams (1988) used a value of 0.5 SD units as acceptable with respect to the reference sample. These issues will be discussed further later in this chapter.

Next, the authors employed a neural network approach to user authentication. They employ a three-layer feedforward architecture employing the back-propagation learning algorithm. They utilized a fixed set of weights between the input and hidden layers (they termed M1) and the same set of constant weights between the single hidden layer and output layer (termed M2 by the authors). The biases for the hidden and output layers were also set to the same value as the weight matrices, which was 0.1 for all experiments reported in this paper. The threshold values for input, hidden, and output neurons were initialized randomly. During training, the average values for each digraph latency were used, and the output neuron was set to 1. After training, the weights and biases were saved for subsequent authentication trials. Note that this was a single class training system, as no negative examples were provided during training. During authentication, the same attributes were extracted (digraph latencies) and passed through the network, and the outputs were computed. The delta between actual and target values was calculated, and a decision threshold was employed to decide whether to accept or to reject the entry. The value of the threshold was not presented in the paper, though, making it somewhat difficult to reproduce this stage of their processing pipeline.

Lastly, the authors employed a statistical test, using confidence intervals (CIs) as per equation 4.22:

$$x_i \pm z\sigma \qquad (4.22)$$

where σ is the SD and z is the standard normal distribution value. All CIs were stored in each user's reference profile and were used subsequently for the authentication phase (testing). When a user attempted to authenticate, the digraph latencies were extracted, and the CI was used to determine whether to accept or reject the authentication attempt.

The efficacy of the authors' approach was based on the type I and type II errors. The authors used most of the combinations of the three methods (excluded the neural and fuzzy combination) to authenticate users – in a parallel fashion. The results are presented in Table 4.6, and yield type I errors ranging from 2% to 20% and type II errors ranging from 6% to 22%. This is one of the earliest (and few) papers that take these calculations one step further – by realizing that when logging into most computer systems, we have more than one attempt available to us. For instance, in Windows, we have three strikes before we are called out (locked out). Most studies to this point in time use single trials as their measurement for FAR/FRR. This will significantly reduce the FRR and possibly reducing the FAR error measurements. The results indicated above were for a single authentication attempt. When two attempts per measurement were allowed, the error rates dropped significantly compared to a separate single trial test. Table 4.6 presents a summary of their data for type I errors (FRR) only.

The results from the Haider study are mentioned principally because it is one of the earliest papers that highlighted the issue of *how* authentication attempts should be generated. In the previous studies mentioned in this chapter, which holds generally across the literature, most

Table 4.6 Summary of an authentication trial comparing single versus two login attempts before an authentication decision was generated (Source: Haider et al., 2000)

	One try	Two tries
Fuzzy	0.26	0.11
Neural network	0.41	0.20
Statistical	0.03	0.02
Fuzzy, neural network	0.36	0.13
Fuzzy, statistical	0.13	0.02
Neural network, statistical	0.21	0.02
Fuzzy, neural network, statistical	0.21	0.02

Note that this data is for type I, FRR measurements only.

studies employ an unrealistic measure of FAR/FRR. Normally, we have three login attempts before a decision is rendered (at least in the Microsoft Windows® world). To make a decision after the first attempt does not reflect the way systems authenticate us. Even though users may be allowed to enter their details multiple times, for the FAR/FRR measurements, each is treated as a single trial. Evidence presented by Brostoff and Sasse (2000) indicated that there was an inherent amount of login failures that appeared to drop off considerably (approaching 1–2%) when the number of login attempts was increased to 10. Also, how we gather imposter results, for instance, may be significantly influenced by how the attempts are collected. Sitting within a single session and typing a login ID/password 10 s to 100 s of times may not be a realistic approach. Fatigue, boredom, and other factors may influence how the entries are made. I can see the issue of testing efficiency – getting as many numbers as possible in the shortest period of time. But what is required are realistic numbers – based on how we actually interact with PCs or even ATMs for that matter. This issue will be discussed further at the summary section of this chapter.

There are several flaws with the Haider study. For one, the number of participants was not indicated. This is a critical piece of information that must be reported – if another laboratory is going to have a chance to repeat the work. The authentication trials probably used training data – this point was not clarified at all in the paper. This would certainly skew the results toward low values for FAR/FRR. It appears that the statistical model provided the best accuracy (see Table 4.6), and the combination with fuzzy and or neural networks served to either maintain or reduce the type I error, though the combination did tend to reduce the type II errors (data not shown). The authors could also explore how to utilize these classification schemes in a serial fashion, where a user would have to pass one or more tests, depending on the required level of stringency. For this approach to work, the relative accuracy of each of the individual approaches will have to be investigated more fully.

In a study by Revett and colleagues (2006), the use of a probabilistic neural network (PNN) as a novel classification algorithm was explored. A PNN is essentially a classifier implemented as a neural network version of a Bayes–Parzen classifier (Specht, 1988, 1990). The general classification problem is to determine the category membership of a multivariate sample data (i.e. a p-dimensional random vector $\mathbf{x}$) into one of q possible groups Ω_i, $I = 1$, $2, \ldots, q$, based on a set of measurements. If we know the pdf $f_i(\mathbf{x})$, usually the Parzen – Cacoulos or Parzen-like pdf classifiers,

$$f_i(x) = \frac{1}{(2\pi)^{p/2}\sigma^p} \cdot \frac{1}{m_i} \cdot \sum_{j=1}^{m} \exp\left(-\frac{\|x - x_j\|^2}{2\sigma^2}\right) \qquad (4.23)$$

the a priori probabilities $h_i = P(\Omega_i)$ of occurrence of patterns from categories Ω_i and the *loss* (or *cost*) parameters l_i associated with all incorrect decisions given $\Omega_i = \Omega_i$, then, according to the Bayesian decision rule, we classify $\mathbf{x}$ into the category Ω_i if the inequality $l_i\,h_i\,f_i(\mathbf{x}) > l_j\,h_j\,f_j(\mathbf{x})$ holds true. The standard training procedure for PNN requires a single pass over all the training patterns, giving them the advantage of being faster than the feedforward neural networks (Specht, 1988, 1990).

Basically, the architecture of PNN is limited to three layers: the *input/pattern layer*, the *summation layer*, and the *output layer*. Each input/pattern node forms a product of the input pattern vector $\mathbf{x}$ with a weight vector W_i and then performs a nonlinear operation, that is, $\exp[-(W_i - x)^\tau(W_i - x)/(2\sigma^2)]$ (assuming that both $\mathbf{x}$ and W_i are normalized to unit length), before outputting its activation level to the summation node. Each summation node receives the outputs from the input/pattern nodes associated with a given class and simply sums the inputs from the pattern units that correspond to the category from which the training pattern was selected, $\Sigma_i \exp[-(W_i - x)^\tau(W_i - x)/(2\sigma^2)]$. The output nodes produce binary outputs by using the inequality

$$\sum_i \exp[-(W_i - x)^\tau(W_i - x)/(2\sigma^2)] > \sum_j \exp[-(W_j - x)^\tau(W_j - x)/(2\sigma^2)] \qquad (4.24)$$

related to two different categories, Ω_i and Ω_j.

The key to obtaining a good classification using PNN is to optimally estimate the two parameters of the Bayes decision rule, the misclassification costs and the prior probabilities. In our practical experiment, we have estimated them heuristically. Thus, as concerns the costs parameters, we have considered them depending on the average distances D_i, inversely proportional, that is $l_i = 1/D_i$. As concerns the prior probabilities, they measure the membership probability in each group and, thus, we have considered them equal to each group size, that is $h_i = m_i$. As in our previous work, we employed an evolutionary technique based on the genetic algorithm to find the smoothing parameters (see Gorunescu et al., 2005b, Gorunescu et al., 2007 for implementation details).

The dataset we examined consisted of a group of 50 subjects (all university students in a computer science department) – 20 acting as authentic users and the balance (30) acting as imposters. We asked the authentic user group to enter a login ID/password of their choice (minimum of six characters each, with a maximum limit of 15 characters for each). This was immediately followed by an enrollment period that consisted of entering their selected user ID/password for 10 trials. We collected a series of attributes (see Table 4.1 for a complete listing) which were to be used during the authentication process. The data samples were collected over a 14 day period, throughout specified periods of the day. We requested that the participants log in during a morning, midday, and late afternoon session in order to replicate the average login times during the course of a normal working day. We maintained a running average of the primary and derived attributes where the oldest sample of 10 was replaced and all derived attributes were recalculated. We invited the imposter group (30 participants) to "hack" into all of the legitimate accounts after providing them with the account holders' login ID/passwords. They were given 1 week to log into all 20 authentic accounts approximately 100 times each (total of 2000 attempts), and the success/failure rates were recorded. More specifically, each participant of the imposter group attacked each account four times for a total of 80 login attempts for each imposter. Therefore, each account will be attacked 120 times. We randomly selected 100 imposter login attempts for each account and used these values in all subsequent calculations in order to keep the numbers in multiples of 100. This was used to estimate the average FAR for the user group. In addition, the authentic users were asked to log into their own accounts 100 times during the same period. This data was to be used for estimating the average FRR for the user group. The resultant data will contain 2000 FRR attempts and 2000 imposter login attempts. We then used this data to train our PNN algorithm to perform the required class discrimination task. We cross validated our results and we reported the average results from these experiments. The particular version of the PNN we employed in this paper was the same as that employed in previous work (Gorunescu et al., 2005, Revett et al., 2005b). We also applied a modified version of our PNN algorithm, which used separate smoothing factors for each class (authentic and imposter). We report both results in this work and found that using a separate smoothing factor provided consistently better classification results. To provide a direct comparison of the PNN results with another recognized classification technique, we developed a three-layer multilayer perceptron neural network trained with back propagation. The following parameters were used for the MLFN: the input layer contained a minimal number of nodes 23; the hidden layer had 14 nodes, and the output layer 2 nodes (corresponding to the two decision classes). Please note that the actual number of potential input nodes really ranges from 23 to 45 in this particular dataset. We therefore used the minimal number of digraphs (10) and trigraphs (8) as per Table 4.2. The learning parameter was $\eta = 0.2$, and there was no momentum term used. The acceptable error rate was set to 0.01. The actual data (extracted attributes) that was presented to both authentication systems is summarized in Table 4.2. Note the difficulty one encounters when using a fixed architecture like an MLP when the number of digraphs varies as is the case with a variable length user ID/password. The results were assessed using 10-fold cross validation, and the results presented in this paper are the average values for each network (PNN or BPNN).

In addition to the classification task per se, we also sought to investigate the information content of each of the attributes that were acquired during the enrollment phase. We therefore tested a variety of combination of attributes (see Table 4.2 for a summary of the collected attributes). The digraphs were recorded during as the time in milliseconds between the release of two successive keystrokes, with an accuracy of 1 ms. The trigraphs were recorded in the same way, based on the release time between the first and third keys. The speed was measured as the total time taken to enter the login ID and password divided by the total number of characters, excluding the return key and the interval between entering the login ID and password. The edit distance was recorded as per Bergadano (Bergadano et al., 2002) using trigraphs only. Briefly, the edit distance is an indication of the entropy different between two typing samples. The trigraphs entered, which span across the login ID/password boundary, are arranged in order of ascending order of time. Then the number of rearrangements required to order the trigraphs is measured and divided by the total number of trigraphs that are available for a string of a given length. The specific details of which attributes and their combinations were tested are described in detail in the results section. These attribute combinations were used for classification purposes with both versions of the PNN and the MLFN as indicated.

We first describe an experiment where we examined which division was used in the PNN and whether a single or separate smoothing factor gave us the best classification accuracy. For this experiment, we used the full set of attributes (see Table 4.2 for details). We selected random samples for training and testing (50/50 in this case) and applied our PNN algorithm to these random samples. More specifically, we selected 200 samples of FAR and FRR data for the training/testing purposes, repeating this process until all samples were utilized (10 trials). The data in Tables 4.7A and 4.7B indicate that the classification accuracy was essen-

Table 4.7 FAR/FRR values as a function of the division level (the same values reported in Table 4.3) (Source: Revett et al., 2007 IJESDF. © Inderscience)

A)

Divisions	Training error	Test error
10	0.0107	0.1153
20	0.0001	0.0884
30	0.0000	0.0942
40	0.0003	0.0923
50	0.0100	0.0961
60	0.0009	0.1153
70	0.0087	0.0903
80	0.0917	0.1003
90	0.0093	0.1076
100	0.0101	0.0923

B)

Division points	False acceptance	False rejection
10	0.0483	0.0481
20	0.0192	0.0197
30	0.0576	0.0376
40	0.0576	0.0566
50	0.0576	0.0483
60	0.0001	0.0021
70	0.0576	0.0598
80	0.0481	0.0483
90	0.0288	0.0312
100	0.0480	0.0427
	0.0422	0.0394

The values in the last row of the rightmost columns are the averages of their respective columns. In panel A), the results were obtained using a different smoothing factor for training/testing, and in panel B) using the same smoothing factor for each.

tially independent of the number of divisions employed for this dataset. Please note that the modified PNN algorithm (separate smoothing factors for each category) yielded consistently higher results than one that employed the same smoothing factor for both classes. The results presented in Table 4.7 indicate that our FAR/FRR is on the order of 4%, and the data in Table 4.6 indicate a slightly higher error rate of approximately 6.8% (average between FAR/FRR errors).

We also investigated the ability of a multilayered neural network running the back-propagation learning algorithm on the data that was collected and previously analyzed with the PNN algorithm. The data extracted from the user input is summarized in Table 4.3. The dataset was sampled 50/50 training/testing and repeated using n-fold validation, and the results are reported as the average values. The data for the MLFN classification experiment is presented as in Table 4.8. Note that the same set of subsamples was used in both experiments. Note that the average accuracy from the samples yielded an accuracy of approximately 91%. This value is approximately the same for the average from resampling the entire dataset without replacement (92.1%). We then repeated the comparison experiments (using the dual smoothing factors only for the PNN) but varied the particular attributes that were used. In particular, we were interested in what effect the various attributes contributed toward the classification accuracy and whether the particular classification technique would be differentially influenced by the attribute selection process. The attributes that were used in this study were digraphs, trigraphs, dwell time, total login ID time, total password time, and total authentication attempt time. Table 4.8 presents a summary of the various attributes that were tested, along with the classification accuracy (reported as the average of the FRR/FAR results) for the PNN and the MLFN, both trained as per the previous results.

Lastly, there is the issue of computational time – both for training and the classification tasks. Generally speaking, the PNN training time was significantly lower than that for the MLFN – 1.4 minutes versus 5.6 minutes for training on 400 objects – 200 for each class. The classification task was approximately the same for each classifier – with an average value of 8 seconds (Table 4.9).

In this study, we have employed our modified PNN to a small dataset of login ID/password samples. The modified classifier performed better than the standard PNN algorithm by a considerable margin (4% versus 8% approximately). These results are comparable to traditional neural network approaches as well as more "modern" approaches such as SVMs. We

Table 4.8 Summary of the attributes employed in this study (both primary and derived) (Source: Revett et al., 2007 IJESDF. © Interscience)

Attribute type	Primary or derived
Digraphs	Primary
Trigraphs	Primary
Dwell time	Primary
Entropy (edit distance)	Secondary
Login ID time	Primary
Password time	Primary
Total entry time	Primary
Power law terms	Secondary

Table 4.9 Summary of the classification accuracy for the PNN and MLFN classifiers when using various combinations of primary and derived attributes (Source: Revett et al., 2007 IJESDF. © Inderscience)

PNN – primary	MLFN – primary
92.2%	93.7%
PNN – primary + derived	MLFN – primary + derived
95.7%	97.1%

The values are presented as absolute classification error, using a 70/30 training regime for the PNN and MLFN. These results are with respect to the test set.

also used the same dataset to test the classification accuracy of standard implementation of the MLFN trained with back propagation. The results from this study indicate that the PNN is superior to the MLFN with respect to the classification accuracy and training time. It must be noted that these results were obtained without any data preprocessing. We simply collected the data, selected a random subset for training 50% and 50% for testing. This algorithm is time efficient when login ID/password credentials are used for authentication purposes. It is a well-known fact that the training phase of the PNN algorithm begins to degrade in terms of time efficiency when the sample numbers are large. But in this area of application, where we have a relatively small number of samples for training (on the order of 100–200) and can select an equal number of testing samples, training performance is not an issue. This is in contrast to other techniques such as the back-propagation algorithm that requires a substantial number of training data in order to generate an accurate classification. These advantages make the PNN a very suitable candidate for a novel machine learning algorithm in the context of keystroke dynamics authentication.

With regard to the attribute used in this study, we found that the derived attributes such as digraph/trigraph times, speed, and edit distance were more effective compared with primary attributes such as dwell time, time of flight, and scan codes. The edit distance attribute produced results with the lowest error rate for both the PNN and MLFN. Although not statistically different from using all attributes, the data from this study suggest that this attribute is quite important in the classification task when using these types of classifiers. This data is consistent with the results published by Bergadano et al. (2002). Clearly, there is a trend in the results from this study to investigate a variety of first- and second-order attributes before selecting a classifier tool. Not all attributes produce the same classification accuracy over different techniques.

Another aspect of keystroke dynamics-based biometrics entails how to collect samples for classification. In this study, we attempted to collect data from users in a manner consistent with normal daily computer usage. It may be fairly unrealistic to ask imposters to hack into a system for 100 consecutive attempts. Most computer systems turn off access opportunities after three failed login attempts, so attempting 100 is an unreasonable situation. In addition, when does one count a login attempt as a failure? Is it after three continuously failed attempts or after each single failed attempt. In this study, we used single failed attempts. If one counts only three failed attempts before considering the attempt as a failure, then both FAR/FRR rates will be significantly different from what we report. As long as the authors make it clear what their criterion is, then different laboratories can meaningfully compare their results.

The neural network approach has been applied quite successfully to keystroke dynamics-based authentication systems. The statistical method has not been as prevalent, though early studies have applied a simplified statistical measure of the difference between an authentication sample and the reference sample (see Leggett & Williams, 1990). The use of fuzzy logic-based systems has been applied successfully, and the next section explores a few case studies.

4.5.5 Fuzzy Logic

de Ru and colleagues (1997) published a paper in 1997 describing experiments using fuzzy logic-based user authentication. The authors employed a multivariate approach to attribute extraction: digraph latencies and typing difficulty. They defined typing difficulty according to the following criteria: i) number of keys separating the successive characters entered and ii) whether the character was created using key combinations, such as capitalized characters. The text entered was short strings consisting of the login ID and password. The total difficulty time is the sum of the first key distance (criterion i), and if multiple keys were employed, an additional factor of 5 was added to the key distance metric. The fuzzy categories that were employed were **somewhat short**, **moderately short**, **short**, and **very short** for the digraph latency. For the difficulty attribute, the authors state that this attribute is not as significant as the digraph latency, so they use a single category subset of **high**. The output categories were the following: **low**, **medium**, **high**, and **very high**. This classification was dependent on the experience level of the typists – based solely on their typing characteristics – not on a survey of their typing qualifications. With these categories in place, what is left is to develop a set of rules that map the inputs to the outputs. This requires the development of the membership functions, which were derived by examining repeated trials for each login ID/password pair. Once the fuzzy memberships have been determined, the center of gravity is calculated, which yields a crisp numeric value for each input. A rule set is generated and stored as the user's reference value. There were a total of 20 fuzzy rules, but the preliminary results indicate that typing difficulty was not very useful and removed those rules, resulting in a net of five rules for their fuzzy classifier. When a user attempts to authenticate, the same attributes are extracted and applied to the fuzzy rule assigned to that login ID/password. The decision outcome was based solely on whether the input was successfully parsed by one of the fuzzy rules. In their experiment, there were 25 participants, each of which selected a login ID and password (which was to contain eight or more characters, where at least one required a complex key press [two keys such as in capitalization]). To build the reference profile, 25 typing samples were entered, all within a single session. To measure FRR, the users logged into their own account 25 times. To calculate FAR, each user logged into the other 24 accounts 25 times, yielding a total of 600 FAR attempts/user account. The results produced an FRR of 7.4%, with a FAR of 2.8%. These results were quite reasonable, but were much higher than those obtained in the Haider study (Haider et al., 2000). Whether this is due to the difference in methodology can only be determined by exchanging data between the two studies. It is clear that this study did employ test data that was different from the training data, and from this perspective provides a more accurate experimental paradigm for determining FAR/FRR results.

The use of SVMs has been successfully applied to keystroke dynamics-based user authentication. According to Yu and colleagues, SVMs provide a similar authentication accuracy as neural networks, but with much less computational overhead (Sung & Cho, 2006). In their 2006 paper, Yu and Cho used a combined approach where an SVM was applied to a reduced set of attributes, extracted using a wrapper feature. Their wrapper was genetic algorithm based, and hence their system was dubbed "GA-SVM wrapper approach for feature selection." (Sung & Cho, 2006, p. 3). In addition, the authors employ an ensemble model based on feature selection. We first start with an explanation of their SVM approach.

SVMs have been successfully employed to solve a range of classification tasks (for a review, see Cristianni & Shawe-Taylor, 2000). The task at hand entails a one-class decision problem, where we have data from the authentic user – but very little is any data from imposters. To solve this problem, most researchers train their system with a set of imposter data obtained by other subjects employed within the study. Generally, this is not a feasible approach as most users are not willing to distribute their passwords. In such cases, a one-class version of the classifier must be utilized. Schölkopf and colleagues published work indicating how the standard SVM can be used for one-class decision making – turning it into a novelty detector (for details, see Schölkopf et al., 1999, 2000). This results in two clusters of data – one containing the most consistent examples of the authentic user and the other containing imposter data and outliers from the authentic user. Generally, to enhance the efficacy of the model, some preprocessing is performed to remove outliers. This typically results in a reduction in the amount of usable data to build a model of the user. This is a luxury in some cases, especially when the amount of user data is minimal. Sung and Cho (2006) opted for a different approach to outlier removal, where they utilized a feature subset extraction method (for a different approach, see Revett, 2007), which entailed searching through the attribute space identifying features that were optimal with respect to the authentic decision class. They employed a GA-SVM wrapper to perform the attribute reduction process. The wrapper approach searches through the parameter/feature space evaluating various combinations of features against some task-specific performance measure. The task-specific performance measure in this instance is the SVM. This approach may be somewhat expensive in terms of computational costs – but as previously mentioned, the SVM algorithm is very efficient compared to other learning systems based on neural networks. It therefore becomes feasible to generate a collection of SVMs, each of which evaluates the attribute/feature space with respect to the classification task. This is the fundamental approach taken by Yu and Cho in their 2004 work. In addition, to avoid any over-fitting, the authors employed an ensemble method. The authors opted for their ensemble method to provide a balance between diversity and accuracy. To this end, the ensemble method was based on the differences between feature subsets, using the Hamming distance as the metric.

The data used in this study consisted of dwell and digraph latency times. Data from owners and imposters were collected for 21 passwords, ranging in length from 6 to 10 characters (at 1 ms resolution). Participants were asked to enter their password 150–400 times. For imposter data, a separate collection of users (15) were asked to enter a password five times (after training), yielding a total of 75 imposter samples per password. In addition, the password owners were asked to enter a test set of password entries (75) for testing the resulting classification system (in addition to the pure imposter samples). Note the passwords consisted of a variety of phrases selected by the researchers.

The authors compared the performance of a neural network-based classification system, which generated a higher average error rate and took three orders of magnitude longer to train (on average 10–100 seconds for the neural network) versus 0.1 seconds for the GA-SVM. The average error rate for the SVM was 0.81%, compared to 1.21 for the best neural network (four-layer **Auto-associative MLP**) (Yu & Cho, 2003). In addition, the feature selection process also reduced the attribute space, selecting 6 out of 17 features on average. This essentially amounts to selecting particular dwell times and/or digraph latencies for particular entries within the password text. The average FRR results for the feature selection (GA-SVM wrapper) was 3.54%, when FAR was set to 0%. Note that these results were generated using the training data. For the testing calculations, 50 entries were selected randomly, and were divided into 35 for training and 15 for testing. The results of this experiment yielded an average FRR of 5.67% (with FAR = 0%), with a range of 0.00–5.67%. These results are quite promising and on par with other experimental approaches discussed in this chapter and published elsewhere in the literature.

Considering the complexity of the task set forth by Yu and Cho, it is quite surprising that the algorithm succeeded in training the GA-generated SVM model so quickly – 0.1 s. Unfortunately the authors did not specify explicitly the attributes that were used – though one assumes it would be the full range of dwell time and digraph times (17 was the maximal number of attributes from which their reduction was produced). A key issue is the requirement that users enter their login details 150–400 times. This does seem to be somewhat excessive, compared to many other studies, where 10–15 appears to be the norm (Gaines et al., 1980, Brown & Rogers, 1993, Gunetti & Picardi, 2005). It would be an interesting experiment to vary the number of entries per user account and to measure the average performance of their system.

Other single-class methods have been applied to keystroke dynamics-based user authentication. Lee and Cho (2006) have successfully applied the 1-LVQ algorithm as another novelty detector approach to user classification. The authors utilized data acquired after a user was assigned a password – generally there would be some failed login attempts that occur through user error. The purpose was to see if using these "pseudo-imposter login attempts" can help improve the classification accuracy (this is the retraining aspect of this work). In this study, the authors compared the one-class LVQ algorithm with the support vector data description (SVDD) algorithm, a modified SVM algorithm. The dataset and experimental paradigm were essentially the same as those used in Yu and Cho (2004). The 1-LVQ algorithm seeds codebooks such that they belong only to the normal data, as that is assumed to be the only data available. The thresholds for each Voronoi region must be explicitly determined, and must be made as tight as possible, such that only normal patterns are contained within them. The results from the 1-LVQ, when applied to the same set of data used in the Yu and Cho (2004) paper, yielded an average integrated error of 0.43% and 0.59%, respectively. Note that the first figure (0.43%) refers to the case where the system was trained with authentic and imposter data and the second with only authentic data. Their SVDD approach yielded a similar error of 0.62% for both authentic only and authentic and imposter data combined.

de Oliviera and colleagues (2005) have applied SVM and artificial neural networks to keystroke dynamics-based authentication. They utilize dwell time and digraph latencies extracted from login ID/password-based user accounts (each entered 10 times). The classification results using the SVM yielded an average FAR for all users of 7%, and an average FAR of about 9%. These results were not as significant as the Yu and Cho study, but the authors did not provide any explanation for this discrepancy, though it must be stated that the Yu and Cho study discussed previously employed an ensemble method, along with the GA wrapper. It should also be noted that in this study, the users entered their login details 10 times, as opposed to 140–400 times. It would have been interesting to compare the present results with users entering their login details in a manner similar to that in the Yu and Cho (2004) study. In addition, the authors also employed the LVQ1 algorithm to their datasets. The results yielded an average FRR of approximately 14% and a FAR of 7%. These results again are not quite as accurate as previous studies (see Yu & Cho, 2004), which might reflect the much smaller sample size and entry repetition rate.

The last algorithm to be explored in this chapter is based on the idea of feature extraction (similar to Yu & Cho, 2004) using a novel algorithm in the biometrics field, based on rough set theory. There are a number of publications that have compared the use of particular attributes such as dwell time versus digraph latency (Gaines et al., 1980, Leggett & Williams, 1991, Revett et al., 2005, 2007), various values of n for n-graphs (n ranging from 2 to 4), and typing difficulty (Bergadano et al., 2002, Gunetti et al., 2003). In addition, there are reports that have examined the proportion of n-graphs that must pass significance in order to assign the decision to the authentication attempt (Umphress & Williams, 1985, Napier et al., 1995). These studies have examined the attribute set in isolation, without a methodology that was designed for such an examination. In some instances, the same dataset was used to examine a parameterized range of values for the attribute(s), such as the value of n in n-graphs. This approach tends to be the exception, and generally, several experiments are performed, each examining an attribute value in isolation. The results from these types of studies are difficult to compare as there will be inter-study variations, which makes this type of analysis difficult at best. The primary reason for these difficulties is a lack of a proper experimental design. Mahar and colleagues (1995) and Napier and colleagues (1995) each published papers on the topic of keystroke dynamics-based user authentication in 1995. These works in these papers utilize a full experimental deign where order effects and variable interactions were quantified using multiple analysis of variance (MANOVA) techniques, which provided statistically valid information regarding any interactions within a multivariate design study. More will be said in this regard later in this chapter on the section of keystroke dynamics standards.

4.5.6 Rough Sets

In the current context, the use of rough sets provides an alternative method for examining the attribute space, which is inherently nonstatistical. For a comprehensive review of rough sets, see the review by Komorowski et al. (1999). Very briefly, rough sets is utilized as a data mining technique that extracts classification information from datasets in the form of decision rules (similar in structure to fuzzy rules). The algorithm operates on a decision table, which necessitates a supervised learning mode. This requirement dictates that the algorithm is generally applied to cases where all classes are present in the dataset (i.e. a two-class approach: authentic users and imposters). This requirement can be alleviated if one chooses to generate association rules, which are less stringent in terms of the amount of information that can be extracted from the dataset (see Komorowski et al. for a detailed discussion). What is relevant here is that rough sets can be used to extract useful attributes from datasets containing any amount of attributes. The dataset is arranged such that the columns represent attributes, including a decision class, and the rows represent examples of the data (e.g. all attributes extracted for a user). From this augmented dataset (termed a decision table in rough sets nomenclature), rules are extracted that preserve the mapping between the attributes and the decision class. The algorithm guarantees to find the minimal attribute set that preserves the relationship between decision attributes and the corresponding decision class. An example of the application of rough sets is presented next.

In this study, we asked users (approximately 100) to enter a passphrase (login ID) that consisted of a string of 14 characters ("ensouspopulare"), which is composed of three words in Portugese, through an intranet-based portal. Please note that all subjects that participated in this study were native Portugese speakers. A subset of the users (10) was designated as the owner of this passphrase and was asked to enter the passphrase on numerous occasions (approximately 50). The entries were collected over a 7-day period to ensure that we acquired a robust sampling of the variations of the input style for passphrase entry. For each passphrase entry, we collected all of the digraphs, the time elapsing between **entering (keypress event)** successive keystrokes (data summarized in Table 4.10). This table presents a sample of five legitimate users ("1" in the Legit? column) and five illegitimate users (with a "0" in the Legit? column). All other values in the table are the digraph times in milliseconds. Please note that there are five additional attributes not included in this table for the sake of presentation clarity. The additional attributes are W1 (first word), W2 (second word), W3 (third word), WH (half the total time), and TT (total time). The Tx in this table represents the digraph number. Legit refers to whether the entry was made by the designated owner of the key presses (13 in total), along with thetime taken for each of the words in the passphrase (three in total), the total time spent in entering the passphrase, and the halfway time point. These formed the objects in our decision table, which included a binary decision class based on whether the entry was from the legitimate user or not.

Our rough sets software, Rosetta (v 1.4) and RSES (Rough Sets xploration System, v 2.2.1), has a limitation of 500 objects, so we split the decision table into legitimate and illegitimate

Table 4.10 Sample digraph times for the first 13 digraphs collected from a random sampling of 10 users (Source: Revett et al., 2005 WIC/ACM (403). © ICGePress University of East London)

T1	T2	T3	T4	T5	T6	T7	T8	T9	T10	T11	T12	T13	Legit?
281	344	297	218	375	266	328	266	234	313	515	282	281	1
343	266	875	297	250	719	593	250	235	312	281	282	250	1
375	359	250	328	328	469	406	282	265	344	359	344	359	1
250	328	266	234	375	328	516	266	234	297	312	297	235	1
391	250	578	297	250	328	297	265	282	312	594	265	438	1
390	344	266	312	297	313	375	312	266	531	547	453	235	0
546	625	297	344	360	343	641	313	296	344	469	500	219	0
344	359	266	266	312	266	344	265	266	312	266	438	234	0
531	501	843	344	344	453	656	297	750	344	453	328	297	0
390	344	297	281	297	313	453	312	266	391	390	532	265	0

The legit column (last column) refers to whether or not the digraphs were collected from the legitimate owner ("1") or an imposter ("0"). Data taken from Revett et al. (2005).

Table 4.11   Results from high-pass filtering of the rules based on support (Source: Revett et al., 2005 WIC/ACM (403). © ICGePress University of East London)

Filter threshold (based on support)	Accuracy (%)	Number of rules
≤0	99.1	74 392
≤4	97.8	2401
≤10	97.5	604
≤20	96.8	452

We excluded all rules that had a support less than the specified filter threshold. Note that the accuracy was reduced by just over 2%, but the number of rules was reduced to 0.6% of the default value.

users (approximately 500 of each) and randomly selected 250 objects from each decision class. We repeated this process 10 times, and report the average results when applicable in this paper. We then discretized the attributes (except for the decision attribute) using an entropy/minimal description length (MDL) algorithm. We then split the decision table up in a 70:30 split (legitimate and non-legitimate entries, respectively). We generated reducts using the dynamic reduct option, exhaustive algorithm. We then generated decision rules that were then applied to the testing set. Since the critical factor in this study is the information content of the rules, we were interested in yielding a rule set with minimal cardinality, while obviously maintaining high accuracy levels. To achieve this aim, we filtered the rules based on support since the initial rule set contained over 74 000 rules – too large to be of practical use.

The principal result of this study is summarized in Table 4.11, where a sample of the objects in the decision table, for the sake of clarity, does not present the values for the word lengths, total time, and the halfway time. The data in the decision table was discretized using the entropy/MDL option in Rosetta, on all attributes except for the decision class. The decision table was split 70:30, which we used for training and testing purposes, respectively. We then generated dynamic reducts (using the exhaustive calculation RSES) option in Rosetta. Lastly, rules were generated from the reducts. Without any filtering, 74 392 rules were generated. Since the primary goal of this study was to determine if a set of rules could be generated that would allow a software-based biometric system to distinguish legitimate from non-legitimate users, to make the system computationally tractable. In Table 4.11 below, we present data on the relationship between the number of rules (filtered on support) and the classification accuracy.

The accuracy of the classification task (with maximal filtering), segregating legitimate from non-legitimate users, was approximately 97%. Table 4.12 below presents a randomly selected confusion matrix that presents the key summary statistics regarding the classification accuracy of the resulting classifier. The primary result of this study was the rule set that was used to distinguish a legitimate from an illegitimate login attempt. The primary attributes used in this study were digraphs – the amount of time required to depress two keys. We collected all digraphs (13 in all), plus the time taken for each word in the login ID, the total time, and the halfway time point for entering the login ID. We present summary statistics in Figure 4.4 below, which depicts a frequency plot of the occurrences of the various digraphs that were found in the resulting rule set. Additionally, we examined the attributes to determine if any were more representative of the rule set than others. We found that attributes 7 and 8 occurred

Table 4.12 A sample confusion matrix for a randomly selected application of the rule set generated using rough sets (Source: Revett et al., 2005 WIC/ACM (403). © ICGePress University of East London)

Outcomes	0	1	
0	74	3	0.96
1	2	71	0.97
	0.97	0.96	0.97

The top entry in the third column is the sensitivity; the value below that is the specificity. The entry at the bottom of column two is the positive predictive value (PPV); the last entry in column three is the predictive negative value (PNV), and the lower right-hand corner is the overall classification accuracy.

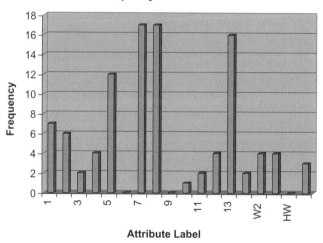

Figure 4.4 Frequency plot for all attributes from the rules (17 in total) corresponding to the legitimate login entries. Please note that there are a total of 392 instances of all 17 rules for legitimate login attempts (Source: Revett et al., 2005 WIC/ACM (403). © ICGePress University of East London)

in 100% of the rules 7, 8, and 13 occurred in 94.6% of the rules, and attribute set 5, 7, 8, and 13 occurred in 72.4% of all instances of the rules (392 instances of 17 rules). This key result indicates that a subset of the attributes, primarily 5, 7, 8, and 13 are the most frequent occurring attributes and may therefore serve as a signature for a legitimate login attempt, for this particular login. We performed this same analysis on the illegitimate login attempts, which we summarize with regard to the attribute frequency in Figure 4.5.

The analysis of the non-legitimate login rules is not as straightforward as for the legitimate login rules. For one, there are many more of them – 175 versus 17 for the legitimate login attempt rules (this excludes the nondeterministic rule set consisting of 260 rules). In addition, the average rule length increased from five attributes to eight. Even with these differences,

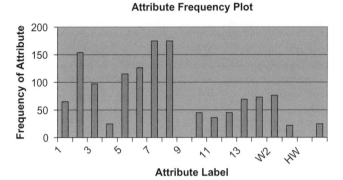

Figure 4.5 Attribute label versus frequency for illegitimate login attempts. Note that the total number of unique rules for the deterministic non-legitimate access classification is 175. The values indicate the number of occurrence(s) of each attribute in the total rule base (Source: Revett et al., 2005 WIC/ACM (403). © ICGePress University of East London)

we can account for 65% of the data by focusing on attributes 2, 3, 5, 6, 7, and 8 a reduction of 6/16 attributes (63.5%). Lastly, there were a significant number of nondeterministic rules which were not able to map attribute values to specific decision classes. There were a total of 260 of such rules, and their examination proved to be quite useful as they highlighted bordering cases between the decision classes. Specifically, we found that in many instances, the same attributes that were significant in the crisp rule set were mapped to different decision classes. After careful, inspection, we found that the difference was based on the magnitude of the attribute which in this decision table represents the digraph time. For the non-legitimate login attempts, all digraphs were on the low end of the discretization range. For the legitimate login attempts, this trend generally held as well, accept for digraphs 5 and 7. It was found unanimously (see Table 4.13 for details) that for the legitimate user, the digraph values for attributes 5 and 7 were sufficient to distinguish the login attempt in virtually 100% of the cases, that is, the typing speed, reflected in the digraph values, was sufficient to distinguish a valid from an invalid login attempt, when combined with a specific digraph pattern. In this particular case, the combination of typing speed for digraphs 5 and 7 was sufficient to discriminate between legitimate owners and attackers/non-legitimate owners of the login ID.

In this pilot study, rough sets was deployed to datamine a small database of keystroke-based biometric data – using only digraph times. The resultant decision rules were able to predict with a high degree of accuracy whether the attempt was legitimate or (97% or more classification accuracy). The most interesting result from this study indicates that the digraph times and specific digraphs (see Table 4.13 for details of the rules) were sufficient to determine whether a user was legitimate. As can be seen in Table 4.7, the decision class "1" – the non-legitimate owners, took the least amount of time in entering the characters of their login ID, compared to that of a non-legitimate owner. In addition to typing speed, there appears to be unique digraphs that are sufficient to distinguish the actual owner versus an imposter – the essence of keystroke dynamics. This implies that instead of using all of the digraphs in a signature for verification, we may only require a subset of them, depending on the particular login ID characteristics of the owner. This implies that all decision thresholds must be generated locally for each user and for each particular attribute collected for a given user. This

Table 4.13 A random sample of six rules (generated filtering on support ≥20)

Rule	Decision
T2([*,391)) AND T3([*,399)) AND T5([*,238)) AND T6([*,282)) AND T7([*,274)) AND T8([*,235)) AND T12([*,368)) AND T13([*,317) AND W1([*,704)) ⇒	0
T1([*,391)) AND T2([*,269)) AND T3([*,399)) AND T4([*,274)) AND T5([*,238)) AND T7([*,274)) AND T8([*,235)) AND T13([*,317)) ⇒	0
T2([*,269)) AND T3([*,399)) AND T5([*,238)) AND T6([*,282)) AND T7([*,274)) AND T8([*,235)) AND TT([*,4204)) ⇒	0 and 1
T2([*,269)) AND T4([*,274)) AND T5([*,238)) AND T6([*,282)) AND T7([*,274)) AND T8([*,235)) AND T13([*,317)) AND W1([*,704)) ⇒	0 and 1
T3([*,399)) AND T5([246, 289)) AND T7([274,*)) AND T8([*,235)) AND T12([*,368)) AND T13([*,317)) ⇒	1
T5([246–289)) AND T7([274, *) AND T8([*,235)) AND T11([*,430)) AND T12([*,368)) AND T13([*,317)) ⇒	1

Note that there is a mixture of deterministic (with a single decision "1" or "0") and nondeterministic rules with two decisions: "1" and "0." The "*" refers to either 0 if it appears on the left of a tuple, or the maximal value following discretization if it appears on the right end of a tuple. All rules are generated in conjunctive normal form from discretized data. (Source: Revett et al., 2005 WIC/ACM (403). © ICGePress University of East London)

reduction in the number of attributes that must be stored and searched through reduces the computational load of the verification system. The use of rules generated from rough sets-based classifiers can be enhanced by the addition of more attributes into the decision table. With these encouraging results, we are expanding our analysis using much larger datasets, both in terms of the number of objects, but also by the inclusion of additional attributes. We hope to discover what attributes are critical for particular login IDs in order to tailor the system so that it can emphasize those keystroke dynamic features that are indicative of the legitimate owner. For instance, in addition to individual digraphs associated with particular keys, we also investigated obtaining composite attributes such as the total time and half time for the entry of the login ID. Although these attributes did not appear significantly in the rule set, there was clearly a trend for these higher-order attributes to segregate across different class decision boundaries. We will continue to explore the addition of higher-order attributes into our decision table in order to help increase the classification accuracy of our biometrics-based security enhancement system.

The studies cited in this chapter all work with raw data derived from a user's typing style. This data is used to generate a model, which is used as a reference in a classification algorithm. One critical issue is the security of the stored reference profiles. If these can be ascertained, then it is feasible for an attacker to extract all the required information to hack into a user's account. Monrose proposed a mechanism that makes this task virtually impossible – and termed their approach *password hardening* (Monrose et al., 2001). Instead of storing the login details along with the desired reference profile, Monrose stores an extended version of the login details that directly incorporates the required profile information, in encrypted format. Monrose claims that "they provide no additional protection against an attacker who captures system information related to user authentication and then conducts an off-line dictionary attack to find the password" (Monrose et al., 20002, p. 70). The essence of their idea is to "salt" the password by adding to it information in encrypted format that is difficult to de-encrypt, yet contains sufficient information to allow the authentication process to proceed to completion. As is required for keystroke dynamics-based authentication, the "salt" is a function of the typing characteristics of the legitimate owner of the login details. If these vary to an appreciable degree from the reference value, then the user will not be authenticated. To generate the hardened password, the typical login features discussed in previous studies are gathered whenever the person logs into the computer system. The authors claim that what is central to their scheme are *distinguishing features*, as measured using some statistical metric in this case (such as whether or not the value falls within the CI). This process ensures that the search space for an attacker must include the typing variability features inherent to the users when entering their login details. The variability must be quantified such that it can be mapped into a form that is suitable for incorporation into the user's login details, ideally in an encrypted format. In essence, the authors proposed the use of a secret sharing scheme, similar to that of Shamir (1979). The results from this study indicate that the ability of an attacker to gain full access to the system has been considerably reduced. The authors presented relative information regarding the exact degree of enhanced difficulty this system provides but did not provide any direct data indicating how this system provides enhanced protection from a dictionary attack. But clearly, any encryption method will serve to slow down this sort of attack.

The surveys presented so far only scratch the surface of the research efforts published in the field of keystroke dynamics-based user authentication. Space has provided a practical limit to how much of the work can be presented in a single chapter on the subject. The general consensus is that this technology can provide a considerable amount of security within a totally software-based approach. For instance, fast fingerprint-based methodologies provide an EER on the order of 5%, consistent with the values generated from a keystroke dynamics-based approach, but without the requirement for specialized hardware. This is indeed an impressive result by itself. But these sort of results do not appear to occur consistently across studies. The variability is substantial, with FAR values ranging from virtually 0% to 40%. What is the reason for such a range of values? Is it that the data is simply not reproducible? Is the approach inherently variable, or is it due to methodological considerations? It is this author's opinion that we cannot address these issues until the methodologies have been sorted properly. The methodologies employed in most studies in this domain are highly variable to say the least. Studies employ different number of users, a variety of attributes, users with a variety of skill levels, from professional typists to students at university, and a wide range of classification algorithms, with their inherent variability in parameter space. Lastly, the input data used for these studies are so variable that it would seem a difficult task indeed to compare the results of two studies, let alone produce unequivocal conclusions as to the viability of this line of research. It is interesting to note that there is no dataset available at the University of California, Irvine (UCI) database for classification algorithm studies (http://www.uci.edu/). Please note that this author has recently made a request to upload a dataset to this site in order that a variety of classification schemes can use this data to provide a systematic appraisal of the algorithmic process. To this end, a paper published by myself and colleagues is presented as the last paper in this series of reviews, which focuses on the need for an – a working definition of the processes by which researchers deploy keystroke dynamics-based user authentication as a valid line of research. This paper is simply the request for a dialogue

– it is certainly not definitive, but it asks the right questions. It is up to us, as members of this research community, to get together and decide if this topic is simply fodder for conference publications, or is it a legitimate area of research?

4.6 Standards

As discussed in Chapter 1, biometric industry standards are essential for generating an atmosphere where data can be shared – and even more – that multiple biometric technologies can be integrated into a proper multimodal system. In addition to simply storing format type, a considerable amount of additional information is required in order to allow various implementations of any behavioral biometric solutions to be shared among various institutions. For instance, with respect to keystroke dynamics, the exact nature of the attributes such as digraphs and trigraphs, durations must be known in order to compare results across different authentication schemes. In addition, there are several different methods for acquiring digraphs (see Figure 4.1). For instance – do you count the press event or the release event as the starting point? The measurement accuracy (temporal resolution) is another required attribute which may vary depending on which algorithm is utilized in extracting timing information (low-level assembly code versus Visual Basic, for instance). In addition to the attribute extraction process, how the data was acquired during the testing phase of the algorithm design is an extremely critical factor. This issue is analogous to the experimental design module in the microarray gene expression data Microarray gene expression data (MGED) ontology. There is currently no universal method for alpha and beta testing of keystroke/mouse stroke/point dynamics. The accuracy of the resulting biometric is dependent on the results obtained during the development phase of the software. A considerable number of alpha tests are performed – followed by one or more beta tests before the system is ready for production and distribution.

With respect to keystroke dynamics, there are several critical issues when testing an implementation. For instance, how many subjects should be used in the study to validate the results statistically? This issue is compounded by the need for subjects to act as authentic users (to measure FRR) and imposters (to easure FAR). This is a critical factor not only in the design phase but also when researchers report their results. Herein lies a conundrum that requires resolution: many researchers report results of tests they have performed using their fully implemented biometric system. What happens if the results are not reasonable for a particular sample population? Generally speaking, most researchers will attempt to determine the factors that are responsible for generating unacceptable results and tweak the system appropriately. But in essence, this is really an ongoing part of the testing phase. The issue here is that many biometric systems reported in the literature are *still* in the development phase. Therefore, comparing one biometric implementation versus another should take into account exactly *how* the testing is to be performed. In addition to a variable number of subjects, what protocol should be used for generating FRR/FAR results? In our research, we have found that when generating data for FRR, it is important to simulate as much as possible the actual environment the system will be used in. For instance, if you assume 100 self-login (for generating FRR) data are appropriate, how do you schedule these self-logins be attempted? Clearly, 100 continuous logins is inappropriate as it does not emulate the way users log in during the course of a given day. Our recommendation is to have several trials at various sessions during the course of a 5 day period (Revett et al., 2007). A morning, noon, and early evening schedule with a minimal number of logins at each of the three sessions (5–10) is the most appropriate regime for a typical office environment. Other environments might vary from this regime, and hence the testing protocol must emulate any particular regime it is to be deployed in. Similar issues exist when making FAR determinations. One has to consider whether the "three strikes and you are out" rule applies. If so, asking a test participant to login 100 times in a single session into a given account produces meaningless results. There is also the issue when multiple accounts exist – do the test subjects test each account randomly? Do they test a specific account *N* times before moving onto the next account? Does switching between different accounts impact the results because of possible confounding effects caused by residual learning from previous accounts? These are again critical issues – and will have a potentially significant impact on the quality of the data that is generated from these experiments.

4.7 Conclusions

The most important conclusion to be derived from this brief survey of the keystrokes dynamics-based literature is that it works – examples of implementations with extremely small values for FAR/FRR exist. This is a very promising result, indicating that in many cases, this technology provides the same measure of security provided by moderate physiological implementations such as fingerprint scanners. Whether the technology will be able to compete with high-end physiological biometrics such as iris scanners is a matter of further research. It should be remembered that keystroke dynamics is a software-only biometric that adds an invisible layer of security. It can be deployed in a variety of scenarios, and in particular is very well situated to be deployed within an e-commerce-based (remote access) platform. In such a scenario, users can be authenticated over the Internet, without the need to purchase any special hardware.

What is also clear is that the performance is dominated by two factors: the extracted attributes and the classification algorithm. The principal attributes utilized in virtually all keystroke dynamics-based authentication systems are *n*-graphs, dwell times, typing time, and typing speed. Typing time refers to the time taken to type in the login ID, password, and possibly their combination. Whether these attributes are collected via a short text or long text entry, or whether a continuous extraction method is employed does not have a significant impact on the classification error. There are only a few derivative attributes reported in the literature such as the edit distance, power law terms, and slope shape. Together, these attributes represent the typing style of a particular user. A critical issue in their use as a discriminating factor is their inherent variability – an issue that may hinder this technology as a viable candidate for authentication. From the results of the implementation survey presented in this chapter, much of the variability can be removed from the data, provided the sample space is sufficient. Outliers can be removed either by a global or local process. Generally speaking, most modern approaches apply a local method, where each attribute is assessed directly for the variability associated with it, and this process is repeated for all attributes, and for each user. With the data preprocessed in this manner, a number of sophisticated machine learning algorithms have been applied quite successfully. These algorithms range in complexity from basic statistical tests (i.e. *t*-test) to SVMs. In addition, hierarchical or heterarchical techniques have been applied, rendering an extremely accurate classification scheme producing EER at approximately 1%. With modern day computer technology, even the sequential application of several machine learning algorithms can be performed within acceptable time frames for online user authentication to occur. The technology appears to be ready for deployment, and indeed there are several commercial products in the market such as Psylock™ and BioPassword™, among others. Still, the question remains – can this technology be driven further, with the aim of reducing still further FAR/FRR values? Unlike physiological biometrics per se, behavioral biometrics is more dynamic – as it is not based on the assumption of constancy as is the case for fingerprints, face recognition, and related technologies. Can we exploit this key difference between the two forms of biometrics? Or is a multimodal approach, where a variety of different biometrics are combined, enhancing the strengths of each broad class of biometrics? This important issue is discussed in more detail in Chapter 7 of this text.

I think the answer is yes – but requires that the research community enters into a more collaborative approach. For instance, there are no consistent protocols by which researchers in the field perform their experiments. Studies employ a variety of participants, with a variety of enrollment methods, and a range of attributes. This makes comparing results from different studies virtually impossible. In order to facilitate the transfer of information within the research community, standards such as the Keystroke Dynamics Format (Table 4.14) for Data Interchange (INCITS M1/05-0303) should be adhered to (see Reynolds, 2005 for details on this standard). This standard has been specifically designed to allow keystroke dynamics-based authentication systems to be interoperable with other CBEFF compliant biometrics. If more researchers adhered to this standard, then possibly it could be extended such that it could serve the majority needs of researchers within the field. It would allow data to be shared among the relevant community, for the purpose of testing various classification algorithms. It would certainly reduce the duplication and multiplicity of efforts that appear so frequently within this literature. It should be noted that even though there is possibly a financial interest in maintaining a proprietary stance with respect to the development of standards and the sharing of data, BioPassword™ has spearheaded the development of Keystroke Dynamics Format for Data Interchange. It is up to the research community to make use of this standard and to extend/modify it as the need arises.

4.8 Research Topics

It is hoped that this brief survey of keystroke dynamics-based authentication approaches will generate an interest in furthering this exciting research area. There are a number of areas that could be addressed by researchers at all levels: both at the undergraduate and graduate level, as well as professional scientific practitioners. Below is a small selection of broad topics that could be considered:

1. Exploration of the attribute space – are we limited to dwell time and key-press latencies only? What about second-order and higher-order attributes?
2. Examination of the enrollment process – are there other formats for enrollment that might provide a more accurate and yet flexible model of the user's typing dynamics?

Table 4.14 Summary of the Keystroke Dynamics Format, providing the named fields, size (in bytes), valid values, and summary notes (Source: Reynolds, 2005)

Field	Size	Valid values	Notes
Format identifier	4 bytes	0xB445200 ("K," "D," "R" 0×0)	"KDR" keystroke dynamics record
Version of this standard	4 bytes	N n n 0×0	"XX"
Length of total record in bytes	2 bytes	28-65535	0x001c to 0xFFFF
CBEFF product identifier	4 bytes		CBEFF PID (registry managed by IBIA)
Input type identifier	1 byte		See document (table 6.4.5)*
Manufacturer's type ID	2 bytes		See document (table 6.4.6)*
Model type identifier	2 bytes		See document (table 6.4.7)*
Keyboard country identifier	2 bytes		Refer to ISO 3166
Biometric process identification	1 byte		See document (table 6.4.9)*
Biometric process status	1 byte		See document (table 6.4.10)*
Input code type identifier	1 byte		See document (table 6.4.11)*
Time resolution	1 byte		Millisecond, microsecond, or nanosecond
Number of input events	2 bytes		
Reserved byte	1 byte		Set to 0
Input event types	1 byte		See document (table 6.5.1)*
Input code	1 or 2 bytes		As determined by input code type ID
Time stamp	4 or 8 bytes		As determined by the time resolution field

Please note that the items in the last column with "*" refer to tables in the reference (see Reynolds, 2005).

3. Exploration of other classification algorithms – either alone or in combination, with respect to enhancing the classification accuracy.
4. Development of enhanced data format standards that extend the functionality of INCITS M1/05-0303.
5. Examine how keystroke dynamics may be deployed as part of a multimodal biometric scheme.

5

Graphical-Based Authentication Methods

5.1 Introduction to the Graphical Authentication Approach

Textual-based passwords are by far the most common form of knowledge-based authentication. Most people are used to providing a password in order to gain access to computer accounts or to gain access to automated teller machines (ATMs). They are easy to implement – and do not require any special hardware other than the use of a keyboard/keypad device. Does the user community feel that a password-based system provides the protection that they need? Considering the number of reports indicating how relatively easy it is to hack into trusted computer systems, which are password protected, one might begin to wonder just how safe they really are. The question addressed in this chapter is whether an alternative to textual-based password, *graphical passwords*, can enhance the level of security of trusted computer systems. To address this question, a brief discussion of the security issues associated with textual-based passwords is presented, focusing on usability and memorability.

Numerous studies have provided unequivocal evidence that the level of security afforded by textual-based passwords is directly influenced by its content (Brostoff & Sasse, 2000, Wiedenbeck et al., 2005a,b), that is, there are variations in the quality of a password. There are obvious features such as password length, which typically varies from six to eight characters. This value reflects the prevailing view from years of research in cognitive science, and to a certain degree, human–computer interaction (HCI) research, which can be summarized by Miller's (1956) law of 7 ± 2 – the amount of information that we can hold in working memory. However, the issue of Miller's "magical number" is still a matter strongly debated within the cognitive science research (Posner, 1969, Wickens, 1984, Cowan, 2001). Current research indicates that the magical number may be closer to 4 ± 1, as opposed to Miller's 7. In addition to length, the character composition will have a significant impact on the ability of an attacker to try and guess the password. There are typically 95 printable characters on a standard PC keyboard, and hence the number of possible combinations of strings of length 8 is 95^8 (6.6×10^{15}). This is a substantial space to search through – though not impossible in a comprehensive off-line attack, using a collection of machines and enough time. What matters is the fraction of this search space that is actually used in the generation of passwords.

Behavioral Biometrics: A Remote Access Approach. Kenneth Revett
© 2008 John Wiley & Sons, Ltd.

For instance, in the often cited Klein's (1990) case study, approximately 25% of the 14 000 passwords were cracked using a dictionary containing three million entries. These dictionaries contain collections of passwords that are ordered by likelihoods and generally contain words typically found in dictionaries, along with common passwords obtained through user surveys. Such an attack can take less than 1 second on a fast single processor (see Van Oorschot & Thorpe, 2005 for a detailed analysis of a similar study). These and similar studies indicate that the actual password space utilized by typical users in the generation of their passwords does not encompass the full space available to them (Manber, 1994, Monrose et al., 1997, Brown et al., 2004). This is probably a direct reflection of the requirement to memorize your password – making help desk calls is generally frowned upon! The issue is confounded by having to remember several passwords – and related pieces of access granting information such as PIN numbers, etc. How can these issues be circumvented in a manner that enhances security without placing undue cognitive constraints on users?

What is required is a password system that utilizes a significant amount of the possible search space while maintaining a level of memorability that suits the typical user. Blonder (1996) suggested the use of graphical passwords in his 1996 patent application. His suggestion was simple – graphical-based passwords can overcome the memory difficulties associated with textual passwords. It is (and was at the time) common knowledge that people are much better at recognition than recall (Paivio et al., 1976, Card et al., 1983, Cowan, 2001). Further, people are better at recognizing images than words. There is a very large body of research in the cognitive science domain that can be called upon to begin to address the issues of memorability (see Cowan, 2001 for a comprehensive survey). The issue is how can recognition or recall be implemented in a textual-based password system? The possibility of cues could be deployed to assist users in remembering their password – but how are we to implement this in a simple and time-efficient manner? Pictures/images were therefore suggested as a means for cueing the user – relying on our superior ability to recognize and/or recall images/pictures over text.

Exactly how much easier is it for humans to work reliably with images as opposed to characters? That pictures appear to be more memorable than words is captured in the phrase "a picture is worth a thousand words!" This common place idea has been the subject of numerous scientific investigations to determine if this is indeed the case, and if so, what is the underlying neurophysiological basis for this often cited phenomenon? It has been termed the "picture superiority effect" in the cognitive science literature (Paivio et al., 1968, Paivio & Csapo, 1973, Nelson et al., 1977, Monrose, et al., 2001, McBride & Dosher, 2002). One of the first theories of the picture superiority effect was suggested by Paivio in 1968. This theory, termed the dual-coding theory, proposes that pictures are more readily remembered because they are stored in two different encoding formats, as opposed to a single format for words (which are only coded verbally). Pictures are encoded both by a verbal aspect *and* an image code (McBride et al., 2002). Having two distinct routes for accessing information increases the likelihood that it will be retrieved during a memory task (such as identifying elements of your login credentials). Nelson and colleagues (Nelson et al., 1977) introduced the sensory-semantic theory to explain the picture superiority effect. He claimed that pictures were superior to words in two fundamental ways. First, pictures contain superior perceptual information compared to words. Second, pictures allow access to meaning (in a semantic sense) more readily than words. To determine if these hypotheses were supported by the data, he performed experiments examining the effect of using pictures that possessed differing degrees of similarity to one another. The results indicate that pictures which were dissimilar to one another were retrieved more readily than pictures with more similarity (Nelson, 1979). This supports the basic underlying assumption that pictures are encoded by their information content, and pictures that are dissimilar should therefore cause less interference and hence should be retrieved more readily. There are a host of other theories that have been reported, and a full in-depth analysis is beyond the scope of this chapter (the interested reader is directed toward McBride et al., 2002 for a comprehensive overview of this topic). What can be stated in summary is that pictures elicit a deeper conceptual processing stream than words do. A likely explanation of this effect will involve processes that encompass both the encoding and retrieval systems interacting at some level to enhance recognition and/or picture recall. These scientific studies form the basis for the design and development of image-based (graphical) passwords.

Before exploring a sample of popular case studies, a taxonomic description will provide a framework for analyzing the different approaches reported in the literature. Monrose and Reiter (2005) describe a set of taxonomies for graphical passwords according to the following: those based on image recognition, tapping or drawing, and image interpretation. In this chapter, tapping, which is essentially clicking on a region within an image, is treated as sub-image selection using the mouse and will not therefore be treated as a separate category. In addition, image interpretation can be considered as an example of cued recall, and hence in this chapter, the taxonomy is reduced to recall and recognition strategies. Table 5.1 provides a summary of much of the work in this field, highlighting the principal developers, the name of their product, and a brief description of each implementation.

In addition to recall or recognition of the graphical password, another feature that serves to categorize implementations is the graphical environment from which the users select their password. The presentation environment consists of a collection of small images (selection images) presented either completely within a single image frame or across multiple image frames. As a side note, generally speaking, multi-frame image systems rely on the use of recognition, while single-frame image systems rely on recall. With single image implementations such as Passlogix, the users are presented with a collection of icons/images contained within a larger single image frame and they are required to select a number of icons/images or regions within the image to serve as their password. This is essentially a recall task (possibly cued). The other approach, typified by Passfaces, is to present the user with a multi-frame set of images, where the selection images are usually presented in some geometric arrangement, and the user is required to select one image from each of the series of images. This is clearly a recognition-based task.

Typically, users are allowed to select their own password during the course of the enrollment process, as opposed to having the system generate a password for the users. This is in keeping with the enhanced memorability of graphical passwords. Users have more freedom of choice in their password selection. The same sort of result (small sampling of the total password space during password selection) typically occurs with textual-based passwords, but they are easier to crack using dictionaries and related off-line attack methods (see Chapter 4 for a discussion). With graphical-based passwords, off-line attacks are more difficult and the search space is potentially much larger than textual passwords, so users are allowed more freedom of choice. In general, one must bear in mind that graphical passwords, per se, as a biometric tool, operate under very different assumptions compared to keystroke dynamics and related biometrics.

Table 5.1 A summary of several popular graphical password-based user authentication systems. (Source: Suo et al., 2003)

Techniques	Usability		Security issues	
	Authentication process	Memorability	Password space	Possible attack methods
Text-based password	Type in password, can be very fast	Depends on the password. Long and random passwords are hard to remember	94^K (there are 94 printable characters excluding SPACE, N is the length of the password). The actual password space is usually much smaller.	Dictionary attack, brute force search, guess, spyware, shoulder surfing, etc.
Perrig and Song [9]	Pick several pictures out of many choices. Takes longer to create than text password	Limited user study showed that more people remembered pictures than text-based passwords	N!/K!(N-K)! (N is the total number of pictures; K is the number of pictures in the graphical password)	Brute force search, guess, shoulder-surfing
Sobrado and Birget [12]	Click within an area bounded by pre-registered picture objects, can be very fast	Can be hard to remember when large numbers of objects are involved.	N!/K!(N-K)! (N is the total number of picture objects; K is the number of pre-registered objects)	Brute force search, guess
Man et al. [14] Hong et al. [13]	Type in the code of pre-registered picture objects; can be very fast	Users have to memorize both picture objects and their codes. More difficult than text-based password	Same as the text based password	Brute force search, spyware
Passface [15]	Recognize and pick the pre-registered pictures; takes longer than text-based password	Faces are easier to remember, but the choices are still predictable	N^K (K is the number of rounds of authentication, N is the total number of pictures at each round)	Dictionary attack, brute force search, guess, shoulder surfing

Reference	Description	Memorability	Password space	Attacks
Janse et al. [20–22]	User register a sequence of images; slower than text-based password	Pictures are organized according to different themes to help users remember	N^K (N is are total number of pictures, K is the number of pictures in the graphical password. N is small due to the size limit of mobile devices)	Brute force search, guess, shoulder surfing
Takada and Koike [23]	Recognize and click on the pre-registered images; slower than text-based password. Slower than text-based password	Users can use their favorite images; easy to remember than system assigned pictures	$(N+1)^K$ (K is the number of rounds of authentication, N is the total number of pictures at each round)	Brute force search, guess, shoulder surfing
Jermyn et al. [24], Thorpe and van Oorschot [25–26]	Users draw something on a 2D grid	Depends on what users draw. User studies showed the drawing sequence is hard to remember	Password space is larger than text based password. But the size of DAS password space decreases significantly with fewer strokes for a fixed password length	Dictionary attack, shoulder surfing
Syukri et al. [30]	Draw signatures using mouse. Need a reliable signature recognition program.	Very easy to remember, but hard to recognize	Infinite password space	Guess, dictionary attack, shoulder surfing
Goldberg et al. [27]	Draw something with a stylus onto a touch sensitive screen	Depends on what users draw	Infinite password space	Guess, dictionary attack, shoulder surfing
Blonder [31], Passlogix [32], [33], [34], Wiedenbeck, et al. [35–37]	Click on several pre-registered locations of a picture in the right sequence.	Can be hard to remember	N^K (N is the number of pixels or smallest units of a picture, K is the number of locations to be clicked on)	Guess, brute force search, shoulder surfing

The principal driving assumptions behind graphical passwords are the following: the password space is potentially larger than textual-based passwords; they are harder to divulge by writing them down; they are potentially more resistant to shoulder surfing, and they are easier to remember. It should be noted that most of the implementations presented in this chapter do not have the added facility which keystroke dynamics offer to textual-based passwords: a true underlying biometric facility. If someone were able to shoulder surf and acquire your graphical password, then the user would be able to access the system – as there is nothing inherently individual about the way these systems expect the password to be entered. There is nothing equivalent to the *selection dynamics* that is prevalent within the keystroke dynamics implementations in most graphical password systems (for an exception, see Chapter 6 for a discussion of Match-n-Go). The order in which users select their password entries may, in many instances, not be maintained, but this is implementation dependent. Generally speaking, most recognition-based systems employ an inherent ordering to the selection of the password elements. One must move through a selection of image frames from which the user selects the appropriate element of the password. Whether this implies a serial order depends on the particular implementation – as it could be possible to start from any image frame and move back and forth. For recall-based systems, users typically select their password from a single image frame, and the order of selection is generally considered to reduce the size of the password space (see Monrose & Reiter, 2005 for a discussion on this issue). Therefore, most of the analyses of graphical-based password implementations rely on a different set of metrics to evaluate various implementations.

Monrose and colleagues rely on the use of graphical password space and its impact on potential off-line attacks as a measure of enhanced security (Monrose et al., 1997, 2001). Very few analyses of graphical password systems report false acceptance rate (FAR) values, for instance (see the studies by Revett in Chapter 7 for an exception). The concept of FAR will not exist in this domain if there is no added layer of security beyond the knowledge of the password. This is exactly analogous to plain textual-based passwords. The real protection is afforded by the implementation of the principal driving forces of shoulder-surfing resistance, large password space, and the awkwardness of transcribing them. Therefore, the sample case studies will provide quantitative information along these lines if available. Principal examples of each of these schemes will be presented in this chapter, in the form of detailed case studies.

5.2 Recognition-Based Techniques

In recognition-based systems, users select their password by choosing a collection of images (typically three to six) from a database of images. The images may be realistic images of common objects or they may be randomly generated images with no correspondence to real objects. The images are presented to the user typically one per image frame, and the users are required to identify (by clicking) each element of their password as they are presented, usually in a predetermined order. To enhance the difficulty of the identification process to possible intruders, the password elements are mixed with a collection of decoy or distractor images. These distractor images may belong to the same categories as the password image or may belong to an entirely different category. This factor has an influence on memorability and will be discussed as applicable within the case studies presented below. Another issue is whether the distractor images are preserved across login attempts. That is, are the distractor images the same for each of the image frames presented with the password images? This is typically the case, but the order of the distractor (and password images) images is randomized to prevent *selection attacks*. This is an attack where users observe someone logging in (shoulder surfing) enough times such that they are able to see the images that are constantly present; even if part of the password is learned this way, the password search space can be greatly reduced. Let's move on to discuss some prototypical recognition-based systems, starting off with Passfaces™.

Arguably, the prototypical recognition-based graphical password system is Passfaces™, produced and licensed by Real User Corporation. This multi-image graphical authentication system relies on our ability to recognize faces. The system presents a collection of face images, in a square array, typically 3×3. Each grid of faces contains one element of the users' password, which they selected from a large collection of faces that constitutes their password. Typical passwords contain four to five images, which are selected by the user, and are reinforced during a short enrollment period. The total password space is 59 049, when the password consists of five face images. This is more than the possible number combinations of four decimal digits typical of a four-digit PIN. This value is obtained by the formula indicated in equation 5.1, where P and Q are the image dimensions (e.g. 3×3), and M is the number of images comprising the user's password. When the images are

$$[(P \times Q)/M \times (P \times Q - M)]^N \tag{5.1}$$

presented in a grid (e.g. 3×3), the decoy images are kept constant, but their position is varied. This helps reduce a shoulder surfer from determining which of the images belong to the actual password, as all that would be required is to view which image occurs consistently. To reduce the likelihood of successful shoulder surfing, one could increase the image size (to say 5×5), or alternatively, one could increase the number of images in the password. The choice of a 3×3 grid is a compromise between user memorability and constraints such as physical screen size. The creators of the system instead proposed for other options to reduce the success rate of shoulder surfing. For one, they suggested that the images could be displayed for a brief time interval (0.5 second), and a mask could be superimposed on the entire image. The brief display time is long enough for the authentic user but reduces the likelihood of success for the shoulder surfer. In addition, a mask, in the form of a common mask face, could also be applied with the brief display interval to reduce the success rate of shoulder surfing. These features were not properly investigated in their study, nor by any other as far as this author is aware of. The results published by Real User Corporation were very promising, even after a long delay between enrolling and subsequent authentication. Their results indicate that "if the user is able to log into the system at least twice in the first 2 weeks following enrollment, users were able to log into the system again after more than six months of not using the system" (Real User Corporation, 2001). Whether these results hold true generally is a matter of further research. Fortunately, there has been a considerable amount of research investigating the use of Passfaces™. Some of the key results are presented next (Figure 5.1).

Brostoff and Sasse (2000) published a paper reporting the results of a comparative study between Passfaces™ and textual-based passwords. The authors wished to investigate how well graphical-based passwords compared to traditional passwords, and employed Passfaces as their graphical password system. In this study, 34 participants took part in field trial over

Figure 5.1 A sample of a login image from Passfaces™. One of the face images is an element in the user's login ID. Each screen presents one element of the user's password (Source: PassFaces Website: www.passfaces.com)

a period of 10 weeks. The participants were university students, who were assigned system-generated passwords (which they were allowed to change) and were also granted access to a local implementation of Passfaces. The system was integrated into their coursework submissions, so each participant had a legitimate need to log into the system, at specific times (i.e. when their assignments were due).

The participants were assigned randomly to one of two groups: the PW-PF or the PF-PW (PF = Passfaces and PW = password). The study ran for 10 weeks, and approximately halfway through, the users switched to the other group for the remainder of the study. For the PW group, users were allowed to select their own password, after being briefed about the need to use a secure password. After successfully logging in with their password two consecutive times, the users were considered to be enrolled into the system. For the PF group, users first selected the gender of the faces and then selected four faces to serve as their password. The participants were again required to enter their PF password without prompting, two consecutive times, after which they were considered enrolled into the system. The results from this study generated a login failure of 15.1% for password users (group PW) and 4.9% for Passface users (PF group). Login failure rates were collected in real time and were stored for subsequent analysis. In this case, a login failure was based on a single failure to input the correct password (textual or graphical). The authors did not specify if there was any time dependence effect, such as whether more of the login failures occurred at the beginning of the study and may have changed over time (i.e. any crossover effect). The results did demonstrate a significant order effect (using ANOVA) between the login problem rates of the PW-PF and the PF-PW groups (i.e. whether PW or PF was presented first). Further, the results indicate that the PW-PF group had a slightly (but significant) higher error rate (5.5%) with Passfaces, while the PW-PF group had an error rate of 4.3%. Lastly, the authors indicate the opposite effect with respect to passwords, with the PW-PF group yielding a login error rate of 7.1%, while the PF-PW group yielded a login error rate of 23.6%. The experiment also employed the use of reminders, which is a mechanism put in place to help reduce help desk calls for students who have forgotten their passwords. Participants employing the textual password system had 1/3 more reminder calls then the Passface group.

The results from this study indicate that the use of Passfaces yielded a smaller login error rate than the use of textual-based passwords. Unfortunately, several details have been omitted from this work that are necessary to make a full evaluation of its contribution to the literature. One would like to see a temporal profile of the errors. It could be that at the beginning, users were not used to a graphical method for authentication, and it took time for them to adjust. In addition, when users switched from one method to the other, there might have been a small adjustment period where the error rate was higher than normal. In part, the authors controlled for this by recording the number of reminders – but not all users might have opted for the reminder after a failed login attempt. A temporal profile of errors would serve to clearly indicate if these types of problems occurred during the course of the study. Another issue was the textual passwords that users choose – how secure were the selected passwords? What constraints were placed on their selection? In many organizations, there are strict rules regarding the acceptability of a password, such as its length, mixture of upper and lower case characters, etc. This information is vital if we are going to extrapolate the results from this study to textual passwords generically. Short of these issues, this was a very comprehensive study that directly evaluated textual versus graphical passwords, and the results were strongly in favor of the utility of Passfaces as a viable graphical authentication mechanism.

Other authors have investigated the use of Passfaces in terms of the inherent level of security with respect to off-line attacks (Davis et al., 2004, Monrose & Reiter, 2005). A principal concern with Passfaces is that with a password of five images, on a 3×3 grid, there are just over 59 000 total combinations (9^5) to search through to completely exhaust the search space. On a fast machine, this will take less then 1 minute to complete. In order to make the search space equivalent to that of an eight-character textual password would require 16 or 17 screen presentations. (Elftmann, 2006). This would clearly increase the time taken to enter the password – and increase the likelihood of failed logins beyond acceptable limits. In addition, the actual usable search space of Passfaces may be much more limited than the theoretical limit (see equation 5.1). Monrose and Reiter (2005) point out that people do not tend to exploit the full search space when selecting elements of their passwords. With the Passfaces system, there tends to be gender-specific biases; for instance, males tend to pick female models more often than females select male models. In addition, there are possibly other biases in face selection that might reduce the size of the password space. Monrose and Reiter report that there were significant "race effects," which reflect our inclination to remember people of the same race better than images of faces from different races. These and possibly other related factors may serve to reduce the size of the password space, rendering this technology vulnerable to attack.

Another example of a recognition-based graphical authentication system is the Déjà vu system (Dhamija & Perrig, 2000). The authors proposed the use of a graphical password system based on image recognition, which they argue is stronger than typical textual passwords. The system was developed to solve three specific requirements: i) authentication relies on recognition instead of precise recall; ii) the system prevents the user from selecting weak passwords, and iii) writing down the password becomes very difficult. The system works by generating a collection of images that are generated by Andrej Bauer's Random Art system, which generates a series of random art images using a formula that generates the images based on the selection of a seed (see Bauer, 1998). User select a subset of images (typically four) from the collection, which is termed their *portfolio*. The portfolio images are embedded within a larger collection of images, which serve as distractors or decoys. Typically, the system presents 25 total images, which include the password and decoy images. The images are presented in a randomized order every time the user attempts to authenticate. Users are allowed to practice entering their password, until they felt comfortable entering their password. The users authenticated by selecting the correct portfolio of images constituting their password. Note that each user is allowed a single attempt before a decision of acceptance/rejection is made when reporting any study results. An example of the Déjà vu interface is presented in Figure 5.2.

The authors conducted a study to evaluate the effectiveness of this system as an alternative to PIN and textual password-based authentication devices. The study employed 20 subjects, with a range of typing skills and computer experience. Measurements of the time required to enter the password (either PIN, textual password, or graphical) were recorded, and the failure

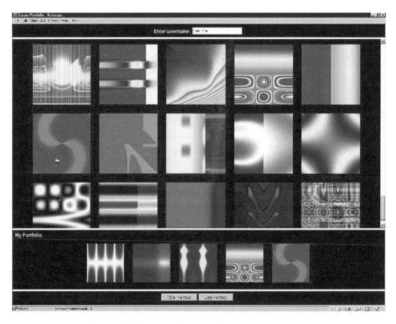

Figure 5.2 Random images used by Dhamija and Perrig's (2000) Déjà vu system. This figure depicts some of the random art generated from a seed using Bauer's (1998) Random Art system (Source: Dhamija and Perrig, 2000)

rates were measured on the day of training and 1 week later. Note that there is an implicit ordering in the password selection process. With respect to time to enter, the graphical version of their password took considerably longer than all other forms of password entry, both on the day of training and 1 week later. With respect to failed logins, the graphical system produced the lowest failure rate at both time points. Even after 1 week, the results indicate that 90% of all participants succeeded using their graphical authentication system, whereas only 70% succeeded using text-based PINS, and 75% were successful for textual password-based access. This was one of the first studies that explored the use of random images as opposed to realistic images or photographs of actual objects. One might expect that the memorability of a collection of abstract surreal images may be diminished relative to a collection of images of things we are familiar with and might see on a regular basis. The results indicate that, at least with the protocol used in their study, the error rate is generally quite acceptable, less than that for PIN or textual (six or more characters)-based passwords. Note that the authors of this study did not divulge much information regarding the details of the passwords, with respect to their adherence to enhanced security features.

As with all graphical-based authentication systems, users will have to spend more time selecting their passwords. In addition, it will take longer to enter your password (in this case 32 seconds for Déjà vu versus 15 and 18 seconds for PIN and textual passwords, respectively. There are also some security issues, with respect to the likelihood of a brute force attack, that need to be addressed as well. In the Déjà vu system, five images produce a search space equivalent to a four-digit PIN, when there are a total of 20 decoy images (25 on screen in total). The probability of guessing five images out of 25 is one in 15 504, compared to 10^4 possibilities for a four-digit decimal PIN. This is a very small search space that could easily be search through exhaustively. In addition, the issue of the seed, which must be stored in an unencrypted format, opens the system up to an off-line attack. Barring these issues in mind, this study indicates that the deployment of random images is a viable alternative to realistic images.

Another recognition-based graphical authentication system, called the Visual Identification Protocol (VIP), was proposed by De Angeli and colleagues (2003). This system was intended to provide improved user authentication within the self-service technology sector (such as PINs). The images were collections of photographs of real objects, which were displayed in color to the user during authentication. The images were displayed such that their arrangement was identical to the keys on a PIN. VIP1 and VIP2 consisted of 10 images, which included four that were the actual password, intermixed with six distractor images. In VIP1, the actual password images were always placed in the same position, but were allowed to vary in VIP2. Also note that by definition, the order of the entry of the password elements was important in this study, as the system was designed to investigate whether images were better than numbers for remembering a PIN. The images were selected from various semantic categories, such as flowers and rocks (De Angeli et al., 2003). Note that the semantic category of the distractors was different from the semantic content of the password images, unless stated otherwise. The VIP3 protocol was similar to VIP2, except that there were a total of 16 images, displayed in a 4×4 grid, containing four password images with 12 distractors from different semantic categories from the target images. De Angeli and colleagues (2003) performed a study to investigate the utility of this system with respect to attitudinal, cognitive, and usability issues. The study included 61 subjects who participated in a study that was designed to compare the use of the various versions of VIP and a simulated ATM device. The subjects were randomly assigned to one of the three protocols or a software-based ATM system (all systems were implemented using a touch screen). The subjects were allowed to enroll by entering their passwords 10 times successfully. Note that success or failure was based on three attempts. The users were then tested 40 minutes after enrollment and 1 week later to measure the memorability of their passwords with respect to each of the systems. The study revealed that graphical-based PINs were more effective with respect to memorability than numeric PINs, as measured at all time points in this study. The performance criteria were based on number of entry mistakes and the time taken to enter the password elements. The authors stated that the sources of error were associated with physical issues, such as the mechanics, double clicking on the image they wished to click on, as well as incorrect sequencing and selection, that is, the users were for the most aware of what image to select; they just found at times they made a mistake due to proximity issues. The number of incorrect selections appeared to be influenced by the scenario complexity, in that the selection error rate increased when going from VIP1 through to VIP3. The authors conclude that wrong-selection errors were principally due to physical proximity issues and/or interference effects. In the former case, items in the password that are close together may be accidentally pressed, yielding an incorrect password. The interference effects may be the result of the similarity between distractor and password entry images, and this effect increases with the complexity of the password images and the semantic content of the images. The interference effect needs to be properly addressed by a controlled study to investigate the effect it has on graphical password memorability. In addition, how does this issue scale when users have several graphical passwords?

As a final survey, Jansen and colleagues (2003) published work on their system, which they call Picture Password. This is a graphical single-image password system that is suitable for deployment on small mobile devices. The image space consists of a set of thumbnail graphics that has an underlying theme, such as "cats and dogs," or "sea and shore." The images can be presented in one of two ways. In one scenario, a single image covering the entire screen is presented after being partitioned into blocks (typically 5×6). The other approach is to generate a collection of thumbnail images (again 30 in a 5×6 grid layout), all different but from a common theme, such as "cats and dogs." Users select a theme and their password, which typically consists of eight images. The users then enroll into the system by entering their password a number of times correctly. After enrollment, the users are then ready to be authenticated. The password space is fairly small as it stands, with a password space of 30^8. In order to increase the size of the password space, the authors suggested adding the equivalent of a "shift key" to the password by allowing the user to select multiple thumbnail images at a time. This expands the number of elements from 30 to 930 (i.e. 30 single elements plus 30×30 composite elements) (Jansen et al., 2003). This increases the password space from 6.6×10^{11} to 5.6×10^{23}, a substantial search space to search through, even for an off-line attack. Note that a 12-character textual password has a space of approximately 5.4×10^{23}. This value is a theoretical limit, and it would be very unlikely that a user could remember all possible combinations of eight-set objects, and hence the password space is much lower than this value. In addition, even without the use of the shift operation, an eight-character graphical password is somewhat difficult to remember – though the authors do not provide any data to contradict this claim. Most typical graphical password systems employ four to five elements, which, depending on the system, may result in a fairly significant amount of forgetting.

It should be noted that picture password employs the National Institute of Standards (NIST) Secure Hash Algorithm (SHA) to compute a cryptographic hash (which results in a 20-byte binary value), which is used to store the user's password on the device itself. Only the hash result is stored on the device, obtained from the enrollment process and used for all subsequent authentication attempts. This system has some interesting qualities, but to date, there have not been any published large-scale studies from which to evaluate the performance of this system.

This brief summary of recognition-based systems is by no means complete. It is hoped that it has covered many of the major systems, many of which have been commercially deployed. These systems tend to be passive with respect to user engagement – selecting elements from the image based solely on recognition. Probably for this reason, multiple images are presented to enhance the security level by reducing shoulder surfing and augmenting the password space. The next section presents a series of case studies involving systems employing recall (or cued recall).

5.3 Recall-Based Techniques

Recall-based systems are typically single image frame systems, which require the user to interact with the system is some cognitively meaningful manner. These systems tend to be more variable than recognition-based systems. The password may be selected via a variety of methods, from clicking on a collection of images that have a memory property, such as telling a story, making a martini, to entering the combination to a safe or drawing a doodle/picture. In a broad sense, these systems too have an implicit order about them, at least during the selection process. Whether the order is used to authenticate the user is an implementation-specific detail. A distinction is often made between recall and cued recall. In this chapter, these two versions of recall-based identification are merely points on the same continuum and are grouped together under the recall umbrella. What follows is a brief survey of several examples of recall and cued recall-based systems.

It is generally held that Greg Blonder (1996) was the first to describe the development and deployment of graphical-based passwords in his 1996 patent application. In his system, a single complex image was presented to the user, which contained various hot spots – regions within the image that would have to be clicked using a mouse.

Each of these hot spots contained a tolerance region, which was a square region around each of the hot spots that was sufficient to activate the hot spot when clicked on (these are the *receptive fields* of the hot spot). Typically, the images were simple and familiar – such as the bust of a horse. The system allowed users to choose their picture and the position of the hot spots ("tap regions") that must be selected (clicked on) in an order-specific fashion. The order of selection is the principal reason why this system is considered to be recall based. Also note that the user could only click within the "tap regions." This flexibility added a personal touch to the selection of the password, ensuring that the system could be tailored to each user's preference(s). This factor may be more important than has been given notice in the literature.

Another example of a single-image system based on recall was proposed by Wiedenbeck in 2005, which was dubbed Passpoints (Wiedenbeck et al., 2005c). This work was essentially an extension of Blonder's work (Blonder, 1996), with the notable change that a user was allowed to click anywhere within the image (in Blonder's proposal, a user could only click within the tap regions). Wiedenstock published a report on a study involving 40 experienced computer users that compared the deployment of Passpoints passwords versus standard textual-based passwords (Wiedenbeck, 2005b, 2005c). The study examined the relative memorability of the two forms of passwords over a period of 4 weeks (times measured at the end of the first session, 1 week, and 4 weeks later). The participants were required to practice using their chosen passwords (both textual and graphical) until they were able to enter it 10 times. The results from this study can be summarized as follows: i) it was easier to create Passpoint passwords than textual-based passwords; ii) it took more trials to enter 10 correct entries with Passpoint than with textual-based passwords, and iii) it took considerably longer to enter the Passpoint password. The authors point out that the study participants were new to the use of graphical-based password schemes, which might have had a negative impact on the results. This is an important point – as many users may have to be trained to use such a system – especially if users have a mixture of different types of authentication protocols to follow, such as textual-based password, PINs, and graphical-based authentication schemes. One advantage of this system is the large password space it incorporates. For instance, with five click points on an image with 1025×752, the password space is somewhat larger than an eight-character textual password. This calculation assumes that the click area around each point had a resolution of 20×20 pixels. In order to increase the password space, the number of click points could be increased. This may cause memorability problems, and would therefore defeat the purpose of graphical-based passwords (Figure 5.3). A field study published by Chiasson and colleagues (2007) did indicate that the tolerance regions around each click point could be reduced to 9×9, without compromising login performance. The other option is to reduce the size of the selection window around each click point. This would probably increase the number of selection errors, which the authors stated was the principal reason for login failure. It should also be noted that this study is one of the few that allowed users to enter the password more than one time (four attempts were allowed in this study) before considering the success or failure of the authentication attempt.

Figure 5.3   The pool image used in the Passpoint system (Source: Wiedenbeck et al., 2005)

In addition, the studies by Wiedenbeck and colleagues (2005a,b,c) and Chiasson and colleagues (2007) examined whether the images used in the Passpoints system would have a significant effect on login success performance. The results from Wiedenbeck and colleagues indicate that login success rates were largely independent of the image category. In the Wiedenbeck study, four picture categories were employed: pool, mural, tea, and map (see Wiedenbeck et al., 2005a for details). The Biasson study, which investigated the effect of image category, employing a total of 17 images, found significant differences between image categories (Chiasson et al., 2007). The range of successful logins based on image category varied from 52% (for their "bee" image) to 94% for the "cars" image. Whether image category actually plays a role with respect to login success rate is still an issue for active research.

VisKey™ is a single-image recall-based graphical authentication system produced by SFR (http://www.sfr-software.de/cms/EN/pocketpc/viskey/). The images are realistic pictures that can be displayed on mobile devices (such as a PDA or phone). User must select a number of click points in the image (typically four) using a stylus or related input device in a specified order to enter their password. Also note that, like Blonder's system, only specific areas of the image can be selected. There is a tolerance associated with each click point, which can be adjusted by the user. Clearly, users must set the tolerance to as low a value as possible to reduce the likelihood of a successful attack. The password space is quite large, depending on the resolution of the screen and the size of the tolerance region (which is a global setting) around each of the click points. Typically, with a four-click point password, the password space is approximately 10^9, equivalent to 30 bits. Clearly, increasing the number of click spots can increase the password space in order to protect against off-line attacks. Again, the balance between security and memorability must be considered – and the data on this critical issue has yet to be published.

Suo and colleagues (2006) report on a system they developed dubbed Recall-a-Formation (RAF). Their system has a dual panel (tables) system (see Figure 5.4). On the right panel (the data table) are icons that contain the user's password and distractors. The images/icons are selected from several thematic categories, such as fruits, animals, starts, and system icons. The left panel (input table) is where icons selected from the data table will be placed. Typical table dimensions are 8×8, which is suitable for most access-controlled devices. The authors report a preliminary study involving 30 users, aged 20–30 years. This study compared the use of RAF and textual-based passwords. The first criterion was the memorability, which compared the ability of the subjects to recall textual-based passwords against their graphical password. The results indicate that half of the RAF users were able to remember their password correctly, after a delay of 1 day. In contrast, all users were able to recall their textual-based passwords. The authors stated that the study participants were free to select their textual password, and that most (29/30) of the textual passwords were easy to remember such as names and birthday dates (Suo et al., 2006). This unfortunately skews the results to the point where the issue of memorability between the two approaches cannot be accurately estimated. In addition, the RAF users had to write down their passwords in order to memorize it for subsequent entry. RAF users also tended to select a low number of icons, typically from the same theme, such as "stars." Even though the password space for RAF is very large, users did not explore the search space very well as it appears from this pilot study. Note that the potential password space was given to be 64^{65}, or equivalently 2.5×10^{117}! The actual space used was a mere fraction of this vast password space. The authors did not explore this issue in this paper, and we are awaiting the results of further study.

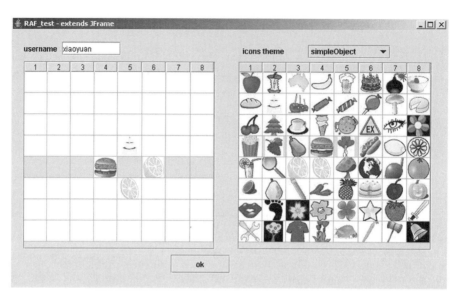

Figure 5.4 An example of the RAF main interface. The right panel is the data table and the left panel is the input table. Note that each cell in the input table can be filled with 1 of the 64 images or the blank from the data table. Since there are 64 cells on the input table, there are 64^{65} unique combinations of icons (Source: Suo, 2006)

In another study, a recall-based system employing the analogy of a safe with a combination lock – dubbed *mouse lock* – was developed (Revett et al., 2008a). In this system, the numbers of the safe dial are replaced with graphic thumbnail images. The system is depicted in Figure 5.5. As with opening a typical safe, the user is required to select the correct position (indicated by the appropriate graphical element) and to move it to the top dial indicator in the appropriate direction. A password is a combination of images and associated with each image is the direction to move the image to the top. For instance: <image 8>L, <image 2>R, <image 5>L, and <image 12>R would constitute a user's password. The direction of movement (L = left or R = right) is indicated by clicking the left and right mouse button, respectively. The user clicks on the appropriate image, then clicks the correct direction button, which then places the image under the dial. Note that this process actually moves the images along the circular dial. It could also be implemented without moving the images, but in this study, the images were moved during password entry whether the correct entry was made or not. An audible sound is produced when the user enters the correct combination (password). In the enrollment process, audible feedback is provided indicating whether or not the correct entry was made – but not when users were attempting to authenticate in the testing phase.

The users were required to select a password that consisted of five images, and the direction was randomly selected by the system. During enrollment, the password was displayed on screen for the users, and they were allowed to practice until they had entered their password correctly five times (not necessarily contiguously). During authentication, no feedback (audible nor on-screen) was provided to the users, and they were allowed a maximum of three failed attempts before the entry was considered invalid. The study group consisted of six subjects (the same participants in the Match-n-Go study). The graphical "lock" consisted

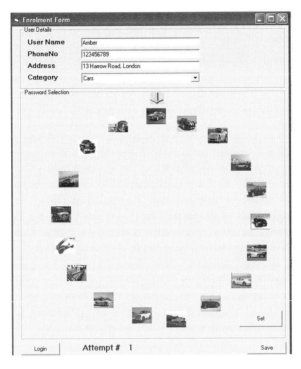

Figure 5.5   The *mouse-lock* system, waiting for user input. (Source: Revett et al., 2006)

Table 5.2   FRR results from each of the six users of the mouse-lock system (Source: Revett et al., 2008a)

Subject number	FRR (%)
1	2.0
2	7.0
3	6.0
4	8.0
5	1.0
6	0.0

The FRR data was generated from 100 trials, and the results are reported as percentages for each user separately.

of 24 small iconic images (each 15 × 15 mm) arranged in a circular fashion (see Figure 5.5), with the position indicator located at the top of the circle. After successfully enrolling into the system (note that the failure to enroll (FTE) was 0%), each user logged into their accounts 100 times, in order to generate false rejection rate (FRR) data. The FRR results from the six subjects is presented in Table 5.2. In order to enhance the security of this system, timing information could be incorporated as a measure of how long it would take for a user to attempt authentication. Reference values from valid users would be stored within the BIR for that account, and compared using the techniques described in Chapter 4. Since this was not attempted yet in this study, there is no FAR data available from this experiment. This task is left for future work.

5.4 Multi-Image Graphical Password Systems

An extension of Blonder's work has been produced under the name Passlogix (Sobrado & Birget, 2002). One of the key issues that Passlogix tried to overcome is shoulder surfing, where a user can gather your password contents by peering over your shoulder while it is being entered (see Suo et al., 2005 for a nice review of this material). In this approach, a collection of objects (termed pass objects) are presented in a single image to the user. The single image contains a number of familiar small icons (pass objects). Note the pass objects presented during authentication are previously selected by the user during the enrollment phase. In order for a user to be authenticated, he or she is required to click within the convex hull formed by all of the pass objects in their password presented in the image (see Figure 5.6). In order to increase the complexity of this scheme, Sobrado and Birget (2002) recommended using 1000 objects, which makes the image extremely busy and distracting for users. In 2006, Passlogix produced a new solution termed V-GO (Passlogix, 2006). This is a cued recall-based system and will be discussed further in this section.

Passlogix produced a new version of its graphical authentication system employing a cued recall-based system. In this version, the user was allowed to create a password by navigating through a single-image scene (as depicted in Figure 5.6). The password was created by clicking and/or dragging items within the image, enacting a particular task such as "mixing a

Figure 5.6 Shoulder surfacing resistance via the Passlogix graphical password scheme (Source: Sobrado and Birget, 2002)

martini," which contained elements typically found in a cocktail lounge. A variety of scenarios were available for the user from which the password could be created. The principal problem with the initial implementation of Passlogix was that it tended to be slow, as there were 1000 objects in the image. In the commercial version (V-GO), the principal problem was the small password space. The image depicted common scenarios in everyday life, which tended to limit the number of possibilities significantly.

Another system developed by Wiedenbeck and colleagues (2006) is the convex hull click (CHC) scheme. Like Passfaces, this system requires the user to select the correct location within a series of images presented sequentially (i.e. a challenge-response scheme). Like their original system, Passlogix, the user is required to click in the convex hull region, which makes this system less susceptible to shoulder surfing. The convex hull is based on three or more of the pass images within each image. One key difference between the two systems is that the pass images within each image are arranged in a more geometric fashion, reducing the cognitive complexity of the images (Figure 5.7).

Another very interesting approach to recognition-based graphical authentication was proposed by Hayashi and colleagues (2007). This system, termed Fata Morgana, was designed for use in small mobile devices. This system relies on our cognitive ability to extrapolate from a degraded version of an image back to the original, fully intact image. This is analogous to the implementation of a one-way hash function (Hayashi et al., 2007, p. 2). After viewing the original, non-degraded image, the user is able to create a "mental trapdoor," enabling the user to recognize the degraded image, even in the absence of the original image. Users who were not exposed to the original image will find this task much more difficult, and should

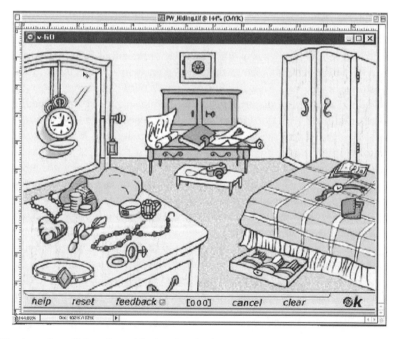

Figure 5.7   A cued recall-based graphical authentication developed by Passlogix (2006) termed V-GO (Source: passLogix website: free access: www.passlogix.com)

Figure 5.8   A collection of three images and their distorted version that are used for training purposes. (Source: Hayashi et al., 2007)

only be able to succeed by pure guesswork. The basic approach of Fata Morgana is to distort a series of user-selected pictures (such as the use of a lossy filter) such that the ability to recognize the distorted image becomes difficult, without having associated the image with the original, undistorted image. The distortion is performed in such a way that it cannot be mathematically converted back to the original image – in essence implementing a one-way hash function. The users are encouraged to select their own images to generate a portfolio. Research indicates that people are better able to recognize images they have personally selected from randomly selected images (Kinjo & Snodgrass, 2000). Figure 5.8 presents an example of three images, the originals (top row) and the corresponding distorted versions. After selecting the set of images to form the user's password (referred to as their portfolio), the users undergo a brief training session, with the goal of facilitating the association between the actual images and the distorted images. Note that the selected images are embedded in a larger set (typically nine images in total) during the training phase. During training, there are a number of decoy images that must be created, which poses a slight technical problem: the issue of how to create the decoy images, which must appear to be similar in appearance to the actual portfolio images. The authors proposed two different methods for decoy production: i) ab initio generate synthetic decoys or ii) apply the same filtering process to photos that are not included in the portfolio set. The authors decided to follow ii), as it is a potentially difficult task to generate reasonable synthetic decoys. Also note that the decoys remain the same until the users change their password to inhibit the intersection attack (Dhamija &

Perrig, 2000, Hayashi et al., 2007). Once users feel comfortable with their password, then they are ready to move onto the authentication phase.

During authentication, the users are presented with their portfolio images, along with a set of decoy images. Whether the decoy images in the authentication phase are the same as those employed in the training phase may impact the memorability of the portfolio images in that the user will have been trained on the entire set of data. The authors do not specify whether this is indeed the case. The success of the system is measured in part by the recognition success rate for the authentic user. The authors conducted a formal usability study to provide the required data.

A group of 54 university students and/or staff members were employed in this study (all from a scientific background, with a mean age of 23, range 18–29). The participants were split evenly into three different groups. For group I, the users were asked to collect three pictures via their cell phone camera, which were used without distortion as their portfolio images, along with 24 decoy images. The group II participants were asked to select three pictures of their choosing, which were distorted and used for their portfolio pictures. The 24 decoy images were selected from a database and were distorted using the same algorithm as was applied to the portfolio images. Note that the decoy images were provided to all the participants of this group. The group III participants were given the same portfolio images as those used for group II. They were also NOT allowed to view the original images, and by definition, did not take the portfolio images. The decoy images for this group were the same as those used for group II. The study spanned a total of 4 weeks, and occurred in four sessions. The first involved portfolio selection and memorization, training, and authentication. The other sessions, occurring at 2 days, 1 week, and 4 weeks later, involved authentication trials. All participants used the same mobile phone, in the same settings (i.e. same classroom). Also note that since there were a total of 27 images, they were presented over three screens (nine images per screen). The images were selected by selecting appropriate keys on the phone's keypad (users were trained in this process).

An authentication attempt was considered successful if the users could identify their three portfolio images within three trials. The results on the authentication rate indicate that all members from groups I and II were able to authenticate (100% success rate) during the entire 4 week period. The members of group III yielded one or two failures starting 2 days after the training period. These results indicate that there might be a tendency for users who either did not take their own pictures, or that were not able to associate the actual images with the distorted image to make mistakes in their password entry. The authors also investigated the login time, which tended to be similar for groups I and II, and considerably longer for group III (though no statistics were gathered for any of these results, so significance and its level were not presented). Also note that for group III, the users tended to do more page flipping while entering their password compared with the other two groups.

Overall, these results indicate that this approach yielded promising results for this particular study cohort. The overall authentication success rate was 89% over the entire course of the 4 week study. The study group was quite large, 54 subjects. But they were from a very homogenous population: university students and/or young staff members. It would be interesting to see if this approach generalizes across age groups. Unfortunately, there was no statistical analysis of the data – though there was sufficient number to do so. Without this validation, only qualitative conclusions can be drawn from these results. For those interested in this system, the authors have a prototype at http://arima.okoze.net/fyeo/.

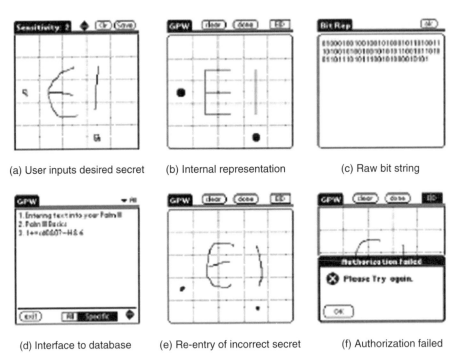

(a) User inputs desired secret   (b) Internal representation   (c) Raw bit string

(d) Interface to database   (e) Re-entry of incorrect secret   (f) Authorization failed

Figure 5.9   DAS technique proposed by Jermyn and colleagues (Source: Jermyn et al., 2001)

Jermyn and colleagues (Jermyn et al., 1999) developed a graphical authentication system called Draw-a-Secret (DAS). This system requires the users to draw a picture on a two-dimensional (2-D) grid, which will become their password as shown in Figure 5.9. This approach is probably most suitable for a PDA-type device, using a stylus for the actual drawing. Since a drawing is used for the users' passport, they do not have to remember any passwords. The freestyle drawing is converted into a set of coordinates, based on a gridding mechanism. An example DAS is presented in Figure 5.9. The basic idea is that the coordinates are extracted while a user draws on the 2-D grid, when the line crosses one of the intersecting lines on the grid. Note that this system decouples the position of the password elements from the temporal order of their input. The authors describe the generation of a password as a collection of strokes separated by a series of pen-up actions. While the pen is down and used in drawing, the coordinates that are crossed are recorded until the user lifts up the stylus. This is the definition of a stroke. The important defining characteristic of a stroke is its *length*, which is defined as the number of coordinates contained within it. The password is defined as a series of strokes, each with their own lengths. The total length of the password then is the sum of the stroke lengths minus the pen-up events. There is also the notion of equivalence classes, where multiple drawings that contain the same stroke sequence are considered identical. It reflects the resolution of the drawing – if it is too high, the users will find it difficult to reenter their password. If it is too low, then the security of the password is compromised. Jerymn and colleagues recommended a 5 × 5 grid, which was evenly partitioned (Figure 5.10). This provides an adequate compromise between reproducibility of the drawing and

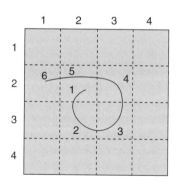

Figure 5.10 A sample password drawn on a 5 × 5 grid using DAS. Figure (Source: Van Oorschot and Thorpe, 2005)

security. The principal restriction of this system is that users should not start too close nor approach the intersection of the grid marks. The reason for this is that if the users vary their input slightly, such as passing below the intersection instead of just above it, the coordinates recorded will differ and the password will not be accepted. There are no restrictions on the selection of a user's password other than that it should be reproducible.

The other novel feature of this system is that the password becomes hardened (encrypted) after it has been produced. The authors employ a SHA-1 hash function (which includes the pen-up characters) to generate the cryptographic key. The key is chosen such that the probability that two distinct inputs generate two different fixed-length keys. The authors then deploy the triple-DES (data encryption standard) algorithm to encrypt and decrypt the password files stored on the PDA using the key. The key selection process works by prompting the user to enter the password onto an empty grid. The key k is derived and a predefined phrase p is encrypted and stored on the PDA. This process is equivalent to setting up your password on the system. When the users wish to gain access to the system after setting their password, they are required to reenter their drawing (password). This results in the production of a symmetric key, which is used to decrypt the encrypted phrase p. If the result of decrypting the phrase results in p, then the symmetric key matches the original key k, and the user is authenticated.

The key advantages of the DAS scheme of Jermyn is that it does not require the user to remember a textual password; it has a potentially very large password space and provides encryption of the password to reduce the probability of success for an off-line attack. For instance, if the user's password contains 12 strokes, then the total password space is 2^{58}, larger than the space of an eight-character password (2^{53}). Clearly, the users are no longer forced to remember a *textual* password, but they must be able to reproduce their drawing, which serves as their password. The memorability of the password can be assessed via controlled studies. The authors of DAS discuss the issue of memorability in terms of passwords incorporating "simple shapes" and those based on "simple algorithms" (Jermyn et al., 1999). The authors stated that simple shapes, such as rectangles, which have semantic content, are thus more memorable than those shapes which do not have a semantic component (more or less similar to abstract art versus realism in more traditional graphical passwords). The results from the Déjà vu graphical password system might argue against this distinction in terms of memorability. Though Déjà vu random art images are used in a recognition task, here we have a recall-based task. Whether this is a critical issue is a matter of further research. The authors discuss this issue in terms of the size of the password space, but not in terms of memorability. The other case for memorability, a short algorithm, focuses on whether or not the password can be generated by the execution of a short set of sequences that describe the manner by which the drawing is to be reproduced, that is, if we can mechanize the reproduction of our password through the enactment of a short "program," that might again help increase the memorability of the password. Again, the authors did not explore this issue in sufficient detail – but did explore the issue of inherent complexity as a factor in memorability. This again is an interesting area for further research.

The password space of a DAS password can be quite large, but this depends on the size of the drawing grid. Typically, a 5×5 grid is employed in most studies evaluating DAS. When evaluating the password space of DAS, the length of the password is the principal factor. The password length, in turn, depends on the number of strokes (termed the stroke count in the literature). Jermyn describes the number of passwords up to some given length, L_{MAX}, as a function of the dimensions of the grid (assuming a symmetric grid, this corresponds to the length of one side). The results of this analysis indicate that a password of length 12 surpasses the number of textual passwords that can be generated from eight characters. This is a theoretical limit, and other authors have investigated how realistic this claim really is.

In a comprehensive study of the DAS system, Van Oorschot and Thorpe (2005) analyzed the password space of DAS based on a set of password complexity properties: password length, number of components, and symmetry (they suggested the number of turns in each component, but did not discuss this issue in this paper). Note by components, the authors are referring to the number of distinct entities contained within the password (such as polygons, etc.). The authors suggested that symmetry is a very integral part of memorability – that people tend to be able to remember objects that contain a high degree of symmetry. This notion is supported by a variety of studies in cognitive psychology (see Tyler, 1996, Cowan, 2001). In terms of symmetry, the authors subdivide symmetry into three distinct categories: local symmetry, pseudo-symmetry, and global symmetry (see Figure 5.11 for an example of each category). The key to this taxonomic scheme is the notion of the proximity to axes, as

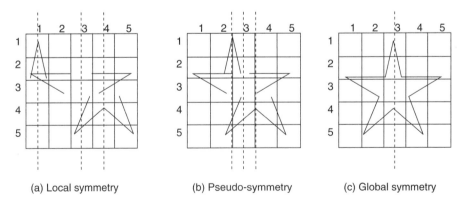

(a) Local symmetry   (b) Pseudo-symmetry   (c) Global symmetry

Figure 5.11   Examples of the three distinct forms of symmetry (Source: Van Oorschot and Thorpe, 2005)

indicated in Figure 5.11. In local symmetry, there is a repetitive motif contained within the image, but it is associated with axes that are far apart. As the symmetry adopts positions such that the axes are closer together, they are referred to as pseudo-symmetrical. When all the elements are symmetric around the same axes, the image is referred to as globally symmetric. Users tend to incorporate symmetry into their passwords, which has the effect of reducing the size of the password space.

In addition, the authors examine the number of strokes of typical DAS passwords, and how this affects the size of the password space. Typically, users tend toward a small stroke count, which tends to reduce the password space considerably. In a study published by Nali and Thorpe (2004), 90% of the users (16 students) selected passwords with a stroke count of six or less. In addition, the data suggested that approximately 56% of the passwords were centered about the midline (central grid) of the drawing space. One solution to the low stroke count problem is to use a technique termed "grid selection." This proposal (Van Oorschot & Thorpe, 2005) entails presenting users with a base grid (termed a *selection grid*), from which they can select a more refined grid, termed a *drawing grid*, onto which they enter their actual drawing. This idea will increase the resolution of the drawing, so that even if the stroke count is low, the chances of drawing the image on the same location in the selection grid as the authentic user will be reduced. This technique may also help to reduce the chances of centering as well.

In another study of the utilization of the possible password space, Chalkias and colleagues (2006) discuss the issue of whether users tend to focus on the central region of the drawing pad when entering their password, resulting in a reduction of the password space. The authors proposed a modified version of the DAS grid system, which would allow users to enter their passwords without focusing on the central drawing region. The results presented in the paper did not unfortunately provide any information regarding whether or not this modification had a positive impact on the size of the password space. The authors did present information from a study of 30 subjects, half in primary school and the other half were university students (engaged in computer-related studies). The DAS system was modified by creating a nested grid with 21 cells, which increased the neighborhood size (in the DAS, each non-edge region was surrounded by four neighboring cells). In addition, they compared the results from the modified grid with a 4 × 6 DAS grid and a text password system. The users were allowed to practice entering their passwords (of all three forms) four times, followed by a 1 hour distraction period before the testing phase began. The results focused on ordering and shift errors, as well as number of strokes, average length, and whether or not the passwords were centered. The results indicate that the technical participants (i.e. the university students) tended to employ longer passwords, more strokes, and generally produced fewer errors (i.e. ordering and shift errors) than their younger study cohorts. Also note that approximately 50% of the study participants were unsuccessful at entering their passwords (DAS version) after 1 hour post-enrollment. In contrast, users with textual passwords had a significantly higher success rate – yielding an average of successful entry rate of 73%.

In addition, Chalkias and colleagues examined the sources of errors when users entered their DAS password, focusing on order and shift errors. Order errors result from entering the password in the wrong order. Shift errors reflect the inexactness with the input of the users' password, missing the appropriate grid cells by some margin that generates a different set of coordinates. Their results indicate that the modification to the DAS system tended to reduce shift errors more than ordering errors (shift errors were reduced to 13% compared to an

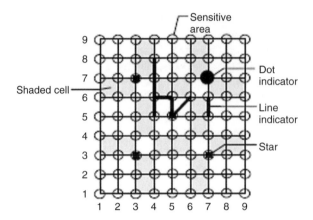

Figure 5.12 Example of a user's password using the Pass-Go system. Note that the password is displayed in a discretized form, displaying only the points and line segments generated by the user's input (Source: Tao, 2006)

average of 26.5% for the modified DAS and DAS systems, respectively). No explanation for this result was provided in the paper, but it may reflect the difference in the grid sizes (24 cells for their DAS implementation) and 21 for the modified DAS system. Further research on the variation of the grid size – in terms of the size of each grid cell and the overall number of grids with respect to the shift error – is required to address this important issue appropriately. The principal result from the Chalkias study is that the grid structure of the DAS system could be modified in such a way as to increase reproducibility while at the same time enhancing the size of the password space, without compromising order errors.

Hai Tao proposed an extension of the DAS scheme called Pass-Go (Tao, 2006, doctoral thesis). The author claims that this system is easier to use than DAS and has a larger password space than the DAS system. This system is also a grid-based system, wherein the user is required to select *intersections* instead of drawing between the intersections, studiously avoiding them in the DAS system. Therefore, the password is a collection of cell intersections. In order to enhance reproducibility, there is a tolerance area surrounding each element of their password. This reduces the required accuracy because in this system, the users are selecting single points as their password elements, which may be difficult for users to be able to reproduce their passwords. The authors state that the sensitive areas (circular) around each password element have a radius of $0.4xd$, where d is the side length of a grid cell (Tao, 2006). One advantage of this system is that the users will reproduce the same drawing whenever they successfully log in. This is because the password consists of a collection of points and lines connecting them, so if the drawing is within the tolerance regions, the image depicted on the screen when the users draw their password is a collection of points and straight lines (see Figure 5.12). Since the password is displayed consistently as the user enters it (assuming it was inputted correctly), the users see the exact same image every time they log in, which might enhance memorability. As indicated in Figure 5.12, the password is

(4,8), (4,7), (4.6), (4,5), (0,0), (4,6), (5.6), (5,5), (6,6), (0,0), (7.7), (0,0), (7,6), (7,5)

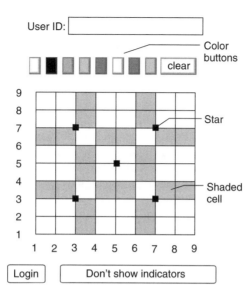

Figure 5.13 An example of an input into the Pass-Go system, with reference indicators designed to assist login entry consistency by providing alignment markers (Source: Tao, 2006)

The password then consists of the set of intersections generated by the user's interaction with the login screen. The (0,0) entries are pen-up events, analogous to the (5,5) entries in the DAS system. The Pass-Go system is defined very much like the DAS system, with password length being the total number of coordinate pairs, excluding pen-up events; the stroke count is the total number of pen-up events; the dot count equals the number of strokes of length 1, L_{MAX}, which is the maximum length, beyond which a password has a zero probability of being chosen, and a neighborhood, with a range of 3–8, depending on the location within the grid. Reference aids are added to the drawing screen, in the form of stars and shaded cells (see Figure 5.13), in order to aid memorability (Tao, 2006). The authors decided to use a 9 × 9 grid, a value derived from the analysis of a user study the author conducted. The 9 × 9 grid results in an image occupying 25 cm^2 (5 × 5 cm), which is suitable for PDAs. This grid size significantly increases the password space relative to a 5 × 5 grid. Lastly, the Pass-Go system also includes eight colors, the default of which is black. This significantly enhances the password space of this system, without apparently reducing usability/memorability. The authors compared the password space of a variety of Pass-Go systems against the standard 5 × 5 DAS system. The results indicate that the password space is 77 bits for $L_{MAX} = 12$, whereas DAS for this same value yields 31 bits. The password encoding scheme is quite efficient, where a numerical code is employed that stores the coordinate location, followed by a direction and number of cells traversed moved in that direction, with intervening pen-up markers (see Tao, 2006, p. 35).

The author set up a user study where 167 university students (computer science and electrical engineering) participated, during a 3 month period during term time at a university. The participants selected their own password, with a minimal length of eight. The study investigated usability and the impact of stroke count on the reproducibility of the system. At the end of the study period, the average successful login rate was 78% (5291/6800 login attempts). The authors noted that the login success rate increased to a steady rate of approximately 90% after the seventh week of use versus 65% success rate in the first week). As expected, the password accepted rate decreased with increasing stroke count (79% for a stroke count less than three and 50% stroke counts greater than or equal to four) (Tao, 2006, p. 51). The average length of the password leveled off at approximately 17 (down from 19 at the start), and this trend also was observed for the stroke count. The effect of color was also investigated in this study, and the preliminary results indicate that 29% of the users actually employed the color option. The authors did not provide any information concerning the impact color had on usability or password entry correctness, however. The users also tended to produce symmetric passwords, similar to the observations of users with the DAS system (41% produced symmetric passwords). In terms of security, the Pass-Go system yields an L_{MAX} of 40, as opposed to the value of 12 for DAS. Depending on what value of L_{MAX} is used and other constraints, it appears, based on the data, that the Pass-Go password space greatly exceeds that of the DAS system (see Tao, 2006, p. 61 for details). Thus, in the final analysis, the Pass-Go system, as an extension of the DAS system, provides a greater level of security, as measured in potential password space. This is accomplished without sacrificing usability (with respect to the number of successful login attempts), although the number for the first week of use was fairly low (65%). The author suggested refinements of the system, for which we will have to wait and see what they decide upon and what results they produce.

Other variations on the password drawing scheme have been proposed, such as Passdoodle, a system where users are allowed to enter their graphical password consisting of handwritten designs, drawn with a stylus-type device on a touch-sensitive screen (Goldberg et al., 2002). Users were required to produce at least two strokes for their password, and could also include color to add variation. Although a potentially interesting system, Passdoodle has not been examined very rigorously (in fact the published data was acquired using pen and paper), and hence this technique cannot be evaluated to the same degree as the other methodologies presented in this chapter.

There are hybrid systems as well that employ both graphical *and* textual elements. For instance, a graphical icon is selected as a password element, and the user associates a corresponding text string. When the user is presented with the images corresponding to their password, the user enters the corresponding text string. One such system is termed "inkblot authentication," proposed and implemented by Stubblefield and Simon (2004).

The inkblot authentication system was based on the Rorschach inkblot test, introduced in the psychology literature over 80 years ago (Rorschach, 1921). In the original Rorschach test, subjects were presented with a set of 10 inkblot images and were asked to tell what they saw when viewing the images, in a free association style. This might allude to a password scheme: present inkblots images and ask users to enter a string that captures what they think about the image. The original Rorschach allowed subjects to input a string of words if so required. This would make formulating a password more difficult – so Stubblefield and Simon (2004) allowed the user to enter a single word association. To generate an actual password, the first letter (or l letters) of each word associated with each image was selected and concatenated to form the password (i.e. a user-defined hash function). This process was used ultimately to form memorable and secure passwords. The authors indicated that at some point, once the user was comfortable with entering the password, the users could enter their password without

Figure 5.14   An example of a computer-generated Rorschach-like image used in the Stubblefield and Simon "inkblot" authentication system. (Source: Stubblefield and Simon, 2004)

the inkblot prompts. The ultimate purpose of this system was really to help users remember difficult passwords.

The inkblots were generated algorithmically, using a hash based on user information and a random seed (see Stubblefield & Simon, 2004, p. 5 for details). An example of one of their images is presented in Figure 5.14. Ten images were presented, and after each presentation, the user would enter the first letter of the word they associated with the image. The word association hash function (and number of inkblot images) defines the password space of this system. The authors stated that the password space is approximately 80 bits, if the user enters two characters per inkblot (i.e. the first and last character of the associated word, yielding 20 character passwords). In terms of memorability, the authors state that no subjects were able to remember less than nine out of the 10 inkblots, even after a substantial delay of several months after generating their passwords. The results from the inkblot authentication system are reasonable – clearly more secure than the Passfaces™ system, with a 3×3 grid and four Passface images.

Another password enabling system with a graphical component is the rebus system (King, 1991). In this system, randomly generated passwords are produced, which consist of one or more nonsense syllables (Gasser, 1974). From the collection of syllables (which together form the password), a keyword set is generated by using an acoustic link (King, 1991, p. 240). Essentially, a phonetic database is examined in order to extract entries that match the pronounceable syllables produced by the password generator. The last step is to associate an image database with the phonetic database (referred to as a picture generator). Then, the pictures associated with the randomly generated password are displayed in order to cue the users for their password. An example of the rebus system is presented in Figure 5.15. Once users become confident with entering their password, the graphical cues are no longer necessary, at least until the password is changed. This technique has been successfully applied to help children learn foreign languages. The author did not explore the usefulness of this approach, though it appears to be a unique methodology for assisting users in remembering their passwords. Whether it can be used for strong memorable user authentication is an open matter, requiring further research.

A related password prompting system with a strong graphical element is a system developed by Man and colleagues (2003). This is essentially a shoulder-surfing resistant approach to password entry, with a graphical component. An image panel is presented with

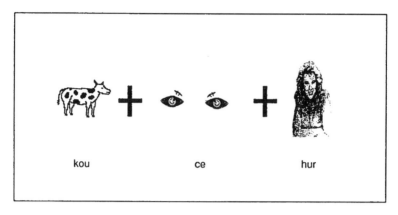

Figure 5.15 A sample password from the rebus system: the password is "kou-ce-hur." The phonetic equivalent is "cow-see-her." (Source: King, 1991)

several hundred small iconic images (called pass objects). User select a number of pass objects for their password, and associated with each pass object is a short text string, which forms part of the user's password. Note that there are a number of variants of the pass objects, and each of the variants has its own associated textual string. When the user authenticates, the pass objects and a number of decoys are presented on the image panel. As each pass object is displayed, the user has to enter the appropriate text string. The principal strength of this approach is that a different set of pass objects is presented every time a user logs into the system, making it resistant to extensive shoulder surfing. Of course, the drawback is that the user has to remember a considerable number of text strings to reliably authenticate.

An extension of the Man system proposed by Hong and colleagues (2004) allows the users to assign their own text string to pass-object variants. Again, a large number of randomly positioned pass objects are displayed on the image panel, and the user must select the pass objects and input the associated text string. Like the Man system, this requires a significant amount of memorization, as there may be several variants of each pass object (Figure 5.16).

5.5 Conclusions

The data from the case studies provided in this chapter support the hypothesis that graphical-based authentication systems are a viable alternative to textual-based authentication. They can be implemented in a variety of devices, from mobile phones to PCs and ATMs. Studies comparing the FRR (or at least the equivalent) between textual and graphical-based passwords suggest that graphical passwords are as easy, if not easier in many instances, compared with traditional textual passwords in terms of memorability. The password space of graphical passwords can, at least theoretically, exceed the password space available on traditional keyboards. A typical PC keyboard (see Appendix B for a discussion of this marvelous device) has approximately 95 human readable characters that can be used as elements of a password. This leads to approximately 2^{53} combinations for an eight-character password. Systems such

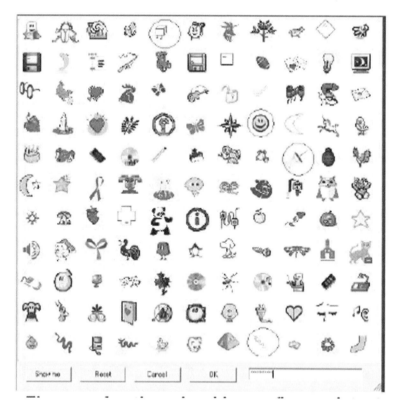

Figure 5.16 A shoulder-surfing resistant scheme developed by Hong (Source: Hong et al., 2003)

as DAS can yield 2^{58} different combinations (i.e. passwords) from a moderately sized value for L_{MAX}. There is theoretically no upper bound for graphical systems, other than the issue of memorability. For textual passwords, the only increase is in the length of the password, which, when beyond eight characters, substantially reduces the FRR, probably above acceptable levels. This translates into a substantially reduced likelihood of successful off-line attacks, provided the passwords are stored in a secure encrypted format. Other security issues, such as shoulder surfing, still need to be addressed within this context. In some cases, the presentation of a large panel of images may expose the system to shoulder surfing. But this issue may depend on the device in which the system is applied to. For instance, mobile phones and PDAs are traditionally quite small, and it should be a relatively easy task to shield suspecting surfers from viewing their password entry. Most people are security conscious at ATMs, so blocking the vision of would-be surfers is more or less a habit for most of us. How to solve this problem for PC graphical password entry is a more difficult matter. There are systems such as that proposed by Man and Hong that help reduce the extent of successful shoulder surfing (Man et al., 2003, Hong et al., 2004). This comes at a cost though, in that the image-panel complexity tends to increase considerably, raising the FRR in many instances. The overall consensus, at least from this author's perspective, is that graphical passwords are clearly a viable alternative to textual-based password authentication systems.

Graphical-based password authentication systems rely on the cognitive ability of *recall*, *recognition*, or *cued recall*. The prototypical graphical password system that relies on *recall* is DAS and its variants. These systems require the users to reproduce their password without any (or at least a modicum of) visual assistance, to within a reasonable tolerance limit. This is arguably the most difficult task to complete in a graphical password-based authentication system. In a recognition-based system, the users are required to identify the elements of their password, which are presented for direct visual inspection, in a more or less passive manner. No additional information is required for a user to interact with a recognition-based approach. *Cued recall* is a compromise between recognition and recall-based memory retrieval. It relies on the presentation of a sufficient amount of information that an *informed* user can exploit in order to aid in the recall task. The issue then is how much information is enough? The general trend is to provide the graphical information, in the form of small icons or images, in a context that tends to mask their information content to the uninitiated. Simply, the users are required to select the icons that form their password from a collection of distractors or decoy images. Therefore, the ratio of distractor to actual password icons is at least a semiquantitative measure of the information content of the graphical password system. Values for this ratio range from 1:9 to 5:1000 (e.g. Passfaces and Passlogix, respectively). When the ratio of decoy to authentic images is low, the system tends to rely on the presentation of multiple image panels, such as the Passfaces system. Further, these systems tend to rely on recognition as opposed to recall. Cued-recall systems tend to rely on a large ratio of decoy to authentic images. But there are practical limits to how many icons can be presented on a screen (especially if the system is to be deployed on small devices such as PDAs and mobiles). Other factors other than this ratio have been exploited to varying degrees of success.

An issue that has not been directly addressed in the context of graphical passwords is the notion of subliminal priming (Seitz & Watanabe, 2003). The developers of Passfaces[TM] intimated that one solution to the inherent surfing problem is to present the image on the screen for a brief time interval (0.5 second). The purpose of such a short presentation issue is to reduce the chance that a shoulder surfer could acquire the password given enough temporal opportunity. It would be a very interesting study to examine the effect viewing time has on memorability. In the cognitive literature, objects can be recognized after a very brief presentation interval, on the order of 100–200 ms (Libet et al., 1967). This interval reflects the time required for conscious perception of an object – that is, the minimal amount of time required for a viewer to be fully aware of the object. Presentation intervals less than this value can still be recognized – but without conscious perception – the hallmark of subliminal perception (Libet et al., 1967, Seitz & Watanabe, 2003). Priming is a technique that is used to provide a bias toward a particular input/output response. This approach could be used in the context of graphical password authentication – provided that a subliminal stimulus is presented along with the input data. This priming is best performed during the enrollment/training phase, as a means of influencing the users' selection of their password elements. Provided the subliminal cues are not directly associated with the element(s) of the password, a shoulder surfer, if they notice them at all, will not benefit from their presentation. In addition, subliminal stimuli presentation will help reinforce the elements of the password when they are presented during the authentication process. This might provide a means for extending the elements of the password from four to six to six to eight or more images. Clearly, any means to extend the cardinality of the password will help reduce the likelihood of attackers (either online or off-line). The issue is whether or not extending the length of the graphical password, to those commensurate with textual passwords, in the context of subliminal priming, would have a negative impact on FRR. This is a very interesting area of research that requires further investigation to determine whether this approach could be used to reduce the FRR (and likewise minimize FARs).

The principal metric used to evaluate graphical password systems is the equivalent of the FRR – though this term is rarely used in this literature. A principal reason for this is that most researchers in this field do not evaluate graphical passwords as a biometric per se; it is simply an alternative to textual-based passwords. Enough data have been published in this field to begin to evaluate this approach as a viable candidate for user authentication. In keeping with other forms of biometrics, both the FRR and FAR data must be made available. The FRR data are available from a variety of studies, and the results indicate that the values are reasonably close to those for other behavioral biometrics – such as keystroke dynamics, signature verification, and speech recognition. The question is how to produce FAR data from this approach. I believe this is the principal impediment to converting this approach into a viable biometric. How can the FAR be produced when the sole level of protection afforded by graphical passwords is direct knowledge of the password itself? In other words, a biometric aspect must be added, akin to the *dynamical* aspect(s) of keystroke dynamics. What aspects are potentially dynamical in graphical password schemes? Clearly, the time taken to enter the password could be considered. Users enter their password typically by clicking with the mouse. This is very similar to entering a key using the keyboard (or related input device). The concept of image-graph, analogous to a digraph in keystroke dynamics, could be measured. This is indeed what the author has done in a system dubbed Match-n-Go, discussed in Chapter 6, multimodal biometrics. Other dynamical data could be extracted such as the total time for password entry, tri-*image-graphs* etc. What could also help in this regard is to ask the user to enter a login ID as well using a graphical interface – providing more data from which to generate a user model. These data could be extracted whether the user employs a mouse or a stylus – as both are generally used in essentially the same way. The use of data obtained from the user of the mouse as the input device, in terms of aiding user authentication, will be described in the next chapter.

5.6 Research Topics

1. Is "subliminal priming" an effective method for enhancing graphical-based authentication schemes?
2. Can the "Stroop effect" be used as a method to confound attacks on user accounts?
3. Do "picture category effects" impact FRRs?
4. How does the cardinality of a graphical password impact the FRR?
5. Explore the use of Fitts's law and the Accot–Zhai steering law in more detail: how does the effect of pointing impact the speed with which a password is entered? What human–computer interface (HCI) elements influence these effects?
6. Integration of dynamical data such that this technology can be properly integrated into the biometrics domain, yielding data on FARs.

7. There is currently no standard for graphical-based passwords – this needs to be developed so that they can be integrated into the Biometric Standards (e.g. INCITS Project 1676-D): "Biometric Profile Interoperability and Data Interchange."

8. Integrating graphical password-based authentication into a larger multimodal biometric scheme. For instance, audio input, mouse dynamics, and other technologies could be integrated with graphical passwords for enhanced memorability and security.

6

Mouse Dynamics

6.1 Introduction

This chapter describes a relatively new approach to behavioral biometrics that relies on the way users interact with their computer using a standard mouse. In most graphical applications, the mouse is the method of choice for program interaction. A substantial amount of human–computer interaction literature exists which explores how to arrange the graphical user interface (GUI) such that the user's interaction with the system is maximized with respect to some parameter (s) (Fitts, 1954, Fitts & Petterson, 1964, Hick, 1952, Card et al., 1983). One common parameter is the interaction speed – how quickly can a user navigate through the GUI-based application? This is the essence of the field of study in experimental psychology termed *interaction ergonomics* (Card et al., 1983, Meyer et al., 1990). For instance, how quickly can a user position the mouse and click on an application icon? If there is a series of menus that must be navigated, what is the best way to arrange them for maximal throughput? These are fundamental questions in computer ergonomics, which has resulted in the formulation of two "laws" within experimental psychology: Fitts' law and Hick's law. Fitts' law has been briefly discussed in the context of keystroke dynamics and graphical authentication systems in Chapters 4 and 5, respectively, and is fully explained in Appendix C. Essentially, this law relates the length of time it takes to perform a task with a pointing device such as a mouse. For instance, how long does it take to move the mouse cursor to a particular position on the screen? The original formulation has been derived from a one-dimensional (1-D) perspective, in that the vertical dimension is assumed to be infinite, and only the horizontal dimension is considered in the timing of the task. A two-dimensional (2-D) version of this model was produced by Accot and Zhai (2003), termed the Accot–Zhai steering law. The derivation of the Accot–Zhai steering law is presented in Appendix C. These laws provide a quantitative estimate of time for task performance, and is used a metric for GUI layout optimization. The findings from these and related studies have by now become an integral part of the way GUI applications are designed.

The human computer interface (HCI) research has also provided another law that relates the amount of time for a decision to be made with respect to selection of an entity (such as an icon) using a pointing device, termed Hick's law (Hicks, 1954). This law (sometimes

Behavioral Biometrics: A Remote Access Approach. Kenneth Revett
© 2008 John Wiley & Sons, Ltd.

referred to as the Hick–Hyman law) is a model that describes the amount of time it takes for users to make a decision as a function of the amount of choices they have available to them. This law is applicable to purely graphical systems (as is Fitts' law) and is mentioned here for completeness – though it belongs in both places. In combination with Fitts' law, these HCI-based models provide quantitative information regarding the thinking time and the motion time for users to interact with a system using a pointing device. To this author's knowledge, there is no comprehensive study employing these laws in the current context.

As mentioned in Chapter 5, the application of Fitts' law can be a useful attribute when examining the dynamical aspects of mouse usage, especially in the context of the process of selecting (via a pointing device) the elements of a graphical password. What other attributes are available, akin to those obtainable from keystroke dynamics? Ahmed and colleagues proposed the average speed against the distance traveled and the average speed against the movement direction (Ahmed & Traore, 2003). The attributes reported in the literature include clicking (left, middle, or center button) and mouse wheel movements (Pusara & Brodley, 2003). Gamboa and colleagues refer to the concept of a *stroke* as the movement of the mouse between two successive clicks (Gamboa & Fred, 2004). In addition, higher-order features such as curvature, angle, and deviation can be acquired and used to capture the dynamical aspects of mouse movements (Pusara & Brodley, 2003, Gamboa et al., 2004). In an interesting approach to user authentication via mouse movements, Syukri and colleagues (Syukri et al., 1998) asked users to write their signature using a mouse. This approach has been discussed in Chapter 3 of this volume and hence will not be discussed further here.

Analogous to keystroke dynamics, once a set of attributes has been extracted, a user profile can be generated (the biometrics information record (BIR) for the user and deployed for authentication purposes. The BIR is generated from data obtained either directly from an enrollment process or through continuous monitoring of the user's mouse activities. Clearly, the enrollment process will depend on how the use of the mouse is integrated into the authentication system. For the most part, the mouse is employed as an interactive device for a graphical application. The user must be trained to use the application, employing the mouse – this is the principal source for enrollment data in most studies. Once the attributes have been incorporated into the BIR, a classification algorithm must be developed to determine whether an authentication attempt is valid or not. Generally speaking, a statistical measure of closeness between the stored BIR and the authentication attempt is employed. In the next section, case studies employing mouse dynamics are presented, with a brief analysis of the results from these studies.

6.2 Case Studies

Hashia and colleagues (2003) published a paper which examined the use of mouse movements as a method for user authentication. The users enrolled in a static fashion, which was immediately followed by an authentication phase. For the enrollment process, the users were required to position the mouse pointer over a set of 10 dots that appeared in random positions on the screen (though for each enrollment trial, the dots appeared at the same position). The initial data that was captured was the movement of the mouse as the user positioned the mouse pointer over the dots in ten target areas). The x–y coordinate position of the mouse was captured every 50 ms and was stored for subsequent online analysis. The data was analyzed with respect to speed, deviation from a straight line, and the angle of movement. Deviation was measured as the perpendicular distance from the point where the mouse was currently positioned to the line formed between the two points between which the mouse was moving. The angle was calculated by the angle between three points, which was either positive (0–180 degrees) or negative (0–180 degrees). The users were required to move 20 times over the 10 points to complete their registration/enrollment. Between each pair of points, the average, minimum, maximum, and standard deviation (SD) of the four attributes were recorded. This yielded a total of 16 values for each point pair and a total of 144 attribute measures (16 attributes for each of the nine pairs of points), which were stored as the BIR for each user. Note that all the data were normalized before being stored in the BIR. For the verification step, the same attributes were extracted and compared to the BIR for that user. As the user moved through the collection of dots, the system checked to see if the attribute values were within 1.5 SDs from the BIR values. If so, a counter was incremented, resulting in a score that was used for authentication purposes. That is, if the score was within the range of values obtained during the authentication phase, the score was accepted and the user was authenticated.

Hashia and colleagues tested their system on a set of 15 students, aged 22–30, in a university setting, employing the same mouse and mouse pad (associated with the same PC). The authors reported an equal error rate (EER) of 20%. The authors also investigated using the average and SD of the resulting counter values (instead of the range), which reduced the EER to 15%. These results are encouraging, but are much higher than the EER obtained from keystroke dynamics and graphical password authentication results. In addition, these authors reported a continuous monitoring system to validate the currently logged-in user. During the enrollment process, mouse movements were collected through a background process over a series of 15-minute blocks. The process calculates where the highest density of mouse movements are, and draws a convex hull around them. These are called states, and the system keeps track of movements between states. The system calculates the speed (average and SD), the average, and the SD of wavering. In addition, it stores the transition state (each assigned a unique number), a count of how many times each state is visited in the 15 minute enrollment time, average speed, and wavering. During user verification, data are collected every 2 minutes and compared to the BIR data. If the speed and wavering is within 1.5 SD units found in the BIR, the user is positively verified. Otherwise, the user can be locked out of the system.

Gamboa and colleagues produced some interesting results deploying the use of mouse movements for user authentication (Gamboa & Fred, 2003, 2004, Gamboa et al., 2004). The approach produced a large number of interesting attributes, which were tuned to each user by a greedy search algorithm, and deployed a unimodal parametric model for authentication. The authors employed the use of a Web-based data acquisition system, built around the Web Interaction Display and Monitoring (WIDAM) system, which recorded all user interactions and stores the data in a file (Gamboa & Ferreira, 2003). The interactions employed in this system were related to mouse movements produced during the interaction with a graphical interactive program (a memory game). The raw data that was recorded was the $\langle x, y \rangle$ coordinates of the mouse pointer position, mouse clicks, and timing information associated with these activities. The authors used the concept of a stroke (analogous to that used in the Draw-a-Secret scheme) to represent the information (the $\langle x, y \rangle$ coordinates) contained between two successive mouse clicks. The authors employed a multistage processing schema in order to generate the data that will be used by the classifier. First, the data was cleansed by applying a cubic spline, which smooths out inconsistencies/irregularities. Next, they extracted spatial and temporal information, and lastly, they applied a statistical model to extract salient features from the data.

A collection of vectors was generated from the data, each of which represented a stroke (or pattern), derived from the spatial and temporal properties of the data. A total of six spatial and nine temporal properties were extracted. The spatial properties (generated from the smoothed data) included the x and y position, the distance from the origin, the angle of the tangent of the point with the x axis, the curvature, and its derivative. For the temporal domain, the extract (from the raw data) included the vector of motions in the x and y directions, the input time vector, the horizontal and vertical velocities, the tangential velocity, the tangential acceleration, the tangential jerk, and the angular velocity. This data was used to generate a 63-dimensional vector that characterized each stroke produced by the user. Each vector was further characterized by statistical measures such as the mean, minimum, maximum, range, and SD. Also note that the authors measured two additional features: the *straightness* and *jitter*. The straightness refers to the ratio of the Euclidean distance between the starting and ending points of the stroke divided by the total path distance. The jitter is the ratio of the actual path length, divided by the smoothed path length. The authors indicated that critical points were also incorporated into the user's feature vector, which measured how many times the derivative was zero during the course of a stroke. Lastly, the authors included the time to click, the number of pauses, the passed time, and the paused time ratio. A pause was indicated when there was a stationary point of at least 0.1 second. The passed time ratio refers to the ratio between the amount of paused time and the stroke time (time between clicks).

With a 63-dimensional input vector available for each stroke, the feature vector was reduced based on how each attribute influenced the EER. Essentially, the authors employed a greedy search algorithm (sequential forward search) algorithm to examine sequentially which attributes produced the lowest EER. This was performed in a bootstrap-like fashion, where each attribute was examined in isolation; the one producing the lowest EER was selected, and then the other attributes were examined sequentially, selecting those that also produced the lowest value for the EER. This process was repeated for all attributes for each user, producing a local set of attributes that best characterized each user in terms of a minimized value for the EER.

With a reduced feature vector modeled for each user, a classifier was deployed to perform the authentication task. The data reported contained both false rejection rate (FRR) and false acceptance rate (FAR) assessments. For FAR data, the imposters were the other users employed in their studies. The authors performed two separate studies, one involving a collection of 25 and the other a collection of 50 volunteers (in the form of separate distributions for authentic and imposter groups). Note that the imposter distribution was based on a mixture model (the Weibull distribution). The data was partitioned 50/50, training and testing, respectively. Bootstrapping was employed, based on the free parameter, the stroke length. Note that on average, there were 180 strokes/user. The bootstrap estimates were based on the stroke length (which was varied from 1 to 200, depending on the study), using 10 000 bootstrap samples from the test set. A statistical model was used, based on the maximum likelihood estimation of the probability that the stroke belonged to one category versus the other, based on a parameterized decision boundary.

The results indicate that the classification accuracy (as measured by the EER) was dependent upon the number of strokes included in the decision model. For instance, when including 50 strokes, the EER was 1.3%, very comparable to results obtained from physiological-based techniques such as fingerprints and hand geometry (Jain et al., 2003). Further, the authors also examined the EER as a function of the surveillance time. The results indicate that a 90 second surveillance time provides an EER on the order of $1:200$, comparable to physiological-based biometrics such as hand geometry and related technologies (Maioa, 2004). Whether these results can be improved upon is a matter for future research.

In a study by Pusara and Brodley (2003), cursor movements and mouse dynamics was examined in order to determine whether these attributes would be suitable for user re-authentication. Re-authentication is a technique suitable for the detection of a hijacking scenario (e.g. someone has replaced the originally logged-in user). The data was collected from 18 subjects working within Internet Explorer (IE). After data collection, a detailed user profile was created for each user, tailored to the way each interacted with the application. Subsequent to model development, a supervised learning approach was used for the purpose of classifying data into authentic or imposter users.

In order to build a profile of user identity based on mouse dynamics, attributes representing discriminatory behavior were collected during an enrollment/training phase. The attributes collected were cursor movements, mouse wheel movements, and clicks (left, middle, and center). The 2-D coordinates of the current mouse position were recorded at 100 ms intervals. From this raw data, secondary attributes such as *distance*, *angle*, and *speed* between pairs of points were recorded. Note that the pairs may be consecutive or separate by some number of data points, k, termed by the authors to be a frequency measure. The mean, SDs, and third moment values were calculated over a window N of data points. In addition, all data points were time stamped. The data was constructed into a hierarchical form, in order to create a template onto which a user profile could be generated. At the top of this hierarchy was the sequence of mouse events for a given user. Next were the clicks, non-click moves, and mouse wheel events, followed by single or double click events. The same statistical measures were again applied to the N data points. This results in a feature set that represents the ensemble behavior of a windowed version of the original raw data.

From this hierarchical model of raw data, a set of features was extracted and used for the authentication/identification task. For each category in the hierarchy, there were six features, corresponding to each of the categories in the hierarchy (e.g. wheel movements, clicks, etc.). The mean, SD, and third moment of distance, angle, and speed between pairs of points were measured, resulting in 63 features. An additional 42 features were derived from statistics on the x and y coordinates of cursor movement data. With the feature vector obtained from the user data, the authors considered performing a supervised versus an unsupervised classification strategy. The authors opted to employ a supervised approach to classification in this study. In this approach, the profile obtained for the current user must be matched to one of the user's models contained within the BIR database. The classification system was applied to a windowed dataset, and each point in the window was evaluated and raised an alarm if the value of the data point was not consistent with the user's profile. If a threshold number of alarms were indicated, the user was flagged as an imposter.

The authors evaluated their system on a set of 18 student volunteers, who provided data that consisted of 10 000 cursor locations. The data was collected from the use of IE from a Windows-based PC (this resulted in 7635 unique cursor locations for the IE interactions alone). The data for each user was split into quarters; the first two were used for training purposes, the third quarter used for parameter selection, and the remaining was used for testing purposes. The authors employed a decision tree classification approach (C5.0). Essentially, the algorithm must find splits within the data based on an information gain ratio, which is an entropy measuring approach. For details on this algorithm, please consult Quinlan (2003). In their first experiment, the authors attempted to build a decision tree classifier that could distinguish between pairs of users. The results indicate that the classification accuracy (based on minimizing EER) was highly dependent upon the characteristics of the user. For instance, if there were a significant number of events recorded within the window, the accuracy was increased. The overall results from this study indicate that the system was able to distinguish between pairs of users with considerable accuracy (with an accuracy of 0% for some pairs of users). In their next study, they examined whether the system could distinguish each user from all other users of the system. The results generated an average false negative rate of 3.06% for all 18 users. The corresponding false positive rate was 27.5%. The authors examined the data to determine the source of the misclassification. This analysis suggests that those users who did not generate a significant number of mouse events were misclassified more often than not. More generally, the authors noticed that users tended to generate similar user profiles – reading the text and then navigating with the mouse. Since the data collected captures *frequency* information only, it ignores user-specific habits, which tend to be smoothed out during the windowing process.

To test this hypothesis, the authors explored the effect of the smoothing window size on the classification accuracy. The data consisted of users who were most dissimilar to one another, based on the analysis of the results from their second experiment (leaving 11 users). The results were improved considerably, yielding an average false positive rate of 0.43% and an average false negative rate of 1.75%. The authors indicated that this improved result was clearly due to the use of a smoothing process over the data. No specific reason why this process improved the results was stated by the authors, but may be in part a consequence of utilizing the "best" subjects from experiment 2. It would have been useful to compare the results of all 18 subjects as well for experiment 3 to quantify this effect on the results. Overall though, these experiments indicate that the false positive and negative rates are within a very acceptable range – comparable to keystroke dynamics and graphical-based biometrics.

Ahmed and colleagues employed mouse dynamics as an approach for intruder-based detection (Ahmed & Traore, 2004, 2005, 2007). The authors measured several attributes with respect to the user's usage when interacting with a graphical-based application such as general mouse movement, drag-and-drop behavior, point-and-click behavior, and silence (Ahmed et al., 2004). Using a variety of machine learning techniques, the authors developed a *mouse dynamics signature* (MDS) for each user. In this study, mouse usage data was collected from 22 participants over a 9 week period (Ahmed et al., 2004). The data that was collected was used in an off-line approach to evaluate their detection system. The detection system relied on the use of average mouse speed (against overall speed and direction), drag-and-drop statistics, mouse movement statistics, and point-and-click statistics. The users were separated into two groups, wherein one group (consisting of 10 participants) represented authorized users and the remaining participants acted as imposters. These features were used to train a neural network to classify users of the system into genuine and imposters. To calculate the FRR, the first half of the sessions was used as reference values, and the remainder was used to test the system. The FRR was approximately 1.3% for this study. The FAR was calculated by allowing the other users of the system to act as imposters, and yielded an average FAR of 0.65%. This approach, though applied to intruder detection, could just as easily have been used to authenticate a user or to perform continuous user authentication.

The author performed several studies deploying the use of a graphical password-based authentication mechanism (see Revett et al., 2006, Revett et al., 2007a,d, Revett et al., 2008a,b). We deployed a different approach to graphical-based authentication, based on a matching scheme. More specifically, a collection of graphical images is presented on one half of the screen, and a similar collection is presented on the other half. The images form a regular grid which is typically a 5×5 set of thumbnail images (see Figure 5.1) on a small device such as a PDA, and a 10×10 grid for a typical 19 inch PC monitor. The user selects a set of images that form their password from a portfolio of images. The images are realistic graphics (JPEG) of common every day items. Typically, users are required to select five images for their password. The password images are integrated into the image montage and are centered on each half of the visual display (forming right and left montages). Both the left and right montages will each contain the same images, so there is no issue of constancy within the image space providing a clue to the password. The order in which the images are inserted into each montage is randomized every time the user attempts to authenticate. Each user has the opportunity to practice selecting his password, through a typical enrollment process. Once users have successfully entered their passwords five times, they are considered ready to use the system for authentication (testing phase). In order to enter their passwords, users are required to match the graphical components (images) of the password by aligning the images contained within the password on the right-hand montage to the corresponding position of the same image on the left montage. For instance, if the password consisted of five images, the user would be required to align each image (possibly in the proper sequence) from the images on the right-hand montage such that they aligned with their corresponding positions on the left-hand montage. In Figure 6.1, in the right-hand montage, the car would have to be moved to the top left-hand corner by clicking on the image of the car and the final location where the car should be placed. The next item in the password would similarly be moved to its proper location with respect to its location in the left-hand montage. The order in which the password elements are moved can be used as well, though in this pilot study, the order was not used for authentication purposes.

We performed a pilot study involving six users, who were computer science undergraduate students (age range 21–33, median 23 years). All users logged into the same type and brand of desktop PCs, with a 19 inch flat screen monitor and a typical three-button mouse. The purpose of this study was to evaluate whether this graphical-based authentication system would be considered a feasible alternative to textual-based passwords. In order to allow these results to be compared to other published studies, all steps toward user authentication were similar to those typically employed in conventional systems. The users were allowed to select their password from a collection of thumbnail images. After the users completed their enrollment phase, when they were allowed to practice entering their passwords (10 successes were considered sufficient), the users were ready for the authentication phase (for the collection of FRR/FAR data). In this study, the thumbnail images were randomly selected from a large collection that included a variety of images from over 20 different semantic domains. The images were all the same size (15×15 mm) and resolution (JPEG). The users were prompted to select five images from a large portfolio of images by clicking on the image with the mouse, which would serve as their password. This password was associated with the user's login ID,

Figure 6.1   The Match-n-Go login screen. Note that the password is contained in the left-hand panel of graphics. The user must locate the graphic in the password by noting the position (x, y coordinate) on the left panel and move the corresponding graphic on the right panel to the same position. This process is repeated for each graphical element in the password. (Source: Revett, 2008b)

which the participants were also allowed to select (using a standard textual interface). The graphical password was then bound to the login ID. During enrollment, the users logged in with their ID, and a screen was then presented to the users, with a random selection of images containing their password. Each user had to enter his password 10 times in order to success-fully enroll. Also note that during enrollment, the images contained within their password were displayed on the screen (top center) to assist the users in memorizing their password. If a mistake was made during password input, they continued until all the elements of their password were selected. After completing the enrollment process, users entered the authen-tication phase, where they were to select their password images, without the mnemonics. The success rate was recorded and used to calculate the FRR, and FAR was collected from the other five users acting as imposters.

As with most graphical-based authentication systems, this system per se does not yet include any biometric information. It simply serves to provide a graphical alternative to textual password-based systems. A careful observer could possibly watch long enough via shoulder surfing (or video recording) to *possibly* determine the elements of the password. The chances are extremely remote that such an event could occur, but there is some finite probability that this could happen. To reduce the likelihood of successful shoulder surfing, or even guessing, timing information is gathered during the enrollment process. The timing information involves calculating the mouse click (press events) times between successive image selections and subsequent positioning. After the first image is located, it must be clicked before it can be positioned. This starts a timer (accurate to within 1 ms) that will stop when the image has been moved to the proper location, indicated by clicking the mouse over the corresponding image location on the montage on the left. Movement occurs simply by clicking on the proper destination location. This system can also be implemented using a keyboard, in which case the images are moved one square at a time using the arrow keys). Unless the destination position is an immediately adjacent square, there will be more than one way to move the image to its final location. When the image is moved to its final location, the timer for that password image stops and the duration is calculated, along with the moves as a set of coordinate positions. The assumption in this model is that image destination distance relative to the starting location will have an obvious impact on the timing and the choice of moves made to arrive at that position. In the work presented here, the focus will be on the mouse click option, where the user selects the item to move by clicking on it, and then the final destination location, again by clicking. A summary of the time taken for the user to select the appropriate images is presented in Figure 6.2.

The reference profile consists of the image number (each has a unique ID number) and the associated timing information for each element in the password. Each *image* graph, as we call it, is averaged and the SD is calculated, both of which are appended to the end of the reference profile. As a first pass toward quantifying the FRR, each participant is requested to log into the system with their selected password 100 times. The selection criteria are whether the input is within the mean $\pm n$ SDs, where n varied from 0.5 to 2.0 in steps of 0.50. These results are presented in Table 6.1. The values for the FAR with the same participants and study details are presented in Table 6.2. The data presented

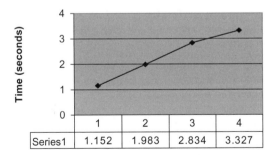

Image size (single dimension)

Figure 6.2 Average image-graph time as a function of the image matrix size. Note that these are the average values for all image graphs, which were averaged across all six participants (i.e. the grand average)

Table 6.1 FRR values calculated and the average for each of the 100 trials for each of the participants are presented as a function of the acceptance threshold (n-SD units, ranging from 0.5 to 2.0 in steps of 0.5)

Participant number	$n = 0.50$	$n = 1.0$	$n = 1.5$	$n = 2.0$
1	9.0%	5.0%	4.0%	5.0%
2	14.0%	8.0%	6.0%	5.0%
3	11.0%	10.0%	4.0%	2.0%
4	8.0%	3.0%	1.0%	0.0%
5	7.0%	3.0%	2.0%	2.0%
6	15.0%	4.0%	3.0%	2.0%

Also note that these values were calculated when users had three attempts to log in to their accounts.

Table 6.2 FAR values calculated and the average for each of the 100 trials for each of the participants are presented as a function of the acceptance threshold (n-SD units, ranging from 0.5 to 2.0 in steps of 0.5). Also note that these values were calculated based on the results of three attempts to log in to the respective accounts

Participant number	$n = 0.50$	$n = 1.0$	$n = 1.5$	$n = 2.0$
1	1.0%	2.0%	4.0%	4.0%
2	0.0%	4.0%	5.0%	9.0%
3	2.0%	8.0%	9.0%	12.0%
4	0.0%	2.0%	4.0%	7.0%
5	1.0%	2.0%	3.0%	5.0%
6	2.0%	5.0%	6.0%	6.0%

indicates that employing this basic authentication metric provides reasonable values for FRR, with an average value of 2.7% (for $n = 2.0$). As with keystroke dynamics, the balance between FRR and FAR must be met such that the EER is minimal. The FAR in this study was measured by allowing each user to log into each of the other five accounts 20 times, yielding a total of 100 imposter attempts per account. The results of FAR as a function of n are presented in Table 6.3.

The best results are generated with $n = 1.0$, yielding an FRR of 5.5% and an FAR of 3.8%. These results are very comparable to textual-based keystroke dynamics-based systems (see previous discussions in Chapter 4). These results were obtained using a standard image size of 15×15 mm (width $\times$ height). We next examined what would happen if the image density was changed by either varying the number of images in a constant viewing area or by changing the size of the images while maintaining a constant image size (thus increasing the viewing area). Obviously, there are screen size limitations that must be adhered to, but within the limits of practicality, we varied these parameters to determine what effect they might have on classification accuracy. The data from this study focused exclusively on PC monitors (19

Table 6.3 FAR and FRR values averaged across all 100 trials for all six participants as a function of the number of images (6×6, 8×8, 10×10, and 12×12) in a fixed region of the screen (6×6 inches). The values in parentheses indicate the SD from the six participants. This data represent the pooled values from six users and 100 attempts each for FAR/FRR

Image matrix size	FRR	FAR
6×6	4.7 (2.3)	2.9 (1.6)
8×8	5.1 (3.3)	2.5 (1.1)
10×10	5.4 (2.9)	2.1 (1.6)
12×12	6.7 (4.2)	4.2 (2.8)

inches), but certainly this work could be extended to include PDAs and even mobile phones. Increasing the number of images from 6×6 to 12×12 incrementally was examined to see how this might effect the user performance.

This test could be used to determine the theoretical limits to the size of the image matrix on small screen devices such as mobile phones. In addition, we wanted to determine if Fitts' law is applicable to this type of computer interaction (Fitts, 1954, Appendix C). In addition, there is an extension of Fitts' law which is more directly applicable to 2-D or bivariate pointing (see Accot & Zhai, 2003). Fitts' law basically states that the time required to perform a task, such as clicking on an object (target) located on a computer screen, is related to the distance of the center of the object from the current mouse/pointer location divided by the width of the target. Fitts' law applies to straight-line movements, and was derived to explain the time requirements for task performance in the human–computer interaction literature. An extension of Fitts' law, termed the Accot–Zhai steering law, provides a more robust measure of performance time when interacting in a 2-D environment. To test the applicability of these two laws, several experiments were performed where the size of the images (larger/smaller) was examined to see how the data fits these models. Very few studies in graphical-based passwords employ these laws, yet this information may prove quite valuable in this context as it may serve to incorporate the substantial body of experimental psychology research into the realm of graphical passwords.

In the first experiment, the viewing space was held constant (each montage was held fixed at approximately 6×6 inches), with a separating line drawn vertically down the middle of the page. The test was performed on a standard 19 inch monitor with 1024×768 SVGA screen resolution, and the images were high-resolution JPEG. The number of images presented in each panel was varied from 6×6 to 12×12 in double-dimension increments. All of the images were the same throughout these experiments. To reduce any practice effect, different sets of students were utilized for each of the four separate experiments, and the results compared between the groups using a standard *t*-test. The test protocols were identical to those mentioned previously, where the users selected their own login ID and a graphical password that contained five pictorial elements. Then, each of the participants (six different subjects for each of the experiments) enrolled by entering their graphical passwords five

Table 6.4   FRR and FAR calculated as the grand average for each of five participants, with 100 entries each for FRR and FAR. The image matrix was fixed as 4 × 4, and the total viewing area was increased according to the figures in column 1. Note that these values are the averages across all users (parenthetical values are the SDs)

Image viewing size (inches)	FRR	FAR
4 × 4	3.6 (1.2)	1.9 (1.0)
5 × 5	3.1 (1.3)	1.5 (0.9)
6 × 6	4.4 (2.1)	0.9 (0.6)
7 × 7	2.7 (1.2)	2.2 (1.8)

times. Note that there were no failure to enroll cases in any of these experiments (failure to enroll, $FTE = 0\%$). The actual password was displayed on the top center of the screen during enrollment, but not during the authentication phase. This was repeated for all four image size matrices, and the FRR and FAR were calculated. After successful enrollment, each of the participants authenticated himself 100 times for FRR calculations, and each logged into the other five accounts 20 times to calculate FAR values. A summary of the results is presented in Table 6.3, where the average FRR and FAR for all six subjects is presented as a function of image size.

The data in Table 6.4 indicate that with respect to the FRR values, taken as an average across all six participants per image matrix size, the values were more or less consistent with one another. There is a clear trend for an increase in FRR, but this was not statistically significant ($P < 0.12$). The same trend was apparent for the FAR values as well, though again the trend was not statistically significant ($P < 0.29$). The information not presented in Table 6.4 is the time it took for each user to select his passwords – which one would expect to increase with increasing image matrix size. For instance, it took on average 1.152 seconds per *image* graph for the 6 × 6 matrix, and 3.327 seconds for the 12 × 12 graph. The average values are presented in Figure 6.2.

The next experiment was to investigate whether there was any effect of total image area size – for this experiment, the images were maintained at the same size (15 × 15 mm), but the number of images was increased, and hence the total viewing area was increased accordingly. This experiment is slightly different from the previous one, in that when the number of images was increased, their size remained constant. In the previous experiment, the opposite holds true. Everything else was the same as in the previous experiment – the subjects employed the same graphical password. The subjects reenrolled in this system, because even though the password elements were the same, the size was varied somewhat (approximately from 4 × 4 to 7 × 7 inch total panel dimensions). The FAR and FRR calculations were performed in the exact same manner as the previous experiment, and the results are presented in Table 6.4.

The results indicate a slightly smaller value generally for both FRR and FAR – again these results are very consistent with high-quality textual-based passwords systems discussed elsewhere in Chapter 4. The best results were achieved with a 5 × 5 inch matrix, which contained

64 images arranged in an 8×8 matrix. This is quite suitable for PC screens, but will these results hold for much smaller, potentially lower resolution and poorly illuminated mobile screens? This is an area for further study, discussed at the end of this chapter.

The results from these two experiments could be fitted quite successfully with the Accot–Zhai steering law, employing a Euclidean distance metric. The task performance time was taken to be the time difference when the user clicked on the password image on the right montage to the time taken to move it to the correct position as indicated on the left montage. The model used in this work was reported by Accot and Zhai in their 2003 paper, and is reproduced here for convenience in equation 6.1:

$$T = a + b \times \log_2\left(\sqrt{(D/W)^2 + \eta(D/H)^2} + 1\right) \tag{6.1}$$

where D is the distance to target; W is the target width, and H is the target height. The parameter a represents the start/stop time; b represents the speed of the device, and η represents a model parameter, which typically takes on a value in the range of 0–1. In the model given in equation 6.2, η can be viewed as a scaling factor and is taken as 1.0 in this study, as the H to W ratio is unity. Typically, when this is the case, the 1-D model of Fitts will generally hold true. We preferred to use the Accot–Zhai law because it would be applicable when the ratio of W to H was not unity. The resulting equation for this system was as follows (note that time is in millisecond):

$$T \approx 732 + 513 \times \log_2\left(\sqrt{(D/W)^2 + \eta(D/H)^2} + 1\right) \tag{6.2}$$

The regression coefficient (Pearson's R^2) was 0.891, quite significant. We did not attempt to vary the ratio of H to W in this experiment, although this work is currently being undertaken in our laboratory.

The results from this series of studies indicate that the users were able to work within this system quite effectively. The results appeared to be robust with respect to the number of images (in the range applied here) and image size. Although this study employed a small number of participants, it is hoped that we will be able to repeat this study with a much larger cohort. In addition, the types of images employed in this study will be varied to see if they have an impact on the speed with which users select their password images (i.e. a Hick's law effect). In addition, a Stroop (1935) effect may be examined using this strategy – particularly when images contain semantic contradictions. This may have an impact on the speed with which users enter their password and may serve to help discriminate authentic users who will adapt to this effect relative to potential imposters.

Lastly, a study by Sylvain and colleagues (2004) examined the use of mouse dynamics as a user authentication technique. The study involved six users, each asked to use a mouse to play a simple game, whereby the user was required to click on a position on a board (presented on a standard PC monitor) that contained an easily identifiable colored object. During the course of the task, records of the $\langle x, y \rangle$ coordinates of the mouse were collected with high temporal precision. The following features were also extracted: horizontal and vertical speed, horizontal and vertical accelerations, the angle between the tangent to the x axis, tangential acceleration, curvature, and curvature derivatives. These attributes were extracted at each time point, forming a collection of feature vectors. The dimensionality of the feature vectors was reduced by taking the minimum, maximum, mean, and SD across each time point for all features. This served as the reference vector for each user. The authentication scheme required the same users to play the game again, and a Euclidean distance metric was deployed to determine which BIR the user matched most closely, given some threshold. The results indicate that the EER was 37.5% for this study cohort. The authors indicate that the results could be improved by deploying an adaptive strategy, which takes into account how users evolve their use of the mouse over time.

6.3 Conclusion

The results from the studies presented in this chapter indicate first and foremost that mouse dynamics can be a very effective means of authentication. With FAR and FRR values of approximately 2–5%, the data has provided evidence that *the way* users interact with computer systems contains sufficient discriminatory power to distinguish authentic users from imposters. What features of a user's interaction with a pointing device can be deployed for user identification/authentication considering that only mouse movements and mouse clicks are available? The studies of Gamboa (2003) and Pusara (2003)indicate that a substantial number of secondary attributes can be extracted. These attributes include the speed, distance, and angles made when moving the mouse within some given time interval. Depending on the temporal resolution, a substantial amount of data can be extracted for classification purposes. In addition, statistical information is typically extracted from the raw data to provide higher-order feature vectors to enhance the discriminatory capability of the classifier (s) employed.

Hashia and colleagues (2003) employed one of the first mouse dynamics-based authentication systems. In their system, mouse movements were collected at particular time intervals (every 50 ms) and were recorded during a 15 minute trial period. In a manner similar to online handwriting analysis, attributes such as speed and direction were collected during the equivalent of an enrollment period. A model was created from this training process and was used for subsequent verification purposes. The results yielded a fairly high EER on the order of 15–20%. This value is probably unacceptably high for commercial applications – but did demonstrate that this approach was feasible – though in need of some methodological improvements possibly.

Gamboa and colleagues have produced a considerable amount of work examining the deployment of mouse dynamics in the context of biometric authentication (Gamboa & Fred, 2003a,b, 2004). These studies extracted a considerable number of attributes such as speed, distance, and direction recorded at particular time intervals (100 ms). Statistical measurements were generated from the raw data, which was collected during the equivalent of an enrollment process. This processing pipeline generated a substantial number of attributes that formed the basis of a user's BIR. The results of the classification process yielded an EER that was dependent on the amount of data recorded during the time window (they call the stroke count, analogous to the Draw-a-Secret scheme). With a sufficiently large stroke count, the EER was recorded to be at the 1:200 range, quite comparable to that for fingerprint systems.

In the Pusara (2003) study, mouse dynamics was employed to re-authenticate users in order to prevent hijacking. They collected data based on frequency information, which examined within some given time interval (100 ms for instance) how many actions were undertaken using the mouse (clicks and movements). Frequency information provides only relative data – the ordering of the events is not considered – only a count frequency of each category of event is measured. This approach proved to be effective in their study, but as the authors mentioned, if the authentic user and imposter user (s) displayed the same basic mouse usage habits, this relative usage scheme may not be able to distinguish the authentic user from the imposter.

Lastly, in the study by the author, a combined graphical and mouse dynamics approach was undertaken. The timing information required to select the elements of the users' graphical password was the principle attribute extracted in this study. Timing was measured in accord to the Accot–Zhai steering law, extracting information regarding how the distances to the destination icons affected task completion speed. The results indicate that FRR/FAR values of the order of 2–5% were obtainable – depending on the image matrix size and the number of images on the selection panel. This study will be expanded to include more subjects (only six were employed in the study reported here), and also we will examine a wider range of attributes, such as those employed by Gamboa and colleagues. This was the first reported study that did specifically utilize the Accot–Zhai steering law, and we also plan to incorporate Hick's law, as well as examine how Stroop effects may be incorporated into the system to examine (Stroop, 1936). The Stroop effect is expected to provide enhanced discriminatory capacity by the general inhibitory/conflicting effect it will have on the untrained versus the trained user. This effect will be most pronounced within a graphical decision context.

Clearly, the deployment of mouse movements, similar to keystroke dynamics, appears to be a viable candidate for behavioral-based biometrics. It has all the advantages of keystroke dynamics and can certainly be utilized in a remote access fashion. Whether alone or in combination with other behavioral (or physiological biometrics for that matter) biometrics, this technology requires further examination to determine more accurately its promise as a behavioral biometric approach to user authentication.

6.4 Research Topics

1. Examine more thoroughly the effect of distance to target (Fitts' or Accot–Zhai steering law) on selection time.
2. What is the relative contribution of Hick's law with respect to the ability of a classifier to discriminate users?
3. Can the incorporation of a Stroop effect – via a graphical selection process – affect the discriminatory capacity of a mouse dynamics-based classification scheme?
4. Integrate the use of mouse dynamics with other behavioral biometrics such as keystroke dynamics, generating a truly multimodal biometric that remains within the behavioral biometric divide.
5. Examine a wider range of machine learning algorithms to enhance the classification accuracy.

7

Multimodal Biometric Systems

7.1 Introduction to Multimodal Biometrics

In this chapter, an overview of the deployment of multiple biometric (multimodal) solutions will be described. Up to this point, all discussions have focused on the development and evaluation of unimodal biometric systems, such as voice recognition, signature verification, or keystroke dynamics. One could argue that the use of multimodal biometrics has to wait until the individual elements have been developed to some desired level with respect to task performance. The data available from most behavioral biometrics indicate that they provide classification performance on par with many physiological-based systems such as fingerprints. For instance, the results from the fingerprint verification competition (FVC2004) fingerprint results produced a false acceptance rate (FAR)/false rejection rate (FRR) of 2% – certainly within the realm of many keystroke dynamics or mouse dynamics results (Bergadano et al., 2002, Revett et al., 2008b). It is possible that there is an upper bound on the classification accuracy of most unimodal biometrics.

Ultimately, the reproducibility, memorability, and related constraints, which are essentially cognitive in nature, *may* have placed a ceiling on the classification capacity of behavioral biometrics. Signatures can vary with time and circumstances; our typing style might change as a result of an accident to our dominant hand, etc. With respect to physiological biometrics, cognitive constraints are not applicable, but there may be other constraints such as the availability of the data (measured as the failure to enroll (FTE)) and the ability to adapt to changing physiognomy. For instance, it is estimated that 2% of the population may not be able to provide a fingerprint due to medical/genetic conditions, accidental destruction, or temporary damage (Maio et al., 2004). Facial features certainly change as a function of age, plastic surgery, and accident-related changes.

In a unimodal biometric system, all potential users are expected to be able to utilize the system (i.e. *FTE* = 0%). If FTE is above acceptable levels, then the deployment of a multibiometric system may be required. For instance, in an iris recognition system, people with glaucoma or related diseases may not be able to authenticate correctly. There is also a finite number of people that because of disease, work habits may not be able to provide reliable fingerprints for fingerprint-based authentication. Clearly, face recognition will face difficulties as a person ages or if there has been some form of medical treatment or disease progression

Behavioral Biometrics: A Remote Access Approach. Kenneth Revett
© 2008 John Wiley & Sons, Ltd.

that has altered the morphology of an individual's facial features subsequent to enrollment. One remedial solution may be for the user to reenroll, but this is expensive and inconvenient as the user will have to reenroll again after recovery. There are also issues of how to handle cases where the data generated from the biometric is identical to that of other enrolled users of the system. Two signatures can be virtually indistinguishable and two faces can be essentially identical. How can these situations be handled within a unimodal biometrics approach? More generally, how does a static unimodal biometric system evolve over time? Clearly, several classes of biometric data are not invariant over time, yet the classification process must be able to cope with an adapting input. The next logical step to enhancing the classification accuracy of biometrics is to employ a combined approach. This is the driving force behind the multimodal biometrics approach. To sum up the approach, one can define multimodal biometrics as "... those which utilize, or are capable of utilizing, more than one physiological or behavioral characteristic for enrollment, verification, or identification" (Mak et al., 2004).

Does the adage "the whole is greater than the sum of its parts" apply to multimodal biometrics? This depends on *which* parts are used and *how* they are integrated into a unified whole. There are a variety of parts – which are essentially any of the unimodal biometrics discussed in this text – and many more that fall under the purview of physiological biometrics. A critical research question is to examine how effectively different unimodal biometrics can be combined in terms of classification accuracy. Is there a linear relationship between the number of unimodal biometrics and classification accuracy? Are certain biometric technologies complimentary with respect to compensating for weaknesses of other biometrics?

Generally speaking, the literature contains examples of combining physiological biometrics together (i.e. face + fingerprints), or physiological and behavioral biometrics (face + keystroke dynamics), but there are very few examples of a purely behavioral fusion approach. Does this reflect an inherent limitation with respect to the fusion of these different classes of biometrics? The search space of unimodal biometrics is quite large – there are over 20 different classes of technologies, yielding 2×10^{18} combinations (order disregarded). Clearly, we have only just begun to explore a small region of this search space. What is required is a systematic approach to evaluating the efficacy of the combination of *any* unimodal biometric.

The systematic approach required is typically instantiated as an analysis framework, based on several distinct stages that are implemented in a serial fashion. These include data extraction, feature extraction, model development, classification algorithms, and a decision module. This processing stream is common to all unimodal biometrics, and literature reports imply that this processing stream can be utilized for multibiometric systems as well (Jain et al., 2005). If this processing stream is applicable to multibiometric systems, how should the separate streams interact with one another?

In Figure 7.1, the distinction between *multimodal-*and *fusion-*based biometrics is highlighted. In a pure multimodal approach, data extraction occurs from *multiple* types of biometric modalities, and each is treated as a parallel stream through the decision-making process. In contrast, the fusion approach takes as input a *single* biometric measurement and analyzes it through several parallel processing streams before rendering a classification decision. Note that in Figure 7.1, prior to the decision stage, a logic phase is invoked, which "fuses" the results together – what this author believes is really part of the modeling process. That is, the model includes as input several features of the original input data that have been

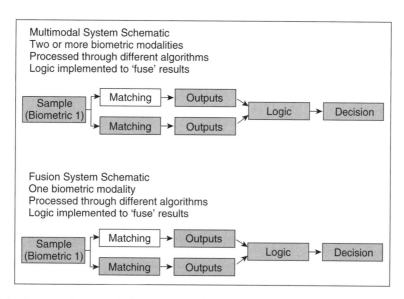

Figure 7.1   An example of two different multimodal biometric systems which differ in the initial data stream that is fed into the biometric pipeline, illustrating the difference between serial (top) and parallel (bottom) processing. (Source: website; International Biometrics Group www.ibia.org)

feature extracted and used as input to a classifier system (s). If there are multiple classification processes, they must be combined in some way prior to rendering a classification decision. The critical issue is how to combine or fuse the various biometric modalities: fusion is potentially a multilevel process that can occur at any stage during the processing stream. Exactly how is this fusion process to be implemented? How are the results affected by the stage at which the fusion process occurs?

7.2 Fusion Framework Approaches

Jain and colleagues (2005) discuss at length the issue of fusion within the context of multimodal biometrics. They identify four processing modules that are universally applicable to any biometric system (uni- or multimodal): sensor, feature extraction, matching, and decision modules (these processing stages are similar to those depicted in Figure 7.1). The fusion process may occur at any one of these processing modules, from a single module to an exhaustive combination of all modules. The sensor module entails the actual deployment of the biometric technology, such as a fingerprint scanner or a keyboard, for the express purpose of collecting raw data from the user. There are several ways in which fusion can occur at this level. In one scenario, multiple samples can be obtained in order to enhance the reliability of the data. Any significant variation in the samples can be removed, yielding clean and statistically reliable data. Statistical reliability can refer to repeated measures of a single source of information. For instance, an enrollment process where users are required to enter their login ID/password 10 times is a suitable example. There is also the issue of coverage, where the acquired data is inherently multifaceted. For instance, in a face recognition system, the particular profile can vary, and the model must be able to handle a variety of poses for accurate classification purposes. Taking multiple images at different pose angles may help reduce error in the classification process by increasing the scope of the input data. In addition, sensor-level fusion can entail the extraction of multiple types of data from a variety of sensors, such as signature samples *and* fingerprints. The data must be combined in some meaningful way in order to enhance the subsequent classification accuracy of the system. Whether this step is feasible depends on subsequent modeling and classification approaches. At the feature extraction module, data from the sensor acquisition stage are combined to yield a complete data profile that is used for subsequent modeling and classification purposes. In the case of repeated measures, the data profile consists of a single unimodal biometric data source. In the case of a multimodal sensor acquisition scheme, the sensor data from multiple sources can be concatenated together to form the data profile for the user.

The transformation of sensor readings into feature data is not always a straightforward manner. Typically, many secondary features are derived from the primary sensor data yielding higher-order features that typically used to enhance the classification process. This is especially true for behavioral biometrics where, for instance, slope shape may be extracted from the data to enhance the cardinality of the sensor space data (see Chapter 4 for details on slope shape transformations in the context of keystroke dynamics). As pointed out by Jain and colleagues (2005, p. 2272), care must be taken to ensure the feature attributes are as uncorrelated as possible at this stage to avoid biasing the classifier. In the case of physiological biometrics, enhancing the sensor data with second-order attributes occurs less frequently, and so this may not be as much of an issue in this context. Another difficulty is how to weight the contribution of each modality in a multimodal feature set. Do we know a priori the relevant importance of each sensor modality with respect to classification process?

Fusion at the sensor or feature stage has been termed pre-classification fusion by Jain (Jain et al., 2005). Fusion at this level may present several difficulties, one being the potential difficulty of merging together data from different biometric modalities. Simply concatenating a large number of attributes may generate a very large feature vector that may increase the computational complexity of the classification process. Generally speaking, this may not present an insurmountable problem, as there are a number of very useful techniques available for dimensionality reduction. For instance, rough sets is a very useful approach that has been successfully applied to extremely large feature vector spaces with great success (Slezak et al., 2002, Gorunescu et al., 2005a,b, Revett et al., 2005a,b). In addition, the application of rough sets to large feature vectors helps to determine which features are important in the classification task, often reducing the dimensionality by focusing on those features that are important with respect to the decision outcome. Whether the curse of dimensionality applies in most cases, especially with respect to behavioral biometrics, is a matter of debate at best. In commercial products, the availability of feature data may not be obtainable, and in this case, fusion may, by definition, have to be postponed to later phases in the processing pipeline.

Fusion can also occur after the feature extraction module, which is referred to as post-classification fusion by Jain and colleagues (2005). Post-classification fusion refers to the process of amalgamating data for the score/matching and decision processes that occur after the post-feature extraction stage, which ultimately produces a verification decision (to authenticate or not). At this processing stage, the input is the values obtained through feature extraction. The task is to ultimately generate a decision outcome, that is, to authenticate or not. There are four general levels in the Jain framework for post-classification processes: dynamic classifier selection, fusion at the abstract level, fusion at the rank level, and fusion at the matching level (Jain et al., 2005). A dynamic classifier selection scheme decides on some a priori basis which classifier is most likely to yield the correct decision, and hence employs a winner-takes-all strategy (Chen et al., 1997). Fusion at the decision level entails integrating multiple sources of information in order to render a decision outcome. There are many approaches employed at this level, such as voting schemes, Dempster–Shafer theory of evidence, and other techniques (Xu et al., 1992, Lam & Suen, 1997). In addition, it may be possible to rank the outcomes of decision, and the decision is based on the rank ordering of the individual components. Lastly, the fusion process can be applied at the matching score level. If there is confidence level associated with each score, then this information can be used to enhance the likelihood of the decision being the correct one. Specific instances of the classification approach will be examined in detail in the case study section. With respect to the verification process, there are two general approaches: one which considers this as a classification task and the other as a combination task (Jain et al., 2005). The classification approach is essentially a parallel approach, where data from each of the biometric modalities is generated independently of one another, and the resulting score is used for subsequent decision making. The combination approach collapses the entire suite of match score values into a scalar value, which is used by the decision module. The combination approach requires that the output scores can be combined in some meaningful way. If this is not the case, then the data may have to be normalized, a process that finds a common domain onto which class the scores can be mapped into. This important issue will be discussed in the case study section by way of example.

Sanderson and Paliwal (2004) provided an alternative approach to the multistage processing stream presented thus far. They provided a three-tiered processing stream, identified as *pre-mapping*, *midst-mapping*, and *post-mapping* fusion. Essentially, the term "mapping" refers to the process of converting data into information whereby a class membership decision is rendered (i.e. authentic or imposter).

Sanderson's pre-mapping fusion essentially incorporates Jain's pre-classification stages, incorporating the sensor-and feature-level fusion processes (Jain et al., 2005). If the feature vectors from a multimodal acquisition scheme are *not* commensurate with one another, the feature vectors can be concatenated; otherwise, they can be combined using a weighted summation scheme. The authors note the same caveats that were in application in the Jain pre-classification scheme, such as finding the proper weighting for the different biometric modalities, the availability of feature vectors from commercial products, and the potential curse of dimensionality.

In the midst-mapping fusion process, a mapping from the feature space onto a model space is produced. The model is used to extract higher-order correlations in the data (e.g. when speech and lip movements are employed) and is typically implemented using extended hidden Markov models (eHMM) (see Wark et al., 2000). Whether midst mapping can be employed prior to the score/classification task depends on the modalities of the biometrics: they must provide synergistic/complementary information that can be incorporated into a larger single data model. This is clearly an interesting area for future research.

The post-mapping fusion scheme (also known as decision fusion), an ensemble of classifiers, is utilized to produce the final decision outcome (imposter or authentic user). This approach is especially useful when dealing with nonhomogeneous classifiers. By using an ensemble of classifiers, it is hoped that each can focus on a particular facet of the data, thus overcoming any shortcomings of individual classifiers. Some examples of these fusion schemes will be discussed in the context of individual case studies, which are presented next.

7.3 Case Studies

In a study published by Ross and colleagues (2001), the levels at which this fusion process can occur are clearly outlined, by way of example, employing three physiological biometrics. In this work, the authors attempt to fuse data derived from fingerprint, face, and hand geometry, in order to demonstrate the process of *information fusion* in the context of multimodal biometrics. The face verification data employed the eigenface approach to extract facial features for subsequent classification (see Turk & Pentland, 1991 for details of this approach). For their fingerprint data, a 500 dpi scanner was employed, and minutiae were extracted for subsequent classification. The hand geometry data was extracted using a high-resolution camera and identifying 14 feature values that were used for subsequent matching purposes. The data was collected from two groups of 50 users, with some degree of overlap between the two groups. The participants in one of the groups (labeled I) were requested to provide face (nine images) and fingerprint data (nine samples of the same finger). The hand geometry data was collected from a second group (labeled II), which consisted of 50 users, but an undisclosed number were from group I as well. They randomly paired each participant from group I with a user in group II. This generated 450 authentic scores and 22 050 imposter scores, for each of the three modalities. All scores (a 3-tuple) were mapped onto a fixed range ([0, 100]) through a normalization process. The data were reasonably well separated when plotted in three-dimensional (3-D) space (each coordinate representing one of the three biometric scores). The authors employed three classification schemes: a sum rule, a decision tree, and a linear discriminant function (LDF). Very briefly, the sum rule calculates that a weighted average of the three scores, using constant coefficients as performance data for each modality, was not available. The decision tree (based on C5.0 algorithm) used 50% of the data for training and the rest for testing purposes. The LDF was used to transform the data into clusters that maximize the distance between each of the data points (in 3-D space), using the Mahalanobis distance rule. The results indicate that the decision tree classifier yielded a combined error rate of approximately 10% (FAR + FRR); the LDF produced a combined error of 0.5%, and the sum rule generated a combined error of approximately 2%.

These results are somewhat surprising in that the error was as high as 10% for the decision tree approach, one that typically performs well in multi-class datasets, especially with such a large number of samples for training. This study raises an interesting question – the unimodal biometrics employed each traditionally yield different levels of classification accuracy, where fingerprints > hand > face, in order of classification accuracy. Typically, fingerprint yields an error on the order of 1–2%, which is essentially similar (same order of magnitude at least) to the results obtained in this study. It appears that combining these three different technologies yields an average classification error essentially equal to the most accurate modality. This assumption would have to be verified by examining each modality in isolation and the relevant combinations. It should be noted that the fusion occurred at the decision model level (or fusion at the score level according to the authors), downstream to the data acquisition and feature extraction level. In addition, it should be noted that the authors did employ a constant weighting factor for each biometric. Whether this approach produces optimal classification error is an issue to be investigated by further study. Lastly, it should also be noted that prior to generating the decision model to score the data, the authors employed a normalization process (on the matching scores) to ensure that the data consisted of elements that were of the same order of magnitude. How important is the issue of normalization with respect to the classification outcome?

Jain and colleagues (2005) extended the Ross study by investigating the effect of a variety of normalization techniques on the resulting decision classification accuracy. The authors asked: what effect does normalization have on the resulting classification accuracy? Normalization in this context is performed prior to combining them for the purpose of scoring. Several normalization algorithms were employed, which will be briefly discussed here (for details, consult Jain et al., 2005). The authors discuss the utilization of the *min–max, decimal scaling, z score, median* and *median absolute deviation* (MAD), *double sigmoid function*, the *tanh-estimator* method, and the *biweight estimator* normalization functions. Only three of these methods will be discussed here, and the interested reader can consult the paper in question and references contained therein.

The min–max normalization technique is the simplest employed in this study, which simply normalizes the data by dividing by the data range (max–min), as depicted in equation 7.1:

$$S'_k = (S_k - \text{min}) / (\text{max} - \text{min}) \tag{7.1}$$

This method is very sensitive to outliers contained within the data used to determine the min/max values. The original data is preserved, along with its distribution, as all scores are simply rescaled onto a single interval, [0, 1]. A similarity score can be generated from this data by subtracting the min–max normalized score from 1.

The z score is a very common normalization technique that requires knowledge of the mean and standard deviation of the matching scores (i.e. it requires prior knowledge of the data). Without prior knowledge, estimates of the mean and standard deviation are required to use this technique. The normalized scores are calculated according to equation 7.2:

$$S'_k = (S_k - \mu) / \sigma \tag{7.2}$$

where μ is the arithmetic mean and σ is the standard deviation. The use of z scores implies that the data (the scores) adhere to a Gaussian distribution, which may not always be the case. In addition, this technique is also sensitive to outliers, and so preprocessing of the sores may be required prior to using this normalization technique. A similar approach, based on using the median and MAD, is more robust to the presence of outliers but is less effective than using the mean and standard deviation. In addition, the original distribution is not retained after this normalization process.

The *tanh estimator* is a very robust normalization technique that is insensitive to outliers. The equation implementing this normalization scheme is presented in equation 7.3:

$$S'_k = \tfrac{1}{2} \{ \tanh(0.01((S_k - \mu_{\text{GH}} / \sigma_{\text{GH}})) + 1 \} \tag{7.3}$$

where μ_{GH} and σ_{GH} are the mean and standard deviation estimates of the genuine score distribution, respectively, as indicated by the Hampel estimators (see Hampel et al., 1986 for details of the Hampel estimators). This is a parameterized approach that requires the estimate of three influence parameters from the distribution of the scores. It is essentially quite robust

Table 7.1 Summary of the genuine acceptance rate (GAR%) when employing a variety of normalization techniques and fusion methods (Source: Jain et al., 2005)

Normalization techniques	Fusion techniques Sum of scores	Max score	Min score
STrans	98.3 (0.4)	46.7 (2.3)	83.9 (1.6)
Min–max	97.8 (0.6)	67.0 (2.5)	83.9 (1.6)
z score	98.6 (0.4)	92.1 (1.1)	84.8 (1.6)
Median	84.5 (1.3)	83.7 (1.6)	68.8 (2.2)
Sigmoid	96.5 (1.3)	83.7 (1.6)	83.1 (1.8)
Tanh	98.5 (0.4)	86.9 (1.8)	85.6 (1.5)
Parzen	95.7 (0.9)	93.6 (2.0)	83.9 (1.9)

Note that these values were obtained when the FAR was set at 0.1%. The values in parentheses are the standard deviations of the GAR.

if there are a small number of outliers, but is not efficient. Likewise, it is efficient, but not robust if there are a significant number of outliers.

The authors examined how the various normalization techniques influence the overall classification accuracy, by recording the FRR at a fixed value for FAR (0.1%). In order to provide a baseline for comparison, the authors investigated the use of face, fingerprint, and hand geometry individually (as purely unimodal biometrics). Their base results indicate that fingerprints > face > hand geometry (with no normalization). The fusion methods employed were the sum of scores, max score, and min score, which were each applied for each of the normalization methods listed at the start of this case study. The results are summarized in Table 7.1. The data in Table 7.1 indicate that the sum-of-scores fusion method was superior to the other two methods, irrespective of the normalization process employed. With respect to the normalization method, the tanh and the min–max outperformed the other methods at low FAR values (Jain et al., 2005). Note that the sum-of-scores fusion method is simply a linear combination of the score vector, according to the following formula: $S = (a_1 s_1 - b_1) + (a_2 s_2 - b_2) + (a_3 s_3 - b_3)$, where s_1, s_2, and s_3 are the corresponding matching scores for face, fingerprint, and hand geometry, respectively. The purpose of the different normalization processes was to determine the values for the coefficients (a_1, a_2, and a_3, and the biases b_1, b_2, and b_3).

The results from this study indicate that normalization can have a significant impact on the classification accuracy, and there are some basic generalizations that can be made with respect to a particular normalization method. For instance, if the data follows a Gaussian distribution, then the z-score normalization method is an appropriate starting choice. If the data contains a significant amount of noise, a more robust method such as tanh may be required. If there is statistical information, such as the mean and standard deviation available, then techniques such as min–max and z scoring can be employed. Nonparametric techniques can be employed such as the Parzen window density estimation method which can be used to convert the scores into posteriori probabilities. This method does not require any knowledge of the underlying structure of the data. But the performance is heavily dependent upon the parameters selected. Lastly, it should be noted that in many instances, the deployment of the sum-of-scores approach yielded better classification accuracy than the corresponding unimodal approach, across all normalization techniques (except for the median–MAD normalization technique).

Sanderson and Paliwal (2004) developed a multimodal approach utilizing speech and face information as a means of identity verification. They wished further to explore how noisy data impacts the efficiency and robustness of various fusion processes. The authors utilized the VidTIMIT (Video Texas Instruments MIT) audiovisual database, which contains recordings of 43 subjects (19 female and 24 male) reciting a selection of short sentences from a corpus (Sanderson & Paliwal, 2002). Three sessions were recorded, with a mean delay of 7 days between the first two sessions and 6 days between the last two sessions (2 and 3). The first two sentences were the same for all subjects, with the remaining eight variable (10 sentences were recited in total). The total time of recording per subject was approximately 43 seconds (corresponding to approximately 106 video frames). The recordings were acquired in a noisy office environment, captured with a high-quality digital video camera. The images were stored as JPEG with a 512×384 resolution. The audio component was stored as mono, 16 bit, 32 kHz wav files.

Since the data consist of voice and face data, the authors employed two different "experts" to capture each of these data channels for subsequent fusion. The speech expert consisted of a feature extraction module and an opinion (decision) generator. The face expert was developed in a similar fashion to the speech expert, except of course that the feature extraction process was different. The speech signal was analyzed frame by frame, generating a 37-dimensional feature vector for each frame. The feature vector consisted on the mel frequency cepstral coefficients (MFCCs), their corresponding deltas, and maximum autocorrelation values (see Chapter 2 in this volume and Reynolds, 1994 for details). This produced a sequence of vectors, which was analyzed using the voice activity detector (VAD), which removes features (attributes) that are associated with silence or background noise (see Haigh & Mason, 1993 for details on VAD).

The opinion generator (decision mechanism) was implemented as a Gaussian mixture model (GMM) for each user. Given a claim of identity, the claim is based on the average log likelihood of that claim being correct. In addition, the average log likelihood of the claimant being an imposter was also calculated, and the difference between the two was recorded. If the difference is greater than some given threshold, then the verification process yields a true result (opinion), else the claim is rejected. Any model parameters were estimated using the expectation maximization algorithm, generated from the training data (Reynolds et al., 2000).

The face expert differs principally from the voice expert in how the features (attributes) were extracted. The authors employed principal component analysis after face localization within the images. The face component of the images was acquired using a template matching algorithm, derived from a collection of face templates of varying dimensions. After the identification of the eyes, an affine transformation was applied such that the distance between the eyes of all images was the same, rendering approximately the same-sized facial image for all subjects. This yielded a 64×56 pixel face window, containing the eyes and the nose. The authors then extracted the D largest eigenvectors ($D = 20$), which was used for subsequent analysis.

In their experimental section, the authors describe the use of clean and noisy data (noisy via the addition of additive white Guassian noise) as a test case to evaluate the effect of noise on the classification accuracy of a variety of fusion models. Accuracy is reported as the equal

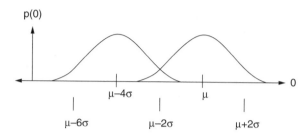

Figure 7.2 The distributions for true claims and imposter claims, delineating the separation of the two distribution on the intervals $(\mu_i - 6\sigma_i, \mu_i - 2\sigma_i)$ (Source: Sanderson and Paliwal, 2004)

error rate (EER) or the total error (TE), which is the sum of the FAR and FRR decision outcomes. They examined the use of a speech expert alone, face expert alone, feature vector concatenation, weighted summation fusion, a Bayesian post-classifier, and a support vector machine (SVM) post-classifier.

Note that for the vector concatenation, there is the issue of different frame rates (100 for speech and 25 for face). The authors decided to increase the frames per second (fps) count for the face data by duplicating face images. The concatenated features were processed using the VAD, as previously discussed. Also note that the opinions were also mapped (normalized) onto the interval [0, 1], using a sigmoid function. They assumed that the opinions for true and imposter claims followed a Gaussian distribution, then the two opinions would be expected to be contained within the intervals $[\mu_i - 6\sigma_i, \mu_i - 2\sigma_i]$, with a 95% probability (see Figure 7.2).

The authors examine a selection of adaptive and non-adaptive fusion techniques and their impact on the opinion (decision) outcomes, as a function of noise contained within the feature space. The overall results indicate that in clean conditions, most of the non-adaptive approaches and performance degrade as a function of the noise level increases. The results also suggest that most of the adaptive approach performance was inferior to the non-adaptive approach or relied on unrealistic assumptions. This prompted the authors to generate a further hybrid approach, where the decision boundary was adjustable based on the expected distribution of the opinions due to noisy conditions. The new approach was embodied as a structurally resistant set of post-classifiers. It was noted that the expert's decision boundaries were directly influenced by the noise levels incorporated into the data. In the adaptive system, assumptions about the expected noise level were incorporated from the training data, which may not generalize to the test data, if it contained a variable level of noise. A piecewise linear (PL) post-classifier was utilized, along with a modified Bayesian approach. These two approaches provided significantly lower EER values than the non-adaptive and adaptive experts. The PL classifier provided performance on par with adaptive methods (based on SVM), but had a fixed structure that was not directly dependent on any assumptions about the noise contained within the data. The modified Bayesian post-classifier also performed well (but not as well as the PL), but it had the ability to generalize to more than two experts (unlike the PL system).

The results from the Sanderson and Paliwal (2002) study indicate that the issue of noise when developing a collection of experts in a multimodal biometrics is significantly influenced by the noise inherent in the biometrics modality. In order to generate a system that is capable of operating correctly (i.e. minimal EER value) within an unknown level of noise, a higher-order opinion (decision) fusion might provide a more robust system. Noise is inherent to all biometric acquisition systems – and further still, each particular instantiation of a particular biometric will impart its own level of noise, independent of the systematic noise. Developing a classifier that takes into account the expected noise level may not be sufficient. Yet there is not a lot of research into this area – not enough to provide some standard reference values for all modalities – especially if the system employs behavioral biometrics as well. Further still, even with this data available, it is not sufficient to guarantee that the noise levels of a particular instantiation of a multibiometric will follow any sort of established standard. Therefore, this type of approach, evaluating each biometrics with respect to some range of noise, is an important task, overlooked in many cases reported in the literature.

Dieckmann and colleagues (Dieckmann et al., 1997, Frischolz & Dieckmann, 2000) developed a multibiometric platform called SESAM (derived from the German Synergetische Erkennung mittels Standbild, Akustik und Motorik). SESAM utilizes three different biometrics (face, voice, and lip movement) from two data sources, face recognition and voice data. Note that voice and lip movement are dynamic features, whereas a face image is obviously a static feature. The three biometrics were used independently, for training three separate classifiers, and ultimately for the classification/verification process. The final decision (opinion) is generated by fusing the matching scores from the three experts, using a 2-from-3 approach. This essentially is a majority voting scheme, where the best two results are used to classify the data if, and only if, there is concordance between at least two of the experts. A principal advantage of using dynamic features is that it helps obviate spoofing attacks, which are easier to implement with static features, such as presenting an image of a particular face, rather than the actual person presenting themselves to the camera.

After the features for face, speech, and lip motion are extracted, a feature vector of 4096 floating point values is utilized for subsequent classification purposes. Very briefly, the face images are extracted, focusing on the mouth as the means for obtaining the lip motion associated with the speech feature. This process entails the use of a template matching scheme, which is used to locate the eyes in the face images. The authors use a commonly reported observation that the distance between the eyes is very similar to the distance between the mouth and the eyes. Once the eyes are located, the mouth is found and, together with the eye information, provides the principal data for the face feature used in this system. The authors employed an optical flow analysis technique to extract the lip motion feature (Horn & Schunk, 1981). A summary of their scheme is depicted in Figure 7.3.

The authors employed the use of the Synergetic Computer system, developed by Haken (see Haken, 1991 for details in this interesting computational platform for classification). Very briefly, synergetic computers are a class of highly parallel computers that are constructed on the basic principles of synergetics in which the analogy between pattern recognition and pattern formation is exploited (Haken, 1991). The authors employ the MELT algorithm, which employs a set of learning vectors (in this case feature vectors), which are class normalized and are orthogonal to one another. The learning vectors in one class (user) are combined forming a prototype vector for that user. The Euclidean distance between each class of learning vectors and an identification/verification request is made and employs a winner-takes-all algorithm to select the best match (i.e. the decision outcome). Their system has been deployed successfully for both identification and verification purposes. For user verification, which is essentially a two-class decision problem, the authentic user data is generated from an

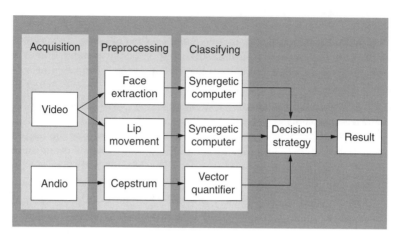

Figure 7.3 A schematic representing the feature extraction and feature fusion process employed by Dieckmann and colleagues (Source: Frischolz and Dieckmann, 2000)

enrollment process that generates 10 samples. The other class, which the authors term the "union-class," is generated from samples of all other users, containing 30 patterns.It is somewhat unclear from the published study results exactly where the 30 patterns originate from. But for each user, there are 10 self samples and 30 nonself samples used for classification purposes. The measure of classification accuracy is a weighted sum of the FAR and FRR values, as indicated in equation 7.4. The value of G, which is a measure of the quality of the classification, ranges from 0 (perfect classification) to 1 (perfect misclassification).

$$G = (2FRR + FAR)/3 \qquad (7.4)$$

The results of a field experiment, which deployed 66 participants, were highly encouraging. Based on 1428 recordings, the best recognition rate (in an *identification* task) with the combined approach (2-from-3) yielded a recognition rate of 93%. This result was superior to the deployment of each of the individual biometrics in isolation (89.6%, 89.0%, and 81.3% for speech, optical flow, and face image recognition rates, respectively). For user verification, the participants were split into three parts. For each subject, 10 patterns were used, and the union-class consisted of randomly selected patterns from the other members of the study. This process was repeated 50 times, for each modality separately, and the best results from each test were utilized to calculate the quality of the verification task. The results for the combined approach (2-from-3) were marginally superior to those from each modality used separately. In addition, the authors employed an *AND* fusion (3-from-3), which provided a slightly lower accuracy than the individual modalities alone and the 2-from-3 approach. The overall FAR was 0.33%, and FRR was 0.21% for the 2-from-3 approach.

The authors have deployed their multimodal verification approach into a commercial product named BioID. It was designed to be deployed within a personal computer environment, utilizing typical add-ons found in personal computers (web camera and microphone). This system was tested on a collection of 150 users for a period of 3 months and yielded a FAR below 1%. For details on this system, please consult the BioID Web site at http://www.BioID.com/.

The results from the Dieckmann study indicate that employing behavioral and physiological biometrics in a multimodal scenario can provide quality classification results, even when employing a majority voting scheme, which is a relatively simple approach to data fusion. The results indicate that the multimodal approach provided classification accuracies that were superior (though marginally in many cases) to the unimodal biometrics deployed in isolation. The approach adopted in the current study was used for a static single-point biometrics authentication scheme (i.e. employees entering a building were to be identified using this method). It suffices to query the authenticity of a user at a fixed time point but does not handle the case when a hijacking scenario may occur. The next case study presents how multimodal biometrics can be deployed for *continuous* biometric monitoring.

7.4 Continuous Verification

Altinok and Turk (2003) presented a model for the deployment of a multimodal *continuous* user verification scenario. The authors deployed a combination of face recognition, voice identification, and fingerprint identification into a multimodal approach to continuous user verification. An underlying issue with multimodal continuous verification/authentication is the temporal profile of each of the unimodal biometrics. Each biometric operates on a unique temporal profile. For instance, keystroke dynamics operates only when the user is interacting with the keyboard. Face recognition can occur continuously, but the quality of the data will depend on the pose angle of the user and related background context. Therefore, if one wishes to obtain, at any point in time, a combinatorial reading of multiple biometric data, then there are issues of temporal integration that must be addressed. Therefore, combining unimodal biometrics over a discrete (in the limit a continuous) timescale may present difficulties that must be addressed when designing such as system. This is the critical issue addressed in this case study.

The authors noted that temporal integration can occur independently of the fusion process. For instance, fusion at the feature level may provide the richest source of data from which to construct a user model; it may be more complex to do so then at subsequent levels (i.e. matcher or decision levels). It may be the case that temporal integration may allow the fusion process to be more effective, even when performed at a later stage during the multimodal authentication process. The authors chose to fuse data at the scores level. Therefore, each channel provides a normalized set of data points, along with a measure of the variance generated from each data channel.

Each channel is modeled as a Gaussain distribution, which is used to map the unimodal scores over time intervals that do not contain sufficient data from unimodal biometric measures. An uncertainty is encountered when a time interval does not contain any biometric data (unimodal or otherwise), and so during these time intervals, the variance associated with the claimant's identity increases. When a score is recorded, it is time-stamped and the variance/uncertainty is computed over the time interval between the current measurement and the last measurement. This diminished certainty is captured using a degeneracy model, which increases with respect to the interval during which data observations are not possible. The authors employed an exponential degeneracy function, which depends only on the mean variability over the last time interval, in order to estimate the parameters for a Gaussian model of the user. A principal parameter of this model is the time interval between successive unimodal recordings (i.e. the length of measurement history).

To determine the efficacy of their model, the authors employed data from face, voice, and fingerprint data from 24 individuals collected independently of one another. The face recognition data was obtained using 20 fps video recording, using a frontal pose for approximately 2 minutes (yielding ~80 frames), 20 of which were used for training purposes. For the voice data, the TIMIT database was employed (Seneff & Zue, 1988). Briefly, the linear prediction coefficients (LPC) cepstrum feature vectors were used, and the energy was normalized to compensate for any differences in loudness. The 16th-order LPC cepstra were calculated from 32 ms frames centered on 16 ms intervals. The feature vector was the rows of the resultant matrix (Altinok & Turk, 200X). Each user was modeled as a Gaussain, and the log likelihoods were the verification scores (taken over 15 seconds of training data). The fingerprint data was taken from the FVC2002 fingerprint verification competition, using minutiae-based features (see http://www.neurotechnologija.com/verifinger.html).

The integrated (multimodal) recognition rates were consistently higher than those for the individual channels. For instance, the integrated system versus voice alone yielded a classification accuracy of 97.74% and 96.61%, respectively. The effect of the history length had a minor impact on the classification accuracy, as long as there was at least one measurement within the time window. This effect is significantly influenced by the model used to extrapolate over the time window – in this case a simple Gaussian distribution was assumed, which has a smoothing effect that has a tendency to reduce the influence of the tails of the distribution on the classification result.

The results from this study indicate that temporal integration of multimodal biometrics can influence the classification accuracy to a certain degree. It must be kept in mind that not all biometrics can be obtained within the same time frame. Any continuous biometric system must accommodate the temporal characteristics of the data. In a multimodal system, this may be less of a problem as the probability of a measurement being available within a recording epoch is enhanced. Yet, if a multimodal system relies on the presence of multiple measurements at some time frame, the possibility of missing data must be taken into account when developing the data model. The authors employed a simple smoothing model (assuming the data follows a Gaussian distribution), which may not be applicable across all biometric modalities. This is an area for further research.

7.5 Standards

The integration of multibiometrics into a universal standard is a critical issue in lieu of increased needs for enhanced border control. As mentioned in previous chapters, the difficulty begins with the production of standards for unimodal biometrics. The production of a large-scale multibiometric standard presents a substantial challenge. This section provides a summary of some of the approaches that have been discussed in the context of developing a multimodal biometric standard. A principal metric for success in the standardization process is interoperability and data exchange formats. This requires walking a fine line between open standards and proprietary protocols. On the one hand, open standards tend to publicize the nature of the underlying technology, making the system appear at last more vulnerable. On the other hand, having a collection of proprietary (secret) protocols makes interoperability difficult at best. Considering the global climate in which biometrics is predominantly applied, one would favor an open standards approach. Unlike unimodal biometrics, case studies involving large-scale, national/international biometric test cases are a difficult and expensive undertaking. One of the principal criteria for multibiometrics is the issue of interoperability. Several such studies have been undertaken, and a brief summary of several such studies will be presented.

In March 2005, the Japanese government conducted a test on the readability of ePassports, focusing on the issue of readability of ePassports at all borders with the country (*Biometric Technology Today*, 2006). The ePassports were developed to conform to the International Civil Aviation Organization (ICAO) specification (for details, see ICAO, 2004). The results indicate that on average, 82.9% of the passports could be read (based on 16 reader vendors and 30 passport vendors). Another ePassport readability study, conducted in Singapore (in November 2005), yielded an interoperability of greater than 90% (based on 140 ePassport specimens and 45 readers) (Dessimoz & Richiardi, 2006, p. 36). There have been (and will be) a number of interoperability tests, which have yielded a variety of degrees of success. A number of international standards organizations have been established to create and test a variety of biometric standards. It is beyond the scope of this work to describe them in detail. Briefly, there is the BioAPI specification version 2.0, which promotes interoperability between vendors (ISO/IEC 19794-1, 2005). This specification consists of four modules: i) a sensor biometric function provider (BFP), ii) archive BFPs, providing access to template databases, iii) BFP processing algorithms, and iv) matching algorithm BFPs. There is the Common Biometric Exchange File Format (CBEFF), which has been discussed briefly in Chapter 4 in the context of keystroke dynamics. This specification consists of the design of a biometric information record, which specifies completely how the data for any given (i.e. included) biometric should be stored for interoperability. There is also the ANSI X9.84 standard, the Biometric Information Management and Security for the Financial Services Industry, which describes how biometrics should be designed to meet the requirements of the financial services industry (ANSI X8.94, 2003). Lastly, the International Standards Organization (ISO) and the International Electrotechnical Commision (IEC), which created the Joint Technical Committee 1 (JCT1) in the early 1980s, have generated several interoperability standards through a variety of subcommittees, many of which are still active. Three such subcommittees, SC17, SC27, and SC37, have been created to manage cards and personal identification, IT security techniques, and biometrics, respectively (see http:///www.jtc1.org). All these subcommittees have working groups that are actively involved in setting many of the extant biometric interoperability standards on an international level in many cases.

7.6 Conclusions

This chapter has highlighted some of the key issues that must be addressed when deploying multimodal biometrics. The critical issues involve finding methods for integrating or fusing multiple data channels together such that a single metric is generated – whether to authenticate or not. In addition, the larger issue is how to integrate unimodal biometrics into a multimodal framework that allows interoperability on a potentially international level. The case studies presented in this chapter are just a small sample of what exists within the literature. What is evident from perusing this literature is the lack of behavioral biometrics as an integral part of the multimodal approach. The majority of multimodal biometrics involves the use of fingerprints and face recognition systems. Each unimodal biometric has its own characteristics, both with respect to the data they produce and their temporal profiles. The deployment of a multimodal approach generally produces more accurate classification results compared with the use of the unimodal biometrics in isolation. This result appears to be independent of the location of the fusion – though there are differences in the ease with which the fusion process can occur.

In addition to static verification, multimodal biometrics has been successfully applied for continuous authentication purposes. The Altinok and Turk (2003) study indicate that using a relatively simple multimodal model, users could be authenticated on a continuous basis, without the need for continuous measurements. Zhang and colleagues (2006) provide another example of continuous multimodal biometrics, employing a more sophisticated model (employing a hidden Markov model), embedded within a Bayesian Framework, produced very satisfactory results, employing purely physiological biometrics.

Further research is required to establish how purely behavioral-based biometrics can be implemented within a multimodal framework. To date, the vast majority of all behavioral biometrics included in multimodal schemes employ voice recognition. Signature recognition has been employed in just a few studies, but there is virtually no inclusion of keystroke or mouse dynamics in this context. Behavioral biometrics do not present any inherent limitation with respect to multimodal biometrics – on the contrary, if they are perceived to be weaker than more traditional physiological techniques, it would be interesting to examine how they work in unison. It is expected that, like their physiological cousins, behavioral biometrics, employed in a multimodal system, would provide more robust authentication results than when deployed in isolation. This is clearly an area of research that needs to be explored in detail.

7.7 Research Topics

1. A critical research question is to examine how effectively different unimodal biometrics can be combined in terms of classification accuracy. Is there a linear relationship between the number of unimodal biometrics and classification accuracy? Are certain biometric technologies complimentary with respect to compensating for weaknesses of other biometrics?

2. Whether midst mapping can be employed prior to the score/classification task depends on the modalities of the biometrics: they must provide synergistic/complementary information that can be incorporated into a larger single data model?

3. Developing a classifier that takes into account the expected noise level may not be sufficient. Yet there is not a lot of research into this area – not enough to provide some standard reference values for all modalities – especially if the system employs behavioral biometrics as well.

4. How should smoothing models be developed and applied to various multimodal biometrics? Can the same approach be used across the range of biometrics? This question becomes very critical when fusing behavioral and physiological biometric modalities.

5. How can datasets be obtained for multimodal biometrics? In a truly multimodal scenario, we require data from each modality for each user involved in a study. There are difficulties

in acquiring a unimodal database – what approaches can we undertake to enhance the production of multimodal databases?

In lieu of 5 above, what ontologies must be created that will allow the seamless integration of a variety of biometric modalities such that data can be shared among researchers in academia and industry alike?

8

The Future of Behavioral Biometrics

8.1 Introduction to the Future of Biometrics

The preceding chapters have presented a brief summary of some of the current technologies available for performing behavioral-based biometrics. The question addressed in this chapter is where do we go from here? Can we extend this technology to provide more accurate and less invasive approaches to user (or object) authentication? The divide between physiological and behavioral biometrics is quickly dissipating, and it may be that behavioral biometrics, based on the *physiology of behavior*, is more flexible than the anatomy – the physiological approach to biometrics. After all, our anatomy is fixed – the thread that runs throughout the literature – and serves as the basis for the supposed superiority of the physiological approach. Are we to acquire new anatomical features in order to expand this horizon? Are there other features we have yet to fully explore? In a paper published by Forsen and colleagues (1977), a listing of the principle biometrics, both behavioral and physiological, was presented. This prescient paper (published 30 years ago) included several physiological techniques such as nail striations, bite patterns, ear structure, as well as a range of other physiological techniques – many of which have not been implemented to any significant degree. Why some of these approaches have not been pursued is an open research question which will not be discussed further in this chapter, as the focus here is on behavioral biometrics.

There are also limitations with the behavioral biometric approach – especially if it is to be utilized in a remote access approach. This limitation is the result of a requirement that behavioral biometrics is a software-only solution, which is a very stiff constraint. If one faithfully adheres to this constraint, there is still considerable room for expansion. If this constraint is relaxed, then the doors open wide – and the possibilities are really open-ended. In what follows, a series of case study-like discussions will be presented, which address both scenarios: adherence to a software-only approach and then an unrestricted approach to behavioral biometrics.

Behavioral Biometrics: A Remote Access Approach. Kenneth Revett
© 2008 John Wiley & Sons, Ltd.

8.2 Software-Only Approach

Take for instance graphical-based authentication systems, a summary of which has been presented in Chapter 6. All of the case studies presented in Chapter 6 utilized two-dimensional (2-D) images, and this trend holds generally in the literature and within commercial implementations. Within the 2-D realm, one could utilize the substantial amount of cognitive psychology literature, such as subliminal cueing theory. As suggested in Chapter 6, the use of subliminal cueing may help to influence a user's attention and mood when interacting with a graphical interface. During the training process, users would be provided with subvisual cues (subliminal) that would help separate out the decoys from the password graphics by biasing the user's selection toward the password elements. Research has demonstrated repeatedly that subliminal cueing has a significant impact on user choice in many paradigms (Dahaene et al., 1998, Hoshiyama et al., 2006). A neutral cue could be presented during authentication, which would be designed to serve as a mild distracter to those not trained with them. The distracter would be too weak to impact the authentic users, but possibly just enough to affect the potential imposter. To this author's knowledge, there are virtually no such systems that have been published in the literature. This is one of many possible paradigms from the cognitive psychology literature that could be explored. To fully explore this approach may require the collaboration between computer scientists and cognitive psychologists.

Another simple modification to 2-D graphical authentication scheme is to add a third dimension. Imagine navigating through a three-dimensional (3-D) version of Passlogix, V-GO, or even Passfaces. First, the realism may provide additional clues that may assist users in remembering their passwords, thus allowing more complex passwords to be generated, augmenting the already large password space of graphical password systems. Simple 3-D worlds can be created very easily using virtual reality markup language (VRML) or X3D – almost as easily as 2-D worlds can be created using Java or C++. The attribute space in a 3-D world is increased considerably over the 2-D version. When interacting in this 3-D world, via a standard mouse (and possibly with keyboard interaction as well), the avatar is immersed in a simulated but quite realistic 3-D world. This enhanced mobility will provide a wider range of choices as the visual scene can be enhanced creating a more "realistic" perspective, allowing more distracters and more subtlety with respect to embedded cues. At the very least, we now have another dimension from which to collect data. It is unfortunate that there is not a lot of published work comparing 2-D and 3-D graphical password systems. This would seem like an obvious extension to the graphical password approach.

8.3 Software plus Hardware Approach

A purely software-based approach to behavioral biometrics may be somewhat of a handicap. If this constraint is relaxed, a number of possibilities open up. In this section, a few technologies will be described, such as a virtual reality environment (VRE), the use of haptic environments, and the use of biological signals (electrocardiogram [ECG] and electroencephalogram [EEG]). Ultimately, the brain–computer interface (BCI) may provide possibilities that are essentially limitless. To add to the formidable repertoire of techniques, a multimodal approach will probably prevail, calling upon a wide variety of techniques that will ultimately provide an insurmountable deterrent to identity theft.

8.3.1 VREs

Although VRML and X3D provide quite realistic 3-D environments, the use of head-mounted displays (HMDs) and data gloves augment the sensory experience of VREs, providing a fully immersive experience for users. There are a number of VRE systems which vary in terms of the degree of immersion and the level of interactions available. The quality of the VRE is dependent upon processing power – as these systems tend to be very processing power hungry. One system that is highly popular within the research community is the cave automatic virtual environment (CAVE) system (Stanney, 2002). Figure 8.1 depicts the prototypical CAVE system, which is a totally immersive VRE.

As an environment of user interaction, VREs provide a unique opportunity to enhance the amount of information extracted from a user for authentication purposes. For instance, Tolba (1999) has used the notion of a virtual system deploying a data glove for a new approach to online signature verification. The HUMABIO system (discussed more in the next section) provides a wealth of authentication approaches, some of which are contained within a VRE.

8.3.2 Haptic Environments

Haptics refers to a feedback mechanism through physical interactions with an object that results in the sensation of touch (somatosensation). Orozco and colleagues (2006) proposed a system based on haptic interactions that could be suitable for user authentication. In their approach, a haptic maze application was deployed as the authentication device (depicted in Figure 8.2). The user is required to navigate through the maze using a stylus. This approach is quite similar to that of signature verification, and a similar set of attributes is extracted during the authentication process. The authors tested this system on a small cohort of users, allowing them to train on the system prior to the testing phase. Note that the haptic system employed is a commercial product using the trade name Reachin®, which utilizes a

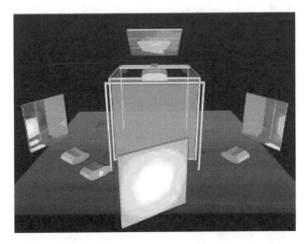

Figure 8.1 The CAVE system, a totally immersive VRE (see Stanney, 2002 for a comprehensive discussion of this system) (Source: Stanney, 2002)

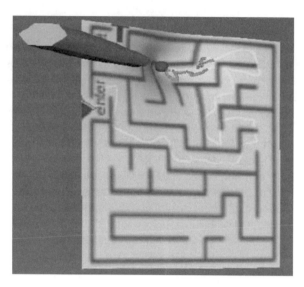

Figure 8.2 The authenticating maze application developed by Orozco and colleagues (2006) based on the Reachin® API system. The user is required to navigate through the maze using a typical stylus (Source: reapin API – web access: www.reachin.se)

combination of VRML and Python scripting with a built-in application programming interface (API) (Reachin Technologies, http://www.reachin.se/). The features that were extracted consisted of the direction, pressure, force, angle, speed, and 3-D position (x, y, z). The data was acquired at 70 Hz and was preprocessed by windowing and the application of the fast Fourier transform (FFT). The result was a set of features that were used to create the reference template (based on three samples), and then were tested on a single authentication attempt. During authentication, a user-defined threshold acceptance criterion was used – and the false acceptance rate (FAR) and false rejection rate (FRR) values were recorded. The results yielded an equal error rate (EER) of approximately 15% when a user-defined threshold was utilized.

Although the EER reported in this study is unacceptably high for serious authentication purposes, the approach explored in this paper indicate that the technology may provide a suitable platform for user authentication. This study was more or less a pilot, which explored a small set of users, with minimal amounts of authentication data. The attributes deployed were not as extensive as those employed in typical signature verification systems, which might have reduced the discriminatory capacity of the system. There are other haptic technologies available (see PHAToM & GHOST at http://www.sensable/) as well as a few more studies in this domain (see Asfaw et al., 2005, Orozco et al., 2006 for more examples). One would expect that there will be more research into this approach which will transcend the pilot study phase and provide some very interesting and competitive EER values.

8.3.3 Biological Signals

The last frontier (at least in the foreseeable future) is the deployment of biological-based signals such as the ECG and the EEG. These signals are generated by the heart and brain, respectively, and are recorded using standard equipment in a generally noninvasive fashion (though there are invasive versions of EEG recordings – this will not be discussed here). The basic approach is to record these signals and to use them directly – as a biometric signature or through training; the signals are modulated in order to provide a medium through which a human can interact with a computer-type device (the basis of the BCI). There are several issues that must be addressed when deploying this approach to biometric-based authentication. For one, what sort of equipment is required? The goal of behavioral biometrics is to minimize (if not eliminate) the amount of specialized equipment required for the authentication process. The second issue is how individual are these signals – are they sufficiently unique to allow them to be deployed for user verification purposes? This issue is critical – in terms of the likelihood of imposter success – and also, with respect to EEG as a tool for the BCI – how adaptable are these signals? Clearly, there are issues of shoulder surfing, variability, etc. that are typical of any biometric system (for a nice review on these issues in the current context, see Thorpe et al., 2005). In the next section, we explore the use of the ECG as a biometric, looking at the inherent variability of this technology with respect to signal production.

The use of the ECG as a biometric was examined in detail by Forsen in 1977 (Forsen et al., 1977), a prescient paper that also discussed the deployment of EEG as a biometric tool. The ECG records the electrical activity generated by the beating heart – generating a characteristic waveform which is depicted in Figure 8.3. This technology has a long and venerable history, beginning officially in 1887 (Waller, 1887). The heart utilizes electrical activity to activate the muscles required to pump blood through the circulatory system. By placing

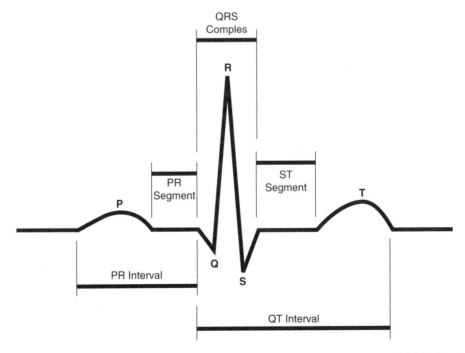

Figure 8.3   A typical ECG pattern for a single heartbeat, with indications of the principle fiduciary marks (Source: wikipedia – free web access)

sensitive recording electrodes at particular regions around the heart, the signals can be detected. The signals generated by the heartbeat form a regular pattern (see Figure 8.3) that records the electrical activity of the heart. This signal was utilized by Forsen in an attempt to determine the individuality of the ECG – if it was determined that the signal was unique – he proposed that this would serve as a useful biometric technique.

In Forsen's approach, the recording of the ECG was accomplished in a very noninvasive fashion – he utilized two electrodes that were attached to the index fingers without the use of a ground lead or electrode paste. Data was collected from subjects at three sessions of 30–40 seconds each. The data was filtered with a 3 KHz cutoff frequency and was digitized for subsequent analysis (for more details, consult Forsen, 1977). Several features were extracted for subsequent classification purposes. A total of 10 features were utilized: five time intervals and five amplitude differences. The time points correspond to the five major deflection points in the signal (labeled P, Q, R, S, and T). The amplitude (along with the frequency) measurements were produced using the same five time point fiduciaries, and the data was digitized for subsequent analysis (for more details, consult Forsen et al., 1977). Several features were extracted for subsequent classification purposes. A total of 10 features were utilized: five time intervals and five amplitude differences. The time points correspond to the five major deflection points in the signal (labeled P, Q, R, S, and T). The amplitude measurements were produced using the same five time point fiduciaries, with the addition of a sixth halfway between S and T deflection points. These features are utilized to produce a reference vector for the individual. When the same user requests authentication, several heartbeats are recorded (takes a few seconds only), and the average of the authentication request trials is compared to the reference vector. The results of this approach, based on type I and type II errors were extremely encouraging, yielding values of 1.2% and 1.1%, respectively. This is a phenomenal result, considering the small number of features utilized.

The results from the Forsen study have been confirmed by other researchers. Silva and colleagues (2001) published results indicating a successful classification rate of over 99% from a collection of 26 subjects, using a contingency matrix analysis approach. Also note that in the Silva study, only just over 1 minutes worth of ECG recording was utilized for this high classification accuracy (63 seconds). A study by Israel and colleagues (2005) examined the stability of the ECG as a biometric modality. Their results indicate that the features extracted for classification purposes were independent of sensor location, invariant to the individual's state of anxiety and unique to an individual. A study by Mehta and Lingayat (2007) yielded over 99% classification accuracy (both in terms of sensitivity and positive predictive value) when using either a single lead or a 12-lead ECG database. There are several other studies that employ ECG as a method for user identification, most of which provide exceptional classification results (greater than 95% accuracy – and many reaching 100%; see Biel et al., 2001, Kyoso & Uchiyama, 2001, Chang, 2005, Kyeong-Seop et al., 2005). This is a desirable quality, as the stability of the signal must be sufficient for robust classification. This issue of stability forms a central research question in the next topic: the EEG (Figure 8.4).

As previously mentioned, Forsen and colleagues (1977) proposed that EEG signals could be deployed for user verification, though Vidal (1973) may be the first to report on the possibility of a brain–computer interaction. Indeed, there are a number of studies that have investigated the use of EEG data in this capacity (Garcia-Molina et al., 2005, Palaniappan, 2005a,b, Palaniappan & Mandic, 2005c, 2007, Marcel & Millan, 2006, Bell et al., 2007, Riera et al., 2007). In a wider sense, EEG signals have been used as a means of allowing

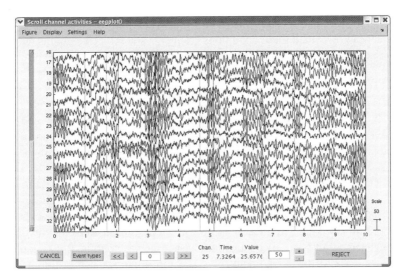

Figure 8.4 Screenshot from the EEGLAB suite of utilities for processing EEG data. The *x* axis is time (in seconds) and the *y* axis is the raw signal amplitude (in μv), measured at a collection of electrodes. (Source: EEGLAB, Delorme et al., 2002)

Figure 8.5 A typical low-resolution EEG cap with all required hardware connections used by the subject to interact with a virtual keyboard through biofeedback (Source: Google image – free web access)

handicapped individuals to interact with computer systems, in what is termed the BCI (Birch et al., 1995, Kubler, 2000, Wolpaw & McFarland, 2004). Both of these issues are directly related and form a very exciting area of research, much of which is applicable to behavioral biometrics. First, a brief discussion of the basis of the EEG is in order.

The EEG is a signal that is generated by the collective activity of neuronal generators. That is, brain activity produces an electrical signal that can be recorded by placing sensitive electrodes on the surface of the scalp (see Figure 8.5). What is required for the signal to be recorded at the scalp is a collection of neurons firing synchronously, and oriented toward the surface of the head. Provided these conditions are met, a stereotyped signal is recorded from an array of electrodes positioned over the entire surface of the scalp. As suggested by Figure 8.4, a tremendous amount of data is generated during an EEG recording. Typically, anywhere from 18 to 256 electrodes are positioned on the scalp, each providing a time series sampled at 0.5–1.0 KHz. Typically, this generates hundreds of megabytes of data that must be analyzed in order to extract useful information. Therefore, the signals that are generated from EEG have to be extensively preprocessed before they can be utilized, and tools such as EEGLAB are remarkably well suited to perform this task. The extent of the preprocessing is contingent upon the task at hand though. EEG as a cognitive psychological tool typically requires the isolation of various components within the EEG signal (see Figure 8.5 for examples of EEG signals). That is, the brain is continuously and spontaneously active. The firing of neurons, which is an electrical process, generates recordable signals that form a background upon which are superimposed the activities of specific collections of neurons that respond according to the engagement of a variety of cognitive tasks, such as reading, thinking of an image, vocalization, etc. The difficulty is identifying specific responses within the ongoing background activity, indicated as a collection of EEG signals, which are reliably correlated with the engagement of a specific cognitive task. Part of the difficulty in performing this task is the issue of spatial resolution. One question to be answered using this technique is where within the brain did a particular identified signal emanate from? The goal here is to associate an anatomical region of the brain with a response – thereby associating function with anatomy. A huge array of researchers has been engaged in this effort, and the research output has been phenomenal. A consistent finding from this research effort is that there are a number of fundamental changes that occur (are superimposed upon) as a result of cognitive processing.

One of the key findings from EEG research is the discovery of an event termed the "P3." The P3 (or P300 as it is also termed) is an example of an event-related potential (ERP) (Sutton et al., 1965, Picton, 1992). An ERP is a signal that indicates a cognitive event has occurred – the P3 is typically produced in what is termed an "odd-ball" paradigm (see Figure 8.6 for a typical P300 image). This is a scenario in which a subject is presented with a stimulus to identify, and a stimulus not related to the expected stimulus is presented in its stead (an odd-ball stimulus). Since the discovery of the P300, a variety of other signals have been uncovered – including visual evoked potentials (VEPs), N400, and auditory evoked potentials (AEPs), to mention just a few (see Nykopp, 2001, Garcia-Molina et al., 2005, Dornhege et al., 2007, Gupta & Palaniappan, 2007 for details). These signals are evoked by a particular stimulus/ response paradigm and are universal in the sense that all humans are able to produce these responses (under normal circumstances), but occur with amazing heterogeneity between individuals. A P300 is a response that occurs approximately 300 ms after stimulus presentation – but this is a rough guide. For some individuals, it will appear at 250 ms, and for others, it might not appear until 450 ms after the stimulus presentation. In addition, the amplitude of the signal can vary considerably from one person to another. Therefore, the requirement of individuality is met by using this technology. Further, it should be noted that the P300 has been utilized as the basis for the "guilty knowledge test" – as a form of lie detection in certain circumstances (Farwell & Smith, 2001).

The ability to record embedded signals within an ongoing EEG recording has been available for well over three decades. There is a considerable amount of research that has moved

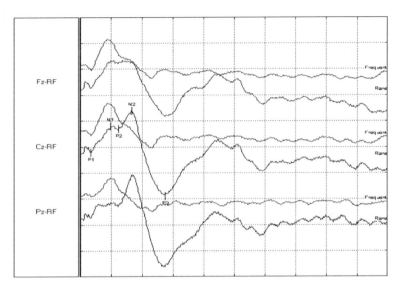

Figure 8.6 A P300 displayed at three different recording locations (along the midline of the brain). (Source: Picton, 1992)

from a classical neurophysiology-based approach to a more practical application approach: which is termed the BCI. Initially, BCI embodied a methodology for allowing people with disabilities to interact with a computer system using limited physical resources. For instance, quadriplegics are able to produce rudimentary communication skills through a training process that allows them to move a computer cursor. By mapping commands onto actions, people are able to interact with their environment in a meaningful and productive way. A framework for this approach is depicted in Figure 8.7, which highlights the key elements in a BCI system. Recently, a number of investigators have utilized the existing BCI framework to address whether or not this approach can be successfully employed as a biometric tool.

A key issue with BCI is the notion of feedback – a form of operant conditioning, where a subject can control to certain degrees the likelihood of generating a controlled event. For instance, a P300 is a positive deflection that occurs approximately 300 ms after stimulus presentation. When the stimulus is presented, at first, it may not produce a reliable P300 event. As a result of training, where the subject is asked to consciously focus on a particular task, and with appropriate feedback (closed-loop BCI), the subject generates the required response more reliably (Felzer, 2001). What is required is that the response is mapped onto a particular command, such as moving a cursor or depressing a key on a virtual keyboard presented on the computer screen. Though much of this work has focused on assisting patients in locked-in states (i.e. patients suffering from a stroke, unable to move their limbs but are cognitively normal), there has been a considerable amount of work in this domain with respect to user identification.

In an interesting paper entitled "Pass-Thoughts, Authenticating with Our Minds," the notion that we may be able to authenticate – for instance one can authenticate using a password based approach simply by *thinking* of the password (Thorpe et al., 2005). The basis of this work is that through the deployment of a BCI-based mechanism, which relies on the use

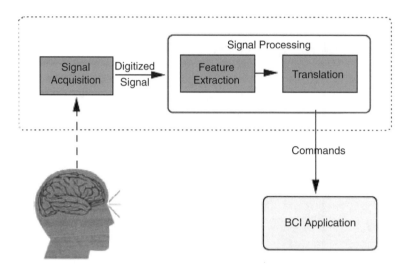

Figure 8.7 A traditional view of the BCI architecture, which includes signal acquisition (typically EEG data), data processing, and the translation of the events with a command sequence (Source: Thorpe et al., 2005)

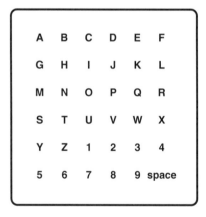

Figure 8.8 The speller system, which employs a BCI mechanism that allows a user – via P300 ERPs – to be able to spell out words (Source: Bierbaumer et al., 1999)

of EEG-acquired signals from a subject, one can authenticate without physically interacting with any device. In their scenario, users authenticate onto a PC by presenting their password through a BCI-type interface. Through the use of a P300 mechanism similar to that employed for a spelling device (see Bierbaumer et al., 1999 for details of the brain speller – and Figure 8.8), subjects can interact with items on a PC desktop when they see part of their "pass-thought" highlighted via the production of P300 signals. The size of the pass-thought pass-word space is obviously limited to the number of characters (as in Figure 8.8) or the number of images that can be displayed on the monitor. As was discussed in Chapter 6, the size of

graphical password spaces can be quite substantial, depending on whether the images are in
2-D or 3-D. The typical bit rate for a BCI system is approximately 4.8–5.0 bits/minute (in a
textual 36-characters-based system as in Figure 8.7) to achieve an accuracy of approximately
90% (see Donchin et al., 2000, Nykopp, 2001, and Kronegg et al., 2005 for details).

Paranjape and colleagues (2001) successfully used this technology to identify a set of 40
subjects. In their work, the subject identification scheme was 100% accurate for training cases
and 80% accurate for test cases. Poulos and colleagues (1999, 2001, 2004) were also able to
accurately identify subjects (classification accuracy between 80% and 100%). Palaniappan
and colleagues (2007) utilized VEP as a means for user authentication. In this study, a collection of 3560 VEP signals were extracted from 102 subjects. The authors employed a variety
of classification schemes to produce the classification results. Typically, the classification
accuracy was well over 95%, independent of the classifier that was employed (k-nearest
neighbors, and neural network-based classifiers were employed).

Riera and colleagues (2007) published a study utilizing the Enobio system, which utilizes
a minimal number of *dry electrodes*, avoiding the use of conductive gels that make the system
much more "user-friendly" from a comfort perspective (Ruffini et al., 2006, 2007). A common
complaint with regard to EEG as a biometric is that the electrode cap must be secured onto
the scalp using conductive gels – this system attempts to eliminate this constraint, allowing
the electrodes to be attached directly to glabrous (hairless) skin. The authors employed a
series of single-channel feature extraction techniques (autoregression and Fourier transform)
as well as dual-channel feature extraction techniques such as mutual information, coherence,
and cross correlation. The authors then combined both feature classes in order to perform the
user authentication task. The classification results yielded a true acceptance rate (TAR) of
95+%, with an EER of 5.5% (Riera et al., 2007).

These results are encouraging – producing high levels of classification accuracy without
significant processing overhead. A commercial implementation of this approach can be found
in the system marketed under the trade name HUMABIO (http://www.humanbio-eu.org/).
This is a total authentication system employing a virtual reality engine, EEG analysis, and a
host of other behavioral and physiological-based biometric technologies. Figure 8.9 presents

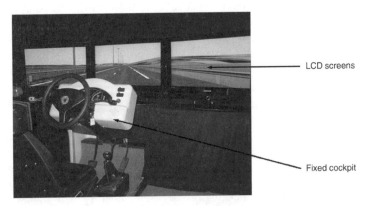

Figure 8.9   The traffic simulator – the heart of the HUMABIO authentication system. This system
employs both EEG and EOG that record users' responses and build a user profile **that** may be used for
subsequent user authentication (Source: HUMABIO website: http://www.humanbio-eu.org)

a component that is the heart of their simulator, which they term "traffic model." This technology is a state-of-the-art approach to user verification, which utilizes a variety of approaches such as indicated below in their traffic simulator. It is capable of performing single and continuous biometric monitoring, using a variety of modalities. This system acquires EEG (28 leads), electrooculogram (EOG) (2 leads) and ECG (1 lead) data and fuses them for subsequent user verification. There is also a voice module that performs speaker verification using **RASTA (RelAtive SpecTrAl)** filtering and an on-board database. There is also a gait authentication module that captures indoor gait data using a stereoscopic camera (which also captures face information as well sufficient for simultaneous face recognition).

The company has plans to develop wireless electrodes for simultaneous EEG and ECG recordings. This will allow the implementation of user-friendly systems that are extremely difficult to spoof and are highly accurate in terms of EER values. It is hoped that this is one of many such systems that will be developed in the near future.

8.4 Conclusions

This chapter has covered several possibilities for the continued development of physiological biometrics. One issue that arises from examining the literature is that the border between physiological and behavioral biometrics may need to be examined more closely. Traditional behavioral biometrics can be enhanced in many ways, such as 3-D graphical authentication systems, and. subliminal cueing It is presumed that these enhancements will increase the classification accuracy of many of the principle behavioral biometric systems. More novel approaches, such as the use of ECG and EEG data, provide another approach – though they entail the use of specialized hardware. The technology is moving toward a wireless interface for both EEG and ECG, and so these limitations will certainly be transcended in the near future.

The deployment of biological signals – either directly or through the process of biofeedback – provides an innovative and practical way of user authentication/identification. Users will no longer have to sign in, enter a password, or select images from a gallery. They may just be able to *think* of their authentication details and these will be transmitted faithfully to the authentication device. The feasibility of such an approach, on a practical level, will have to await advances in the collection machinery (EEG montages, ECG monitors, and related devices). This technology, coupled with a VRE, may provide a unique opportunity to implement multimodal biometrics within a single framework, allowing fusion to occur at all levels. These ideas are already in place – and the components are being developed in laboratories around the globe. It is really up to government agencies and related legislative bodies to decide how this technology will be utilized.

8.5 Research Topics

1. What is the effect of subliminal cueing on users remembering their graphical passwords? Can it be used to enhance the users' ability to remember their password? If so, can this feature be used to create longer passwords to enhance security? How long can the password be before we begin to decrease memorability?

2. Can we devise a system based on EEG data that can be used to differentiate authentic users from imposters? Are there specific signals that are indicative of the authentic user that can form the basis of a classification algorithm?
3. Can proper training using biofeedback enhance the discriminating capacity of EEG as a biometric approach?
4. Since ECG provides robust classification results, can a simple device such as the finger pulse system be used to acquire data for classification purposes? The preliminary data suggests that this is possible – it must be reproduced on a larger scale. Is it possible to modulate the heartbeat pattern with appropriate training using biofeedback training?
5. Can the virtual reality approach be utilized as an authentication approach considering the realistic constraints such as time and hardware such that it could serve as a viable remote access approach? What issues need to be addressed in this context?
6. The deployment of 3-D graphical passwords needs to be explored – to see how they compare with the 2-D approach. How much additional information could be incorporated into a 3-D graphical approach? How does this approach compare to existing graphical-based password systems?
7. Can haptics be utilized in a cost-effective way as a means of user authentication? What issues need to be addressed? How do they fit in with either virtual reality or within the context of EEG/ECG? Can we create haptic scenarios that generate cognitive effects that are measurable at the EEG level?

Appendix

A. Gait Analysis

Gait analysis is a behavioral biometric that captures the way a person walks as a means of identification and/or verification. There are two basic version of this approach: model-based and model-free. The former focuses on developing a static model of the human form – generating silhouettes via an eigen-shape type of approach. The silhouette will be tracked over time – and the translations are captured as a series of vectors which are used to record the movement in 3-D space (see Bobick & Johnson, 2001). The model-free approach utilizes statistical features which tend to focus on the dynamical aspects of the feature space (see Tanawongsuwan & Bobick, 2001, Kale et al., 2003). Another division is whether the system is based on machine vision or is sensor driven. Many systems employ a video recording of the users as they are walking – extracting static information about body movement in space. With the sensor-based approach, a sensor device (typically an accelerometer) is attached to the subject which records the change in 3-D space of the person while in motion. The principal difference between these two approaches is that the former can be deployed for identification while the later is typically employed for authentication/verification purposes. What follows is a very brief introduction via several case studies that depict some of these characteristic features of gait biometrics. This section is included for completeness, as it is generally understood that gait biometrics may not be the most suitable technology to a remote access authentication scheme.

Shutler (2002) investigated the development of a large-scale database generated in order to determine if a ground truth could be generated for subsequent study. The authors generated data from a variety of conditions: indoor, outdoor, and from users on a treadmill. Using high-resolution photography, data was collected for each subject in a variety of viewpoints (front-parallel and oblique angles), silhouette extraction, and still images (side and frontal views). This data served as the basis for the development of their database system, which also served to generate data required to determine if conditions could be enabled such that a perfect extraction could be achieved (ground truth). The goal was to generate data on 100 subjects that contained eight sequences and at least 1.5 steps per subject. The lighting conditions were arranged such as to maximize contrast between the subjects and their local environment. Next, using edge detection filters (Sobel and Canny), the subject's silhouettes were extracted as required. Typically, the ground truth occurs in very controlled conditions (indoors), with

Behavioral Biometrics: A Remote Access Approach. Kenneth Revett
© 2008 John Wiley & Sons, Ltd.

controlled lighting condition, and cinematography conditions at their optimal levels (see Shutler, 2002). The outdoor images are considerably more blurred, as quantified by examining the variance. The authors reported the classification results by evaluating symmetry, velocity moments, and moment-based analysis, yielding greater than 96% classification accuracy except for the moment-based approach, which yielded much lower results (Foster et al., 2002, Shutler, 2002).

Gafurov and colleagues (2006) examined a sensor-based approach to gait analysis using an accelerometer attached to the right lower leg. The advantage of a sensor-based approach over other biometric modalities such as fingerprints is that it is more unobtrusive – it can be acquired from a distance. In this study, the sensor employed was an accelerometer that was attached to the lower leg (though other studies have positioned the accelerometer at the hip, pocket, and hand). The device can record up to 256 Hz, and can respond to changes in gravity to within ±2 g forces, and the data is collected in three orthogonal directions (vertical, backward-forward, and sideways). The authors combined the three orthogonal direction signals into a signal scalar value, the formula for which was determined empirically (see Gafurov et al., 2006 for details), which essentially is the sideways acceleration normalized by the total Euclidean distance. This information is used to build a reference model for the 21 users employed in this study (12 male and 9 female, aged 20–40). The authors also employed the concept of a cycle, which is a collection of recorded data points that represents the notion of a dynamic feature. There were a total of 16 observations per cycle, where a cycle is defined as the time between successive points in time where the acceleration is zero. In addition, a total of 16 such cycles per user (where each cycle is referred to as a cycle group) were collected.

The actual study data consisted of the subjects walking a total of 70 m, and after approximately 35 m, the users had to turn around to return to the starting point. The first 35 m of data were used as the enrollment data, and the second 35 m data was used for authentication purposes. A t-test was used to determine whether or not an authentication attempt was sufficiently close to one of the feature vectors stored in the gait database. There were a total of 21 genuine trials and 420 imposter samples for the determination of FAR and FRR. The results from this study yielded an EER of 5% when the scalar value was used and 9% when the cycle method was employed. The difference was probably related to the inherent variability when collecting a larger array of data points that were based essentially on the same measurement which had a tendency to reduce the discriminating capacity of the feature space. The challenge is to generate a feature vector that is composed of complimentary information. This is somewhat difficult to accomplish within the context of gait biometrics, and the usual solution is to assume a multimodal approach. For instance, when combining gait and voice information, the EER could be reduced to as low as 2%, depending on the background noise levels (Vidjiounaite et al., 2006).

Wang and colleagues (2003) examined the contribution of static versus dynamic features with respect to gait biometrics in a machine-vision approach. The authors explore the differences between static versus dynamic features in constructing a biometric based on gait. The static features capture geometry-based measurements which include body height, stride length, and build (see Bobick & Johnson, 2001). These are features that remain essentially constant throughout the process of walking and running. Dynamic features, on the other hand, measure joint angles of the lower extremities and how they change with gait (see Tanawongsuwan & Bobick, 2001). Typically, gait-based systems employ either static or dynamic

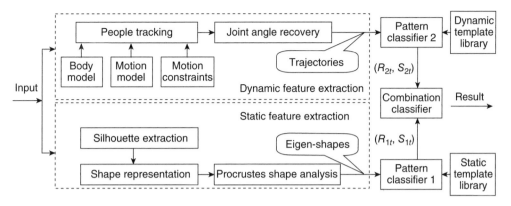

Figure A.1 The gait-based approach which incorporates both static (bottom half) and dynamic features (depicted in the top half) (Source: Wang et al., 2003)

attributes. The purpose of this study was to investigate whether combining these classes of attributes will influence the classification accuracy.

In this study, silhouettes are extracted yielding a static pose, and their changes over time are recorded as a series of vector transformations, using the Procrustes shape analysis method that yields the corresponding eigen-shape (yields the static shape data). The dynamic features were extracted by tracking the walker using a condensation framework along with a human body model used to calculate the joint angle trajectories, which yielded the dynamic features. Their model is presented in Figure A.1.

During the process of generating the static and dynamic features, a feature vector containing the spatial and temporal data was used for classification purposes. The features were extracted from each walking cycle, and a DTW algorithm was employed to align the features within each cycle for reference modeling.

The actual classification approach utilized a nearest-neighbor classification algorithm with exemplars. To measure similarity, the authors employed the Procrustes mean shape distance for the static features and the Euclidean distance for the dynamic features. The authors also explored a fusion approach at the score level, applying the product, sum, minimum, maximum, combination rules to determine which provided the best classification accuracy (see Chapter 7 for details on fusion approaches). The study employed 80 sequences from 20 subjects, with four sequences acquired per subject. The authors calculated the FAR, FRR, and the correct classification rate (CCR). The EER was approximately 10% for static features and 8.4% for dynamic features, without any fusion at either the match or score levels. The best results (with respect to EER) were obtained using the product score summation technique (3.5%).

The results from gait biometrics yield EER rates of approximately 5% in many cases. This may not be suitable for high-end security installations, but is quite reasonable considering the ease with which this technology can be implemented with respect to user involvement. Gait analysis can occur at a considerable distance – one of the few biometrics that does not require that the user directly interacts with the authentication device. The deployment of dynamic features tends to increase the classification accuracy relative to the deployment of static features. When employed in a multimodal approach, gait can be a very convenient and accurate mechanism for implementing bioemtric based security.

B. The History of the Keyboard

The PC keyboard is based on a standard electronic typewriter. The search therefore begins with the first recorded invention of the typewriter. The earliest record of the idea of a typing machine was recorded as a patent application in 1714 by an English engineer Henry Mill (Labanieh & Heer, 2003). Unfortunately, there are no records of this patent manifesting in a working device. The first working typing machine in record is the Pellegrino Turri's typewriter, created ca. 1808 (Bliven, 1954) (Figure B.1). Just over 20 years later, William A. Burt received the first US patent for his typographer. In 1868, Christopher Sholes patented his own version of the typewriter – sometimes referred to as the Sholes–Gliden machine, because his associate Carlos Gliden assisted him in the development of this machine. This machine went into mass production with the assistance of the Remington Corporation – makers of the gun. In order to overcome a mechanical problem – namely, that keys could jam if pressed too quickly – Sholes developed a method to slow down the typist. He argued that by placing keys that were frequently pressed consecutively on separate ends of the keyboard, this would slow down the typist, thereby minimizing key jamming. This was the birth of the "QWERTY" keyboard, which is the principal keyboard in use today on typewriters and PC keyboards. For a more detailed discussion of the history of the typing machines, consult Bliven (1954) and Strom (1992). Note that there were other keyboard layouts, most notably the Dvorak Simplified Keyboard (DSK), invented by August Dvorak in the late 1800s (Figure B.2). Due to financial and training reasons, the DSK keyboard layout has never caught on, and the QWERTY layout remains all that most people are aware of. Subtle refinements over the next 100 years have produced what we are all familiar with – modern typewriters and PC keyboards, along with numeric input pads found at checkout counters and automated teller

Figure B.1   One of the earliest keyboard-type devices (Source: Bliven, 1954)

Figure B.2   A typical Dvorak keyboard (with the QWERTY keys overlaid). (Source: Buzing, 2003)

Figure B.3   A "haptic"-like computer pyramid

machines. Though there are a number of very interesting shapes and versions of keyboards that are in use – but have not reached the mainstream commercial markets. Figure B.3 presents an interesting variant on the "typical keyboard" structure that has the look of a haptic device.

What has evolved more slowly than the development of the technology is the skill required to use the device efficiently. Typing skills have increased marginally over the years – with today's world-leading typist able to type at 200 words/minute, error free. There are several factors that affect our ability to type, and some of these will be described briefly in the next section.

C. Cognitive Aspects of Human–Computer Interaction

I. Power Law of Practice

From the psychological literature, two principal factors have been identified that can explain, in quantitative terms, factors that may impact a person's typing ability. One is referred to as the power law of practice, which basically states that "practice makes perfect" (well it improves performance!) (Martin et al., 2005). The power law is initially derived to explain quantitatively how practice improves performance in a variety of cognitive tasks, such as typing and related cognitive exercises involving memory and motor functions. The general formula for the power law is

$$Y = Ax^{-B} \qquad\qquad\qquad (C.1)$$

where the constant A is the Y intercept and B is the slope of the learning curve, which is linear when plotted on a log–log graph. The constant A indicates the learning rate without any practice. Generally, the power law curve flattens out, indicating that further practice will not provide any appreciable increase in performance (see Figure C.1 for details). Although the use of this law is prevalent within the psychological literature, it has not played a prominent role as a metric in behavioral biometrics generally. It could be employed in several contexts within behavioral biometrics: whenever a pointing device is utilized to make selections, typing, and other interactive processes used for authentication purposes. For instance, if the values of the parameters A and B are determined for a user, an imposter could be identified by having a slightly different value(s) for A and/or B. If the differences were minor, then this difference could be noted and used in conjunction with other features. The collection of such features would be used to make the final arbitration.

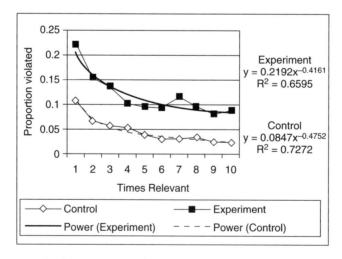

Figure C.1   An example of the power law of practice, demonstrating learning curves for two versions of an SQL-Tutor (Source: Martin et al., 2004)

II. Fitts' Law

While the power law of practice is a generalized model that accounts for improvements in motor activities resulting from practice, Fitts' law describes how choice impacts a user's reaction time, sometimes referred to as movement time (MT). Typically, this area of research has focused on studies involving human–computer interaction – where a subject is required to move a mouse to navigate through a series of computer screens (Fitts, 1954). Mathematically, Fitts' law has been formulated in several different ways. One common form is the Shannon formulation (proposed by Scott MacKenzie [MacKenzie, 1992]), named for its resemblance to the Shannon–Hartley theorem for movement along a single dimension:

$$T = a + b \log_2(D/W + 1) \tag{C.2}$$

- T is the average time taken to complete the movement (Traditionally, researchers have used the symbol MT for this, to mean *movement time.*).
- a and b are empirical constants, and can be determined by fitting a straight line to measured data.
- D is the distance from the starting point to the center of the target (Traditionally, researchers have used the symbol A for this, to mean the *amplitude* of the movement.).
- W is the width of the target measured along the axis of motion. W can also be thought of as the allowed error tolerance in the final position, since the final point of the motion must fall within $\pm W/2$ of the target's center.

From the equation, there is a *speed-accuracy* trade-off associated with pointing, whereby targets that are smaller and/or further away require more time to acquire. This fact has implications in the development of human–computer interface layouts – the principal domain in which this law has been formulated and has been applied quite successfully. The first human computer interface (HCI) application of Fitts' law was by Card and colleagues (1978), who used the index of performance (*IP*), defined as $1/b$, to compare performance of different input devices, with the mouse coming out on top. (This early work, according to Stuart Card's biography, "was a major factor leading to the mouse's commercial introduction by Xerox" (Card, 1980). Fitts' law has been shown to apply under a variety of conditions, with many different limbs (hands, feet, head-mounted sights, eye gaze), manipulanda (input devices), physical environments (including underwater), and user populations (young, old, special educational needs, and drugged participants). Note that the constants a, b, IP have different values under each of these conditions.

Since the advent of graphical user interfaces (GUIs), Fitts' law has been applied to tasks where the user must position the mouse cursor over an on-screen target, such as a button or other widgets. Fitts' law can model both point-and-click and drag-and-drop actions (Note that dragging has a lower *IP* associated with it, because the increased muscle tension makes pointing more difficult.). Despite the model's appeal, it should be remembered in its original and strictest form:

- It applies only to movement in a single dimension and not to movement in two dimensions (though it is successfully extended to two dimensions in the Accot–Zhai steering law).
- It describes simple motor response of, say, the human hand, failing to account for software acceleration usually implemented for a mouse cursor.

- It describes untrained movements, not movements that are executed after months or years of practice (though some argue that Fitts' law models behavior that is so low level that extensive training does not make much difference).

If, as generally claimed, the law does hold true for pointing with the mouse, some consequences for graphical-based interactions design include

- Buttons and other widgets to be selected in GUIs should be a reasonable size; it is very difficult to click on small ones.
- Edges (e.g. the menu bar) and corners of the display (e.g. "start" button in a typical Windows™) are particularly easy to acquire because the pointer remains at the screen edge regardless of how much further the mouse is moved, thus, they can be considered as having infinite width.
- Pop-up menus can usually be opened faster than pull-down menus, since the user avoids travel.
- Pie menu items typically are selected faster and have a lower error rate than linear menu items, for two reasons: because pie menu items are all the same and small distance from the center of the menu, and because their wedge-shaped target areas (which usually extend to the edge of the screen) are very large.

Despite the success of Fitts' law, it was formulated for a 1-D environment, which is a severe limitation in many cases. A recent extension to Fitts' law allows it to be utilized to the same degree in a 2-D graphical environment.

III. Accot–Zhai Steering Law

Fitts' law is inherently 1-D: as used in most GUI-based applications, the width is varied, but the target height is left open (and effectively set to infinity). This leaves one single degree of freedom in movement, yielding a 1-D scenario. This limitation has been transcended by Accot and Zhai (2003) in what is termed the Accot–Zhai steering law. Although there are extensions of Fitts' law into the 2-D realm, they were not general enough to handle all possible 2-D situations found in GUI applications (see Jagacinsiki, 1985, MacKenzie & Buxton, 1992). For instance, previous studies indicate the MT does not depend on the height when it becomes greater than the width and vice versa (see Accot & Zhai, 2003 for details). These and others issues motivated Accot and Zhai to develop a new approach to generalizing Fitts' law in 2-D.

In the final analysis, the Accot–Zhai steering law can be formulated as follows:

$$T = a + b \log_2 \left(\sqrt{(D/W)^2 + \eta(D/H)^2} + 1 \right) \tag{C.3}$$

where a varies in the range [−50, 200], b in the range of [100, 170], and η in [1/7, 1/3] (Accot & Zhai, 2003). This formulation reduces to the 1-D case (i.e. the original Fitts' law) in the case of infinite height (H). The two terms in the above equation (C.3) account for the distance/width ratio (left term) separately from the distance/height ratio (second terms). This form of Fitts' law (termed the Accot–Zhai steering law) has been successfully applied to account for the timing required to make selections in GUI-based applications with considerable success (see Accot & Zhai, 2003 for detailed experimental results). This formulation should be taken into account when designing a GUI-based application – such as those found in graphical-based authentication systems (see Chapter 6 for details). The last issue to discuss in this context is how the number of choices presented to the users affects their response time.

IV. Hick's Law

Hick's law, or the Hick–Hyman law, is an HCI model that describes the time it takes for a user to make a decision as a function of the possible choices he or she has. Given n equally probable choices, the average reaction time T required to choose among them is approximately

$$T = b \log_2(n+1) \tag{C.4}$$

where b is a constant that can be determined empirically by fitting a line to measured data. According to Card et al. (1983), the +1 is "because there is uncertainty about whether to respond or not, as well as about which response to make." The law can be generalized in the case of choices with unequal probabilities p_i of occurring, to

$$T = bH \tag{C.5}$$

where H is the information-theoretic entropy of the decision, defined as

$$H = \sum p_i \log_2(1/p_i + 1) \tag{C.6}$$

Hick's law is similar in form to Fitts' law. Intuitively, one can reason that Hick's law has a logarithmic form because people subdivide the total collection of choices into categories, eliminating about half of the remaining choices at each step, rather than considering each and every choice one by one, requiring linear time. Hick's law has been shown to apply in experiments where the user is presented with n buttons, each having a light bulb beside them. One light bulb is randomly lit up, after which the user must press the corresponding button as quickly as possible. Obviously, the decision to be made here is very simple, requiring little conscious thought.

In more realistic scenarios, Hick's law is sometimes cited to justify menu design decisions. However, applying the model to menus must be done with care. For example, to find a given word (e.g. the name of a command) in a randomly ordered word list (e.g. a menu), scanning of each word in the list is required, consuming linear time, so Hick's law does not apply. However, if the list is alphabetical, the user will likely be able to use a subdividing strategy that may well require logarithmic time. The user must also know the name of the command. Of course, well-designed submenus can allow for automatic subdivision. Yet another situation is when the users do not know the exact name of the command they seek in a menu, but would likely recognize it if they saw it. In this case, the user may or may not be able to use a subdividing search strategy, depending in part on how menu items are categorized and how well the users can use categories to speed their search. This highlights the differences inherent to recall- versus recognition-based systems (see Chapter 6 on graphical-based authentication systems in this volume).

The HCI factors listed in this appendix demonstrate that there are factors that must be taken into account when designing graphical-based applications – in the context here – graphical-based authentication systems. Not only will the design have an impact on the way the user interacts with the system per se – the design may impact on how *effectively* a person interacts with the system. These aspects of GUI design should be incorporated into any standards associated with the biometric – see the end of Chapter 1 for details on biometric standards. At the very least, one must take these and related issues into account when comparing the results from different studies.

References

Accot, J. & Zhai, S. Refining Fitts' law models for bivariate pointing. Proceedings of ACM CHI 2003 Conference on Human Factors in Computing Systems, 5–10 April, 2003, pp. 193–200, 2003. Ft Lauderdale, Fla, USA.

Adler, M.H. *The Writing Machine: a History of the Typewriter?* George Allan & Unwin, London, England, 1973. ISBN 0-04-652004-X.

Ahmed, A.A.E. & Traore, I. A new biometrics technology based on mouse dynamics. Technical Report ECE-03-5, Department of Electrical and Computer Engineering, University of Victoria, British Columbia, Canada, 2003.

ANSIX9.84. *American National Standards Institute, Biometrics Information Management and Security for the Financial Services Industry, ANSI X9.84-2003.* American National Standards Institute, New York, NY, USA, 2003.

Asfaw, Y., Orozco, M., Shirmohammadi, S., El Saddik, A., & Adler, A. Participant identification in haptic systems using hidden Markov models, IEEE International Workshop on Haptic Audio Visual Environments and their Applications, 1–2 October 2005.

Asonov, D. & Agrawal, R. *Keyboard Acoustic Emanations.* Proceedings of the 2004 IEEE Symposium on Security and Privacy (S&P '04), Oakland, CA, 1081-6011/04, 2004.

Atal, B.S. & Hanauer, S.L. Speech analysis and synthesis by linear prediction of the speech wave. *Journal of the Acoustical Society of America* 50(2), 637–655, 1971.

Bar, M. & Biederman, I. Subliminal visual priming. *American Psychological Society*, 9(6), 464–469, 1998.

Bauer, A. Gallery of random art. http://andrej.com/art, accessed 12/1/2007, 1998.

Bell, C.J., Shenoy, P., Chalodhorn, R., & Rao, R.P.N. An image-based brain-computer interface using the P3 response. UWCSE Technical Report # 2007-02-03, University of Washington, Seattle, WA, USA, 2007.

Benzeghiba, M.F. & Bourlard, H. Hybrid HMM/ANN and GMM combination for user-customized password speaker verification, *IEEE International Conference on Acoustics, Speech, and Signal Processing (ICASSP'03)*, 6–10 April, 2003, Hong Kong, Vol. 2, pp. 225–228, 2003.

Bergadano, F., Gunetti, D., & Picardi, C. User authentication through keystroke dynamics. *ACM Transactions on Information and System Security* 5(4), 367–397, 2002.

Berger, Y., Wool, A., & Yeredor, A. Dictionary attacks using keyboard acoustic emanations, CCS'06, October 20–November 3, 2006, Alexandria, Virginia, USA.

Biel, L., Petterson, O., & Stork, D. ECG analysis: a new approach in human identification. *IEE Transactions on Instrumentation and Measurement* 50(3), 808–812, 2001.

Bierbaumer, N., Ghanayim, N., Hinterberger, T., Iversen, I., Kotchoubey, B., Kubler, A., Perelmouter, J., Taub, E., & Flor, H. A spelling device for the paralysed. *Nature* 398, 297–298, 1999.

Bimbot, F., Bonastre, J.-F., Fredouille, C., Grabier, G., Magrin-Chagnolleau, I., Meignier, S., Merlin, T., Ortega-Garcia, J., Petrovska-Delacretaz, D., & Reynolds, D.A. A tutorial on text-independent speaker verification. *EURASIP Journal on Applied Signal Processing* 4, 430–451, 2004.

Biometric Technology Today. Part 1: biometrics and ePassports. *Biometric Technology Today* 13(6), 10–11, 2006.

Birch, G.E., Watzke, J.R., & Bolduc, C. Research and development of adaptive equipment for eprsons with significant disabilities and the elderly: activities conducted by the Neil Squire Foundation. *Technology and Disability* 4, 169–173, 1995.

Bliven, B., Jr. *The Wonderful Writing Machine*. Random House, New York, NY, USA, 1954.

Blonder, G.E. *Graphical password*, U.S. Patent Number 5.559.961, 1996.

Bobick, A. & Johnson, A. Gait recognition using static, activity-specific parameters, Proceedings of the International Conference on Computer Vision and Pattern Recognition, Kauai, Hawaii, December 2001, pp. 423–430, IEEE Computer Society, CVPR'01, 2001.

Bower, G.H., Karlin, M.B., & Dueck, A. Comprehension and memory for pictures. *Memory and Cognition* 3, 216–220, 1975.

Brostoff, S. & Sasse, M.A. Are passfaces more usable than passwords: a field trial investigation, in McDonald S., et al. (editors), *People and Computers XIV – Usability or Else, Proceedings of HCI 2000*, 5–8 September, pp. 405–424, Springer, Edinburgh, Scotland, 2000.

Brown, M. & Rogers, S.J. User identification via keystroke characteristics of typed names using neural networks. *International Journal of Man-Machine Studies* 39, 999–1014, 1993.

Brown, A.S., Bracken, E., Zoccoli, S., & Douglas, K. Generating and remembering passwords. *Applied Cognitive Psychology* 18, 641–651, 2004.

Card, S.K., English, W.K., & Burr, B.J. Evaluation of mouse, rate-controlled isometric joystick, step keys, and text keys for text selection on a CRT. *Ergonomics* 21(8), 601–613, 1978.

Card, S.K., Moran, T.P., & Newell, S. The keystroke-level; model for user performance time with interactive systems. *Communications of the ACM* 23(7), 396–410, 1980.

Card, S.K., Moran, T.P., & Newell, A. *The Psychology of Human-Computer Interaction*, Lawrence Erlbaum Associates, Inc., Mahwah, NJ, USA, 1983.

Chalkias, K., Alexiadis, A., & Stephanides, G. A Multi-grid graphical password scheme. 7th ArtificialIntelligence and Digital Communications conference (AIDC), Thessaloniki, Greece, August 18–20, 2006.

Chen, W. & Chang, W. Applying Hidden Markov Models to Keystroke Pattern Analysis for Password Verification. In: proceedings of the 2004 IEEE International Conference on Information Reuse and Integration, IRI-2004, November 8–10, 2004, las Vegas Hilton, Las Vegas, NV, USA, pp. 467–474, 2004.

Chang, C.K. Human identification using one lead ECG. MS Thesis, Department of Computer Science and Information Engineering, Chaoyang University of Technology, Taiwan, 2005.

Chang, W. Improving hidden Markov models with a similarity histogram for typing pattern biometrics, in proceedings of the IEEE International Conference on Information Reuse and Integration, IRI – 2005, 15–17 Aug. 2005, pp. 487–493.

Chen, K., Wang, L., & Chi, H. Methods of combining multiple classifiers with different features and their applications to text-independent speaker identification. *International Journal of Pattern Recognition* 11(3), 417–435, 1997.

Chiasson, S., Biddle, R., & van Oorschot, P.C. A second look at the usability of click-based graphical passwords. Symposium on Usable Privacy and Security (SOUPS), Pittsburg, PA, USA, July 18–20, 2007.

Chollet, G., Cochard, J.-L., Constantinescu, A., Jaboulet, C., & Langlais, P. Swiss French polyphone and PolyVar: telephone speech databases to model inter- and intra-speaker variability. IDIAP Research Report, IDIAP-RR-96-01, 1996.

Coetzer, J., Herbst, B.M., & du Preez, J.A. Offline signature verification using the discrete radon transform and a hidden Markov model. *EURASIP Journal on Applied Signal Processing* 4, 559–571, 2004.

Connell, S.D. & Jain, A.K. template-based online character recognition. *Pattern Recognition* 34(1), 1–14, 2001.

Cooper, W.E., editor. *Cognitive Aspects of Skilled Typewriting*. Springer-Verlag, New York, NY, USA, 1983. ISBN 0-387-90774-2.

Cowan, N. The magical number 4 in short-term memory: a reconsideration of mental storage capacity. *Behavioral and Brain Sciences* 24, 87–185, 2001.

Cristianni, N. & Shawe-Taylor, J. *An Introduction to Support Vector Machines and Other Kernel-based Learning Methods*, Cambridge Press, Cambridge, UK, 2000.

Dahaene, S., Naccache, L., LeClec'H, G., Kroechlin, E., Mueller, M., Gahaene-Lamvertz, G., van de Morrtele, P.F., & Bihan, D. Imaging unconscious semantic priming. *Nature* 395, 597–600, 1998.

Davis, S.B. & Mermelstein, P. Comparison of parametric representations for monosyllabic word recognition in continuously spoken sentences. *IEEE Transactions on Acoustics, Speech, and Signal Processing* 28(4), 357–366, 1980.

Davis, D., Monrose, F., & Reiter, M.K. On user choice in graphical password schemes, in *Proceedings of the 13th USENIX Security Symposium*, August 9–13, 2004, San Diego, CA, USA, pp. 151–164, 2004.

De Angeli, A., Coventry, L., Johnson, G.I., & Coutts, M. Usability and user authentication: pictorial passwords vs. PIN, in McCabe, P.T. (editor), *Contemporary Ergonomics 2003*, pp. 253–258, Taylor & Francis, London, UK, 2003.

Delorme, A. & Makeig, S. EEGLAB: an open source toolbox for analysis of single-trial EEG dynamics, *Journal of Neuroscience Methods* 134:9–21, 2004.

Deng, P.S., Liao, H-Y., M., Ho, C.H., & Tyan, H-R. Wavelet-based off-line signature verification. *Computer Vision and Image Understanding* 76(3), 173–190, 1999.

Dessimoz, D. & Richiardi, J. MbioD: multimodal biometrics for identity documents. Research Report PFS 341-08.05, June 2006.

Dhamija, R. & Perrig, A. Deja Vu: a user study using images for authentication, in *Proceedings of 9th USENIX Security Symposium*, August 14–17, 2000, Denver, CO, USA, p. 4, 2000.

Dieckmann, U., Plankensteiner, P., & Wagner, T. Sesam: a biometric identification system using sensor fusion. *Pattern Recognition Letters* 18(9), pp. 827–833, 1997.

Doddington, G.R., Przybocki, M.A., Martin, F.A., & Reynolds, R.A. The NIST speaker recognition evaluation-overview, methodology, systems, results, perspective. *Pattern Recognition* 36(2), 383–396, 2000.

Dolfing, J.G.A. Handwriting recognition and verification, a hidden Markov model approach. PhD Thesis, Eindhoven University of Technology, the Netherlands, 1998.

Donchin, E., Spencer, K.M., & Wijesinghe, R. The mental prosthesis: assessing the speed of a P300-based brain-computer interface. *IEEE Transactions on Rehabilitation Engineering* 8, 174–179, 2000.

Dornhege, G., del Millan, J.R., Hinterberger, T., McFarland, D.J., & Muller, K-R. *Toward Brain-Computer Interfacing.* MIT Press, Cambridge, MA, USA, 2007.

Dugad, R. & Desai, U.B. A tutorial on hidden Markov models, University of Illinois, TR SPANN-96.1, 1996.

Durbin, R., Eddy, S., Krogh, A., & Mitchison (Eds) Biological Sequence Analysis, Cambride University Press, 1998, ISBN: 0521620414).

Eddy, S.R., Multiple Alignment Using Hidden Markov Models, In Proc. Third Int. Conf. Intelligent Systems for Molecular Biology, C. Rawlings et al., eds. AAAI Press, Menlo Park. pp. 114–120, 1995.

Elftmann, P., Secure Alternatives to Password-based Authentication Mechanisms, Thesis submitted to the Laboratory for Dependable Distributed Systems RWTH Aachen University Aachen, Germany, October 2006.

El-Yacoubi, A., Justino, E.J.R, Sabourin, R., & Bortolozzi, F. Off-line signature verification using HMM and cross-validation, in *IEEE International Workshop on Neural Networks for Signal Processing*, 11–13 December, 2000, pp. 859–868, Sydney, Australia, 2000.

Farwell, L.A. & Smith, S.S. Using brain MERMER testing to detect knowledge despite efforts to conceal. *Journal of Forensic Science* 46(1), 135–143, 2001.

Felzer, T. On the possibility of developing a brain-computer interface (BCI). Technical Report, Department of Computer Science, Technical University of Darmstadt, Germany, 2001.

Fierrez, J., Ramos-Castro, D., Ortega-Garcia, J., & Gonzalez-Rodriguez, J. HMM-based on-line signature verification: feature extraction and signature modeling. *Pattern Recognition Letters* 28(16), 2325–2334, 2007.

Fierrez-Aguilar, J., Krawczyk, S., Ortega-Garcia, J., & Jain, A.K. Fusion of local and regional approaches for on-line signature verification, *Advances in Biometric Person Authentication*, Springer-Verlag LNCS 3781, pp. 188–196, 2005.

Fitts, P.M. The information capacity of the human motor system in controlling the amplitude of movement. *Journal of Experimental Psychology* 47(6), 381–391, 1954.

Forsen, G., Nelson, M., & Staron, R. Persoanl attributes authentication techniques, in Griffin, A.F.B. (editor), *Rome Air Development Center Report RADC-TR-77-1033*, RADC, Griffins Air Force Base, NY; RADC-TR-77-333 Final Technical Report, October 1977, AD A047645. New York, NY, USA, 1977.

Foster, J.P., Nixon, M.S., & Prugell-Bennet, A. Gait recognition by symmetry analysis. AVBPA'01, pp. 272–277, 2002.

Franke, K. & Rose, S. Ink-deposition model: the relation of writing and ink deposition processes. Ninth International Workshop on Frontiers in Handwriting Recognition, IWFHR-9, 2004, pp. 173–178, October 26–29, 2004.

Franke, K. & Koppen, M. Pen force emulating robotic writing device and its application. IEEE Workshop on Advanced Robotics and Its Social Impacts, 12–15 June, 2005, Nagoya, Japan, pp. 36–46, 2005.

Freeman, W. The physiology of perception. *Scientific American* 264, 78–85, 1991.

Frischolz, R.W. & Dieckmann, U. A multimodal bioemtric identification system. *IEEE Computer Security* 33, 64–68, 2000.

Fuentes, M., Garcia-Salicetti, S., & Dorizzi, B. On line signature verification: fusion of a hidden Markov model and a neural network via a support vector machine, in *Proceedings of the 8th International Workshop on Frontiers in Handwriting Recognition (IWFHR '02)*, pp. 253–258, 2002.

Furui, S. Cepstral analysis technique for automatic speaker verification. *IEEE Transactions on Acoustics, Speech, and Signal Processing* 29(2), 254–272, 1981a.

Furui, S. Comparison of speaker recognition methods using statistical features and dynamic features. *IEEE Transactions on Acoustics, Speech, and Signal Processing*, 29(3), 342–350, 1981b.

Gafurov, D., Helkala, K., & Sondrol, T. Biometric gait authentication using accelerometer sensor. *Journal of Computers*, 1(7), 51–59, 2006.

Gaines, R., Lisowski, W., Press, S., & Shapiro, N. Authentication by keystroke timing: some preliminary results. Rand Report R-256-NSF. Rand Corporation, 1980.

Gamboa, H. & Ferreira, V. WIDAM – Web interaction display and monitoring, in *Proceedings of the 5th International Conference on Enterprise Information Systems*, 23–26, April, 2003, Angers, France, pp. 21–27, 2003.

Gamboa, H. & Fred, A. An identity authentication system based on human computer interaction behaviour, in *Proceedings of the 3rd International Workshop on Pattern Recognition on Information Systems*, Angers, France, 23–26 April, 2003, pp. 46–55, 2003.

Gamboa, H. & Fred, A. A behavioural biometric system based on human computer interaction, in *SPIE 5404 – Biometric Technology for Human Identification*, Jain, A.L. & Ratha, N.K. (editors), Orlando, USA, pp. 381–392, 2004.

Gamboa, H., Fred, A., & Vieira, A.V. Prevention or identification of web intrusion via human computer interaction behaviour – a proposal, in *Proceedings of the RTO SCI Symposium on Systems, Components, and Integration (SCI) Methods and Technologies for Defense Against Terrorism*, RTO-MP-SCI-158, London, UK, 25–27 October 2004, and published in RTO-MP-SCI-158, 2004.

Ganchev, T.D. Speaker recognition. PhD Thesis, University of Patras, Greece, 2005.

Ganchev, T., Fakotakis, N., & Kokkinakis, G., Comparative evaluation of various MFCC implementations on the speaker verification task, in *10th International Conference on Speech and Computer (SPECOM 2005)*, vol. 1, pp. 191–194, 2005.

Garcia-Molina, G.N., Ebrahimi, T., Hoffmann, U., & Vesin, J.-M. Direct brain-computer communication through EEG signals, 2005 IEEE Engineering in Medicine and Biology 27th Annual Conference, Shanghai, China, 2005.

Gardner, J. Detection of vapors and odors from a multi-sensor array using pattern recognition, part 1: principle component and cluster analysis. *Sensors and Actuators B* 4, 109–115, 1991.

Gasser, M. A random word generator for pronounceable words. Technical Report ESD-TR-75-97 MTR-3006, Mitre Corporation, Bedford, MA, USA, 1974.

Gentner, D.R. Keystroke timing in transcription typing, in *Cognitive Aspects of Skilled Typewriting*, Cooper, W.E. (editor), p. 95–120, Springer Verlag, New York, 1993.

Goldberg, D. *Genetic Algorithms in Search, Optimization, and Machine Learning*. Addison-Wesley Publishing Company, USA, 1989.

Goldberg, J., Hagman, J., & Sazawal, V. Doodling our way to better authentication. Conference on Human Factors and Computing Systems, Poster Session: Student Posters, Minneapolis, MN, USA, 20–25 April, 2002, pp. 868–869, 2002.

Goldberg, J., Hagman, J., & Sazawal, V., Doodling our way to better authentication, Proceedings of Human Factors in Computing Systems (CHI), Minnesota, USA, 2002.

Gorunescu, F., Gorunescu, M., Revett, K., & Ene, M., A hybrid incremental/Monte Carlo searching technique for the "Smoothing" parameter of probabilistic Neural Networks, in the Proceedings of the International Conference on Knowledge Engineering, Principles and Techniques, KEPT2007, Cluj-Napoca (Romania), June 6–8, 2007, pp. 107–113, 2007.

Gunetti, D. & Picardi, C. *Keystroke Analysis of Free Text*. University of Torino, Italy, 2002.

Guo, J.K. Forgery detection by local correspondence. Technical Report CS-TR-4122, University of Maryland, College Park, MD, USA, 2000.

Gupta, G. & McCabe, A. A review of dynamic handwritten signature verification. Technical Report 97/4, James Cook University, Townsville, Australia, 1997.

Gupta, C.N. & Palaniappan, R. Enhanced detection of visual-evoked potentials in brain-computer interface using genetic algorithm and cyclostationary analysis. *Computational Intelligence in Neuroscience*, 2007(2), 1–12, 2007.

Haider, S., Abbas, A., Zaidi, A.K. A multi-technique approach for user identification through keystroke dynamics. In: IEEE International Conference on Systems, Man, and Cybernetics, Vol. 2., Nashville, TN. USA, pp. 1336–1341, 2000.

Haigh, J.A. & Mason, J.S. A voice activity detector based on cepstral analysis. *Proceedings of the European Conference on Speech Communication and Technology*, 2, 1103–1106, 1993.

Hampel, F.R., Rousseeuw, P.J., Ronchetti, E.M., & Stahel, W.A. *Robust Statistics: The Approach Based on Influence Functions*, Wiley, New York, NY, USA, 1986.

Hashia, S., Pollett, C., & Stamp, M. On using mouse movements as a biometric. LNCS 2652, pp. 246–254, 2003.

Hayashi, E., Christin, N., Dhamija, R., & Perrig, A. Mental trapdoors for user authentication on small mobile devices. Technical Report CMU-CyLab-07-011, Carnegie Mellon University, Pittsburgh, PA, USA, 2007.

Haykin, S. *Neural Networks: A Comprehensive Introduction.* Prentice Hall, Upper Saddle River, NJ, USA, 1999.

Hecht-Nielsen, R. Neurocomputing, Reading, MA: Addison-Wesley, 1990.

Hermansky, H. Preceptual linear predictive (PLP) analysis for speech. *Journal of the Acoustic Society of America* 1738–1752, 1990.

Hertz, J., Krough, A., & Palmer, R.G. *Introduction to the Theory of Neural Computation*, Addison-Wesley, Reading, MA, USA, 1991.

Hong, D., Man, S., Hawes, B., & Mathews, M. A password scheme strongly resistant to spyware, in *Proceedings of International Conference on Security and Management.* SAM'04, 21–24, June 2004, pp. 94–100. Las Vegas, NV, USA, 2004.

Horn, B. & Schunk, B. Determining optical flow. *Artificial Intelligence* 17, 185–203, 1981.

Hoshiyama, M., Kakigi, R., Takeshima, Y., Miki, K., & Watanabe, S. Priority of face perception during subliminal stimualtion using a new color-opponent flicker stimulation. *Neuroscience Letters* 402, 57–61, 2006.

ICAO. Document 9303 on Machine Readable Travel Document, International Civil Aviation Organization, 2004.

ISO/IEC-19794-1. *International Standards Organization (BioAPI v2.0).* International Standards Organization, Geneva, Switzerland, 2005.

Israel, S., Irvine, J., Cheng, A., Wiederhold, M., & Wiederhold, B. ECG to identify individuals. *Pattern Recognition* 38(1), 133–142, 2005.

Jagacinsiki, R.J. & Monk, D.L. Fitts' law in two dimensions with hand and head movements. *Journal of Motor Behavior* 17, 77–95, 1985.

Jain, A.K. & Ross, A. Multibiometric systems. *Communications of the ACM, Special Issue on Multimodal Interfaces*, 47(1), 34–40, 2004.

Jain, A.K., Bolle, R., & Pankanti, S. Introduction to biometrics, in Jain, A., Bolle, R., & Pankanti, S. (editors), *Biometrics. Personal Identification in Networked Society*, pp. 1–41, Kluwer Academic Publishers, Norwell, MA, USA, 2003.

Jain, A.K., Nandakumar, K., & Ross, A. Score normalization in multimodal biometric systems. *Pattern Recognition* 38(12), 2270–2285, 2005.

Jansen, W., Gavrila, S., Korolev, V., Ayers, R., & Swanstrom, R. Picture password: a visual login technique for mobile devices. NIST Report – NISTIR7030, 2003.

Joyce, R. & Gupta, G. Identity authorization based on keystroke latencies. *Communications of the ACM* 33(2), 168–176, 1990.

Justino, E.J.R., El Yacoubi, A., Bortolozzi, F., & Sabourin, R. An off-line signature verification system using hidden Markov models and cross-validation, in Proceedings of the 13th Brazilian Symposium on Computer Graphics and Image Processing, pp. 105–112, 2000.

Kaewkongka, T., Chamnongthai, K., & Thipakorn, B. Off-line signature recognition using parametized Hough transform, in *Proceedings of the 5th International Symposium on Signal Processing, and its Applications*, pp. 451–454, IEEE Brisbane, Australia, 1999.

Kale, A., Cuntoor, N.P., Yegnanarayana, B., Rajagopalan, A.N., & Chellappa, R. Gait analysis for human identification. 4th International Conference on Audio and Video-Based Biometric Person Authentication, 9–11 June 2003, Guilford, England, UK, pp. 706–714, Springer-Verlag, 2003.

Keller, P. Overview of electronic nose algorithms. International Joint Conference of Neural Networks (IJCNN '99), Washington, DC, USA, 10–16 July, 1999.

Kholmatov, A. A biometric identity verification using on-line and off-line signature verification. MSc Thesis, Sabanci University, Turkey, 2003.

Kholmatov, A. & Yanikoglu, B. Bioemtric authnetication using online signatures, in *Proceedings ISCIS*, pp. 373–380, Springer-Verlag, Kemer-Antalya, Turkey, 27–29 October, LNCS-3280, Springer-Verlag, Heidleberg, Germany, 2004.

King, M.M. Rebus passwords, in *Proceedings of the 7th Annual Computer Security Applications Conference*, pp. 239–243, IEEE San Antonio, TX, USA, 1991.

Kinjo, H. & Snodgrass, J.G. Does the generation effect occur for pictures. *American Journal of Psychology* 6, 156–163, 2000.

Klein, D. Foiling the cracker: a survey of, and improvements to, password security, in *Proceedings of the 2nd USENIX Security Workshop*, Portland, OR, USA, 27 August 1990, pp. 5–14, 1990.

Kohonen, T. Learning Vector Quantization, Neural Networks, 1 (suppl 1), pp. 303, 1998.

Korotkaya, Z. Biometric Person Authentication: Odor. *Advanced Topics in Information Processing*, Lappeenranta University of Technology, Finland, 2003.

Kotani, K. & Horii, K. Evaluation on a keystroke authentication system by keying force incorporated with temporal characteristics of keystroke dynamics, Behavior and Information Technology 24, p. 289–302, 2004

Kronegg, J., Voloshynovskiy, S., & Pun, T. Analysis of bit-rate definitions for brain-computer interfaces. International Conference on Human-Computer Interaction (HCI '05), Edinburgh, Scottland, June 20–23, 2005, 2005.

Kubler, A. *Brain-Computer Communication – Development of a Brain-Computer Interface for Locked-in Patients on the Basis of Psychophysiological Self-regulation Training of Slow Cortical Potentials (SCP)*. Schwabische Verlagsgesellechaft, Tubingen, Germany, 2000.

Kyeong-Seop, K., Tae-Ho, Y., Jeong-Whan, L., Dong-Jun, K., & Heung-Seo, K. A robust human identification by normalized time-domain features of electrocardiogram. IEEE EMBS 27th Annual International Conference of Engineering in Medicine and Biology (EMBS2005), 12–15 May, 2005, Istanbul, Turkey, pp. 1114–1117, 2005.

Kyoso, M. & Uchiyama, A. Development of an ECG identifcation system, in *Proceedings of the 23rd Annual International IEEE Conference on Engineering in Medicine and Biology Society*, pp. 3721–3723, IEEE, Istanbul, Turkey, 2001.

Lam, L. & Suen, C.Y. Application of majority voting to pattern recognition: an analysis of its behavior and performance. *IEEE Transactions on Systems, Man, Cybernetics, Part A: Systems Humans* 27(5), 553–568, 1997.

Lee, H-J. & Cho, S. Retraining a novelty detector with imposter patterns for keystroke dynamics-based authentication. International Conference on Biometrics, 5–7 January, 2006, Hong Kong, pp. 633–639, Springer-Verlag LNCS 3832, Hong Kong, 2006.

Leggett, J. & Williams, G. Verifying identity via keystroke characteristics. *International Journal of Man-Machine Studies* 28(1), 67–76, 1988.

Leggett, J., Williams, G., & Umphress, D. Verification of user identity via keystroke characteristics. Human Factors in Management Information Systems. Ablex Publishing Corp., Norwood, NJ, USA, 1989.

Leggett, J., Williams, G., & Umphress, D. Verification of user identity via keystroke characteristics. *Human Factors in Management Information Systems*, Vol. 28, pp. 67–76, ACM International Journal of Man-Machine Studies, 1989.

Lei, H. & Givindaraju, V. A comparative study on the consistency of features in on-line signature verification, Pattern Recognition Letters, 26(15), 2483–2489, 2004.

Libet, B., Alberts, W.W., Wright, E.W., & Feinstein, B. Responses of human somato-sensory cortex tto stimuli below the threshold for sonscious sensation. *Science* 158(3808), 1597–1600, 1967.

Maarse, F. & Thomassen, A. Produced and perceived writing slant: differences between up and down strokes. *Acta Psychologica* 54(1–3), 131–147, 1983.

MacKenzie, I.S. & Buxton, W.A.S. Extending Fitts' law to two-dimensional tasks. Proceedings of ACM CHI 1992 Conference on Human Factors in Computing Systems, 3–7 June 1992, Monterey, CA, USA, pp. 219–226, 1992.

Magnus, R. An introduction to front-end processing and acoustic features for automatic speech recognition, January 2006.

Mak, M., Kim, J., & Thieme, M. Biometric Fusion Demonstration System Scientific Report, Defence R&D Canada – Ottawa, Contractor Report, DRDC Ottawa CR 2004-056, March 2004.

Mallat, S.G. Zero-crossings of a wavelet transform. *IEEE Transaction on Information Theory* 37(4), 1019–1033, 1991.

Man, S., Hong, D., & Mathews, M. A shoulder surfing resistant graphical password scheme, in *Proceedings of International Conference on Security and Management*. CSREA Press, 23–26 June, 2003, (Hamid R. Arabnia, Youngsong Mun, Eds.) Las Vegas, NV, USA, 2003.

Manber, U. A simple scheme to make passwords based on one-way functions much harder to crack. *Computers & Security* 15(2), 171–176, 1996.

Mandler, J.M. & Ritchey, G.H. Long-term memory for pictures. *Journal of Experimental Psychology: Human Learning and Memory* 3, 386–396, 1977.

Marcel, S. & del R. Millan, R. Person authentication using brainwaves (EEG) and maximum a posteriori model adaptation, IEEE Transactions on Pattern Analysis and Machine Intelligence, Special issue on Biometrics, 2006.

Markowitz, J.A., Voice biometrics. *Communications of the ACM* 43(9), 66–73, 2000.

Martin, A., Doddington, G., Kamm, T., Ordowski, M., & Przybocki, M. The det curve in assessment of detection task performance. Proceedings of the 5th European Conference on Speech Communication and Technology, Rhodos, Greecer, September 1997, pp. 1895–1898, 1997.

Mason, J.S. & Zhang, X. Velocity and acceleration features in speaker recognition. Proceedings of ICASSP'91, 14–17 April 1991, Toronto, Ontario, Canada, pp. 3673–3677, April 1991.

Masuko, T., Tohuda, K., Kobayashi, T., & Imai, S. Speech synthesis using HMMs with dynamic features. Proceedings of ICASSP-96, 7–10 May 1996, Atlanta, GA, USA, pp. 389–392, 1996.

Masuko, T., Hitotsumatsu, T., Tojuda, K., & Kobayashi, T. On the security of HMM-based speaker verification systems against imposture using synthetic speech, in EROSPEECH '99, pp. 1223–1226, 1999.

Matsui, T. & Furui, S. Speaker adaptation of tied-mixture-based phoneme models for text-prompted speaker recognition. Proceedings of ICASSP-94, 19–22 April, 2004, Adelaide, Australia, pp. 125–128, 1994.

McBride, D.M. & Dosher, A.B. A comparison of conscious and automatic memory processes for picture and word stimuli: a process dissociation analysis. *Consciousness and Cognition* 11, 423–460, 2002.

McCabe, A. Implementation and analysis of a handwritten signature verification technique. Honours Thesis, James Cook University, Townsville, Australia, 1997.

McCabe, A. Markov modelling of simple directional features for efficient and effective handwriting verification, in Mizoguchi, R. & Saney, J. (editors), *PRICAI, LNAI 1886*, August 28–September 1, 2000, p. 801, Springer-Verlag, LNCS 1886, 2000.

Mehta, S.S. & Lingayat, N.S. Comparative study of QRS detection in single lead and 12-lead ECG based on entropy and combined entropy criteria using support vector machine. *Journal of Theoretical and Applied Information Technology*, 3(2), 8–18, 2007.

Mermelstein, P. Distance measures for speech recognition, psychological and instrumental, in Chen, C.H. (editor), *Pattern Recognition and Artificial Intelligence*, pp. 374–388. Academic, New York, NY, USA, 1976.

Meyer, D.E., Smith, J.E.K., Kornblum, S., Abrams, R.A., & Wright, C.E. Speed-accuracy tradeoffs in aimed movements: toward a theory of rapid voluntary action. In Jeannerod, M. (ed.), *Attention and Performance* XIII, pp. 173–226. Lawrence Erlbaum, Hillsdale, NJ, USA, 1990.

Miller, G.A. The magical number seven, plus or minus two: some limits on our capacity for processing information. *Psychological Review* 63, 81–97, 1956.

Miller, N.E. Learning of visceral and glandular responses. *Science* 163(688), 434–445, 1969.

Minsky, M. & Papert, S. *Perceptrons*. MIT Press, Cambridge, 1969.

Modi, S.K. Keystroke dynamics verification using spontaneous password, MSc dissertation, Purdue University, May 2005.

Monrose, F. & Rubin, A.D. Authentication via keystroke dynamics. *Proceedings of the Fourth ACM Conference on Computer and Communication Security*. Zurich, Switzerland, 1997.

Monrose, F. & Reiter, M.K. Graphical passwords, in Cranor, L. & Garfinkel, S. (editors), *Security and Usability*, Chapter 9, pp. 147–164, O'Reilly, Media, Inc., USA, 2005.

Monrose, F., Reiter, M.K., & Wetzel, S. Using voice to generate cryptographic keys, Password Hardening Based on keystroke Dynamics, 1997.

Monrose, F. et al. Password hardening based on keystroke dynamics. *International Journal of Information Security* 1(2), 69–83, 2002.

Nakanishi, I., Nishiguchi, N., Itoh, Y., & Fukui, Y. On-line signature verification based on discrete wavelet domain adaptive signal processing, ICBA 2004: International Conference on Biometric Authentication, Hong Kong (15/07/2004), Vol. 3072, pp. 584–591, 2004.

Nali, D. & Thorpe, J. Analyzing user choice in graphical passwords. Technical Report TR-04-01, Carleton University, Canada, 2004.

Nalwa, V.S. Automatic on-line signature verification. *Proceedings of the IEEE* 85(2), 215–239, 1997

Napier, R. Keyboard user verification: toward an accurate, efficient, and ecologically valid algorithm. *International Journal of Human-Computer Studies* 43, 213–222, 1995.

Newell, A. & Rosenbloom, P.S. Mechanisms of skill acquisition and the law of practise, in cognitive skills and their acquisition, in *Cognitive Skills and Their Acquisition*, Anderson, J.R. (editor), pp. 1–56, Lawrence Erlbaum Associates, Hillsdale, NJ, USA, 1981.

Niels, R. Dynamics time warping. MSc Thesis, Radbound University Nijmegen, the Netherlands, 2004.

Niels, R. & Vuurpijl, L. Using dynamic time warping for intuitive handwriting recognition, In A. Marcelli & C. De Stafano (Eds.), Advances in Graphonomics. *Proceedings of the 12th Conference of the Internatonal Graphonomics Society (IGS2005)*, (pp. 217–221), Salerno, Italy, 2005.

Niesen, U. & Pfister, B. Speaker verification by means of ANNs. European Symposium on Artificial Neural Networks (ESANN), Bruges, Belgium, pp. 145–150, April 28–30, 2004.

Nixon, M.S. & Carter, J.N. On gait as a biometric: progress and prospects. *EUSIPCO* 2004, 1401–1404, 2004.

Nykopp, T. Statistical modelling issues for the adaptive brain interface. MSc Thesis, Helsinki University of Technology, Finland, 2001.

Obaidat, M.S. & Macchairolo, D.T. A multilayer neural system for computer access security. *IEEE Transactions on Systems, Man, and Cybernetics*, 24(5), 803–816, 1994.

Orozco, M., Graydon, M., Shiromohammadi, S., & El Saddik, A. Using haptic interfaces for user verification in virtual environments, in *Proceedings IEEE International Conference on Virtual Environments, Human-Computer Interfaces, and Measurement Systems*, pp. 25–30, IEEE Computer Science Series, La Coruña, Spain, 2006.

Orsag, I.F. Biometric recognition systems, speaker recognition technology. Doctoral dissertation, Brno University of Technology, Czech Republic, 2004.

Ouzounov, A. An evaluation of DTW, AA, and ARVM for fixed-text speaker identification, pp. 3–10, Sofia, Bulgaria, 2003.

Ortega-Mendoza, R.M., Villatoro-Tello, E., Villaseñor-Pineda, L., Montes-y-Gómez, & Morales, F. On the use of dynamic information for speaker identification, http://ccc.inaoep.mx/~mmontesg/publicaciones/2007/DynamicInformationForSpeakerIdentification-Core07.pdf, 2006.

Ozgunduz, E., Senturk, T., & Karsligil, E. Off-line signature verification and recognition using support vector machines, 13th European Conference on Signal Processing (EUSIPCO 2005), 4–8 September, 2005, Antalya, Turkey, 2003.

Ozgunduz, E., Senturk, T., & Karsligil, E. Efficient off-line verification and identification of signatures by multiclass support vector machines. Lecture Notes in Computer Science 3691, pp. 799–805, 2005.

Paivio, A. & Csapo, K. Picture superiority in free recall: imagery or dual coding? *Cognitive Psychology* 5, 176–206, 1973.

Paivio, A., Rogers, T.B., & Smythe, P.C. Why are pictures easier to recall then words? *Psychonomic Science* 11(4), 137–138, 1968.

Paliwal, K.K. & Atal, B.S. Frequency-related representation of speech. Eurospeech'03, pp. 65–68, Geneva, Switzerland, 2003.

Paranjape, R.B., Mahovsky, J., Benedicenti, L., & Kolesapos, Z. The electroencephalogram as a biometric. Canadian Conference on Electrical and Computer Engineering, 13–16 May, 2001, Vancouver, British Columbia, Canada, pp. 1363–1366, 2001.

Parizeau, M. & Plamondon, R. A comparative analysis of regional correlation, dynamic time warping, and skeletal tree matching for signature verification. *IEEE Transaction on Pattern Analysis and Machine Intelligence* 12(7), 710–717, 1990.

Passlogix. http://www.passlogix.com, accessed on January 29, 2006, 2006.

Picton, T.W. The P300 wave of the human event-related potential. *Electroenchephalography and Clinical Neurophysiology* 9, 456–479, 1992.

Pineda, L., Villaseñor-Pineda, L., Cuétara, J., Castellanos, H., & López, I. DIMEx100: a new phonetic and speech corpus for Mexican Spanish, in *Proceedings of the 9th Ibero-American Conference on Artificial Intelligence* (IBERAMIA 2004), pp. 974–983, Pueblo, Mexico, Springer-Verlag, LNCS 3315, Heidelberg, Germany, 2004.

Plamondon, R. & Parizeau, M. Signature verification from position, velocity and acceleration signals: a comparative study, in *Proceedings of the 9th International Conference on Pattern Recognition*, Vol. 1, Rome, Italy, pp. 260–265, 1988.

Posner, M.I. Abstraction and the process of recognition, in Bower, G.H. & Spence, J.T. (editors), *Psychology of Learning and Motivation*, Vol. 3, pp. 43–100, Academic Press, New York, NY, USA, 1969.

Poulos, M., Rangoussi, M., & Alexandris, N. Neural network based person identification using EEG features. *Proceedings of the IEEE International Conference on Acoustics, Speech, and Signal Processing*, 2, 1117–1120, 1999.

Poulos, M., Rangoussi, M., Alexandris, N., & Evangelou, A. On the use of EEG features towards person identification via neural networks. *Medical Informatics and the Internet in Medicine* 26(1), 35–48, 2001.

Pusara, M. & Brodley, C.E. User re-authentication via mouse movements, Conference on Computer and Communications Security, Proceedings of the 2004 ACM workshop on Visualization and data mining for computer security, 29 October, 2004, Washington, DC, USA, p. 1–8, ACM, New York, NY, USA, 2003.

Quek, C. & Zhou, W. Antiforgery: a novel pseudo-outer product based fuzzy neural network driven signature verification system. *Pattern Recognition Letters* 23(14), 1795–1816, 2002.

Quinlan, R. Data mining tools (see 5 and C5.0), C4.5: Programs for machine learning, Morgan Kaufmann, New York, 1993.

Rabiner, L. & Shafer, R. *Digital Processing of Speech Signals.* Prentice Hall, Inc., Englewood Cliffs, NY, USA, 1978.

Rabiner, L.R. A tutorial on hidden Markov models and selected applications in speech recognition. *Proceeding of the IEEE* 77(2), 257–286, 1989.

Rahman, M.S. & Shimamura, T. Linear prediction using homomorphic deconvolution in the autocorrelation domain, circuits and systems, 2005. ISCAS 2005. IEEE International Symposium on Circuits and Systems, Vol. 3, 23–26 May 2005 pp. 2855–2858, 2005.

Rahman, M.S. & Shimamura, T. Speech analysis based on modelling the effective voice source. *IEICE Transactions on Information and Systems* E89-D(3), 1107–1115, 2006.

Rangayyan, R.M. *Biomdeical Signal Analysis, A case study Approach.* Wiley-IEEE press, Piscataway, NJ, USA, 2002.

Real User Corporation. The science behind Passfaces. http://www.realusers.com., accessed December 2, 2002, 2001.

Revett, K. On the use of multiple sequence alignment for user authentication via keystroke dynamics. International Conference on Global eSecurity 2007 (ICGeS), April 16–18, 2007, University of East London, pp. 112–120, 2007e.

Revett, K. & Khan, A. Enhancing login security using keystroke hardening and keyboard gridding. Proceedings of the IADIS MCCSIS 19–23 April, 2005, pp. 194–199, 2005.

Revett, K., Gorunescu, F., Gorunescu, M., El-Darzi, E., & Ene, M. A breast cancer diagnosis system: a combined approach using rough sets and probabilistic neural networks. Proceedings of Eurocon 2005 – IEEE International Conference on "Computer as a tool," Belgrade, Serbia, November 21–24, pp. 1124–1127, 2005b.

Revett, K., Magalhães, S., & Santos, H.M.D. Critical aspects in graphic authentication keys. International Conference on I-Warfare, University of Maryland Eastern Shore, March 15–16, 2006, pp. 212–217, 2006.

Revett, K., Gorunescu, F., Gorunescu, M., Ene, M., Tenreiro de Magalhães, S., & Santos, H.M.D. A novel machine learning approach to keystroke dynamics based user authentication. *International Journal of Electronic Security and Digital Forensics* 1(1), 55–70, 2007a.

Revett, K., Tenreiro de Magalhães, S., & Santos, L. Graphical based user authentication with embedded mouse stroke dynamics. 2nd International Conference on Information Warfare and Security (ICIW 2007), pp. 171–176, Monterey, CA, USA, March 8–9, 2007b.

Revett, K. & Jokisz, I. A bioinformatics based approach to behavioural biometrics, Frontiers in the Convergence of Bioscience and Information Technologies (FBIT2007), October 11–13, 2007, Cheju Island, Korea, pp. 665–670, 2007b.

Revett, K., Tenreiro de Magalhães, S., & Santos, L. Graphical based user authentication with embedded mouse stroke dynamics. 2nd International Conference on Information Warfare and Security (ICIW2007), March 8–9, 2007, Monterey, CA, USA, pp. 171–176, ISBN: 978-1-905305-41-4, 2007d.

Revett, K., Jahankhani, H., Magalhaes, S., & Santos, H.M.D. User dynamics in graphical authentication systems. 4th International Conference on Global eSecurity 2008 (ICGeS'08), June 24–26, 2008, University of East London, 2008a.

Revett K., Jahankhani, H., Magalhaes, S., & Santos, H.M.D. A survey of user authentication based on mouse dynamics. 4th International Conference on Global eSecurity 2008 (ICGeS'08), June 24–26, 2008, University of East London, 2008b.

Reynolds, D. Experimental evaluation of features for robust speaker identification. *IEEE Transaction on Speech and Audi Processing* 1(3), 639–643, 1994.

Reynolds, S. Keystroke dynamics format for data interchange. Biopassword, 2005.

Reynolds, D., Quatieri, T., & Dunn, R. Speaker verification using adapted Gaussian mixture models. *Journal of Digital Signal Processing* 3(1), 19–41, 2000.

Riera, A., Soria-Frisch, A., Caparrini, M., Grau, C., & Ruffini, G. Unobtrusive biometric system based on electro-encephalogram analysis. *EURASIP Journal on Advances in Signal Processing*, 2008 (1), Hindawi Publishing Corporation, USA, 2007.

Rigoll, G. & Kosmala, A. A systematic comparison between on-line and off-line methods for signature verification with hidden Markov models, in *Proceedings of the 14th International Conference on Pattern Recognition*, Vol. 2, pp. 1755–1757, Brisbane, Australia, August 16–20, 1998.

Rigoll, G., Kosmala, A., Rottland, J., & Neukirchen, C. A comparison between continuous and discrete density hidden Markov models for cursive handwriting recognition, in *Proceedings of the IEEE International Conference on Pattern Recognition (ICPR '96)*, Vienna, Austria, Vol. 2, p. 205, 1996.

Rorschach, H. *Psychodiagnostik*. Bircher, Bern, Switzerland, 1921.

Rosetta. http://www.idi.ntnu.no/~aleks/rosetta, accessed January 6, 2006.

Ross, A. & Jain, A.K. Information fusion in biometrics. *Pattern Recognition Letters*, Special Issue on Multimodal Biometrics 24(13), 2115–2125, 2003.

Ross, A., Jain, A.K., & Qian, J. Information fusion in biometrics. Proceedings of the 3rd International Conference on Audio- and Video-Based Person Authentication (AVBPA), pp. 354–359, Halmstad, Sweden, June 6–8, 2001.

Rosell. http://www.nada.kth.se/~rosell/courses/rosell_acoustic_features.pdf, accessed January 10, 2008.

de Ru, W.G. & Eloff, J. Enhanced password authentication through Fuzzy Logic. *IEEE Expert* 12(6), 38–45, 1997.

Ruffini, G., Dunne, S., & Farres, E. A dry electrophysiology electrode using CNT arrays, Sensors and Actuators, A: physical 132(1), pp. 34–41, 2006.

Ruffini, G., Dunne, S., & Farres, E. ENOBIO dry electrodephysiology electrode, first human trial plus wireless electrode system, in *Proceedings of the 29th IEEE EMBS Annual International Conference*, Lyon, France, IEEE EMB, Piscataway, NJ, USA, pp. 6689–6693, 2007.

Rumelhart, D.E. & McClelland, J.L., editors. *Parallel Distibuted Processing: Explorations in the Microstructure of Cognition*, Vol. 1. MIT Press, Cambridge, MA, USA, 1986.

Sanderson, C. & Paliwal, K.K. Information fusion and person verification using speech and face information. Research Paper IDIAP-RR 02-33, IDIAP, September, 2002.

Sanderson, C. & Paliwal, K.K. On the use of speech and face information for identity verification. Research Paper IDIAP-RR 04-10, IDIAP, March, 2004.

Schölkopf, B., Platt, J., Shawe-Taylor, J., Smola, A.J., & Williamson, R.C. Estimating the support of a high-dimensional distribution. Technical Report MSR-TR-99-87, Microsoft Research, Redmond, WA, USA, 1999.

Schölkopf, B., Williamson, R.C, Smola, A.J., Shawe-Taylor, J., & Platt, J. Support vector method for novelty detection, in Solla, S.A., Leen, T.K., & Müller, K.-R. (editors), *Advances in Neural Information Processing Systems*, Vol. 12, pp. 582–588, MIT Press, Cambridge, MA, USA 2000.

Seitz, A.R. & Watanabe, T. Is subliminal learning really passive. *Nature* 422, 36, 2003.

Seneff, S. & Zue, V. Transcription and alignment of the time TIMIT database, in *Proceedings of the Second Symposium on Advanced Man-Machine Interface through Spoken Language*, pp. 1–9, IEEE Computer Society, Oahu, Hawaii, 1988.

Shakespeare, H. *King Henry VI*, Part 2, act 3, ca. 1590–1591.

Shannon, C. Prediction and entropy of printed English. *Bell Systems Technical Journal* 30, 50–64, 1951.

Shamir, A. How to share a secret. *Communications of the ACM* 22, 612–613, 1979.

Shao, Y., Srinivasan, S., & Wang, D. Incorporating auditory feature uncertainties in robust speaker identification, in *Proceedings of ICASSP'07*, 15–20 April 2007, Honolulu, Hawaii, IEEE, pp. 227–280, 2007.

Shutler, J.D. Velocity moments for holistic shape description of temporal features. PhD Thesis, University of Southampton, UK, 2002.

Silva, H., Gamboa, H., & Fred, A. Applicability of lead V_2 ECG measurements in biometrics, Proceedings of the International Educational and Networking Forum for eHealth, Telemedicine and Health ICT – Med-e-Tel, Luxembourg, April, 2007, 2001.

Sim, T. & Janakiraman, R. Are digraphs good for free-text keystroke dynamics, IEEE Conference on Computer Vision and pattern recognition, 2007 CVPR '07, 17–22 June 2007, Minneapolis, MN, USA, 2005.

Sim, T. & Janakiraman, R. Are digraphs good for free-text keystroke dynamics? IEEE Conference on Computer Vision and Pattern Recognition, 2007. CVPR apos;07. June 17–22, 2007, pp. 1–6, 2007.

Sobrado, L. & Birget, J.-C. Graphical passwords. *The Rutgers Scholar, An Electronic Bulletin for undergraduate Research*, Vol. 4, Camden New jersey, USA, 2002.

Sommerich, C. M., Marras, W. S., & Parnianpour, M. Observations on the relationship between key strike force and typing speed. *American Industrial Hygiene Association Journal* 57, 1109–1114, 1996.

Song, D., Wagner, D., & Tian, X. Timing analysis of keystrokes and timing attacks on SSH, in 10th USENIX Security Symposium, pp. 337–352, 2001.

Specht, D.F. Probabilistic neural networks for classification mapping or associative memory. *Proceedings of the IEEE International Conference on Neural Networks* 1, 525–532, 1988.

Specht, D.F. Probabilistic neural networks. *Neural Networks* 3, 110–118, 1990.

Stanney, K.M., editor. *Handbook of Virtual reality Environments: Design, Implementation, and Applications*, Lawrence Erlbaum Associates, Inc., Mahwah, NJ, USA, 2002.

Stevens, S.S., Volkman, J., & Newman, E.B, The Relation of Pitch to Frequency, A Revised Scale, *Journal of the Acoustical Society of America* 8(3), 185–190, 1937.

Strom, S.H. *Beyond the Typewriter: Gender, Class, and the Origins of Modern American Office Work, 1900–1930*. University of Illinois Press, Urbana and Chicago, IL, USA, 1992.

Stroop, J.R. Studies on interference in serial verbal reaction times. *Journal of Experimental Psychology* 18, 643–662, 1935.

Stubblefield, A. & Simon, D.R. Inkblot authentication. Microsoft Technical Report MSR-TR-2004-85, Microsoft Research, Redmond, WA, USA, 2004.

Suo, X., Zhu, Y., & Owen, G.S. *Graphical Passwords: A Survey*. Department of Computer Science, Georgia State University, Atlanta, GA, USA, 2003.

Suo, X., Zhu, Y., & Owen, G.S. Graphical passwords: a survey. 21st Annual Computer Security Applications Conference (ACSAC), December 5–9, 2005.

Suo, X., Zhu, Y., & Own, S. Analysis and design of graphical password techniques. ISVC 2006, LNCS 4292, pp. 741–749, 2006.

Sutton, S., Braren, M., Zubin, J., & John, E.R. Evoked potential correlates of stimulus uncertainty. *Science* 150, 1187–1188, 1965.

Syukri, A.F., Okamoto, E., & Mambo, M. A User identification system using signature written with mouse, in *Proceedings of the 3rd Australasian Conference on Information Security and Privacy*, LNCS 1438, pp. 403–414, Springer-Verlag, Heidelberg, Germany, 1998.

Tanawongsuwan, R. & Bobick, A. Gait recognition from time-normalized joint-angle trajectories in the walking plane. Proceedings of the International Conference on Computer Vision and Pattern Recognition, 8–14 December 2001, Kauai, Hi, USA, pp. 726–731, 2001.

Tao, H. Pass-Go, a New Graphical Password Scheme, Master thesis, University of Ottawa, Ottawa, Ontario, Canada, June 2006.

Teo, A., Garg, H., & Puthusserypady, S. Detection of humans buried in rubble: an electronic nose to detect human body odor. Proceedings of the IEEE 2nd Joint EMBS-BMES Conference, 23–26 October, 2002, pp. 1811–1812, Houston, TX, USA, 2002.

Thorpe, J., Van Oorschot, P.C., & Somayaji, A. Pass thoughts: authenticating with our mainds, in Proceedings of the ACSA 2005 New Security Paradigms Workshop, Sept. 2005, Lake Arrowhead, California, USA, 2005.

Tilton, C.J. *White paper: Biometrics Industry Standards*. SAFLINK Corporation, Kirkland, WA, USA, 2003.

Tolba, A.S. GloveSignature: A virtual-reality-based system for dynamic signature verification. *Digital Signal Processing* 9(4), 241–266, 1999.

Trevathan, J. & McCabe, A. Remote handwritten signature authentication, in *Proceedings of the 2nd International Conference on EBusiness and Telecommunication Networks (ICETE '05)*, pp. 335–339, Kluwer Academic Publishers, Reading, UK, 2005.

Turk, M. & Pentland, A. Eigenfaces for recognition. *Journal of Cognitive Neuroscience* 3(1), 71–86, 1991.

Tyler, C. Human symmetry perception, in Tyler, C. (editor), *Human Symmetry Perception and Its Computational Analysis*, pp. 3–22, the Netherlands, 1996.

Van Oorschot, P.C. & Thorpe, J. On the security of graphical password schemes. Technical Report TR-05-12, Carleton University, Canada, 2005.

Vidal, J. Toward direct brain-computer communication. *Annual Review of Biophysics and Bioengineering*, 2, 157–180, 1973.

Vidjiounaite, E., Makela, S.-M., Lindholm, M., Riihimaki, R., Kyllonen, V., Mantyjarvi, J., & Allisto, H. Unobtrusive multimodal biometrics for ensuring privacy and information security with personal devices, in *Pervasive, Computing 2006*, 7–10 May, Dublin, Ireland, pp. 233–238, Springer-Verlag, Heidelberg, Germany, LNCS, 2006.

Wahl, A., Hennebert, J., Humm, A., & Ingold, R. Generation and evaluation of brute-force signature forgeries. LNCS 4105, pp. 2–9, 2006.

Waller, A.D. A demonstration on man of electromotive changes accompanying the heart's beat. *Journal of Physiology (London)*, 8, 229–234, 1887.

Wang, L., Ning, H., Tan, T., & Hu, W. Fusion of static and dynamic body biometrics for gait recognition. Proceedings of the 9th IEEE International Conference on Computer Vision, 13–16 October, 2003, Nice, France, vol. 2, p. 14491454, 2003.

Wang, L., Ning, H., Tan, T., & Hu, W. Fusion of static and dynamic body biometrics for gait recognition. *IEEE Transactions on Circuits and Systems for Video Technology* 14(2), 149, 158, 2004.

Wark, T., Sridharan, V., & Chandran, V. The use of temporal speech and lip information for multi-modal speaker identification via multi-stream HMM, in *Proceedings International Conference on Acoustics, Speech, and Signal Processing*, IEEE Standards Office, Istanbul, Turkey, pp. 2389–2392, 2000.

Wassner, H. & Chollet, G. New cepstral representation using wavelet analysis and spectral transformation for robust speech recognition, in Proceedings of the Fourth International Conference on Spoken Language (ICSLP96), October 3–6, 1996, pp. 260–263, 1996.

Wickens, C.D. Processing resources in attention, in Parasuramna, R. & Davies, D.R. (editors), *Varieties of Attention*, pp. 53–102, Academic Press, New York, NY, USA, 1984.

Widrow, B. Generalization and information storage in networks of adaline "neurons," in Yovitz, M.C., Jacobi, G. T., & Goldstein, G.D. (eds), *Self-Organizing Systems*, pp. 435–461, Spartan Books, Washington, DC, USA.

Wiedenbeck, S., Waters, J., Sobrado, L., & Birget, J. Design and evaluation of a shoulder-surfing resistant graphical password scheme, Proceedings of the working conference on Advanced Visual Interfaces, Venezia, Italy pp. 177–184, 2006.

Wolpaw, J.R. & McFarland, D.J. Control of a two-dimensional movement signal by a noninvasive brain-computer interface in humans. *Proceedings of the National Academy of Sciences of the USA* 101(51), 17849–17854, 2004.

Wu, T. A real-world analysis of Kerebros password security, in *Proceedings of the 1999 ISOC Symposium on Network and Distributed System Security*, pp. 723–736, 1999.

Xafopoulos, A. Speaker verification (an overview). TICSP presentation, 2001.

Xu, L., Kryzak, A., & Suen, C.Y. Methods for combining multiple classifiers and their application to handwriting recognition. *IEEE Transactions Systems, Man, Cybernetics* 22(3), pp. 418–435, 1992.

Xuhua, Y., Furuhashi, T., Obata, K., & Uchikawa, Y. Constructing a high performance signature verification system using a GA method. ANNES'05 – Second New Zealand International Two-Stream Conference on Artificial Neural Networks and Expert Systems, 1995, 20–23 November, 1995, Dunedin, New Zealand, pp. 170–173, 1995, IEEE Computer Society, 1995.

Xuhua, Y., Furuhashi, T., Obata, K., & Uchikawa, Y. Selection of features for signature verfication using a genetic algorithm, *Computers & Industrial Engineering*, Vol. 30(4), September 1996, pp. 1037–1045.

Yamazaki, A., Ludermir, T., & de Suonto, M. Classification vintages of wine by an artificial nose using time delay neural networks. *IEE Electronics Letters* 37(24), 1466–1467, 2001.

Yang, L., Widjaja, B., & Prasad, R. Application of hidden Markov models for signature verification. *Pattern Recognition Letters* 28(2), 161–170, 1995.

Yeung, D-Y., Chang, H., Xiong, Y., George, S., Kashi, R., Matsumoto, T., & Rigoll, G. SVC2004: First International Signature Verification Competition. Proceedings of the International Conference on Biometric Authentication (ICBA), Hong Kong, July 15–17, 2004.

Yu, E. & Cho, S. Novelty detection approach for keystroke dynamics identity verification. Fourth International Conference on Intelligent Data Engineering and Automated Learning, IDEAL 2003, 5–7 January 2006, Hong Kong, 2003.

Zhang, S., Janakiraman, R., Sim, T., & Kumar, S. Continuous verification using multimodal biometrics. International Conference on Biometrics, 7–11 November, 2005, Alexandria, VA, USA, LNCS 3832, pp. 562–570, 2006.

Zhuang, L., Zhou, F., & Tygar, J.D. Keyboard acoustic emanations revisited, in CCS '05: Proceedings of the 12th ACM conference on Computer and communications security, pp. 373–382, ACM Press, New York, NY, USA, 2005.

Index